The Word on the Streets

The Word on the Streets
The American Language of Vernacular Modernism

BROOKS E. HEFNER

University of Virginia Press
CHARLOTTESVILLE AND LONDON

Quotations from letters from Claude McKay to James Weldon Johnson, April 30, 1928, and to Langston Hughes, April 3, [1928], are used with the permission of the Literary Estate for the Works of Claude McKay. Quotations from Dashiell Hammett's unpublished writings are used by permission of the Literary Property Trust of Dashiell Hammett. Quotations from Erle Stanley Gardner's correspondence are used by permission of the Estate of Erle Stanley Gardner and Queen Literary Agency.

University of Virginia Press
© 2017 by the Rector and Visitors of the University of Virginia
All rights reserved
Printed in the United States of America on acid-free paper

First published 2017

9 8 7 6 5 4 3 2 1

Library of Congress Cataloging-in-Publication Data

Names: Hefner, Brooks E. author.
Title: The word on the streets : the American language of vernacular modernism / Brooks E. Hefner.
Description: Charlottesville : University of Virginia Press, 2017. | Includes bibliographical references and index.
Identifiers: LCCN 2017011908 | ISBN 9780813940403 (cloth : alk. paper) | ISBN 9780813940410 (pbk. : alk. paper) | ISBN 9780813940427 (e-book)
Subjects: LCSH: American literature—20th century—History and criticism. | Modernism (Literature)—United States. | Americanisms in literature.
Classification: LCC PS228.M63 H42 2017 | DDC 810.9/112—dc23
LC record available at https://lccn.loc.gov/2017011908

Cover photo: Sixth Avenue, looking south from 40th Street, Manhattan, May 18, 1940. (NYC Municipal Archives, Borough President Manhattan Collection, image bpm_1445-1)

For Bethany and her vanishing accent

It is too late to be studying Hebrew; it is more important to understand even the slang of to-day.
—HENRY DAVID THOREAU, "WALKING" (1862)

Contents

	Acknowledgments	ix
	Introduction: Toward a Theory of American Vernacular Modernism	1
1	"The Steady Reaching Out for New and Vivid Forms": H. L. Mencken and the American Revolution of the Word	35
2	"Never Mind the Comical Stuff. . . . They Ain't No Joke about This!": Ring Lardner, Anita Loos, and the Comic Origins of Vernacular Modernism	62
3	"I Didn't Understand the Words, but My Voice Was Like Dynamite": Anzia Yezierska, Mike Gold, and the Jewish American Break with Realism	102
4	"Say It with Lead": Carroll John Daly, Dashiell Hammett, and Modernism's Underworld Vernacular	139
5	"The Necromancy of Language": Realist Uplift and the Urban Vernacular in Rudolph Fisher and Claude McKay	179
	Conclusion: Modernism's Familial Relations	215
	Notes	223
	Bibliography	251
	Index	271

Acknowledgments

An argument about the "language of the streets," this book is necessarily the product of a cacophony of voices: the multilayered, multiethnic voices of American writers of the early twentieth century. And like any book of its kind it is also an effort to wrangle together the voices of literary figures and literary critics into a kind of coherence. But even that attempt at coherence masks another set of voices, an even louder cacophony: the voices of numerous friends, colleagues, and mentors who served as readers and interlocutors as this project grew and developed. Without those conversations, this project would certainly not have taken the form it has today.

Like most first books, this project developed in graduate school, and the guidance of Marc Dolan at the CUNY Graduate Center was essential to its coming into being. Mentors, colleagues, and friends who provided insightful feedback as well as welcome distraction both during and after graduate school include Sari Altschuler, Sean Grattan, Heather Hendershot, Casey Howard, Jessica Ingram, Christopher Leslie, Bridget McGovern, Neil Meyer, Erin Lee Mock, Robert Reid-Pharr, and Jon-Christian Suggs. I have been fortunate to find an equally supportive community at James Madison University, where colleagues have been generous with time and encouragement as the project transformed. In particular, the advice and guidance provided by John Ott, Mark Parker, and Matthew Rebhorn sustained me through the long process of rewriting, reconceptualization, and revision. Other colleagues in my department and across campus—including Dabney Bankert, Liam Buckley, Allison Fagan, Laura Henigman, Kristen McCleary, Bill Van Norman, and Siân White—read drafts or talked with me as I worked out particular ideas that appear here. I'd also like to thank my editor at the University of Virginia Press, Eric Brandt, for his commitment to and support of this project. Research for this project was supported by a number of sources, for which I am extremely grateful. Research for chapter 4 was supported by the Erle Stanley Gardner Endowment for Mystery Studies Fellowship at the Harry Ransom Center at the University of Texas in Austin, while a summer grant from JMU's College of Arts and Letters made possible additional research for chapters 4 and 5. Part of chapter 2 appeared in *PMLA* 125.1 (2010): 107–20, and is reprinted by permission of the copyright owner, The Modern Language Association of America. An earlier version of part of chapter 3 appeared in *MELUS: Multi-Ethnic Literature of the United States* 36.3 (2011): 187–211.

Support comes in many forms, and the encouragement of my parents, Ellis and Carlean Hefner, also forms the bedrock of this project. They have come to be cheerleaders and advocates for my professional work, as well as sympathetic ears during successes and struggles. I reserve my final thanks for my toughest reader and most incisive interlocutor, my partner, Bethany Hurley. Her support, her interest, and her ruthless editing are matched only by her brilliance, her sharp questions, and her loving encouragement. She's supported my work in more ways than I can begin to describe, and because of our ongoing and unending conversations I dedicate this book to her.

Introduction

Toward a Theory of American Vernacular Modernism

> *The distinguished trait of the American is simply his tendency to use slang without any false sense of impropriety, his eager hospitality to its most audacious novelties, his ingenuous yearning to augment the conciseness, the sprightliness, and, in particular, what may be called the dramatic punch of his language.*
>
> —H. L. MENCKEN, "THE AMERICAN: HIS LANGUAGE" (1913)

In the summer of 1929 the transatlantic little magazine *transition* published its celebrated "Revolution of the Word" issue (number 16/17, June 1929). Edited by expatriate American Eugene Jolas, *transition* was quickly becoming "the most important of the American expatriate 'little' magazines," especially since the *Little Review* and the *Dial*, two major organs of modernism's dissemination in the United States, ceased publication in 1929, since editors of both magazines felt that the work of these journals was largely complete.[1] Appearing in Paris a month after the *Little Review* closed up shop, this issue of *transition* is one of the most bombastic in a history of aggressive and confrontational feats that carried on the legacy of the *Little Review*. In its effort to continue the bold modernist experimentation pioneered by earlier little magazines, *transition* was noteworthy for printing excerpts from Joyce's *Finnegans Wake* (completed and published between covers in 1939) under the title "Work in Progress," as well as for its regular inclusion of pieces from Gertrude Stein, including "Four Saints in Three Acts," published in this "Revolution of the Word" issue.

The issue gets its title from the opening section of the magazine, which includes Jolas's editorial "Proclamation," one of the great modernist manifestos. "Tired of the spectacle of short stories, novels, poems and plays still under the hegemony of the banal word, monotonous syntax, static psychology, descriptive naturalism, and desirous of crystallizing a viewpoint," Jolas and the now mostly obscure cosigners of this modernist manifesto laid out a twelve-point plan for a literary revolution rooted in language experiments. Jolas's lacerating document works both as a descriptor of many characteristics and assumptions of what has come to be known as modernism and as a laundry list of the specific nineteenth-century tropes that modernists found so detestable: "the banal word, monotonous syntax, static psychology, [and] descriptive naturalism." In response, Jolas posited complete freedom for the creative mind, "the plain reader be damned." "The writer expresses," the "Proclamation" claims, "he does not communicate."[2]

Alongside Jolas's manifesto the opening section of *transition* includes a number of pieces designed to demonstrate the claim that "the revolution in the English language is accomplished fact." These are, in fact, attempts to demonstrate and elaborate on this "Revolution of the Word": they include difficult (and, at times, incomprehensible) prose poems and other pieces, including Stuart Gilbert's commentary on Joyce's "Work in Progress," poems by the Baroness Elsa von Freytag-Loringhoven, and Harry Crosby's "The New Word," where he describes the "New Word" as "the Panther in the Jungle of Dictionary who pounces upon and devours all timid and facile words."[3] One of these contributions, however, stands out as particularly interesting in light of the apparent attempt by these highbrow, internationalist writers and artists to alienate the "plain reader." Near the end of the "Revolution of the Word" section, only a few pages before the first publication of Gertrude Stein's "Four Saints in Three Acts," appears a piece entitled "Slanguage: 1929."[4] Acknowledged as a reprint from the *New York World,* this list, credited to Theodore D. Irwin, is a glossary of contemporary American slang words and phrases with definitions on the facing page. These include terms like "wowser," "to make whoopee," "everything is copesetty," and "to be Chicago'd" (the latter meaning "despatched [sic] via machine gun or automatic").[5] As originally published in the *New York World,* a list like this might make for an interesting lifestyle piece; in the "Revolution of the Word" issue of *transition,* it takes on an entirely different meaning. Filled with words originating in American ethnic and working-class communities, its inclusion suggests a vital—and essentially unacknowledged—connection between the revolutions of modernism and the revolutionary nature of American street slang.

Jolas himself acknowledged this curious connection in later issues of *transition,* publishing his own "Revolution of the Word Dictionary" (with many neologisms derived from Joyce's work) in 1932, and emphasizing the importance of the "language of the street" in a 1930 article responding to his critics. Here, Jolas directly connects the proclamation with innovations in American slang, writing:

> I do not demand that every writer henceforth invent his own vocabulary. I merely believe—and that was the impulse of my *proclamation*—that he has the right to make lexicographical changes if there is an organic necessity for it in the substance of his work itself . . . and if the subject he is treating seems to require it, to use the language of the street, of erotic-physiological processes, of the prison, of the tenement-house, of the baseball-grounds, of slang, to give voice to the irrational both of his own and of the collective mind of a people, to organize all this into an art of the word rooted deeply in the living movement of things.[6]

Other modernist figures agreed that the language of modernism was inextricably linked to "the language of the street." For Joseph Freeman, a Jewish American journalist who worked as an editor with influential leftwing little magazines the *Liberator,* the *New Masses,* and *Partisan Review,* twentieth-century literature was distinguished by its distance from the elite and "lofty" language of proper education. In his 1936 memoir, reflecting on learning English as a child in New York City, he writes

> At home we spoke Yiddish; in the street a form of American with a marked foreign accent, a singsong rhythm and the interpolation of Yiddish phrases; in public school we read and recited an English so pure, so lofty, so poetic that it seemed to bear no relation to the language of the street. Literature was the enemy of the street until years later, when postwar fiction and poetry gave the language of the street the dignity of art, when Joyce and Hemingway replaced Longfellow and Whittier.[7]

For Freeman, modernist writers depended on "the language of the street," while modernist magazines like *transition* equated this "slanguage" with radical modernist experimentation. Such combinations and permutations of a modernism of the street—and in particular of the multiethnic streets of New York—are a far cry from narratives of modernism that emphasize the elite separation from the ordinary. At one level, "Slanguage: 1929" appears to be a "found object," like Marcel Duchamp's "readymades"; however, its placement in this "Revolution of the Word" issue and Jolas's follow-up suggest a more intense alliance between the high modernist experiments of Joyce and Stein and the powerful and contemporary American vernacular. This manifesto section, after all, claimed that "the literary creator has the right to disintegrate the primal matter of words imposed on him by text-books and dictionaries" and that "he has the right to use words of his own fashioning and to disregard existing grammatical and syntactic laws."[8] Both critics of and advocates for the American vernacular would use much the same terms to describe the operation of slang.

Jolas's bibliographic recoding of vernacular language as revolutionary experimentation suggests that even the highest of high modernists ("The plain reader be damned!") were seeing reflections of their own aesthetic and linguistic experiments in the popular language and culture that surrounded them. It was not a matter of a separation from the realm of what critics have termed "mass culture"; rather, these modernist figures demonstrated respect for—and even a debt to—not just popular culture in general, but popular forms of language. An examination of the vast print culture in America during the modernist era makes it clear that the little magazine crowd was not the only group thinking about language in experimental ways. In fact, as many of these high modernists themselves recognized, a great deal of popular fiction of the era had begun asking modernist questions about the arbitrariness and externality of language, the limits of linguistic experimentation, and the failures of the realist aesthetic. In *The Word on the Streets,* I examine a host of what might be generally termed vernacular fiction of the modernist era. I argue that American popular writers long thought of as working in the nineteenth-century traditions of realism and naturalism were, in fact, experimenting with language in much the same way that their European and internationalist counterparts were doing. These "vernacular modernists," working in popular genres and ethnic literary traditions in the 1910s and 1920s, were building a self-consciously American modernism out of what Joseph Freeman called "the street form of American." Writing for popular audiences now denigrated as low- and middlebrow, writers like Ring Lardner, Anzia Yezierska, Dashiell Hammett, and Claude McKay rejected the "banal word" with the same enthusiasm as Jolas and the contributors to *transition,* exploring the experimental possibilities of the vernacular languages they encountered (and adapted). Writing across traditional boundaries of race, class, ethnicity, and cultural value, these writers built a group of unique but related forms of American vernacular modernism out of the colorful and complex possibilities presented by the American vernacular languages, forms both celebrated and described in the popular linguistics of American critic H. L. Mencken.

On Modernist Plurality

It has become critical commonplace to speak of a multiplicity of modernisms, rather than of a single, monolithic thing called "modernism." On the one hand, this turn toward the plural encompasses, as it does for critics like Peter Nicholls and Michael Levenson, the variety of competing, contradictory, and mutually constitutive avant-garde and experimental movements in the late nineteenth and early twentieth centuries. In a prescient 1983 essay, Malcolm Bradbury argued convincingly for a plurality of experimental practices, writing that

> what we call Modernism is, however, a variety of movements and individual performances, from a variety of countries, in a variety of arts, at a variety of times; the term thus gives coherence to a collage of different tendencies and movements, often epistemologically at odds with or in revolt against others, arising from a variety of different traditions and lineages, different political and cultural situations, different stages in modern historical evolution, different periods themselves segmented from each other by the cataclysm of a world war, and with deeply various views of what the modern situation is and so of the nature and species of the artistic expression it should duly call forth.[9]

Likewise, Nicholls rejects "a sort of monolithic ideological formation" of modernism.[10] And while Michael Levenson's most recent survey emphasizes the capital-M Modernism of its title, it acknowledges the plurality of styles, calling modernism "a heterogeneous episode in the history of culture. It depended as much on its enemies as on its proponents, on audiences as much as artists, on a network of little magazines, on the attentions of reviewers in the mainstream press, on patrons as well as on publishers."[11] This "heterogeneous episode" is another delineation of the vast complexities of formal experimentation that characterize modernist writing.

While these critics have considered a variety of formal modernisms, other articulations of the multiplicity of modernisms have described these differing strains in terms of culture, allowing for a studied removal from one of the defining elements of modernist literature, its ability, in Terry Eagleton's words, to "derange ... its forms to forestall instant consumability."[12] The move away from form toward an emphasis on cultural and ideological readings of texts from this era has meant that critical definitions of modernism have broadened to encompass almost anything produced during the period. This is perhaps most succinctly described by Daniel Joseph Singal, who noted in 1987 that "put simply, Modernism should properly be seen as a *culture*—a constellation of related ideas, beliefs, values, and modes of perception—that came into existence during the mid to late nineteenth century, and that has had a powerful influence on art and thought on both sides of the Atlantic since roughly 1900."[13] The journal *Modernism/Modernity*, founded in 1994 as the unofficial voice of the New Modernist Studies, extends its study of modernist culture back to 1860 and also emphasizes the broader culture of modernisms. This cultural focus frequently signals a move away from formalist identifiers of modernism and allows critics to speak of pop modernism, bad modernism, pulp modernism, ethnic modernism, melting-pot modernism, border modernism, pragmatic modernism, sensational modernism, virtual modernism, and many more subcategories of modernist culture.[14]

What is interesting about these two different conceptualizations of the plurality of modernisms is that they each stress fundamentally different aspects of literary and cultural production. Nicholls (and others) tend to identify the plurality in a variety of forms and distinct formal innovations, highlighting European movements like symbolism, futurism, expressionism, and Dada. The cultural model of modernisms, on the other hand, sees this plurality primarily (although not exclusively) in terms of content and ideology. This cultural model has become nearly hegemonic in the current study of American modernism, which lacks the formal and aesthetic infighting of its European counterparts. To speak of modernism in 1970 meant to address a recognized and agreed-upon group of experimental writers. To do so in the twenty-first century is to speak of a broader cultural phenomenon that knows virtually no boundaries, even if the emphasis still largely falls on that same group of writers. Fortunately, the trend toward cultural definitions certainly critiqued and broadened the canon, bringing a variety of new subjects and methodologies to the study of modernism.[15] At the same time, however, that trend has muddled the characteristics that these writers and artists themselves saw as central to their own experimental practice. After all, as Astradur Eysteinsson notes in his detailed survey *The Concept of Modernism* (1990), "surely we can imagine a traditional realistic text that fulfills the thematic requirements" of the "culture" of modernism, such as those articulated by Singal and others in more recent scholarship on American modernism.[16] While a handful of scholars of American modernism—Michael Denning, for example—have managed to walk the fine line between formalist and cultural definitions of modernism, an overemphasis on the cultural aspects of modernism threatens to divorce the term from any consideration of experimental form whatsoever. When formalism is abandoned and new writers are added to the modernist canon based solely on their encounter with the culture of twentieth-century modernity, critics often fail to attend to the formal properties of the writers' work in any significant way. Modernist inclusion now involves a sort of backhanded compliment: now that formal or stylistic innovation is off the table, writers from previously underrepresented groups are suddenly asked to sit with Eliot, Pound, Stein, Joyce, and others.

With the rise of what Marjorie Levinson has characterized as the "new formalism," which "seek[s] to reinstate close reading both at the curricular center of our discipline and as the opening move, preliminary to any kind of critical consideration," the study of modernism is pivoting back toward the canon, toward works that correspond to more traditional, formal notions of modernist experimentation.[17] Such a move threatens to eliminate some of the more valuable gains by viewing modernism as a broader cultural phenomenon. From a strictly formalist standpoint, the assumption is that newly included works—particularly popular and ethnic writing—generally conform, to varying (and critically uninteresting) degrees, to the formal standards of realism. However, as Eysteinsson notes, "Labeling the whole so-called culture industry 'realistic' hardly seems productive. Those who endorse this dichotomy often do not address the question of popular culture at all."[18] To treat these works as formless (or, by default, realist) is to ignore both the history of ethnic and genre fiction and to flatten out the formal innovations these works present.

The Word on the Streets is an attempt to bridge the gap between these two competing notions of modernism(s). The development of the cultural model of modernism had a profound and positive impact on how modernism is studied and taught; it rightly criticized the traditional modernist canon for its overwhelmingly white and male representation, and it troubled the elitism of the avant-garde by redirecting its focus into other areas. But while more recent modernist studies have consistently acknowledged the value of popular culture during the early twentieth century, the terms by which the noncanonical or newly canonized work has been valued tends to reject the frameworks through which modernist writers themselves understood their own aesthetic practice. Rather than introducing a newly discovered writer into the modernist fold and placing her alongside a repackaged group of well-recognized modernists, *The Word on the Streets* takes such critical repackaging to task: too often the discussion has focused on how "major" writers have translated the popular culture surrounding them into "great" literary work, through some form of modernist alchemy. Such a model is an injustice to both the canonical figures and the culture surrounding them. It frames the canonical figures as cultural predators and the popular work around them as mere raw material, unformed until touched by the hand of genius. Also, as Bakhtinian dialogic practice, it suggests influence moving in only one direction, rather than the multidirectional flow and exchange that characterizes dialogue. In response, *The Word on the Streets* seizes on the term "vernacular modernism" as way of characterizing an alternative framework for imagining an American modernism that can simultaneously preserve the gains of canon expansion while recognizing the unique formal and linguistic innovations of American popular fiction in the 1910s and 1920s, just as Eugene Jolas and *transition* recognized an important part of their own "Revolution of the Word" in "Slanguage: 1929."

Toward a Theory of American Vernacular Modernism

Vernacular modernism, a term common in architecture and film studies but relatively new to the field of literary criticism, provides a model for rethinking modernist boundaries, not by the inclusion of a single representative writer from a previously marginalized group but instead by fully considering the modernist project of experimentation with language across race, class, and ethnicity in American popular writing of the 1910s and 1920s. The writers discussed in *The Word on the Streets* all represent groups that fall outside the standard narratives of modernism, and only a handful of these writers have been called modernist at all. Additionally, their readers—working-class, middlebrow, ethnic—certainly do not fit the mold of the transatlantic, cosmopolitan character to whom magazines like the *Little Review* catered, with its motto "Making No Compromise with the Public Taste."[19] Indeed, this argument returns—at its origins at least—to a nationalist framework that has fallen out of favor in more recent, transnational approaches to American literature; as such it might seem overly exceptionalist to readers accustomed to hemispheric or transatlantic approaches. This national focus grows out of a respect for the language and the conceptual structures the writers themselves used: for transnational expatriate Eugene Jolas, British novelist Virginia Woolf, and American critic H. L. Mencken there was something about the *American* vernacular that spoke to experimental concerns in ways that other vernaculars did not. This refocusing also stems from a desire to attend to the historical realities of American publishing—these writers were promoted as American writers and published first and foremost for an American readership—as well as to address concerns with defining the moving target of an "American language" in the period.

The little magazine *transition*'s fascination with American slang demonstrates, however, that this "national" language had an international reach and, as language chroniclers from Mencken to Yezierska noted, a transnational dimension, incorporating and being transformed by foreign words and phrases into a language acutely adapted to modernity. Such a vision resonates with Randolph Bourne's vision for a "Trans-National America" in an article published as both Mencken and Yezierska began their investigations and experiments in the polyglot American language.[20] Transnational writers like Jamaican-born Claude McKay—whose first novel, *Home to Harlem,* observes the linguistic innovation of the Harlem streets from the perspective of a Caribbean outsider—even transported the politics and aesthetics of a cross-class, cross-ethnic, and cross-racial experimentation associated with the "American" language into an international setting in his novel *Banjo,* discussed in chapter 5. Rejecting the prototypical modernist locus of the expatriate community of high modernists, this vernacular modernism poses a quite explicit democratic reframing of modernist experimentation, rejecting the cultural elitism commonly associated with canonical figures while employing many similar and analogous techniques in works written for a mass audience. These writers form an alternative genealogy to standard modernist narratives; instead of forging a path into fascism, as Ezra Pound did, these writers—with their largely proletarian narrators and protagonists, their multiethnic worldviews, and their commitment to the experimental power of (s)language—form a latent prehistory to the leftward movement of American literature in the 1930s, what Michael Denning has called "the cultural front."[21]

The term vernacular modernism poses some problems of definition. Recent criticism has begun to use the term more frequently, associating it with film, music, and other nonliterary cultural productions, and even Cyril Connolly's *Enemies of Promise* (1938, revised 1948), an early study of "the modern movement," splits an international group of canonical writers into camps called "mandarin" and "vernacular."[22] In American literary history, however, the middle of the twentieth century also saw a number of efforts to characterize the importance of American vernacular language to the American literary tradition. Modernist writer, chronicler, and critic Malcolm Cowley described the phenomenon in a 1945 essay titled "The Middle American Style." In discussing manifestations of this literary language, from Davy Crockett through John Hersey, he claimed that this "Midwestern style ... is something more than a dialect, and it does not depend for its effects on misspellings or on violations of English grammar."[23] He also closely associated this with fiction—not poetry—and with a national literary language, noting that "the novelists try with more or less success to speak United States."[24] Following Cowley, Richard Bridgman's *The Colloquial Style in America* (1966) sought to trace the lineage from early practitioners of dialect writing like Joseph Neal through celebrated modernists like Gertrude Stein and Ernest Hemingway. To be sure, Bridgman's text has served as a foundation for many later arguments (including my own), but *The Colloquial Style*'s emphasis on both a singular colloquial style and the relatively phonographic representation of actual speech patterns and tropes obscures the ways in which vernacular language(s) offered a variety of experimentally modernist—not merely realist—representational possibilities.[25] While he concludes his argument with Stein and Hemingway, in his emphasis on the replication of colloquial speech patterns, Bridgman nevertheless fails to see the broad influence the American vernacular exerted on literary experimentation in the early twentieth century.

In *The Word on the Streets,* the word "vernacular" should evoke a number of distinct but related meanings. In its more familiar usage, the term suggests the common language of the streets, as opposed to the elite language of the academy. The very term "streets" serves here as an important metaphorical marker for both this project and for the writers discussed therein. Both Freeman and Jolas deploy the phrase "the language of the street" in their efforts to describe a form of democratic linguistic experimentalism, one that emerges not from libraries, academies, or literary salons but from the lived experience of largely working-class spaces. This language, however, appears not in a single monolithic street but in a host of public spaces shaped by social discourse: the streets of Harlem and New York's Lower East Side; the mean streets of crime-ridden and hardboiled urban locales; and the public spaces of amusement, like movie theaters and ballparks. The metaphorical streets of the title of this study, then, embody the vernacular by highlighting its public and popular orientation, along with a spatial dynamic that emphasizes the encounters between and across languages marked by class, race, and ethnicity and normally considered out of the purview of elite literary language.

Important to this argument, as well, is the crucial distinction I will make between vernacular language and dialect. Dialect literature, popular in the nineteenth century, emphasized difference between the reader and the speaker; by nature, dialect is the language of an outsider, a subaltern.[26] As such, dialect was frequently quarantined or "caged" by quotation marks or other orthographic marks.[27] Vernacular language, by contrast, is a more widely used and widely understood common language, and is, like any "universal" language, a linguistic fiction; the early twentieth century (as we shall see) was full of studies trying to identify common American vernacular.[28] Naturally, vernacular, with its Latin root meaning "a home-born slave" (*OED*), also evokes class and racial considerations that are crucial to concerns of elitism, cosmopolitanism, and primitivism in high modernism. In *The Word on the Streets* I do not intend to suggest that these writers all employ a uniform vernacular; rather, they all turn toward culturally and generically different vernacular representations—different "slanguages"—out of a similar impulse to explore the boundaries of linguistic representation.

Simultaneously, I wish to draw on the term "vernacular" as it appears in the discipline of musicology. Since the late 1960s musicologists have used the terms "cultivated music" and "vernacular music" to differentiate between music produced by and/or for academy-educated musicians ("cultivated") and the enormous amount of popular and folk musics ("vernacular").[29] According to the *Grove Music Dictionary*, "Unlike musics known and practiced by a socio-cultural and professional elite, vernacular music is accessible to the majority of people because of their familiarity with its forms and functions and because they are able to acquire knowledge of it through everyday practice, that is, without any specialized skills."[30] While this binary is analogous to problematic literary critical concepts like high/low or modernist/popular, as well as sociological concepts like autonomous/heteronomous, it eliminates contradictory constructions like "low modernism" or "pop modernism," phrases that have the potential to reinscribe the long-standing hierarchies of value in modernist studies. It also untangles the difficulties that arise when works thought of as exemplary of high culture, like Stein's *Autobiography of Alice B. Toklas* (1933), become commercial successes and when works intended for a popular audience result in commercial failures. Vernacular modernism, then, consists of identifiably experimental work written by popular but not self-consciously elite authors, published by major commercial magazines or presses, and read by the general public (or by a public far broader than the audience for high modernism). Its formal innovations are tied to a variety of manifestations of vernacular language—the language of the streets—all while highlighting the experimental power of working-class and ethnic language to transform literary representation. This particular manifestation of experimental modernist practice stands in a curious relation to what critics conventionally describe as "high modernism," texts self-consciously written by and for a literary elite: at times friendly and mutually appreciative, at times hostile and combative, these two strains of American modernism consistently define themselves in a dialectical relationship to one another.[31] Additionally, vernacular and high modernist practices show a great deal of cross-pollination, with vernacular writers drawing on high modernists, just as high modernists voiced great appreciation for these vernacular writers and often mined their work for ideas and forms.

While the term "vernacular" serves a multifaceted function as a descriptor of the language, content, and cultural and publishing contexts of the texts, I would also like it to carry the weight of another critical concept, that of the "multiaccentuality" of the linguistic and ideological sign, as theorized by the Russian linguist (and member of Bakhtin's circle) V. N. Vološinov. As Vološinov writes, "Class does not coincide with the sign community, i.e., with the community which is the totality of users of the same set of signs for ideological communication. Thus various different classes will use one and the same language. As a result, differently oriented accents intersect in every ideological sign. Sign becomes an arena of class struggle."[32] Vološinov's "accents" have an explicit political orientation and suggest a political analogue of what have come to be known as "reading communities." Along these lines, Michael Denning has drawn on the notion of multiaccentuality in his important work on dime novels and working-class readership.[33] Multiaccentuality is useful here because vernacular modernism depends on linguistic self-consciousness and an awareness of the ways that nonstandard, "accented" vernacular speech can have radical formal and aesthetic influence on literary production. This does not empty the concept of its political weight—indeed, my notion of vernacular modernism is an effort to understand and seek value in the reading preferences of nonelites—but it adds an additional aesthetic dimension to Vološinov's concept. These literary accents rely on the ways in which different classes of readers encounter a text: we might, for example, read Joseph Conrad's *Heart of Darkness* (1899) as an adventure tale (as many did), while another reader may see it as a protomodernist psychological meditation on colonialism.[34] What Vološinov sees as the variant political accents present in all signs can simultaneously be seen as a politically charged aesthetics.[35]

These connections—between the accented vernacular language deployed in texts and the vernacular cultural status from which the texts originate—enable a critical approach that allows for an original discussion of experimental aesthetics in popular fiction. Critics have long acknowledged the productive and constitutive intersection between popular culture and high modernism. However, such studies often have the effect of both troubling the boundary between high and popular culture while simultaneously policing it. In other words, the great gains of modernist canon expansion have more frequently generated critical reconsideration of long-canonized works than they have produced thoughtfully close, formal analysis of these newly examined popular contexts. And, while Andreas Huyssen's argument about the "Great Divide" between modernism and popular culture has become, in T. Austin Graham's words, "a straw man argument to be knocked down," significant strains of modernist criticism have continued to emphasize the ways in which high modernists sought to differentiate themselves from the commercial output of popular fiction and so-called "mass culture." Two influential texts in this regard are Thomas Strychacz's *Modernism, Mass Culture, and Professionalism* and Mark McGurl's *The Novel Art*. For Strychacz, modernist writers drew strongly on mass-cultural forms in order to "articulate an opposition between them and mass culture."[36] Similarly, McGurl claims that "modernism's constitutive fascination with the low" served to underwrite the production and thematization of "literary sophistication" in the art novel.[37] For both these critics, modernists may have cannibalized the raw material of a compelling and all-encompassing mass culture, but they nevertheless sought to differentiate their work strongly from it.

Strychacz and McGurl offer models for the complex engagement that modernist scholarship has to mass culture; indeed, they demonstrate that critical discussion of what Huyssen called "vernacular and popular culture" normally happens in order to offer a richer understanding of canonical literary production.[38] Whether charting the influence of dialect poetry or the music hall on the work of T. S. Eliot (as Michael North and David E. Chinitz have done), tracking the tropes of popular magazines and advertising in avant-garde journals (Mark S. Morrisson), or seeing John Dos Passos's work as drawing on the popular chorus-girl novel (Graham), modernist critics often emphasize a single trajectory in this productive and porous interrelation: canonical figures (the subjects) transform the raw material of a broader modernist culture into a self-conscious and experimental modernist aesthetic.[39] Meanwhile, the popular texts that provide this rich thematic material seldom receive any attention for their own experimental aesthetic practice. As a result, popular works like dime novels and pulp fiction have long been treated by critics as "unauthored discourse" or "industrial production" in contrast to the "esoteric writing strategies" that Strychacz has seen as central to the "professional" nature of modernist writing.[40] The shift to the multivalent notion of the term "vernacular" in *The Word on the Streets* foregrounds the experimental possibilities of language present across a host of popular texts in the modernist period and allows for these texts to stand up to formalist critical approaches generally reserved for the long-canonized subjects of literary modernism.

Dialect Realism, Vernacular Modernism

Central to my argument about vernacular modernism is the long-standing opposition between realism and modernism. That this binary is problematic is not new; critics have been unpacking this symbiotic relationship for decades. However, it is no exaggeration to claim that high modernist writers were eager to throw off what they perceived to be the chains of mimetic realism in their search for new forms. Some preferred pure abstraction, while others claimed that emergent psychological devices made modernism a purer representation of reality than the stilted and genteel style associated with realism, the difference, in short, between what Virginia Woolf characterized as "real" and "lifelike."[41] Whether William Carlos Williams was advocating for "not 'realism' but reality itself" or Eugene Jolas was advocating a break with the staid traditions of "descriptive naturalism," modernists were quite sure of one thing: while they may have been getting closer to "the real thing," they were no realists.[42]

Following the lead of these high modernists, I place vernacular modernism in contrast to realist aesthetics, what I call "dialect realism." This distinction—like the opposition between realism and modernism—is far from perfect. It is clear, for example, that realists and naturalists (such as Theodore Dreiser in *An American Tragedy*) dabbled with modernist modes, and the work of high modernist writers frequently depended on realist aesthetics to hold together narrative. In certain cases, formal experiments like Harold Loeb's *Doodab* (1925), initially written with extensive dream sequences and with as few definite and indefinite articles as possible, were made more conventionally realist by editorial intervention.[43] And realism continued to exert influence on American writing throughout the twentieth century, becoming a particularly valuable mode of representation for politically engaged writers of the 1930s and 1940s, as Chris Vials has convincingly argued.[44] Ultimately, though, the question of a realist/modernist divide was an integral aspect of modernist self-definition, even if such a simple dichotomy has been seriously complicated—if not largely abandoned—by contemporary scholarship.[45] By yoking together the terms "dialect" and "realism," however, I hope to draw attention to the differences between vernacular writing and dialect writing and to tie these two concepts more explicitly to the ways in which realism and modernism use similar language to different purposes.

American realist writing of the late nineteenth century was, as critics like Gavin Jones have demonstrated, underwritten by dialect language. While realism and dialect writing developed at the same time in the nineteenth century and certain figures (for example, Mark Twain and Charles Chesnutt) are central to both modes, the connections between the two run far deeper. The godlike narrator of many realist and naturalist texts creates characters in his image, with one small variation: their language. As such, realist texts are characterized by Bakhtin's notion of heteroglossia, the layering of languages within novelistic productions, especially those of the nineteenth century. "The novel," Bakhtin writes, "can be defined as a diversity of social speech types (sometimes even a diversity of languages) and a diversity of individual voices, artistically organized."[46] What realist texts accomplish, however, is an often-implicit hierarchy of characters through language, where sympathetic or identificatory characters speak languages most similar to the narrator, and characters meant to be marginal, unsympathetic, or problematic veer from the standard language of the narrator. June Howard notes, for example, that "the narrator, in naturalist novels as in others, is generally the 'character' who is closest to the reader."[47] In works dominated by dialect, this difference is easy to see in the distinction between genteel narrator and dialect speaker or storyteller, a hierarchy emphasized by the frequent use of frame narration, a frame that, according to Richard Bridgman, "established an invidious comparison that was sustained by interchanges between the dialect animal and the genteel man."[48] In more subtle and nuanced realist texts, language marks characters as others, sometimes on the basis of race or ethnicity but just as often on the basis of class and education. In a text like William Dean Howells's *The Rise of Silas Lapham* (1885), the plot revolves around a figure whose upcountry language ultimately prevents him from ascending the social ladder in Boston and finally banishes him from the urban (and urbane) future in its conclusion.[49] Ultimately, as Gavin Jones argues, "while appearing to represent a democratic desire to record America's multifarious speech-ways, much literary dialect attempted to reinscribe a qualitative hierarchy between standard and nonstandard speech."[50]

The emphasis on language as a marker of difference runs hand-in-hand with one of the central concerns of realism and naturalism: the increasing exposure of class and racial difference in nineteenth-century America. Whether it is the crushing poverty of the city or new consumer spaces, realism must, as critics from Amy Kaplan to Russ Castronovo have noted, confront social and economic difference.[51] Spoken language, as Henry James discovered in his return to the United States in 1905, is a pivotal marker of these differences.[52] Dialect provides an outlet within realism that allows writers to maintain social distinctions that are increasingly under threat in the Gilded Age. By marking characters as dialect figures, realists remain able to push them to the margins or, at the very least, reduce sympathy with such characters among an educated and enlightened readership. Indeed, Nancy Glazener's *Reading for Realism* emphasizes the ways in which the print culture of realism (on the part of the so-called *Atlantic* group) solidified the class hierarchies present in realist narratives by "consolidating privilege" through "new practices of distinction."[53] In realist and naturalist fiction, dialect characters become, in large part, *objects* of interest, lacking the subject position of the narrator and characters speaking more standardized forms of English.[54] Mark Twain's work—easily the most radical and experimental dialect writing in nineteenth-century America—comes closest to breaking with these traditions, and, in a sense, forges a path later taken up by H. L. Mencken and the vernacular modernists, but he remains dependent upon the presence of an organizing, editorial consciousness reporting the language of an uneducated storyteller. In an era when a genteel public was striving toward what Kenneth Cmiel has called "democratic eloquence," the presence of dialect in largely unsympathetic (and, at times, immoral) characters helped reinforce social distinctions and buffet an increasingly incoherent American society.[55]

Realism's "social construction," to invoke Amy Kaplan's powerful argument, operates as a containment strategy at the level of language. Realist writers sought to represent, as Howells would claim in one of his more famous editorials, the "real grasshopper," and to reject "the ideal grasshopper, the heroic grasshopper, the impassioned grasshopper, the self-devoted, adventureful, good old romantic cardboard grasshopper."[56] Works of nineteenth-century American realism, however, are populated almost exclusively by genteel grasshoppers; characters exhibiting differences in race, ethnicity, or class stand as linguistic deviants, whose utterances mark them as outside the realm of refinement. This aspect of realism came under intense criticism by naturalists like Frank Norris, but

Norris and others merely shifted the gaze away from bourgeois culture to the culture of poverty. The protagonists, now ethnic and working-class figures, still spoke a dialect that alienated them from the sophisticated narrative voice, and, presumably, from the genteel readership. As Gavin Jones has argued, "American nervousness about the stability and correctness of spoken standards stemmed from the deep fear of linguistic contamination, the fear that subaltern forms were radiating upward, affecting the language of the elite."[57] In realist and naturalist writing, these dangers remained containable: by keeping the dialect speakers on the margins or under the control of a genteel narrator, realist writing effected a temporary solution to the dangers presented by immigration and proletarianization in the United States of the late nineteenth century.

The term "genteel" carries a great deal of weight in the modernist critique of realist aesthetics and nineteenth-century American culture. While the terms "*genteel* and *gentility* slowly took on negative connotations after 1850," according to Kenneth Cmiel, writers of the modernist era took up the terms in force as they looked back on a late nineteenth-century culture that seemed overly cultured and largely "feminized."[58] Although Nancy Glazener notes that the realist mode was already being critiqued as overly "genteel" in the last decade of the nineteenth century, modernist writers and intellectuals took up this position with a vengeance.[59] The term gained new traction following George Santayana's 1911 essay "The Genteel Tradition in American Philosophy," which imagined a genteel world of "American Intellect" that stood in opposition to the commercialized "American Will" of business and progress.[60] This "genteel tradition" informed Van Wyck Brooks's notion of "highbrow" and "lowbrow" in *America's Coming-of-Age* (1915), Vernon Parrington's idea of nineteenth-century American Brahminism (which he called "the reign of the genteel"), and, perhaps most importantly for American literary history, provided the title for Malcolm Cowley's anthology *After the Genteel Tradition: American Writers, 1910–1930* (1937).[61] Like other modernists, Cowley translated Santayana's characterization of culture to the world of literature, calling the "genteel tradition" "the persistent enemy and slow poisoner of good writing in America" during the nineteenth century.[62] The collection featured Cowley's foreword, entitled "The Revolt against Gentility," as well as selections from a number of contributors writing on figures from Theodore Dreiser to H. L. Mencken to John Dos Passos. Highlighting Sinclair Lewis's 1930 Nobel acceptance speech, where he railed against "Victorian and Howellsian timidity and gentility in American fiction," Cowley notes that the writers surveyed in his volume "made it possible for young Americans to write without a side-glance at London or Oxford, to speak in their own language about everyday matters, to be accurate, coarse, even bawdy, without too much fear of having their books suppressed."[63]

In his foreword, Cowley also yokes the notion of gentility to class and ethnic identity. "In the conflict of racial strains," he writes, "the genteel writers all represented the older immigration. They were English by descent, except for a few whose forebears were Scottish or Knickerbocker or Huguenot, and they looked down in a kindly way on the Irish and the Germans." Opposing this group, "the new literary movement was a revolt of the lower middle classes against conventions that did not fit their personal lives and that prevented them from telling the truth about their world." Ultimately, Cowley's "new literary movement" does not line up perfectly with modernist historiography (he includes writers like Dreiser and Lewis), but the opposition between nineteenth-century conceptions of gentility and twentieth-century literary revolt remains clear. And for Cowley, those in revolt against the genteel tradition, "instead of being inspired by English models . . . tried to create an American myth, in the American language."[64] Cowley's argument is clear: the writers he values—his contemporaries—saw themselves (and their American language) in stark opposition to the nineteenth-century American world of Victorian gentility, rooted in elite literary journals and a slavish imitation of "English models."[65]

Vernacular modernism sought to undermine the subject/object power dynamic present in dialect realism by removing the narrative frame and embracing a new valuation of nonstandard "American" language. With an incorporation of multiethnic and cross-class slang and vernacular phrases, the vernacular modernists called into question the very nature of linguistic hierarchy that defined realism. In vernacular modernism, the language of the street is given value through its use as a standard narrative voice, as a consistently innovative way of representing modernity, and as an experimental strategy used to cope with the twentieth-century world. Whether employed by humor writers looking to transform the relationship readers had to formally marginalized figures or by African Americans seeking to bring value to the experimental vernacular of the Harlem streets, vernacular modernists self-consciously engaged discussions of an American vernacular language and practiced a modernist critique of what high modernist Eugene Jolas called the "banal word" and "monotonous syntax" of realism.

Slang Lexicography and Modernist Paratexts

In the modernist era, the language of the streets began to take precedence, not only in literary productions but also in the study of language itself. As Julie Coleman's multivolume *History of Cant and Slang Dictionaries* has demonstrated, the slang dictionary in English has a long history that reaches back into sixteenth-century England. The vast majority of slang dictionaries before 1900 were produced in England or derived from English sources; this included dictionaries and glossaries of American slang. To that point, American linguists appeared to shy away from slang in an effort to preserve the "genteel tradition" in American language study. With the publication of H. L. Mencken's *The American Language* (1919), however, American amateur and professional lexicographers began producing word lists, like Irwin's "Slanguage: 1929," that appeared in all manner of publishing venues. The "first self-contained dictionary of American slang compiled without reference to earlier British dictionaries" was Clement Wood and Gloria Goddard's *A Dictionary of American Slang* (1926), a volume produced as part of socialist publisher E. Haldeman-Julius's Little Blue Book series.[66] Wood and Goddard's dictionary is a playful look at mid-1920s slang, defining, for example, a "cake-eater" as "a tea-hound, lounge-lizard, lady-bug" and including a subsection at its conclusion on "Baseball Slang."[67] Soon after the publication of Wood and Goddard's volume, dictionaries of general American slang as well as specialized argot began appearing in droves.[68]

Academic interest in slang also spiked in the mid-1920s, as most clearly demonstrated by the founding of the journal *American Speech* in 1925. Part of what Joshua L. Miller has called "an avalanche of linguistic scholarship" in the postwar period, *American Speech* was designed to be, in the words of founding editor Louise Pound, "a journal of the LIVING language. . . . There are enough of the formal kind of philological journals, dealing mainly with the past, already."[69] The founding of the journal was inspired by H. L. Mencken's *The American Language,* and Mencken's letters and short contributions were a regular feature of the journal's early years.[70] *American Speech* operated as an alternative to the longstanding journal *Dialect Notes,* then the official journal of the American Dialect Society. Even if the contents of the journals could be similar, the difference in titles underscores the shift in thinking about the value of nonstandard language, from a nineteenth-century consideration of "dialect"—with its longstanding subordinate relationship to "standard" language—to the living "American Speech," a vital, vibrant, and contemporary phenomenon of modern American life. The journal regularly featured glossaries and word lists drawn from specialized groups, from criminals and hoboes to college students and musicians. Unlike nationalist efforts at linguistic standardization, *American Speech* operated along descriptive lines, regularly publishing features on working-class and ethnic word lists.

The explosion of slang lexicography in the United States appears curious in an era that seemed to be obsessed with linguistic standardization. In *Accented America*, Joshua L. Miller yokes the 1920s interest in slang and nonstandard vernacular language to the push for English-only education among immigrant groups. It is true that the various forms of slang and vernacular language documented and taxonomized by works like Wood and Goddard's *Dictionary of American Slang*, the journal *American Speech*, and Mencken's *The American Language* were all variants of English; however, the celebration of working-class alternatives to the bourgeois language taught to immigrants demonstrates a significant rejection of linguistic standardization in the first place; as Joseph Freeman reminds us, his street language was "a form of American with a marked foreign accent," and immigrant writers like Anzia Yezierska celebrated the degree to which the American language could be destabilized and reinvented by foreign influence.[71] As one slang dictionary supplanted another over the late 1920s and 1930s, it became clear that the American language was a moving target, a language of continual invention and reinvention, subject to a promiscuous influence from other languages. Indeed, the study and celebration of working-class and ethnic slang falls more in line with the "descriptive linguistics" of Franz Boas and Edward Sapir (among others), who worked "to counter racialized binaries of civilizational superiority and primitivism. . . . Their work," Miller writes, "was organized around rigorous description and documentation, particularly of ignored and stigmatized languages, in order to demonstrate the richness and validity of their cultural particularities."[72] The explosion in the production of these taxonomies and glossaries also shares some characteristics with the modernist era's emphasis on the "interventionist literary anthology," which Jeremy Braddock has shown to represent one of the "most prominent forms of modernist collecting."[73]

The novels and stories considered throughout *The Word on the Streets* all display an investment in slang and multiethnic vernaculars, deploying specialized and obscure terms and linguistic forms in ways that create a richer textual experience for their readers. In cases like Rudolph Fisher's *The Walls of Jericho* (1928) or Zora Neale Hurston's "Story in Harlem Slang" (1942), the textual apparatus appears in the form of a glossary of words and phrases with which the reader may be unfamiliar. The "Baseball Slang" of Wood and Goddard's slang dictionary, Ring Lardner's sample of "Baseball-American" (in Mencken's second and third editions of *The American Language*), and Lardner's early Jack Keefe stories all partake in the same fascination with the peculiar and colorful language of American sports. Criminal slang—integral to hard-boiled crime fiction—was routinely charted in books, pamphlets, casual lists, and even pulp serials like Henry Leverage's "Dictionary of the Underworld," which appeared in *Flynn's* magazine (later *Detective Fiction Weekly*) in 1925. Even professional journals like *Writer's Digest* offered glossaries for its aspiring genre fiction writers and featured advertisements for the magazine *Hot Dog*, which sought "stories written in American slang, the most picturesque and most forceful medium of expression evolved since the beginning of the English Language."[74] The great number of slang dictionaries and glossaries of the 1920s provide a broad discursive network of paratexts that allowed readers richer access to the experimental street language of vernacular modernist fiction.

Slang glossaries of the period—from Rudolph Fisher's "Introduction to Contemporary Harlemese" to Leverage's "Dictionary of the Underworld"—effectively operate as analogues to the high modernist paratext, that characteristic textual apparatus that serves as a guide for difficult and impenetrable modernist masterworks. From T. S. Eliot's notes to *The Waste Land* (1922) and William Faulkner's maps and genealogies to semiauthorized "guides" to James Joyce's *Ulysses* or Ezra Pound's *Cantos*, high modernist writing is filled with difficult texts that demand (and often include) an explanatory apparatus.[75] These interpretative and explanatory additions can often transcend Gerard Genette's definition of a "paratext" as "a zone between text and off-text"; for these modernist works, the explanatory apparatus is frequently an integral part of the reading experience and necessary for a coherent interpretation of the text itself.[76] In some cases, the author provides the textual apparatus; in others, it is provided by editors or critics, often working in close contact with the author. Regardless of who produces the textual apparatus, the difficult texts of high modernism generate paratexts that are slightly different from those that precede them. No longer are paratextual notes "a supplement, sometimes a digression, very rarely a commentary"; in modernist examples like Eliot and Faulkner, they are a necessity for textual interpretation, and they cross the threshold between paratext and text.[77]

Likewise, the preponderance of slang dictionaries, glossaries, and taxonomies produced during this era operate as paratextual "keys" to an understanding of the slang-laden discourse of vernacular modernist texts. As the chapters that follow will show, vernacular modernist writers deployed a barrage of colorful and inventive terms to expand the boundaries of linguistic representation. In many cases, this involved transforming the purported purity of American language by incorporating other linguistic words and forms to adapt it to the realities of modernity, introducing "foreign" language and structures "to express more vitally the rush of new experience," as Anzia Yezierska argued.[78] In other cases, this meant resorting to the thieves' slang of Dashiell Hammett's fiction in an effort to demonstrate the emptiness of bourgeois clichés in a world marked by expressionist violence and filled with linguistic deception. Importantly, *The Word on the Streets* presents vernacular modernism as a multiplicity of overlapping but decidedly different (s)languages; far from a singular "American language" (as posited by Mencken), vernacular modernism emerges on different streets, in different subcultures, but with similarly modernist goals. Ring Lardner's "Baseball-American" is a far cry from Claude McKay's transnational "necromancy of language," but both are rooted in the cultural shift toward slang and vernacular language as a vital and experimental part of American literature.

Toward a Political Economy of Modernist Reading

Traditional characterizations of the modernist reader draw strongly on the notion of experimental writing as set apart from the commodified world of mass culture, the "great divide" of Andreas Huyssen's famous argument.[79] Indeed, the *Little Review*'s two famous mottos—"Making No Compromise with the Public Taste" and "The Magazine That Is Read by Those Who Write the Others"—clearly emphasize the magazine's identity as one of Anglo-American modernism's "shared instructional structures" and paint its readership as an educated coterie of creative talent sharing strong affiliations with the avant-garde writers appearing in its pages.[80] Whether those readers were like-minded aesthetes and experimentalists or, later, a part of what Lawrence Rainey has called the "institutions of modernism," they were some version of Richard Poirier's "grim readers," who, in Thomas Strychacz's words, "set out to enjoy the intellectual challenge" of difficult writing.[81] Modernists, as Laura Frost has recently argued, sought a "redefinition of pleasure: specifically, exposing easily achieved and primarily somatic pleasures as facile, hollow, and false, and cultivating those that require more ambitious analytical work."[82] As a result of this new kind of reading practice, "modernism," James F. English has noted, "finds its adherents above all among practicing artists and university professors."[83] This intellectual challenge of confronting difficult writing, rooted in what Pierre Bourdieu called a "pure aesthetic," stands in opposition—even in the most sympathetic readings of popular culture—to the characterization of readers encountering the broader swath of cultural production of the modernist era.[84] Readers of pulp magazines, in particular, were often singled out for ridicule in middlebrow venues like *Vanity Fair*, which in 1933 called these working-class (and ethnic) readers "those who move their lips when they read."[85] This seems to confirm Peter Bürger's claims in his influential study of the avant-garde that "the relation between serious and pulp fiction is barely thematized, precisely because both are assigned to distinct spheres from the beginning."[86] Such pernicious assessments seem to reinforce the rather entrenched cultural hierarchies promoted in the period and beyond, and to validate Bourdieu's notion of a stark divide within the field of cultural production between "autonomous" and "heteronomous" zones.[87]

Despite the seeming gulf between cultural spheres as different as the *Little Review* and pulp magazines of the period, marketplace boundaries remained far more porous, suggesting that the movement between these entrenched cultural spheres—the movement made by Irwin's "Slanguage: 1929"—remained possible for work with unacknowledged experimental potential. Anita Loos's comic masterpiece *Gentlemen Prefer Blondes* (1925), discussed in depth in chapter 2, presents an interesting example of this political economy of literary value in the mid-1920s. Loos, as she describes in her "Biography of a Book," initially submitted her first chapter of this novel to H. L. Mencken's cultural journal the *American Mercury*. The *Mercury*, edited by Mencken and George Jean Nathan, was a major player in the 1920s intellectual scene. Mencken and Nathan had previously worked as coeditors on the *Smart Set*, taking over after Willard Huntington Wright (who later became popular detective novelist S. S. Van Dine) had published too many European experimentalists, alienating the readers of a publication known as "A Magazine of Cleverness" and sinking the magazine's circulation. Mencken and Nathan also tired of mere "cleverness" and, after leaving the *Smart Set*, used the *Mercury* to satirize American mores. Given this, the vapid (but successful) protagonist of Loos's novel seems ideally suited for Mencken's journal charting the idiocies of what he famously called the American "boobacracy." Publication in a magazine like this—its readers self-styled intellectuals—would lend a certain cultural value to Loos's work.

Yet Mencken balked at the perceived explicitness of the piece, reportedly telling Loos, "You're making fun of sex and that's never been done before in the U.S.A. I suggest you send it to *Harper's Bazaar*, where it'll be lost among the ads and won't offend anybody."[88] *Harper's Bazar* (spelled thusly until 1929), like many popular magazines of the 1920s, was loaded with advertisements. In the issue where Loos's first chapter appeared, the table of contents is preceded by over fifty pages of advertising. *Harper's Bazar* also exemplified a very different sort of cultural capital. Founded as "a ladies' *Harper's Weekly*," *Harper's Bazar* primarily featured articles about fashion and travel, as well as a selection of fiction targeting women readers: largely formulaic romance stories.[89] In his study of American magazines, James Playsted Wood notes of *Harper's Bazar* that "some attention is given to people and ideas, usually the wealthy and the social life of the wealthy, women in their roles as dowagers, matrons, debutantes or subdebutantes, but the emphasis is all on clothes and beauty modes."[90] In a 1925 report to the Audit Bureau of Circulations, the editors of *Harper's Bazar* defined the magazine as "an international publication of authoritative styles and smart fiction appealing to the discriminative women of means and influence."[91] A venue tied directly to the marketplace—and therefore to Bourdieu's "heteronomous field"—it is *definitely* not the place a modernist scholar might go looking for experimental writing.[92]

The differences between *Harper's Bazar* and the *American Mercury* are manifold. Loos herself even nods at these differences in the novel's second chapter, when she has Lorelei's friend Dorothy meet Mencken for lunch: Lorelei dismisses him as "Mr. Mencken from Baltimore who really only prints a green magazine which has not even got any pictures in it."[93] While the *Mercury* had no pictures (and very few ads), *Harper's Bazar* had very little text and an overwhelming number of images and ads. At fifty cents a copy, *Harper's Bazar* was one of the pricier slick magazines, doubly commercialized for its glossy pages, full color images, and heavy amount of advertising. Other slick magazines, like the *Saturday Evening Post*, for example, cost merely five cents a copy, subsidized by the high price of advertising for a magazine with such wide circulation and subscriptions. The *American Mercury*, however, also cost an astounding fifty cents a copy (five dollars for a year's subscription), despite the fact that it used cheaper paper, no color, and virtually no image reproductions. As with many of the European little magazines, Mencken's magazine courted the reader who was willing to pay for an intellectually superior periodical.[94] *Harper's Bazar*, on the other hand, sold high-class commercial entertainment and fashion news. Both cost fifty cents a copy, but readers were buying very different things for the same price. Mencken's magazine was also published by Alfred A. Knopf, at the time an up-and-comer in the book publishing world and one of the main outlets for American modernism.

If the story of Lorelei Lee had ended in the pages of *Harper's Bazar*, it's unlikely that we would have any knowledge of it at all now. After all, how many stories from *Harper's Bazar* in the 1920s remain in print today? But the telling moment was Loos's publication of the novel with Boni & Liveright at the end of 1925. According to Loos, this came out as "a sort of 'vanity' edition" and sold much more quickly than anyone had imagined it would.[95] But to move from the pages of *Harper's Bazar* to the covers of Boni & Liveright was to straddle a significant cultural divide. "By 1920," according to Gorham Munson, "Boni & Liveright had been heard as a clarion in the publishing world. To the book trade the firm represented the new ferment and the new figures in American letters."[96] Though the publishing house eventually failed in the early 1930s, it stood throughout the 1920s as one of the most—if not *the* most—experimental publisher in America, a reputation burnished by their publishing of T. S. Eliot's *The Waste Land* in 1922. Boni & Liveright's book list from 1925 alone reads like a who's who of American literary celebrity: Sherwood Anderson, *Dark Laughter*; H.D., *The Collected Poems of H.D.*; Eugene O'Neill, *Plays: Anna Christie, All Gods Chillun Got Wings, Diff'rent*; and Ernest Hemingway, *In Our Time*. During this year, Boni & Liveright also published Theodore Dreiser's quasi-modernist *An American Tragedy*, as well as minor modernist works like Harold Loeb's *Doodab*. None of these "highbrow" works, though, achieved the bestseller status that Loos's novel did.

The literary and cultural value of a text like Loos's *Blondes* amplifies with what Jerome McGann calls "bibliographical codes" (as opposed to more traditionally literary "linguistic codes"): in this he includes the material conditions of the text, such as "ink, typeface, paper, and various other phenomena that are crucial to the understanding of textuality."[97] But these bibliographical codes are also bound up in an economic and cultural matrix—a political economy of literary value—that determines what critics allow themselves to see.[98] What did initial publication in one magazine or another mean for a text's literary value? How can one determine the literary reputation of a given magazine or book publisher? How did the transition from magazine serialization to publication between covers impact the text's viability as a cultural object? The example of *Gentlemen Prefer Blondes* raises questions about Bourdieu's "field of cultural production," especially as it represents not only the historical shift in the nature, definition, and value of "literary language," as John Guillory has charted in his study of canon expansion.[99] Loos's novel suggests the possibility of a simultaneity of value in the modernist era. Here there is no "great divide"; instead, her novel achieves success both in a commercially oriented fashion magazine and in a modernist publishing house; its success is simultaneously economic (it was a bestseller) and cultural (it was highly praised by critics). Its publication contexts and its reception by a modernist public confer on Loos's novel forms of "legitimacy" that appear mutually exclusive in Bourdieu's construction of the cultural field.[100]

Both Loos's contemporaries and current modernist scholars see her work as exceptional in this regard (and exceptionally interesting); at the same time, the path this work traveled in the publishing industry is a sign of the permeability of modernist boundaries. Admirers of Loos's text like William Faulkner and Edith Wharton no doubt read the novel between covers, authorized by the Boni & Liveright imprint, and not in the pages of a fashion magazine like *Harper's Bazar*. Had Mencken published it in the *Mercury*, its initial impact might have been larger; but then again, its improbable rise from the advertisements and stories about and for "women in their roles as dowagers, matrons, debutantes or subdebutantes" (and its quality as a brilliant naïf piece) might also have played a large role in its broad popularity. If Loos's text—rejected by Mencken for being what Lorelei might call too "riskay," hidden among the ads in an American fashion magazine that probably had few readers on Paris's bohemian Left Bank—could become a bestseller under the modernist-inflected Boni & Liveright imprint, how might this spur us to reevaluate our ideas about literary value and commercial publishing? *Gentlemen Prefer Blondes*, at the very least, suggests that the formal experiments associated with literary modernism might be found in unlikely places, and the emphasis on language in Loos's novel looks toward the juxtaposition of modernist and vernacular language in *transition*'s "Revolution of the Word" issue. For Loos and other vernacular modernists, literary experimentation could happen in popular contexts as easily as in avant-garde ones. Though bibliographical codes might put literary critics off the trail of the experimental aspects of work like hers, the rubric of vernacular modernism allows for these formal and aesthetic elements to emerge more clearly in service of a broader understanding of literary modernism.

It's important, I think, to say that modernist writers had modernist tastes; many of the vernacular writers discussed here were popular among the canonized modernists. Gertrude Stein was an aficionado of detective fiction, James Joyce was an admirer of the humor of Anita Loos, William Faulkner and Ernest Hemingway were avid readers of pulp fiction, and Virginia Woolf was highly impressed with the work of humorist and sportswriter Ring Lardner.[101] Of course, critics have frequently outlined how these popular forms influenced the work of these major writers. Stein tried her own hand at the detective novel (*Blood on the Dining-Room Floor* [written 1933, published 1982]); Joyce famously included a host of references to lowbrow culture in *Ulysses* (1922) and *Finnegans Wake* (1939); and Faulkner (in *Sanctuary* [1930], *Pylon* [1935], and *Intruder in the Dust* [1948]) and Hemingway (in *To Have and Have Not* [1937]) adopted and transformed popular formulas from pulp magazines.[102] However, an insistence that these modernist writers were "slumming" when they picked up a detective novel or a humor story not only ignores the publishing realities, but threatens to continue an already entrenched ossification of the modernist canon. Still, while it is certainly evidence of some sort of modernist affinity, the kind of validation offered by a modernist writer's appreciation for one of the popular writers discussed in *The Word on the Streets* is, by itself, not nearly enough to confer the mark of vernacular experimentalism on them. As such, my choice of writers and genres is selectively attuned to identifiable literary innovations present in the period: many popular writers of the era demonstrated no interest in formal and linguistic experimentation, and many popular genres did not undergo radical transformation alongside the rise of high modernism. Nevertheless, the vernacular modernists considered here were experimentalists in their own right, as the formal readings in this study will demonstrate. And the realities of publishing—what I have grouped under the notion of the political economy of modernist reading—make this case even more strongly. Whether they were overtly compared to high modernists, published under the same imprint, anthologized with them, or advertised in experimental little magazines, the vernacular modernists under discussion here demand a rethinking of modernist principles. For, as *transition*'s "Slanguage: 1929" shows, the boundary between writers like Gertrude Stein and James Joyce and the language of the streets might not have even existed in the first place.

Uncovering the modernist experimentation of the language of the streets requires looking at a number of popular genres that have traditionally been isolated in literary study: genres that underwent profound formal and thematic transformation in the modernist era. Methodologically, *The Word on the Streets* uses the term "genre" in two related (but distinct) modes. Standard literary genres appear in chapters 2 and 4: humor writing and the crime novel are identifiable generic practices with a history of conventions. These genres, however, have been largely segregated from traditional literary histories—due in part to their appeal to nonelite, and particularly middle- and lowbrow, readerships. As these chapters will demonstrate, these popular genres experienced substantial changes in the early twentieth century, revolutions in style and content that renovated and rewrote the generic conventions themselves. Robert Scholes has called such generic transformation "formulaic creativity," a modernistic practice that "occurs in that middle ground between larger structures established by tradition and the adaptations of structure and texture that a writer uses to make an individual work out of such structures."[103] *The Word on the Streets* argues for an even stronger understanding of these innovations; for writers like Ring Lardner, Anita Loos, Carroll John Daly, and Dashiell Hammett, these "adaptations" were more than the efforts of a writer to put an individual imprint on an example of formula fiction; these writers sought to modernize the genres themselves, transforming and redefining the very forms of representation that underwrote the formulas. For American writers working in humor and crime fiction in this period, the "structure and texture" of their experiments in the genre were built around innovations in vernacular language.

Chapters 3 and 5 follow a more sociological notion of genre, addressing two groups that also tend to fall outside of historically standard narratives of modernism and have only been incorporated within canon expansion since the 1980s. The Jewish American fictional memoir and the African American urban novel both could be conceived as literary genres, but as formal categories they also serve as windows into specific anxieties experienced by ethnic groups and demonstrate modes of understanding the particularly complex relationship these groups had to ideologies of realism. This latter notion of genre is informed, to a degree, by Richard H. Brodhead, who argues for a "history of literary access" in *Cultures of Letters: Scenes of Reading and Writing in Nineteenth-Century America* (1993). This involves examining "the history of the processes by which literary writing has had different cultural places made for it, and so has had different groups placed in different proximities *to* it."[104] The era that spawned modernist writing also saw increased interest in immigration (as both immigrant advocacy and the nativist Immigration Acts of 1921 and 1924 demonstrate), as well as a fascination with African American culture, when, as Langston Hughes phrased it, "the Negro was in vogue."[105] These phenomena alone did not create "cultural places" for these writers but contributed to the literary access that, itself, enabled aesthetic transformations in the received traditions with which these writers were engaged.[106] Such "cultural places" also became battlegrounds for representation in which vernacular language, with its strong racial, ethnic, and class associations and markers, played a pivotal role. The organizational principle of this project, while ostensibly chronological, is designed to emphasize the cross-race and cross-class models of vernacular modernism in American writing, suggesting larger and more inclusive ways of considering modernist aesthetics that do not require isolated (and isolating) subcategories.

Ultimately, *The Word on the Streets* hopes to shift the terms of the debate back to the experimentation that dominated wide varieties of modernist discourse before canonization limited the number of writers considered sufficiently interesting or "experimental." Vernacular modernism is a peculiarly American mode or current running parallel to and intersecting with transnational high modernism; it engages canonical writers as these writers engage vernacular forms. Most importantly, this concept hopes to acknowledge the wide-ranging modes of literary and linguistic revolutions happening across broad swaths of early twentieth-century American literary culture, building on criticism that has successfully brought popular culture and underrepresented groups into the broader discussion of modernist culture. By extending such critical reconsiderations and shifting a focus toward formal experimentation, I hope to offer vernacular modernism as a concept—and as a particularly American literary mode—that acknowledges something long overdue: there was a great deal more literary production, circulating in and across working-class and ethnic communities, that demonstrated the experimental power of the language of the streets.

The opening chapter of this study operates as an extension of the theory of vernacular modernism posed in this introduction, situating the shifts in both the theoretical understanding and the practical use of the American vernacular in the popular linguistic work of H. L. Mencken. Mencken himself advocated for Mark Twain as the preeminent figure in American literary history, so the chapter will first read Twain as Mencken read him: with an emphasis on the politics and poetics in works like *Roughing It* (1872) and *Adventures of Huckleberry Finn* (1885), both examples of what Twain called the "vigorous new vernacular." Mencken's research into the American vernacular began in 1910, just months after Twain's death. The product of this research, Mencken's *magnum opus, The American Language* (1919), follows as a logical extension of the linguistic play of Twain. In *The American Language,* published in four different editions and two supplements over a thirty-year period, Mencken lays out what I call a "vernacular modernist manifesto" in which he characterizes the American vulgate as exhibiting "a constant experimentation, a wide hospitality to novelty, a steady reaching out for new and vivid forms."[107]

Mencken's characterization of the "vigorous" language that originates in literature with Twain is analogous to many modernist manifestos in that it wholeheartedly rejects nineteenth-century gentility, realism, and—for Mencken—the pernicious influence of a staid and academic British language. For Mencken, the American language—with its unique hospitality to "foreign words and phrases"—is *the* modern language, and despite his well-known distaste for American idiocy, his fascination with the language is palpable and sets up the 1920s as a period ripe for vernacular experiments.

The first true examples of vernacular modernism appeared in the writing of one of Mencken's favorite writers, humorist Ring Lardner. No single writer of the period is more influential and less critically examined than Lardner, whose work was almost universally praised by high- and lowbrow critics alike. The second chapter examines Lardner's specific impact on the long-popular genre of American humor writing, particularly the ways his writing provides a critique of nineteenth-century realist humor and its emphasis on explicitly framed dialect stories. In its place, Lardner's work, such as the epistolary baseball novel *You Know Me Al* (1916), foregrounds individual subjectivity—representing the growth and development of their narrators through broken and reconstructed language—that challenges realist assumptions about the innocence of the linguistic sign. Following Lardner, Anita Loos's *Gentlemen Prefer Blondes* (1925) utilizes a vernacular narrator—iconic blonde Lorelei Lee—to parody notions of gentility and provide an opportunity for Lorelei to examine the clash between genteel sensibility and an emerging modernist consciousness. Using a narrative mode derived from Loos's own theories of writing for silent film, this novel narrates while simultaneously obscuring crucial narrative events through the sophisticated misapplication of language and heavy-handed intervention by the fictional diarist. Although critics—from Hugh Kenner to Michael North—have long connected silent slapstick comedy to modernism, my reading of Loos, whose silent film specialty was the writing of title cards, shifts away from this emphasis on the purely visual to a consideration of the interplay between image and text.[108]

The third chapter retains the emphasis on language and subjectivity in its discussion of popular Jewish American autobiographical fiction. While pioneering writers like Abraham Cahan and Mary Antin relied on the standards of realism to articulate the problems of assimilation into American society, Jewish American writers of the 1920s and 1930s, such as Anzia Yezierska, rejected a purely realistic mode for a more complex narrational strategy that layered English vocabulary onto Yiddish syntax. Critics have suggested that Yezierska's work lacks a self-conscious aesthetic, but I argue that her work demonstrates an acute aesthetic self-consciousness about the influence of foreign words on English: as she writes, "The foreign mind works on an old language like the surging leaven of youth. It rekindles and recreates our speech." For Yezierska, the hybrid language of immigrants is a modernist language, constantly renovative and specifically attuned to twentieth-century realities. Yezierska's characters challenge notions of standardization among English speakers; indeed, the stories in *Hungry Hearts* (1920) allow characters to speak "modernistically," piecing together foreign words and phrases into abstract forms of representation, giving new life and transnational overtones to the American language, echoing Mencken's claims. Like Yezierska, Mike Gold utilizes working-class and Jewish vernacular characters in his collection of "proletarian sketches" *120 Million* (1929) and his novel *Jews without Money* (1930). Normally considered a party-line proletarian writer, Gold's early (and largely unacknowledged) work in experimental theater—including work with the Provincetown Players and his constructivist-expressionist minstrel play *Hoboken Blues* (1927)—roots his aesthetics more firmly in a realm of politically engaged modernist experimentation. With an awareness of Gold's early connection to the avant-garde, I read *Jews without Money* as a text that grows out of Gold's fusion of the avant-garde and the political, one that combines brutal, expressionist images of urban degradation with an impressionist, almost Proustian nostalgia. Unifying the free play of memory in Gold's narrative is his use of a collective vernacular voice of New York's Lower East Side Jews.

The urban grotesques of Gold provide a transition to the hard-boiled crime narratives in the following chapter. Chapter 4 begins with a discussion of a pulpwood magazine that Mencken and George Jean Nathan founded to offset losses incurred by the *Smart Set*. This magazine, *Black Mask*, became a pioneer in the development of the hard-boiled detective story, a style that has become synonymous with American crime fiction. This style first emerges in the work of largely unknown Carroll John Daly, whose early short fiction shows a conscious shift from the haunted genteel narrator to the hard-talking tough guy who would dominate American detective narratives in the twentieth century. Born into a truly modern network of social, political, and economic corruption, this figure grapples with this world through a laconic, slangy form of narration. In the hard-boiled mode, not only is the ability to represent the world with any sort of accuracy seriously compromised, the world assumes a form that appears incomprehensible to language itself. Dashiell Hammett's work in the genre moves this style out of the pages of the pulp magazine with attempts, as he wrote, "to make 'literature' of it." Hammett's work was admired by modernists like Gertrude Stein and Ernest Hemingway, and his work made the transition from the pages of *Black Mask* to hardback publication with Knopf and later the Modern Library. In novels like *Red Harvest* (1929), Hammett's working-class detectives encounter nearly illegible worlds filled with expressionist violence and opaque criminal cant. Hard-boiled narration becomes a means of negotiating and manipulating a world corrupted by the smooth talk of genteel power, and Hammett's fiction poses serious questions about how language represents, and presents, epistemological puzzles that cast doubt on the ability to know and narrate an increasingly confusing and corrupt modern world. In environments where corruption runs rampant, the best a hard-boiled detective can hope for is to mitigate disaster through linguistic and narrative performance.

Chapter 5 moves away from the usual subjects of African American modernism (Jean Toomer, Sterling Brown, Langston Hughes) and looks to novels of "Black Manhattan" for signs of vernacular modernist experimentation. In this chapter, I consider the simultaneous emergence of the first Harlem "glossaries" and the most spirited debates about black aesthetics and the politics of representation in the pages of the W. E. B. Du Bois–edited journal the *Crisis*. While critics like James Weldon Johnson all but declared dialect writing dead, and journals like the *Crisis* advocated strongly for a focus on middle-class lives in African American fiction, the last half of the 1920s saw a surge of interest in African American slang, particularly in the pages of Harlem-based fiction. Carl Van Vechten's notorious *Nigger Heaven* (1926) was at the center of both of these debates, incensing black critics over its controversial subject matter and providing a "glossary" of slang terms, but it was African American writers like Rudolph Fisher and Claude McKay who exploited the potential of the intersection between slang and aesthetics in an effort to push working-class characters to the center of African American fiction. Rudolph Fisher's *The Walls of Jericho* (1928) challenges the propriety and norms of early Harlem Renaissance fiction by elevating the drama of urban vernacular characters to the level of middle-class "dickties." Fisher's novel, where characters use "any language you had the ingenuity to devise," also includes a clever glossary (a nod to Van Vechten) that sends readers in a circle of referentiality. Claude McKay's *Home to Harlem* (1928) and its quasi-sequel *Banjo* (1929) emphasize the interconnectedness of the black writer and the vernacular figure; through these two novels, which scandalized African American literary culture, his aspiring modernist expatriate Ray (an exile from Haiti) all but rejects his literary pretensions for the more interesting and vital "necromancy of language" invented by a transnational group of working-class figures and itinerant musicians. While *The Word on the Streets* emphasizes national literary contexts, McKay's presence here—as an international and diasporic figure—suggests the political and aesthetic possibilities for a vernacular American language in a global setting. For, though it's clear that McKay sought to intervene in debates about black aesthetics in the United States and to court controversy among American readers with his bawdy language and themes, his use of working-class vernacular in *Banjo* internationalizes American vernacular modernism in intriguing and radical ways.

This new articulation of an American vernacular modernism allows a wholesale rethinking of the relationship of modernist aesthetics to popular culture in American writing. Far from operating merely on a model of cultural appropriation, high modernists recognized in the vernacular writers an exciting possibility—that of yoking the American language (as celebrated by Mencken) to trends of experimentation current in Europe. As *transition*'s publication of "Slanguage: 1929" indicates, conventional divisions—even among high modernists—were beginning to fall away by the end of the 1920s. The conclusion examines how the rubric of vernacular modernism might operate if applied to more recognizable canonical figures in American modernism. William Faulkner's 1929 novel *The Sound and the Fury* places high and vernacular modernist modes side-by-side, in a familial relationship that reveals the important connection these modes would have in the 1930s, as many modernist writers turned leftward and began to explore proletarian narratives, to blend the high and the vernacular, and to embrace a modernism that could incorporate and value languages across race, ethnicity, and class. Vernacular modernism, in its most utopian form, imagines a narrative of American literary history where ethnic and working-class voices represent the true experimentation that transforms the conventions of nineteenth-century American literary production.

1 / "The Steady Reaching Out for New and Vivid Forms"

H. L. Mencken and the American Revolution of the Word

> *American thus shows its character in a constant experimentation, a wide hospitality to novelty, a steady reaching out for new and vivid forms. No other tongue of modern times admits foreign words and phrases more readily; none is more careless of precedents; none shows a greater fecundity and originality of fancy. It is producing new words every day, by trope, by agglutination, by the shedding of inflections, by the merging of parts of speech, and by sheer brilliance of imagination.*
> —H. L. MENCKEN, *THE AMERICAN LANGUAGE* (1919)

The fallout from Eugene Jolas's "Revolution of the Word" manifesto was both swift and palpable. Shortly after the publication of this famous issue, which included Irwin's "Slanguage: 1929" among its experimental pieces, the leftist journal the *Modern Quarterly* took issue with the manifesto's bold proclamation in a fall 1929 symposium devoted to *transition*'s "Revolution of the Word." If anything, Jolas's 1930 response to his *Modern Quarterly* critics produces a stronger bond between *transition*'s avant-garde literary polemics and the innovations of the American vernacular. Titled "The King's English Is Dying—Long Live the Great American Language," Jolas's point-by-point response to V. F. Calverton concludes with a memorable invocation. He writes,

> The mysticism surrounding the "purity of the English language" has, I believe, lost its force. In the crucible of the immense racial fusion of indigenous and immigrant America there is occurring [*sic*] today an astounding creation that ultimately will make the American language, because of its greater richness and pliancy and nearness to life, the successor of British English. This is already happening in speech, and as soon as the age-old delusion that there must be a difference between written and spoken words has had its day we will probably see the American language colonize England and all English-speaking countries.[1]

In making these claims, Jolas provides a telling footnote: "See H. L. Mencken's *The American Language.*" Jolas's argument here is not far off of Mencken's in his masterwork; Mencken too would celebrate the American language for what Jolas called its "immense racial fusion of indigenous and immigrant America" and for its ability to colonize, to become globally dominant. What is striking in this, however, is Jolas's insistence that the American language, with "its great richness and pliancy and nearness to life" is, in effect, the *lingua franca* of modernism itself. He concludes the essay by claiming that the intersection of racial and immigrant groups in the United States "will bring to fruition the language of the century to come."[2]

Jolas's invocation brings Mencken and his *American Language* squarely into the discussion of avant-garde aesthetics. While this might seem surprising, particularly to modernist scholars who have largely ignored the importance of Mencken to the period, it is not unique. Mencken was a veritable obsession among writers and intellectuals of the modernist era, and Jolas was not the only avant-garde figure to cite Mencken's popular linguistics as a useful analogy for experimental writers. A 1923 article by Matthew Josephson, editor of the little magazine *Broom*, claims that "the temper of the age, which is one of prodigious social transformation, must be contributing far more in the way of new names, technical and colloquial, new compounds, neologisms, word-structures. Another period of language expansion, such as occurred in the sixteenth century, has set in. (The reader is here referred to H. L. Mencken's The American Language)."[3] If anything, Mencken's linguistic work provided modernists like Jolas and Josephson a popular and well-respected analogue for the innovations they championed in little magazines like *Broom* and *transition*. At the same time, it reinforces the strong connection between manifestos like the "Revolution of the Word" and slang and vernacular dictionaries like Irwin's "Slanguage: 1929."

This chapter considers the popular linguistics of H. L. Mencken, whose landmark study *The American Language* offers a theoretical voice to the concept of vernacular modernism. Additionally, the chapter serves as an extension of the theoretical issues raised in the introduction and a practico-theoretical bridge between the introduction and the case studies that follow. Mencken's work, however, would not likely have been possible without the influence of writers like Mark Twain. Twain's literary praxis operates as a precursor to vernacular modernism, critiquing the linguistic assumptions of realism from within a largely realist framework. In what follows, I consider Twain's linguistic experimentation in texts like *Rough-*

ing It (1872) and *Adventures of Huckleberry Finn* (1885) as a background to the linguistic and philological work of Mencken, whose *American Language* (1919), researched and published at the birth of high modernism, operates as a vernacular modernist manifesto. In analogous modes, Twain and Mencken sought an American "Revolution of the Word," one that punctured the pretensions and elitism of dialect realism, offering in its place an experimental American vernacular that would provide the raw material for a peculiarly American modernist innovation.

"The Vigorous New Vernacular": Mencken Reads Twain

> *A nation's language is a very large matter. It is not simply a manner of speech obtaining among the educated handful; the manner obtaining among the vast uneducated multitude must be considered also.*
> —MARK TWAIN, "CONCERNING THE AMERICAN LANGUAGE" (1882)

For the purposes of this argument, it is a rather convenient coincidence that the year 1910 witnessed two crucial moments in the history of the American vernacular: the death of Mark Twain in April and the first of H. L. Mencken's *Baltimore Evening Sun* articles on the American language in October. Mencken was soon to become the editor of the *Smart Set* and later the *American Mercury* and well on his way to becoming one of the most prominent cultural figures of the 1920s, and these publications would be the first in a lifelong engagement with questions of language and culture in America. Though Mencken's bombastic and polemic writing style shared little with Twain's work, it was clear in Mencken's multiple appreciations of him that Mencken saw Twain as the greatest American writer to date. Twain was, according to Mencken, "the largest figure that ever reared itself out of the flat, damp prairie of American literature."[4]

For Mencken, Twain's literary genius rested, unsurprisingly, on the latter's distinct prowess in the use of vernacular language. Twain is one of Mencken's major sources in his popular linguistics, and he singled Twain out in the early editions of *The American Language*, noting that "in all his writings, even the most serious, he deliberately engrafted its greater liberty and more fluent idiom upon the stem of English, and so lent the dignity of his high achievement to a dialect that was as unmistakably American as the point of view underlying it."[5] Here Mencken highlights Twain's early travelogue *Roughing It*, where he notes that Twain was "celebrating 'the vigorous new vernacular of the occidental plains and mountains'" (*AL* 1:16–17, *AL* 2:20, *AL* 3:21). These celebrations of Twain tie Mencken's popular linguistic project to Twain's work, collecting and reproducing the vernacular speech of the West and old Southwest; they also point to Twain's thematic concerns, which, in Mencken's reading, overlap with his own intellectual project.

Like most American literary critics of the early twentieth century, Mencken's literary assessment of Twain found its primary source in *Adventures of Huckleberry Finn*. In 1913 he called the novel "one of the great masterpieces of the world . . . the full equal of *Don Quixote* and *Robinson Crusoe*," and in 1919 he wrote that it was "a truly stupendous piece of work—perhaps the greatest novel ever written in English."[6] Mencken's estimations of the novel anticipate later celebrations of it by modernists like William Faulkner and Ernest Hemingway, who claimed in *Green Hills of Africa* that "all modern American literature comes from one book by Mark Twain called *Huck Finn*."[7] While the study of Twain has long moved beyond the exclusive consideration of his masterpiece, it is important to reconsider and reconstruct Mencken's reading of Twain—and of works related to *Huckleberry Finn*—as central to his own popular linguistics, and, by extension, a vital precursor to what I have termed vernacular modernism.

Additionally, Mencken's understanding of Twain shares an affinity both with his own intellectual project of the 1910s and 1920s and with influential critical readings of Twain that coalesce around concepts like "genteel" and "vernacular." For Mencken, Twain is the model of the debunker:

> What a sharp eye he had for the bogus, in religion, politics, art, literature, patriotism, virtue! What contempt he emptied upon shams of all sorts—and what pity! He regarded all men as humbugs, but as humbugs to be dealt with gently, as humbugs too often taken in and swindled by their own humbuggery. He saw how false reasoning, false assumptions, false gods had entered into the very warp and woof of their thinking, how impossible it was for them to attack honestly the problems of being; how helpless they were in the face of life's emergencies.[8]

Mencken cannily anticipates mid-century readings of Twain, such as Henry Nash Smith's influential thesis that Twain's work is structured around the conflict between genteel and vernacular values, generally siding—in his most celebrated work, at least—with vernacular characters and language. Channeling Van Wyck Brooks's argument that bifurcated the nature of American life along the terms "highbrow" and "lowbrow," Smith emphasizes that Twain's work charts the "two levels of experience":

"the realm of the ideal, the locus of values, and the realm of everyday reality, the locus of facts."[9] Twain scholars—including James M. Cox, Michael Egan, David R. Sewell, and many others—have long been indebted to this particular characterization of Twain, even if they have complicated and revised Smith's initial argument.[10] Sewell, for example, situates Twain's work in the complex nineteenth-century relationship between speech and writing and complicates Smith's hard-and-fast distinction between these vernacular and genteel registers.

Smith's argument has been adapted since its publication in 1962, but it continues to structure readings of Twain, whether those oppositions are seen in terms of vernacular/genteel or oral/written.[11] What remains suggestive about Mencken's reading of Twain is the way in which this celebration of Twain's ability to debunk pretention and hypocrisy is connected to his strategic and virtuosic use of vernacular language. Mencken's description of Twain's virtues uncannily resembles Mencken himself; this is in fact a version of Twain crafted in Mencken's own image. Compare his description of Twain's value, for example, to Mencken's own assessment of "the daily panorama of human existence, of private and communal folly" of life in the United States: "the unending procession of governmental extortions and chicaneries, of commercial brigandages and throat-slittings, of theological buffooneries, or aesthetic ribaldries, of legal swindles and harlotries, of miscellaneous rogueries, villainies, imbecilities, grotesqueries, and extravagances."[12] For Mencken—and for Mencken's reading of Twain—the exposure of what he called the *"boobus Americanus"* is somehow subtly linked to the celebration of a "vigorous new vernacular" that would become Mencken's *American Language.*[13]

Because Mencken tied Twain's genius to *Roughing It* and *Adventures of Huckleberry Finn*, a reading of such texts—along the lines Mencken might have read them—will serve as a useful means of conceptualizing the development of vernacular modernism (and of Mencken's linguistic studies) from Twain's experimental model. Given the underlying assumptions of this project, it might be better to describe Twain's work as representing the limits of dialect fiction, rather than exemplifying that of the vernacular. Of course, Twain's rampant experimental use of dialect blurs these boundaries and gives rise to further experiments in vernacular fiction of the twentieth century. It remains important, however, to see Twain operating in a tradition that encompasses both dialect fiction and the literary realism of figures like his friend William Dean Howells. As Jonathan Arac has written, "Only during Howells's own career, beginning after the Civil War, did an ethnographically serious dialect literature arise, what we call local color."[14] For, while popular humor movements of the first half of the century turned on dialect to mark racial and regional difference (and the political and social hierarchies such difference suggested), the rise of a realist aesthetic in the 1870s and 1880s meant that literary work—determined to represent the real world in mimetic forms—would also begin to include the "commonplace" language that had previously been excluded from serious literary endeavors. In efforts to democratize literary representation, realism often went beyond the simple inclusion of a dialect-speaking servant figure or backwoodsman; serious novelists began emphasizing dialect in protagonists, and talented dialect writers like Mark Twain became literary sensations. As Gavin Jones has argued, "Late nineteenth-century America was crazy about dialect literature."[15]

The link between dialect writing and realism is unmistakable: both depend on photographic (or phonographic) representation, both assume the ability of language to accurately represent this world, and both orient themselves around hierarchy within linguistic groups. So, even in the most genteel of realist texts, the introduction of commonplace language, whether marking country naïveté or ethnic difference, marks social differentiation, education, and value of characters. As Elsa Nettles has written,

> Howells's faith in the power of realism to promote brotherhood seems based on an unswerving allegiance to principles of unity and equality which he championed throughout his life. Yet his theory of realism, when put into practice, reveals an inherent conflict.... As his own fiction shows, nothing more immediately establishes differences among characters than different habits of speech. Unless all the characters speak in the same way, dialect at once divides the speakers of the standard language from the non-standard speakers.[16]

Even in realist texts where the protagonists are marked with dialect (like Howells's *The Rise of Silas Lapham* [1885]), these characters are routinely judged—and in Lapham's case, ultimately banished—by the genteel narrative voice. The major realist writers of this era generally held to this particular sense of language hierarchy, where, according to Gavin Jones, "the assumption of Howellsian realism that dialect was democratic, energetic, and native means of expression was undercut by another view of nonstandard speech as the humorous sign of cultural degeneration."[17]

Howells and Twain were closely associated in the late nineteenth and early twentieth centuries, a fact solidified by Howells's publication of his tribute *My Mark Twain* in 1910, almost immediately after Twain's death.

Mencken's reading of Howells's relationship to Twain varied over his career. In *The American Language,* he linked them as champions of the American language over British English. There, he called Howells's novels "mines of American idiom," and noted that "his style shows an undeniable revolt against the trammels of English grammarians" (*AL* 1:17, *AL* 2:20, *AL* 3:21). Earlier, however, Mencken saw these figures as crucial opponents in an American linguistic legacy. In a review of Howells's *My Mark Twain,* Mencken highlighted what he called "the abysmal difference between the straightforward, clangorous English of Clemens and the simpering, coquettish, overcorseted English of the later Howells."[18] Certainly, this distinction—on the basis of language—is a crucial one in that it parses the difference between Twain, whose "clangorous English" is far preferable to the "overcorseted" language of Howells, echoing descriptions Mencken would later give British English. Not surprisingly, Mencken was at the beginning of his research on the American language when he reviewed *My Mark Twain,* and, despite his endorsement of Howells in later linguistic work, this dichotomy is not only a useful way of understanding Twain's relatively radical realist aesthetics: it also anticipates critical assessments of Howells that highlight hierarchical character distinctions modeled on linguistic stratification.

For Mencken, Twain is both an integral part of the Howellsian realist tradition that elevated "commonplace" language to the forefront of American literature culture *and* the purveyor of a sophisticated autocritique of that realist aesthetic. For, while Howells could, on the one hand, produce "mines ... of the American idiom," his work could also—in contrast to Twain's—seem conservative and "overcorseted." Twain, then, operates within the tradition I have described as dialect realism, but he constantly pushes the boundaries of this tradition, producing a "clangorous English" that can barely be contained by the realist aesthetic that defines it. It is in the two Twain texts most celebrated by Mencken that these challenges to traditional dialect paradigms become clearest.

In his 1872 Western travelogue *Roughing It,* Twain begins his earnest experiments with language and narration. From its first scenes of difficult communication, through Horace Greeley's unintelligible handwriting near the conclusion, questions of language and communication help structure the text. Critics like Lee Clark Mitchell have noted how important language is to *Roughing It,* calling it "the west of words"; indeed, the twists and turns of language is one of the major themes throughout the book.[19] Twain not only draws on the conventions of Southwestern humor, he also foregrounds these conventions as they occur. The speech/writing divide in nineteenth-century dialect writing is at the center of this text; Gavin Jones has noted that the text "is a remarkable document of philological self-consciousness that enacts, rather than merely refers to, the linguistic debates of Twain's era."[20] Twain uses his narrator's encounters to suggest the inadequacies of standard language in the new western environment, the new rules surrounding discourse in the West, and the problematic assumptions of dialect realism in general.

Twain's emergent critique of dialect realism begins at the onset of *Roughing It*'s loosely organized plot. Hardly out of the St. Joseph, Missouri, stage station, the narrator and his brother soon encounter a radically different linguistic world. Sharing the coach with these two figures are three days' worth of mail bags, "almost touching our knees, a perpendicular wall of mail matter rose up to the roof" of the stage, as well as an unruly "Unabridged Dictionary" that will soon injure them on their bumpy travels.[21] But the written word—the correspondence of the east intended for points west—is not all that will accompany the narrator on his first day in the stage. In the evening, a woman boards the coach for a short time. The narrator refers to her as the "Sphynx," because her stony quiet disturbs the narrator and the other passengers. As the passengers sit through a lengthy silence, the narrator finally breaks the ice, resulting in an absolute torrent of language from the Sphynx. Her language—riddled with the grammar of a backwoods dialect—immediately becomes the focal point. She was just as confused about the silence of the men as they were about her. She says, "Fust I thot you was deef and dumb, then I thot you was sick or crazy, or suthin', and then by and by I begin to reckon you was a passel of sickly fools that couldn't think of nothing to say" (*RI* 9). The social and linguistic codes here are indicative of Twain's sophisticated use of dialect strategies. One day into their journey west from St. Joseph, Missouri, the men, too proper and self-conscious to begin a conversation with this unknown woman, have already encountered new modes of discourse and new rules of social interaction. Like many of Twain's genteel narrators, they fail to understand the codes and are made to look like "a passel of sickly fools" precisely because they "couldn't think of nothing to say." The inability to speak—and to speak in appropriate ways—is apparently worse than being "deef and dumb" or "sick or crazy." It is, in fact, the worst thing one could be in the West. As Philip Burns has argued, "The Western vernacular becomes a mode of experience, an aberration that impinges upon the narrator's consciousness," and Twain's narrator has yet to recognize the new linguistic terrain he has entered.[22]

Despite her censure of the "sickly fools" in the stagecoach, the Sphynx is summarily dismissed by the narrator in a fashion that characterizes how dialect characters were often treated by realist narrators throughout nineteenth-century American fiction. According to Twain, "The Sphynx was a Sphynx no more! The fountains of her great deep were broken up, and she rained the nine parts of speech forty days and forty nights, metaphorically speaking, and buried us under a desolating deluge of trivial gossip that left not a crag or pinnacle of rejoinder projecting above the tossing waste of dislocated grammar and decomposed pronunciation" (*RI* 9). Twain and his companions "suffered" at the hands of this woman and her "dislocated grammar and decomposed pronunciation."[23] A minor incident in *Roughing It*, the encounter with the Sphynx anticipates things to come, an early warning of the ways in which language will be transformed and social and linguistic codes will be upended by the West. This is far from the last time that Twain's narrator will play the tenderfoot fool in the face of a language and culture he has not quite mastered.

As *Roughing It* proceeds, however, the narrator's perspective begins a dramatic transformation. Soon, he no longer characterizes this language as "dislocated grammar and decomposed pronunciation," but instead begins to speak of "the vigorous new vernacular of the occidental plains and mountains," a phrase quoted by Mencken in every edition of *The American Language* (*RI* 26). This shift is a profound one in the context of dialect literature of the nineteenth century; it essentially inverts the hierarchies of language that underwrite dialect realism. *Roughing It* upends traditional expectations: readers expecting a humorous account of backwoods miners receive a rude awakening when Twain begins to appreciate and even idolize the language and customs of the West. The educated nineteenth-century reader does not find a stable point of genteel identification that maintains class hierarchies. Instead, Twain's text increasingly becomes complicit with the corrupting influence of western dialect. In set pieces devoted to Scotty Briggs and other figures, the narrator's conversion from genteel Eastern tenderfoot into devotee of the Western vernacular becomes obvious. No longer does the narrator look down on the language of the West; Twain starts drawing out the complexities of dialect and its connection to power relationships as he depicts other bewildered Easterners unable to adapt to this "vigorous new vernacular."

The funeral preparations for Buck Fanshaw draw out Twain's linguistic preferences in very explicit ways; indeed, the conversation between Scotty Briggs and the young minister, found roughly halfway through the text, is central to many critics' understanding of language in the novel. Twain prefaces his encounter with a discourse on the importance of slang to the silver-mining communities. These communities are crucibles for the preservation and development of slang:

> Now—let us remark in parenthesis—as all the people of the earth had representative adventurers in the Silverland, and as each adventurer had brought the slang of his nation or his locality with him, the combination made the slang of Nevada the richest and the most infinitely varied and copious that had ever existed anywhere in the world, perhaps, except in the mines of California in the "early days." Slang was the language of Nevada. It was hard to preach a sermon without it, and be understood. Such phrases as "You bet!" "Oh, no, I reckon not!" "No Irish need apply," and a hundred others, became so common as to fall from the lips of a speaker unconsciously—and very often when they did not touch the subject under discussion and consequently failed to mean anything. (*RI* 309)

If slang is the language of Nevada, it is also the most valued language of *Roughing It*, and Scotty Briggs's negotiations with the young minister ("the duck that runs the gospel-mill . . . the head clerk of the doxology-works" [*RI* 310]) is *Roughing It*'s most explicit encounter between vernacular and genteel figures. For Sewell, "Twain's major object in this chapter was to create a tour de force of Western slang, the success of which is certified by his contemporaries' appreciative response. But the object of satire here is language itself, which creates as much opportunity for misunderstanding as for communication."[24] The notion of linguistic interference, of a multiplicity of viable languages, emerges in this chapter as a counterpoint to the narrator's first experience with the Sphynx. And the minister's bookish language, like the Unabridged Dictionary, is utterly useless in an environment of linguistic experimentation and flexibility like this one.

If *Roughing It* begins to challenge the dominant paradigms of dialect realism in the form of a self-deconstructing travelogue, Twain's most celebrated novel, *Adventures of Huckleberry Finn* (1885), more explicitly dismantles these realist expectations through its sophisticated vernacular narration. This text opens in a celebrated, if peculiar, fashion. On a page titled "Explanatory," "The Author" notes the following:

> In this book a number of dialects are used, to wit: the Missouri negro dialect; the extremest form of the backwoods Southwestern dialect; the ordinary "Pike County" dialect; and four modified varieties of this last. The shadings have not been done in a haphazard

fashion, or by guesswork; but painstakingly, and with the trustworthy guidance and support of personal familiarity with these several forms of speech.

I make this explanation for the reason that without it many readers would suppose that all these characters were trying to talk alike and not succeeding.[25]

Published in 1885, a high point of realism in American publishing, Twain's introductory remarks serve both to remind readers of the important symbiotic relationship between realist aesthetics and dialect and to satirize the notion that such a meticulous, photographic version of realistic art is even possible. Some critics have sought to identify all seven of these dialects, but such a task seems absurd.[26] For why would we take the word of "The Author" after the "Introductory" note ("By Order of the Author") tells us that "Persons attempting to find a Motive in the narrative will be prosecuted; persons attempting to find a Moral in it will be banished; persons attempting to find a Plot in it will be shot" (*AHF* xxxiv)? Instead of taking Twain at his word—always a dangerous approach—we might consider this Twain's satire of the expectations of a dialect specialist. To look for the seven dialects in *Huckleberry Finn* is to be taken in by Twain's joke, like so many of his genteel narrators are by the dialect figures of the West, Southwest, and South. In this opening, Twain performs a mastery of dialect writing, while simultaneously satirizing the expectations that come with such mastery: consistency was certainly difficult for even the most talented dialect writer working with eye dialect and phonetic representations, and Twain's opening caveat already absolves him of any inconsistencies in linguistic representation under the guise of a heightened realism.

Twain's opening "Notice" and "Explanatory" also serve an additional purpose: they replace the standard genteel frame that accompanies virtually all dialect writing during this period. Dialect realism, with an interest in marking linguistic difference, depends on a hierarchy of voices within the dialect text. Usually, this operates in much the same way as Twain's early work in the mode of Southwestern humor. A genteel figure—effectively the educated reader's representative in the world of the text—typically frames the tale, and the dialect figures, themselves often storytellers like Jim Blaine of *Roughing It* or Simon Wheeler of "Jim Smiley and His Jumping Frog," inhabit this world. The sharp distinction between the language of frame narration and that of the dialect storyteller reinscribes the class, regional, and/or ethnic distinctions between these two spheres, making a text of dialect realism what Bakhtin would call a "zone of contact."[27] The frame narrator, educated like the author and the reader, has the ability to represent dialect accurately; this figure is an incarnation of the aesthetics of dialect realism. Even in texts that do not employ the genteel first-person frame narrator, the language of third-person narration closely resembles the speech of educated characters, while the dialect speakers are, if not linguistically marginalized, nonetheless disposed of through narrative strategies that cannot allow such a figure to dominate an otherwise genteel realist text.

It is here that *Adventures of Huckleberry Finn* pushes the boundaries of the narrative frame as far as they can go at this historical juncture. Huck is ostensibly our storyteller; his relationship to the writing of the text, though, remains confusing. After all, both the "Notice" and the "Explanatory" at the text's opening are signed by "The Author," and neither one exhibits a language even close to that of Huck's. That said, chapter one opens unabashedly in Huck's voice: "You don't know about me, without you have read a book by the name of 'The Adventures of Tom Sawyer,' but that ain't no matter. That book was made by Mr. Mark Twain, and he told the truth, mainly" (*AHF* 1). Huck's vernacular voice opens with a reference to the "real" textual production of Twain, and Huck challenges Twain's veracity in telling a story that readers know full well is a fiction. Twain's satire of realism and realist expectations is on full view here as his fictional creation challenges the creator's ability to record fictional events accurately ("mostly a true book; with some stretchers," Huck says [*AHF* 1]). But Huck's opening lines beg the question: Who is writing *this* book, *Adventures of Huckleberry Finn*? While the author's notes at the opening suggest the presence of an authorial force that looms over Huck, this authorial presence essentially vanishes throughout the remainder of the text, allowing Huck to control the narrative. But is Huck *writing* here, or is he *telling* this story to the authorial consciousness that appears in "Note" and "Explanatory"?

Twain's less celebrated and less successful sequels to *Huckleberry Finn* make the relationship of author to narrator somewhat clearer. *Tom Sawyer Abroad* (1894) is "By Huck Finn/Edited by Mark Twain" and *Tom Sawyer, Detective* (1896) is "as told by Huck Finn."[28] In both of these cases, the presence of Twain—as editor or ethnographic collector/auditor—is made clear, and Huck's role as dialect storyteller conforms more comfortably to the standards of dialect realism. After all, realism's strategy of class and ethnic containment generally permits dialect characters the ability to speak, but not to write. In *Adventures of Huckleberry Finn*, certainly Twain's most ambitious and experimental Mississippi story, Huck's role remains relatively undefined: he is both literal author (in early stages, Twain referred to the text as *Huck Finn's Autobiography*) and contained dialect figure.[29] Is the variation in dialect due to Huck or "The Author" of the prefatory "Note"? Is the use of eye dialect ("sivilize," for example) meant to imply Huck's misspelling or—as it often was in dialect work—to heighten the distance between uneducated speakers and educated readers? How do we square the seeming linguistic contradictions between the genteel prefatory Author and Huck, who speaks of "what a trouble it was to make a book" at the novel's conclusion (*AHF* 362)? Anticipating what I have called vernacular modernism, Twain pushes the genteel frame as far to the margins as he possibly can and leaves readers on unstable ground in a world where dialect realism is often strictly governed by the speech/writing divide.[30]

Huck's most important scene of writing in the novel contributes to the text's intentional lack of clarity. After escaping from the King and the Duke and discovering that Jim has been sold and effectively re-enslaved, Huck considers writing to Miss Watson. Another in a series of scenes about Huck's ongoing ethical transformation (a transformation rudely interrupted by Tom Sawyer's "evasion" plot), Huck finally decides to write a letter, telling Miss Watson where Jim is. His decision-making process begins with a failed prayer: "I was letting *on* to give up sin, but away inside of me I was holding on to the biggest one of all. I was trying to make my mouth *say* I would do the right thing and the clean thing, and go and write to that nigger's owner and tell where he was; but deep down in me I knowed it was a lie—and He knowed it" (*AHF* 269). In spite of his inability to "*say*" that he wants to turn Jim in, Huck still manages to *write* the letter. As he contemplates the letter in front of him, he remembers the adventures he and Jim have enjoyed together, how Jim "would always call me honey, and pet me, and do everything he could think of for me" (*AHF* 270). Huck's memories of his time with Jim, the memories that dominate the first part of this spoken/written text, finally help Huck make a decision: he tears the letter up, and in the process resigns himself: "All right, then, I'll *go* to hell" (*AHF* 271). Huck's rejection of the written word here dramatizes Twain's challenge to the standards of dialect realism that insists on dialect speech inside (and subordinated to) genteel writing: Huck's writing (like Unabridged Dictionaries) would effectively support the written laws that have enslaved Jim to begin with. When Huck says, "I knowed it was a lie," he means not only his prayerful intention to do the right thing, but the written laws that create the structures of slavery.

Huck's destruction of the letter represents a preference for the spoken and the vernacular over genteel pretention and hypocrisy in its written forms.

Ultimately, though, *Adventures of Huckleberry Finn* ends on a comprised note, where Huck's vernacular values are subordinated to Tom's insistence on doing things "the way all the best authorities does"—in other words, by the book (*AHF* 299). Tom's bookish principles script a story that endangers both the boys and Jim in the service of genteel cultural scenarios, the historical romances that Tom has devoured as historical truths. Steven Blakemore has written that in the "evasion" plot that concludes the novel, "Jim literally becomes the prisoner of writing, locked in a linguistic dungeon of Tom's devising."[31] This dynamic between Huck and Tom is central to Twain's sequels, as well, though Huck's implicit critique of Tom's genteel nonsense is diminished, if not completely effaced. Sewell even argues that the presentation of Huck, Tom, and Jim in *Tom Sawyer Abroad* makes them "disappointingly unlike the trio in *Huckleberry Finn*."[32] Still, at one more interesting moment, after Jim has fallen asleep listening to Tom ramble on, Huck notes that "a person always feels bad when he is talking uncommon fine, and thinks the other person is admiring, and that other person goes to sleep that way. Of course he oughtn't to go to sleep, because it's shabby, but the finer a person talks the certainer it is to make you sleepy."[33] "Talking fine," Tom's specialty, stands in opposition to Huck's vernacular language. When they are not putting Huck and Jim to sleep, Tom's bookish language and logic serve, like the Unabridged Dictionary of *Roughing It*, to interrupt and endanger others in the service of scripted and textually licensed adventures.

In *Roughing It* and *Adventures of Huckleberry Finn*, Twain inverts traditional dialect hierarchies, upsetting the classist and racist notions that inform realism's use and abuse of dialect characters. His most innovative work anticipates H. L. Mencken's modernist celebration of the vernacular by demonstrating the complex narratological and representational possibilities offered by vernacular protagonists. But Twain only pushes so far; it remains difficult for Twain to break out of the dialect standards, and even in *Huckleberry Finn*, where his experiments are most intense, he inserts a silent but crucial editorial presence that maintains a realist dichotomy between the written and the spoken word. Still, Twain pushes this editorial frame as far as it will go, allowing Huck's language to define and dominate the linguistic consciousness of the novel. Twain would go on to experiment in most of the genres discussed in *The Word on the Streets*. His influence on humor writing is undeniable, and his impact on the depiction of African American dialect is also central to his critical reputation. He also crafted narratives of cultural encounter (*Roughing It, The Innocents Abroad* [1869]) as well as detective stories (*Pudd'nhead Wilson* [1894]; *Tom Sawyer, Detective*). But Twain's linguistic legacy would be formidably taken up by a theorist of the American language, a critic who would expand on Twain's practice with a serious theoretical and philological consideration of the American language in a thirty-year project that framed the "vigorous new vernacular" of America as an overt challenge to its English roots, to nineteenth-century gentility, and to realist aesthetics. H. L. Mencken's *The American Language* was a vernacular modernist manifesto, rooted in the experiments of Twain and connected to the experimental vernacular that entered popular culture in the 1910s.

"When Things Get All Balled Up": H. L. Mencken's Modernist *American Language*

> *Thus the American, on his linguistic side, likes to make his language as he goes along, and not all the hard work of his grammar teachers can hold the business back. A novelty loses nothing by the fact that it is a novelty; it rather gains something, and particularly if it meets the national fancy for the terse, the vivid, and, above all, the bold and imaginative.*
> —H. L. MENCKEN, THE AMERICAN LANGUAGE (1919)

Citations throughout Mencken's popular linguistic work suggest that Mencken saw himself as the inheritor and chronicler of a tradition best exemplified by Twain. Mencken's literary preferences ran toward the realism and naturalism of writers like Twain and Theodore Dreiser, rather than the modernist experiments that were appearing during the height of his career. Indeed, Mencken displayed a rather complex and evolving relationship toward the notion of realism throughout his career. In an early essay on Twain, Mencken linked Twain's vernacular language with the very idea of realistic representation, asking, "Where, in all fiction, will you find another boy as real as Huck himself?"[34] Later, however, Mencken followed the path of many other literary critics, who, in the 1920s, began to have doubts about the purely mimetic function of language. He began a 1926 article entitled "On Realism" with the statement, "One of the strangest delusions of criticism is to be found in the notion that there is such a thing as realism—that is, realism grounded on objective fact in the same way that a scientific monograph, say, or the report of a law trial, is grounded upon objective fact."[35] Nevertheless, he reaches a conclusion that his idea of "realism" has less to do with a measurable objectivity and more to do with "intellectual honesty in the artist," a common position among realists and naturalists of the early twentieth century.[36]

Despite this shifting relationship to realism, Mencken never wholly endorsed the high modernist experimentation that emerged alongside his own rising celebrity as a cultural critic. While he gave Joyce's *Portrait of the Artist as a Young Man* (1916) a positive review in the *Smart Set*, noting that "there is not the slightest hint in it of the usual structure of prose fiction; it is new both in plan and in detail," he absolutely hated *Ulysses*, calling it "deliberately mystifying and mainly puerile.... I have never been able to get over a suspicion that Joyce concocted it as a kind of vengeful hoax."[37] Mencken's own literary preferences—his prejudices, as he might call them—remained rather Victorian throughout his life. Of his contemporaries, he preferred the literary work of naturalist Theodore Dreiser and realist and debunker Sinclair Lewis, and he had little use for new experimental art forms, whether they were (like jazz) commercial products or (like Joyce's *Ulysses*) emblematic of a more elite literary avant-garde.

Mencken's literary tastes became, by the middle of the twentieth century, largely unfashionable, and contemporary scholars rarely cite Mencken as an authority on any matters of literary value, despite his influence during the 1910s and 1920s. Around the same time that his taste in literature went out of style, his increasingly controversial political positions further marginalized him in the American mainstream. His marginalization as both a literary and cultural critic and a political and social thinker has only increased with the revelation of some of Mencken's more controversial views about Jews and World War II; for all intents and purposes, he has become a *persona non grata* in American literary studies. Unlike other cultural figures of the era, Mencken has not received as much attention from American studies scholars as he did from his contemporaries. In American studies scholarship of the last thirty years, only Chip Rhodes's *Structures of the Jazz Age* (1998), Mark McGurl's *The Novel Art* (2001), and Joshua L. Miller's *Accented America* (2011) deal with Mencken at any length. This is somewhat surprising, given that Mencken was probably the most influential and well-known social and cultural critic of the 1920s and served as editor of the *Smart Set* and *American Mercury*, two periodicals that set standards for both literary and intellectual discourse in the American mainstream in the early decades of the twentieth century.[38] In a 1921 article, Edmund Wilson styled Mencken as a modern Walt Whitman, calling him "the civilized consciousness of modern America, its learning, its intelligence and its taste, realizing the grossness of its manners and mind and crying out in horror and chagrin."[39] In the popular American mind, at least, the 1920s were not the famous "Pound era" of Hugh Kenner's description, but almost undeniably the "Mencken era."[40]

When Mencken is addressed in criticism, the results are frequently predictable. An avowed Nietzschean, contemptuous of American culture and the Americans who embraced it, Mencken's name has become synonymous with the concept of "debunking," a popular fascination of the 1920s. With his series of essays *Prejudices* (1919–27) as well as his commentary in *American Mercury* (on, among other things, the Scopes trial), Mencken's reputation has long been that of the gritty and crusading realist, driven to explode myths and expose idiocy wherever he saw them. Indeed, when Mencken's work has seen republication in the twenty-first century, it is along these lines: the S. T. Joshi edited volume *Mencken's America* (2004); *A Religious Orgy in Tennessee* (2006), which collects Mencken's writings on the Scopes trial; Marion Elizabeth Rogers's new edition of Mencken's 1926 *Notes on Democracy* (2008); and the two-volume Library of America edition of *Prejudices* (2010) all reinforce his position as ruthless critic of American culture. Unfortunately, Mencken's status as harsh cultural critic has largely limited the ways in which his importance to the modernist era has been discussed. Beyond the hackneyed characterization of him as the ultimate "debunker" and leader of a movement that historian Frederick Lewis Allen called in 1931 "The Revolt of the Highbrows," it is difficult to situate him in the contemporary milieu of modernist studies where race, class, gender, sexuality, and ethnicity constitute a cultural matrix in which modernist writers and thinkers attempt to reconfigure the changing world around them.[41] As a result, both American studies scholars and New Modernist critics do not quite know what to make of him.

Unlike so many other major figures in the American 1920s who were literally trying to make the world "new," Mencken remained locked into a schizophrenic Victorianism. While railing against an American "boobacracy" of Puritan values in his work, he lived much of his private life in line with nineteenth-century genteel bachelorhood. Because of these contradictions (as well as the controversy surrounding anti-Semitic remarks in his posthumously published diary) biographies of Mencken outnumber critical studies of his work by more than two to one. Of course, the inconsistencies in a subject's life are far easier to explore than are contradictions in his work and thought. And Mencken's work is almost unbelievably varied: his writings encompass reportage, literary journalism, philosophical biography, literary criticism, popular linguistics, cultural criticism, travel writing, memoir, and dramatic burlesques (among others). The studies that do attempt to bring together Mencken's varied work inevitably end up in a familiar place. Writers like Frederick J. Hoffman in *The Twenties* (1965) and Edward A. Martin in *H. L. Mencken and the Debunkers* (1984) essentially reinscribe Allen's 1931 thesis that Mencken was "the keynoter of this revolt [of the highbrows], its chief tomtom beater."[42]

Almost inevitably left out of any "comprehensive" study of Mencken's work is his magnum opus, *The American Language*.[43] Initially published in 1919, this book is one of the first in a series of books by major figures in American intellectual history that suggest an early articulation of American cultural "exceptionalism" after World War I.[44] *The American Language* does not fit conveniently into any of the rubrics for understanding Mencken as a man or as an intellectual. It is neither polemic nor burlesque; it is seldom cranky or hostile. It is, in many ways, Mencken's most earnest attempt at creating a literary and intellectual legacy. As Raymond Nelson has noted in one of the few scholarly considerations of *The American Language*, "Mencken came to believe it would be the single work for which he would be remembered."[45] Such a position does not jibe with the common notion of Mencken as the self-appointed scourge of the *boobus Americanus*. Even in Mencken biographies, *The American Language* gets short shrift.[46] The critical avoidance of this work is somewhat surprising, considering that Mencken worked on versions of it for most of his career. Beginning with journalistic musings in the *Baltimore Sun* in 1910, it evolved into a special series of articles in 1914 and became a book-length study by 1919. The next four years saw two new editions (1921 and 1923), and, while writing influential cultural criticism during the late 1920s, Mencken continued to amass material toward the fourth and final edition, published in 1936 at a moment when Mencken's public reputation (and Germanophilia) had become increasingly unpopular. While this has become the standard edition (and has remained in print into the twenty-first century), Mencken published two "supplements" in 1945 and 1948 and followed these with a series of "postscripts" in the *New Yorker* from 1948–49, his last major publications. Mencken's engagement with *The American Language* (1910–49) covers nearly his entire professional life, far more time than his influential editorships at the *Smart Set* (1914–23) and at the *American Mercury* (1924–33), or his acclaimed essay series *Prejudices* (1919–27). And though scholars have not managed to position *The American Language* within the larger corpus of Mencken's thought, reviews of the first edition saw the study as typically Menckenian, noting that "never has the flourishing personality of H. L. Mencken been so happily exercised as in this big book on the living speech of America."[47]

More recent interest in the politics of modernist language has brought

Mencken back into the spotlight in Joshua L. Miller's *Accented America*, where he places Mencken in the fraught context of "English-only Americanism." Miller's reading of *The American Language* exposes the text's notion of an exceptionalist and yet "ethnically white, masculine, normative vernacular."[48] Miller's reading offers a valuable recovery of the importance of this text to the broader culture of American literary modernism, and it effectively links Mencken's troubling racial politics and critical blind spots—his anti-Semitism, his ignorance of African American vernacular—to the "invention of a standardized and racialized national vernacular" in language education of the twentieth century. Nevertheless, Miller tends to overread this work as "a curiosity piece, a hair-raising, pseudoscholarly work" and ignores the long and serious prehistory of the first edition of *The American Language,* as well as its broad appeal across the lines of race and ethnicity.[49] At the same time, Miller's emphasis on Mencken's problematic relationship with ethnic and racial difference obscures the important work that *The American Language* does in elevating a working-class language to the realm of a national one. For Mencken, the term "English" itself posed a number of problems, as the multifaceted language he describes in his project emerged, in fact, as a direct challenge to notions of linguistic purity.

The American Language, invisible though it may be in many studies of Mencken, ought to be placed at the center of American modernist studies, for virtually no other critics of this period weave together concerns of linguistic and literary independence with questions of linguistic experimentation in quite the way that Mencken does. Moving between subjects as diverse as histories of pronunciation and debates in poetry journals about the use of slang in American novels, *The American Language* reinforces longstanding ideas about a modernist era in which issues of language and experimentation were paramount. *The American Language* consciously rejects the cultural criticism for which Mencken is better known today. His interest in language does not appear to be a part of his "mediaeval but unashamed taste for the bizarre and indelicate, [his] congenital weakness for comedy of the grosser varieties" that he describes as his somewhat perverse reasons for remaining in the United States in his essay "On Being an American."[50] Rather, his linguistic study—as unsystematic as it is—is rooted in two other tendencies: Mencken's desire for a unique and independent American culture, separate from English influence, and the revolutionary and experimental power of a vernacular language that is always in a process of innovation. In an era filled with bombastic attempts to define and promote new forms of linguistic and literary experimentation, *The American Language* assumes the form of a homespun, vernacular variation on the modernist manifesto.

Mencken's first series of articles that would become *The American Language* does not strike one as necessarily revolutionary; these pieces include (as does *The American Language* itself) extended lists of variable meanings between American and British English. He begins this series relatively humbly: "Words change and their meanings change. Idioms decay, dry up and blow away. Grammatical forms give birth to new grammatical forms. The same verb is conjugated differently in different ages, in different countries, on different sides of the street. The English people speak an English which differs enormously, in vocabulary and idiom, from the English spoken by Americans."[51] The articles that followed "The Two Englishes" fell along the same lines, with Mencken pointing out the differences in English and American slang in "England's English" (October 14, 1910), creating conjugation charts for vernacular American usage in "Spoken American" (October 19, 1910) and "More American" (October 20, 1910), and contrasting the variant uses of pronouns in "American Pronouns" (October 25, 1910). While Mencken occasionally exhibits some of his notorious contempt for the American public—for example, when he writes that "any spoken language, however barbarous, is worthy of investigation"—the overall impression of these pieces is that Mencken has developed a real fascination with the independence of the American vernacular from its English roots.[52]

Indeed, Mencken would later expand his ideas and celebrate the idiosyncrasies of American English in a *Smart Set* article entitled "The American: His Language," published in August of 1913. Here, Mencken notes, "Such is American, a language preeminent among the tongues of the earth for its eager hospitality to new words, and no less for its compactness, its naked directness, and its disdain of all academic obfuscations and restraints."[53] Embracing novelty and innovation, rejecting nineteenth-century academicism, the American language is, in Mencken's characterization, a language built for modernity. Strangely, this article appears in a series (entitled "The American"), in which Mencken has few positive things to say about American character. In other articles in this series, subtitled "His Morals," "His Ideas of Beauty," "His Freedom," and "His New Puritanism," Mencken savages virtually every element of American life in the early twentieth century. Only in "His Language" does Mencken praise some element of the culture he made a career out of criticizing.

In his articles on American English, Mencken seizes upon the ways in which it quite literally declares independence from the English of England. The issue of linguistic independence, particularly in the vernacular uses of the language, remains central in all of the later incarnations of Mencken's language studies. "The American: His Language" would become the basis of a short first draft of *The American Language*, written in 1915 and 1916 and held in typescript at the Enoch Pratt Free Library in Baltimore. In articles produced over the next two years, Mencken would continue to argue for linguistic independence in wartime articles like "Nothing Dead about Language U.S. Boys Take to the Trenches," published in the New York *Evening Mail* in September 1917. In contrast to the "English dialect of English," which is "conservative and unyielding," "the American dialect . . . is extraordinarily hospitable to change. It bends to every wind. It absorbs every flying particle. It is astoundingly fluent, resilient and porous. . . . In slang, too, American is a much more enterprising language than English—so much so, in fact, that fully a half of the annual crop of new slang in England is imported from America."[54] Mencken's article is illustrated by two cartoons. The first, depicting an Englishman fleeing "A New Word," contains the caption "the English resent the use of a new word." The second, which might illustrate much of Mencken's evolving thought about the American language, depicts Uncle Sam bound with a gag reading "No Slang." Its caption reads, "Without Slang America Could Not Talk."[55] Of course, given Mencken's own political distaste for England and oft-discussed Germanophilia, this emphasis on linguistic independence could be read as a means of extricating his own American identity from too close an association with England. At the same time, however, his interest in the American vulgate suggests a set of larger concerns about the manner in which American language provides a way out of a stale, conservative gentility that still dominated American literature and culture in the first decades of the twentieth century.

In its first three editions, *The American Language* takes this critique further, as Mencken develops an argument for the "superior imaginativeness" of American over English (*AL* 1:82, *AL* 2:97, *AL* 3:100). The early editions of Mencken's text—more radical in their description of linguistic innovation than the fourth and final edition—consistently echo the calls for modernist experimentation; according to Mencken, Americans have no trouble making their language new and consistently remaking it at a moment's notice.[56] As he notes, "The American vulgate is not only constantly making new words, it is also deducing roots from them, and so giving proof, as Prof. Sayce says, that 'the creative powers of language are even not now extinct'" (*AL* 1:23, *AL* 2:31).[57] That consistent innovation of language is what characterizes the American language and what feeds into, for example, *transition*'s celebration of American "slanguage" published a decade after Mencken's first edition of *The American Language*.

Mencken opposes this American innovation most explicitly to the "English" language. Sections of the book—as well as of Mencken's earlier articles—use columns to demonstrate the different words used in America and England. But Mencken is not merely interested in making these distinctions; his emphasis is in associating American with change, transformation, and modernity. "English now has the brakes on," Mencken writes, "but American continues to leap in the dark, and the prodigality of its movement is all the indication that is needed of its intrinsic health, its capacity to meet the ever-changing needs of a restless and emotional people, constantly fluent in racial composition, and disdainful of tradition" (*AL* 1:28–29, *AL* 2:37, *AL* 3:39). The American language, he notes here, differs from English because it is not static but ever changing. Hospitality to various kinds of foreign influence ("constantly fluent in racial composition") and the wholesale rejection of linguistic traditions characterize American as modern, multiethnic, and multiracial.[58] By extension, English, with its "brakes on," is emblematic of a monoracial linguistic past, of the gentility and aristocracy that Mencken loathed, traditions that troubled modernist writers as well.

Mencken's oppositions—between a static and homogenous English language and an ever-changing and racially complex American one—not only mirrored the high modernist theory of the 1910s and 1920s; avant-garde experimentalists also cited Mencken as an authority on the powerful transformations in modernist language. As noted in the introduction, avant-garde figures like Matthew Josephson and Eugene Jolas referenced Mencken in their own arguments that the American language might just be the basis of a new, experimental language for "the temper of the age" as well as being "the crucible of the immense racial fusion of indigenous and immigrant America." For these modernists, Mencken provided more than a model of cultural critique of American Puritanism and hypocrisy; his work on linguistics offered opportunities to consider the experimental possibilities inherent in the American vernacular.

Although modernists saw immense possibility for vernacular language in their own experimental approaches, Mencken's work charted how slowly the innovative American vulgate had entered the literature of the United States. He notes, "Literature in America, as we have seen, remains aloof from the vulgate. Despite the contrary examples of Mark Twain and Howells, all of the more pretentious American authors try to write chastely and elegantly; the typical literary product of the country is still a refined essay in the *Atlantic Monthly* manner, perhaps gently jocose but never rough—by Emerson, so to speak, out of Charles Lamb—the sort of thing one might look to be done by a somewhat advanced English curate" (*AL* 1:305, *AL* 2:361, *AL* 3:370). This characterization of most American literature demonstrates Mencken's own sense of the modernity of the American vulgate. Outside of Twain and Howells, American literature has embodied the American nineteenth century of Emerson, the British nineteenth century of Lamb, the gentility and propriety of "a somewhat advanced English curate," and the refinement of the Boston-based journal *Atlantic Monthly* (ironically enough, known for regularly publishing both Howells and Twain).[59] The vulgate, largely missing from American literary production, stood ready to challenge these stultifying tendencies in American literature, and other writers and thinkers at this moment had also begun noting the potential power that American vernacular language might have in modernist literary circles.

As Mencken's first two editions appeared, debates raged in a wide variety of publishing contexts over the trend toward the use of the American language more forcefully in serious American literary productions. In the second edition of *The American Language*, for example, Mencken cites a lengthy passage from a 1920 article in the journal *Poetry* by Richard Aldington (*AL* 2:19, *AL* 3:19–20). Aldington, Imagist poet and husband of the American Imagist H.D., had earlier pondered the literary differences between English and American writing in an article on H.D. entitled "A Young American Poet" (1915), but this article, "English and American," articulates a position even closer to that of Mencken.[60] In the passage from "English and American" cited by Mencken, Aldington reinforces the arguments in *The American Language*:

> Language is made by the people; it is only fixed by writers and orators. When language, especially that of the poetry, is too far removed from that of the people, it becomes conventional and hieratic, like church Latin; or languid and degenerate, like modern official French poetry. When language is conventionally used by writers it becomes burdened with clichés and dead phrases. If American soldiers, newspapers and popular novels are evidence, it is clear that the American people is evolving a new language, full of vigorous and racy expressions.[61]

For the English Aldington, though, this new literary language could be as difficult to follow as the most complex modernist poem. In a statement that might just as easily apply to high modernist texts like *The Waste Land* or *Ulysses,* Aldington notes, "New [American] novels are bewildering with vigorous but incomprehensible expressions."[62]

Aldington's multiple uses of the adjective "vigorous"—like Twain's "vigorous new vernacular"—mark American as a language uniquely suited to the demands of twentieth-century modernity and simultaneously opposed to a "conventional" language "burdened with clichés and dead phrases." Emerging from "newspapers and popular novels" and making their way into poetry and more serious narrative, these "vigorous and racy expressions" are the core of Mencken's notion of *The American Language,* and the stuff of vernacular modernism itself. The "vigorous but incomprehensible expressions" mentioned by Aldington are, in effect, the same kinds of expressions that make it into the *transition* piece "Slanguage," discussed in the introduction. American slang, in effect, had already been singled out as providing a possible "Revolution of the Word" long before Jolas decided to juxtapose his manifesto with a glossary of contemporary slang terms.

In the first three editions of *The American Language,* Mencken devotes a crucial chapter to the discussion of "American Slang"; this is one part of the text that grows with each edition and that assumes an even larger role in the 1936 fourth edition. For Mencken slang is rooted in individual creativity, not larger social trends. "Slang originates in an effort, always by ingenious individuals, to make the language more vivid and expressive" (*AL* 1:309, *AL* 2:365, *AL* 3:375). In the three early editions, he links this to the power of newspapers, and he is loath to grant the American public with the power to produce interesting slang. In discussing "the slang of baseball," for example, he claims that "there is not enough imagination in that depressing army [of baseball fans] to devise such things; more often than not, there is not even enough intelligence to comprehend them" (*AL* 1:311, *AL* 2:367, *AL* 3:377). Though Mencken's disdain for the *boobus Americanus* dominates this discussion, his fascination with slang as the best and most experimental example of American vernacular language remains a strong theme througout his study In "The American: His Language," he notes that the "striving for vividness and forcefulness, when applied to the sentence instead of to a single word, produces the extraordinarily lush and vigorous thing called American slang."[63] Twenty-four years later, Mencken's argument for the power of slang remained compelling; he noted in the fourth edition of *The American Language* that slang "originates in the effort of ingenious individuals to make the language more pungent and picturesque—to increase the store of terse and striking words, to widen the boundaries of metaphor, and to provide a vocabulary for new shades of difference in meaning" (*AL* 4:563).

American slang—or the American "slanguage" as *transition* might have it—provides a modernist tool for countering the dead weight of realist language. Mencken's advocacy for the "vigorous" language of American slang anticipates, in a sense, the "Revolution of the Word" manifesto, which—like Mencken's conception of American slang—challenges "the banal word, monotonous syntax, static psychology, [and] descriptive naturalism." While equating Mencken's writings on American slang with the bombastic theoretical statements of Jolas and others might seem, at first, to be a perverse use of these writers, there is some suggestion that Mencken saw his work as a manifesto of its own kind. In the second (1921) and third (1923) editions of *The American Language*, Mencken included an appendix titled "Specimens of the American Vulgate," a nod toward his own proclivity for writing burlesques throughout the 1910s. Designed to display the American language in practice, these sections included pieces by humorist Ring Lardner, poet John V. A. Weaver, and Mencken himself. Lardner's pieces, "Baseball-American" and "Ham-American," demonstrate different kinds of specialized argot (among baseball players and actors), and Weaver's poem shows how vernacular language might appear in serious poetry. Mencken's pieces, on the other hand, are actually "translations" of historical American documents into the slang of the 1920s. The piece that appears in both editions, which would be later reprinted as a "burlesque" in *A Mencken Chrestomathy* (1949), edited by Mencken himself, is his translation of the American Declaration of Independence.

Early on in the second edition of *The American Language*, Mencken sets the stage for this "burlesque" by referencing a 1920 *Harper's* article by Rupert Hughes (*AL* 2:22–23, *AL* 3:23). Hughes's article, "Our Statish Language," opens with a flourish: "A new Declaration of Independence is needed"; it proceeds to challenge prevailing notions that "Americanisms are not nice, and are not written by well-bred little writers." After citing Mencken's first edition of *The American Language*, Hughes closes on a note that seems to anticipate Mencken's attempt to transform the Declaration into the vulgate: "Let us sign a Declaration of Literary Independence and formally begin to write, not British, but Unitedstatesish."[64] Hughes's argument, like Mencken's, sets American against British English and calls for, quite literally, a "Revolution of the Word." Mencken closes his second edition by providing one. By "translating" the Declaration into contemporary American vernacular, Mencken demonstrates the vigorous and imaginative nature of what he calls "the American vulgate" and invokes the Declaration's call for independence from British rule, aristocratic pretention and privilege, and the past. In essence, Mencken's Declaration is the vernacular modernist manifesto for the "American Revolution of the Word."

Mencken's rationale for such a translation is interesting: "It must be obvious that more than one section of the original is now quite unintelligible to the average American of the sort using the Common Speech" (*AL* 2:388, *AL* 3:398). This claim of unintelligibility points toward an almost evangelical use of translation; because no one can understand this liberating document, Mencken implies, he will liberate the document (and its readers) by rendering it in a language with a more nuanced contemporary meaning. His opening operates simultaneously as a burlesque and a declaration of independence for vernacular modernists: "When things get so balled up that the people of a country have to cut loose from some other country, and go it on their own hook, without asking no permission from nobody, excepting maybe God Almighty, then they ought to let everybody know why they done it, so that everybody can see that they are on the level, and not trying to put nothing over on nobody" (*AL* 2:388, *AL* 3:398–99). Mencken's translation removes the Enlightenment language of the original document, substituting in its place a series of highly idiomatic expressions. His entire translation, full of ephemeral slang, much of which has long passed out of use, almost needs its own set of annotations for an early twenty-first-century reader. Like so many other bombastic statements in this age of manifestos, Mencken's declaration rejects a realist language for a set of vernacular metaphors that draw attention to themselves as much if not more than the content they purport to communicate. "When things get all balled up," as they often do in the language of genteel realism, only a vernacular language, a modernist aesthetics of slang, can liberate them.

In the context of debates surrounding the use of slang and vernacular language in American literary production, Mencken's declaration is a manifesto, growing out of ten years of research into the ways in which the American language challenges the staleness and sterility of a nineteenth-century American culture that modeled itself on British gentility. A language seemingly built for modernity, "American ... shows its character in a constant experimentation, a wide hospitality to novelty, a steady reaching out for new and vivid forms. No other tongue of modern times admits foreign words and phrases more readily; none is more careless of precedents; none shows a greater fecundity and originality of fancy" (*AL*

1:26, *AL* 2:35, *AL* 3:37). The American language is also the language of modernist experimentation and aesthetic novelty, "producing new words every day by sheer brilliance of imagination" (*AL* 1:26, *AL* 2:35, *AL* 3:37).

Mencken's construction of a modernist American vernacular informs the writers discussed throughout *The Word on the Streets*. Across the editions of *The American Language,* he emphasizes the importance of figures like Ring Lardner, whose baseball columns led to his own experimental humor; silent film titles, which inform Anita Loos's work; criminal cant and popular fiction, both important to the development of the hardboiled style in the pages of *Black Mask* (a magazine Mencken started with George Jean Nathan); and the incorporation and transformation of "foreign tongues" into the "constantly fluent . . . racial composition" of *The American Language,* issues that dominate my chapters on Jewish American and African American writing.[65] In the interest of charting these relationships, for example, Mencken corresponded with Abraham Cahan, pioneering Jewish American realist writer and editor, over the interchanges between Yiddish and American English. Ultimately, Mencken's "American vulgate" crystallizes a way of thinking about vernacular American language as inherently experimental, a modernist challenge to the prevailing standards of genteel realism. The vernacular modernist manifesto that appears in the second and third editions of *The American Language* shares space with other "specimens of the American vulgate," including contributions by one of Mencken's favorite writers, Ring Lardner. And it is in Lardner's largely unacknowledged revision of American humor that the theory of vernacular modernism first becomes practice.

2 / "Never Mind the Comical Stuff.... They Ain't No Joke about This!"

Ring Lardner, Anita Loos, and the Comic Origins of Vernacular Modernism

> *In fact, the most of the successful authors of the short fiction of to-day never went to no kind of college, or if they did, they studied piano tuning or the barber trade. They could of got just as far in what I call the literary game if they had of stayed home those four years and helped mother carry out the empty bottles.*
>
> —RING LARDNER, PREFACE, *HOW TO WRITE SHORT STORIES (WITH SAMPLES)* (1924)

In his 1879 study *Hawthorne*, Henry James makes the now-notorious list of the "absent things in American life" that hamper the development of a serious novelist in the United States. Here, he argues that America lacks the rich usable past of Europe, and without a long history, the creation of a complicated, literary novel is impossible in the young society of the United States. He does note, however condescendingly, that despite lacking all these important historical and cultural legacies of Europe, Americans are not completely without culture. "The American knows that a good deal remains; what it is that remains—that is his secret, his joke, as one may say. It would be cruel, in this terrible denudation, to deny him the consolation of his natural gift, that 'American humour' of which of late years we have heard so much."[1] James's somewhat snide dismissal of the popularity of American humor set the tone for much of the discussion of humor in American literature throughout the nineteenth and twentieth centuries.

James is almost certainly referring to traditions like that of Southwestern humor, particularly popular in the 1830s and 1840s, but heavily influential on the work of Mark Twain, whose "Jim Smiley and His Jumping Frog" became a national sensation in 1865.[2] As I have argued in chapter 1, Twain provides a literary ancestor for vernacular modernism, while James's influence on modernist aesthetics remains an influential part of modernist historiography. James's idealization and centralization of the figure of the artist and his interest in chronicling the inner lives of the European and American elite lead almost directly to the work of figures like Pound, Stein, and Woolf. Indeed, Pound saw his own poetry as deriving from the prose of James.[3] Twain's work, on the other hand, establishes a somewhat different legacy. His specialty in creating "authentic" character speech (particularly of children, African Americans, and rural figures) informs a major strain of American humor and the larger tradition of vernacular modernism as defined here, and his particular brand of humor is a clear antecedent to the humorists of the modernist era.[4]

In the 1910s and 1920s, Ring Lardner and Anita Loos transformed the nature of American humor writing, foregrounding its textuality in contrast to the orality of earlier humor texts like Twain's. Influenced by the modern technological transformations of motion pictures and sound recording, these two writers pushed language to new extremes, emphasizing a humorous narrative subjectivity that was itself fragmented, incomplete, and wholly unreliable. While James dismissed humor as a bastard form of culture, the only uniquely American development, Lardner and Loos demonstrated the degree to which James's own modes of psychological interiority, complex subjectivity, and textual manipulation could transform the experience of humor. Both favorites of canonized literary figures and of the general public, these two humorists created a subjective, textually self-conscious form of humor that revels in the linguistic exuberance of Mencken's modernist slang. As a result, Lardner and Loos worked to transform the traditions of American humor, moving away from the conventions of realist representation, and ultimately they inaugurated a new and highly influential mode of vernacular modernism that has influence across multiple popular genres.

"I'll Explain It to Ye": Realist Aesthetics and American Humor

> *Somewhere between the two—that is to say, forninst th' gas-house and beyant Healey's slough and not far from the polis station—lives Martin Dooley, doctor of philosophy.*
> —FINLEY PETER DUNNE, MR. DOOLEY IN PEACE AND IN WAR (1898)

Following the dismissal of American humor by James, the history of American humor writing (outside of the figure of Twain) has received relatively scant attention in the mainstream of American literary history. When critics approach humor, they frequently do so in the realm of "humor studies," a literary critical subspecialty that isolates humor from the rest of American literature. A foundational text in this regard, Constance Rourke's *American Humor: A Study of the National Character* (1931), sees humor as central to conceptions of American identity and American literary history. For Rourke, however, humor is almost inevitably regional; in *American Humor* she identifies three distinct nineteenth-century character types or strains that ultimately overlap and intertwine in the twentieth century: the Yankee, the backwoodsman, and the "Negro."[5] Representing the North, the West, and the South respectively, these types ultimately inform fiction of the late nineteenth and early twentieth centuries; her analysis anticipates (by over fifty years) the dialogic work of the 1980s as she identifies the ways in which these popular comic types make their way, however subtly, into the work of such canonical writers as Poe, Hawthorne, Melville, and even Henry James (!).[6]

While such comic types, and the history of American humor itself, remained important to the writers of the early twentieth century, Rourke does not complete a full survey of contemporary humorists in *American Humor*. In a section entitled "Round Up," quite possibly a reference to the well-known 1929 collection of Ring Lardner's short stories of the same name, she devotes as much time to Willa Cather and Sinclair Lewis, writers with considerable literary credibility, as she does to humorists Lardner and Finley Peter Dunne.[7] She frequently insists, however, on seeing humor as something necessarily situated in the past. For Rourke, humor serves as a part of the raw material of American character that contemporary literature cannibalizes; this actually prefigures the complex problematic of literary influence and dialogical models discussed in the introduction, but it fails to consider how humorists of the early twentieth century engaged with and transformed the aesthetic assumptions of American humor in new twentieth-century modes. Had Rourke spent a greater deal of time examining the most successful and influential humorists around the time of the publication of *American Humor*, her discussion would likely have centered on two major figures in 1920s humor: Ring Lardner and Anita Loos. Both favorites of H. L. Mencken, these two writers suggest a continuity with some of the traditions of American humor as well as a significant break with many of the formal and structural assumptions of the comedic tropes of the nineteenth century. Informed by a host of transformations in media and literature, it was humor that first harnessed the vernacular modernist potential highlighted in Mencken's writings on the American language.

To a degree, humor writing in America has always been interested in American speech; its generally regional focus highlights the ways in which language, representation, narration, and identity are necessarily intertwined. For example, the Southwestern humorists of the 1830s and 1840s, many published in William T. Porter's anti-Jacksonian *The Spirit of the Times*, frequently lampooned Jackson's backwoods constituency from the perspective of a genteel, Republican narrator, creating a Bakhtinian "zone of contact" with a specific political goal. The dialect and malapropisms of the frontier figures signified an ignorance that forestalled reader identification and created explicit textual hierarchies largely consistent with the dialect realism of the late nineteenth century. But Southwestern humor rarely operated in such a reductionist manner. Many of these tales, such as Twain's first published works, satirized the genteel narrator's inability to understand the community and language of the frontier. In these situations, the narrator, feeling himself superior to the frontier figures, often gets in over his head. The consequences of this may be as innocuous as being mocked in front of a group of backwoodsmen or as serious as physical violence.[8] In both cases, the humor relied on a distinct linguistic and textual difference between the genteel (and sometimes quasi-anthropologic or ethnographic) narrator and the regionally specific frontier characters.

Indeed, a great deal of humor throughout the nineteenth century turned on the difference between languages and their textual representation, a difference that would in some ways anticipate and ultimately parallel the standards of literary realism itself.[9] Brom Weber argues that comic writers of the nineteenth century were more than "popular funny men whose prime comic stock in trade was butchery of the English language by means of gross misspellings and other crude linguistic shenanigans."[10] Many popular writers, including rural humorists like Bill Nye and "misspellers" like Artemus Ward, employed elements of satire that were frequently highlighted by their publication in newspapers alongside actual political commentary.

As was true with much of the humor throughout the nineteenth century, late nineteenth-century literary humor often appeared in dialect tales, focusing on racial, ethnic, and regional groups increasingly marginalized by political, economic, and cultural modernity.[11] With its emergence as a Midwestern metropolis, Chicago actually became the center of American humor at the turn of the twentieth century, producing a number of nationally famous humorists. In 1898 Chicago newspaperman Finley Peter Dunne became a national sensation with the publication of *Mr. Dooley in Peace and in War*, a collection of social and political commentary written in a thick Irish brogue under the pseudonym "Mr. Dooley."

This book, derived from articles published around the turn of the twentieth century, operates as a running commentary on American involvement in the Spanish-American War, as well as a general set of observations on working-class Chicago society.

Following a tradition common in nineteenth- (and twentieth-) century humor, *Mr. Dooley* uses formal strategies to create an intentionally blurred notion of authorship. Dunne's name appeared on neither the newspaper articles nor the book, suggesting that "Mr. Dooley" himself is, in fact, the author of the text. Like the various introductions to Twain's *Huckleberry Finn,* the book's preface, signed "F.P.D.," complicates this even further. Is Dunne posing as editor or author here? Even the use of language in the preface blurs some of these distinctions. It begins "Archey Road stretches back for many miles from the heart of an ugly city to the cabbage gardens that gave the maker of the seal his opportunity to call the city 'urbs in horto.'" Though it opens with this commanding and controlling voice of the narrator of nineteenth-century literary realism, the narrative quickly introduces the dialect that will dominate the majority of the text: "Somewhere between the two—that is to say, forninst th' gas-house and beyant Healey's slough and not far from the polis station—lives Martin Dooley, doctor of philosophy."[12] As if charting the interdependence of dialect and realism in the late nineteenth century, the Irish brogue of Dooley himself seeps into this dominant narrational voice, but only in an appositional phrase, prefaced by "that is to say." Thus, the dialect, describing the location of Dooley's home, appears in Dooley's own voice as a modified quotation. Like other instances of dialect in this preface, the punctuation of this first appearance sets the dialect off from the language of the realist narrator, seeing it at a distance as something foreign and fundamentally different from the genteel language that Dunne predominantly uses in the remainder of the preface.

The function of the preface in a book of dialect humor like Dunne's is of central importance to the project of literary humor during the realist era. In a sense, this resembles the practice of the Southwestern humorists, who mediated their dialect with a genteel narrator that could interpret the language of the frontiersman for the literate readership, while effectively "quarantining" it from standard language.[13] However, in works like *Mr. Dooley* the heavy mediation of the narrator who becomes a kind of fictional ethnographer gives way to a more subtle form of textual and narrational mediation. Through prefaces, indication of dialogue, and impression of recorded speech, humorists maintained the dichotomies of realism (literate *langue*/subliterate *parole*) while de-emphasizing their own narrative involvement. Unlike Twain, Dunne does not go to such lengths to complicate the idea that he is recording speech. Instead, the Mr. Dooley sketches are all indicated as dialogue; the opening sketch begins with a characteristic trope of the Dooley pieces: "'I'll explain it to ye,' said Mr. Dooley."[14] As a result, while the text is almost completely dominated by the voice of Mr. Dooley himself, there is a mediating force, however slight, between the reader's experience of Dooley's language and of the text. Because the sketches are presented as dialogue, readers might assume that the speech is somehow reported and the "F.P.D." of the preface retains ultimate control over the representation of Dooley's words.[15] Like other dialect figures in realist or regional writing, Dooley remains a character in need of introduction and interpretation, and his language requires a buffer (however slight) to prevent any misapprehension by the reader.

At the same time, Dunne's humor—like a majority of dialect writing—turns on a particular kind of semiotics that the vernacular modernism of Lardner and Loos works to disrupt. The Dooley stories operate on the assumption that they do, in fact, sufficiently articulate the ideas of Mr. Dooley, whom Dunne calls in his preface "the traveller, archaeologist, historian, social observer, saloon-keeper, economist, and philosopher, who has not been out of the ward for twenty-five years 'but twict.'"[16] As a result, the authorization of Dooley's "expertise," however satirical, means that the language of the sketches can be understood as a function of a comprehensible dialect semiotics. In other words, the reader must work through Dunne's representation of Dooley's thick brogue to arrive at a clear understanding of the ideas being communicated. The assumption remains that Dooley has articulated a complete and closed idea; the job of the reader is to engage the language at the level of semiotic substitution (refiguring pronunciation, unpacking idiomatic expressions, etc.) to gain access to a definite signified.

While Dunne was, in a sense, working fully within the nineteenth-century dialect tradition of writers like Joel Chandler Harris and others, George Ade, another Chicago newspaperman, had also begun to reconceptualize and revise some of the assumptions associated with nineteenth-century humor. Beginning as a Midwestern urban regionalist, writing fiction about the experience of Chicago life, Ade became the most popular humorist in America in the first decade of the twentieth century, largely due to his highly successful series of humorous fables. The title of Ade's most famous work, *Fables in Slang* (1899), certainly suggests his importance to the notion of vernacular modernism, and his work, like Lardner's and Loos's, was praised by Mencken. In *Prejudices: First*

Series (1919), Mencken called him "one of the few genuinely original literary craftsmen now in practice among us," and said that his work "is as thoroughly American, in cut and color, in tang and savor, in structure and point of view, as the work of Howells, E. W. Howe or Mark Twain."[17] However, the role of slang in the *Fables* is—despite its title—minimal.[18] Rather than following the tradition of dialect story, Ade's stories employ a disinterested, realist third-person narration and remain largely consistent with Victorian norms.

In some respects Ade explicitly objectifies language; his use of italics in titles and comic deployment of specialized language in the fables generates humor from the extreme objectification of nonstandard language. In "*The* Fable *of the* Professor *Who* Wanted *to be* Alone," Ade's objectification of specialized language is apparent: "One day a Professor, preparing to make a Grand Ascension, was sorely pestered by Spectators of the Yellow-Hammer Variety, who fell over the Stay-Ropes or crowded up close to the Balloon to ask Fool Questions. They wanted to know how fur up he Calkilated to go and was he Afeerd and how often he did it. The Professor answered them in the Surly Manner peculiar to Showmen accustomed to meet a Web-Foot Population. On the Q.T. the Prof. had Troubles of his own."[19] Rather than presenting this "slang" as a form of experimental representation, the narrator presents these terms as curious novelties, whether specialized terminology ("Stay-Ropes"), general vernacular expressions ("Q.T."), or dialect pronunciation ("Calkilated"). In each case, the terms that seem to suggest a diversion away from realism become the objects of realistic investigation. However, Ade replaces standard English with idiomatic expressions, assuming a nearly one-to-one correspondence between the two linguistic signs. Ade's objectification of these words, by their capitalization, operates in a manner analogous to the frame created by implicit or explicit quotation in the vast majority of dialect tales. The unusual capitalization of these words—hearkening back to eighteenth-century conventions—becomes a marker that confirms the fables' connection to the older conventions of dialect realism.

While literary humor was struggling in the work of Dunne and Ade to break free of the assumptions of nineteenth-century realism, with its standard English/dialect binary and frame narration, other media provided models of how writers might create and dramatize comic situations under entirely different structural, narrational, and representational principles. The 1890s saw the emergence of sound recording and motion pictures, major forms of mass media that would transform not only American comedy, but the majority of American popular culture as well.[20] At first these new technologies struggled with the adaptation of contemporary elements of popular culture; one of the primary inspirations for many early films and sound recordings was one of the most dominant popular culture forms of the time, vaudeville. Still, as producers in these new media discovered, the experience of a song, a comedic sketch, or a scene from a minstrel or stage show was profoundly different when experienced absent of the expected sound or visual cues, the frame devices that helped identify humor. The limitations of these media, both in time and in content, forced their producers to reconsider the elements of vaudeville comedy that would work in each of the new media. The resulting developments produced two new forms of twentieth-century comedy, the comic monologue (on cylinders or recorded discs) and slapstick comedy (in film).

Humor recordings, such as Cal Stewart's popular "Uncle Josh" series (1897–1919), engage their listeners under a set of limits created by sound recording technology.[21] Unlike the vaudeville routines from which they derive, humor recordings lacked the framing device of the proscenium or visible audience. Like the vast majority of realist-inflected literary humor, which used frame narrators, vaudeville humor was mediated in ways that constantly reminded its audience of the artificiality of the performance. Indeed, it was often seen as a stark contrast to emerging theatrical naturalism of the late nineteenth century. Henry Jenkins's history of vaudeville and early sound film comedy emphasizes the interplay between performers and audiences, "the active role of popular response in shaping vaudeville performances."[22] Beyond spatial markers like the visible proscenium and surrounding audience members, vaudeville shows included structural indicators as well: regular shifts between acts and, at times, a speaker who introduced and interpreted or commented on the acts. These performances provided visual and situational semiotic clues, reminding the audience when to laugh and when to wait for the punch line. Sound recording was another matter entirely. As Patrick Feaster has noted, "Because phonograph recordings were among the first experiments at translating live performances of any kind into mass-mediated ones, their producers had to pioneer new conventions for framing discourse, using sound to compensate for the lack of visual and contextual cues."[23] Recording technology introduced artificial limits; the three-minute maximum recording time on the cylinders and discs necessitated an abridgement of acts and an elimination of the mediating cues to which audiences had become accustomed. The "straight man" or commentator was often the first to be cut.[24] This resulted in a more direct form of comedy that created a profoundly different experience for its listeners. Without a straight man or other mediating elements (such as an audience), the listener was laughing *at* the performer as opposed to laughing *with* another performer or fellow audience members.

The absence of semiotic clues such as the straight man (in routines like the "Uncle Josh" performances) meant that individuals listening to these mechanically reproduced comic routines encountered more complicated difficulties involving identification. This, of course, was added to the "amazement and even fear" that the new technology presented.[25] Feaster has linked this experience of early sound recording to R. Murray Schafer's notion of "schizophonia," a "cognitive disorientation" engendered by the alienating effect of this technology.[26] Although some listeners almost certainly experienced these records in groups, the invention of the phonograph was itself a means to bring entertainment into the private sphere. These isolated listeners encountered comics like Uncle Josh without an audience or a straight man to guide their laughter. According to Mark Katz, "Solitary listening was another facet of the phonographic experience that challenged early users ... [and] contradicted centuries of tradition."[27] Often, this anxiety was mildly ameliorated by the laughter of the comic monologist himself. Still, this presented the individual listener with a problem: given only one person (the comic) with whom to identify, what happened when this person was also the butt of the joke? Lacking any form of mediation, listeners were forced to identify both with and against figures like Uncle Josh, a problem that texts and performances during the realist era self-consciously avoided through their insistence on mediating dialect humor. As Jason Camlot has argued, "In this in-between space the [recorded comic] monologue is both objectified and received from a distance, and yet is also potentially something performed by the audience itself."[28] The only laughs in the records are Uncle Josh's, laughing, as one critic has noted, "at his own rigid behavior in the face of modernity, at the same time providing a suture between the listener and the modern apparatus of the phonograph."[29] In these recordings, the listeners' only possible source of identification was Uncle Josh himself; this meant that listeners laughing at Uncle Josh were also, in effect, laughing at themselves.

Paralleling the development of sound recording, early comic film negotiated similar issues with identification, form, and representation. Modernist critics from Hugh Kenner to Michael North have connected the slapstick film to the developments of modernism, and what Tom Gunning has called the "cinema of attractions" was one of the most explicitly "avant-garde practices" of the era.[30] In the first decade of the twentieth century, slapstick dominated nickelodeons; Eileen Bowser notes that these comedies "constituted 70 percent and more of the fiction films" of this period. More than anything else, these films were notable for their "vulgar, amoral, and anti-establishment" nature, which would cause serious problems when social censorship became a part of the industry.[31] The chaos and anarchy (and potentially ensuing social disruption) of these early slapstick films were the major causes of a shutdown of New York City nickelodeons in 1908. The disruptions inherent in these films, however, were of more than just a moral nature; as silent comic film developed, the navigation of highbrow/lowbrow dichotomies and the problematic relationship of image to text provided models for high modernists and vernacular modernists alike. Like comedic sound recordings, slapstick film comedy influenced the development of comic literature in the United States by resetting the subject/object position of comedy from a relatively stable vaudeville model to something direct, immediate, and inherently experimental.

The modes of literary humor emerging alongside these new media technologies provided innovative models that were fundamentally different from their realist predecessors. These modernist forms of humor focused on an individual figure, encountered without traditional forms of textual or contextual mediation. In large part because of the early technological limitations of these nascent media, this new humor rejected the dramatic frame of vaudeville, the political frame of the newspaper, and, frequently, the explanatory frame of narrative. This shifted comedy away from the notion that the humorous figure must necessarily be objectified in relationship to some other subject (the genteel narrator of the dialect tale, the editorial staff of a newspaper, the straight man, or the vaudeville announcer). Instead, as with the "Uncle Josh" recordings, this figure could embody a subjectivity that demanded identification from the audience, precisely because the text offered no alternatives. The resulting emphasis on the subjectivity of the comic individual, the elimination of the comic frame, and the disturbance of other realist conventions created the background for what would emerge in literary humor as comic vernacular modernism.

These revolutions in American humor, influenced by both technological and literary innovations, led to the first true example of vernacular modernism in the work of Ring Lardner, who developed the experimental dialect realism of Twain in ways that reconfigured the experience of literary humor. The ways in which these new media eliminated the need for some form of mediation as well as some of the basic elements of narrative meant that even literary humor could do away with the restrictive narrators and prefatory notices that characterized humor during the realist period. What results, however, is a crisis in identification; in the work of Lardner and Anita Loos, it often becomes difficult to identify at whom readers should be laughing. When the single, unmediated version of the story originates in text produced by the comic object her/himself, the realist norms of nineteenth-century American humor become tremendously warped. The product of this is a new brand of twentieth-century American humor and a pioneering demonstration of the experimental possibilities of the language of the streets.

"I Can't Figure Out If He Is Kidding or in Ernest": Ring Lardner, Baseball-American, and the Subjectivities of Vernacular Modernism

> *Whatever Ring's achievement was, it fell short of the achievement he was capable of, and this because of a cynical attitude toward his work. How far back did that attitude go?—back to his youth in a Michigan village? Certainly back to his days with the Cubs. During those years, when most men of promise achieve an adult education, if only in the school of war, Ring moved in the company of a few dozen illiterates playing a boy's game. . . . However deeply Ring might cut into it, his cake had exactly the diameter of Frank Chance's diamond.*
> —F. SCOTT FITZGERALD, "RING" (1933)

> *It may shock Mr Lardner to know that he has done in little what Mr Joyce has done on the grand scale in* Ulysses.
> —GILBERT SELDES, *THE SEVEN LIVELY ARTS* (1924)

The story of Ring Lardner is itself a complex and twisted narrative of literary success and disillusionment during the modernist era. As he worked his way up in the sports pages of the Chicago newspapers and became one of the first nationally known sportswriters of the twentieth century, Lardner's literary aspirations (first glimpsed in plays he wrote as a young man) did not disappear with this new career. Instead, he took the raw material of his experience as a baseball reporter and turned it into one of the most successful examples of literary humor of the period. His epistolary baseball novel *You Know Me Al* (1916) made him a sensation, and his later work became some of the most highly sought-after magazine fiction of the 1920s. The few biographers and critics who have considered him generally divide Lardner's career into three or four phases: the Keefe stories of the mid-1910s (including *You Know Me Al*); the "wise boob" stories of the late 1910s and early 1920s (including *Gullible's Travels* [1916], *The Big Town* [1921], and "The Golden Honeymoon" [1922]); the dark satire of his later collections, *How to Write Short Stories (With Samples)* (1924) and *The Love Nest and Other Stories* (1926); and the nonsense plays, a genre that Maxwell Geismar once termed "native dada."[32] The standard narrative of Lardner's career follows an evolutionary model, with the later, satirical work more broadly appreciated for its ruthless critique of middle-class Americans.

Like other humorists, Lardner is difficult to fit into literary history, and the fact that he never "graduated" (in F. Scott Fitzgerald's metaphor) into more easily canonized works like Twain did with *Adventures of Huckleberry Finn* makes him a peripheral figure, even in 1920s literary studies.[33] In a 1924 review of *How to Write Short Stories,* Edmund Wilson reveals both Lardner's acknowledged debt to Twain and the great question about Lardner's career, asking, "Will Ring Lardner, then, go on to his *Huckleberry Finn* or has he already told all he knows? . . . Here is a man who has had the freedom of the modern West no less than Mark Twain did of the old one, who approaches it, as Mark Twain did, with a perceptive interest in human beings instead of with the naturalist's formula. . . . If Ring Lardner has anything more to give us, the time has now come to deliver it."[34] Although Lardner himself downplayed his debt to Twain, the link between the two was a natural for literary critics: as Richard Bridgman has noted, "Dozens of writers in this century have been identified as Mark Twain reincarnated, but none more so than Lardner."[35] His inability to deliver "anything more" than short fiction, however, has left him out of most literary histories of the modernist era. As a result, his late collection *Round Up* (1929) is seen as representative, though it contains only six stories (out of thirty-five) that appeared before 1924 and completely ignores Lardner's breakthrough work *You Know Me Al,* constructing Lardner's literary legacy as a pure satirist in the conventional mode of realism, the preferred style of his later career. *Round Up* writes out Lardner's dependence on his baseball background, or, as Fitzgerald called it, "Frank Chance's diamond." Even Lardner himself said in a 1917 interview, "I'm tired of this sort of writing. I'd give anything to be able to stop writing dialect stories. And I'm tired of writing in the first person. I'd like to write in the third person."[36] Given the prevailing standards of realism in humor writing in the 1910s, this evaluation of his vernacular writing should come as no surprise, and his reluctance to include much of this work in *Round Up* shows the degree to which he maintained a distance from his early work.

Still, while Lardner's satire certainly became sharper later in his career, his aesthetic approach in much of the later work was far more conventional, utilizing third-person narration that shared many of the assumptions and representative modes of nineteenth-century realism and of later practitioners like Sinclair Lewis. This move away from the vernacular humor of his earliest successes raises a curious question: Why, if this work was so successful and innovative, did he reject it once he found a high degree of success in the 1920s? From his own statements, it appears that Lardner retained the nineteenth-century view that dialect humor constituted a more debased form of literary production. Marketplace considerations may have influenced this shift as well; as Lardner sought better-paying venues for his work, he may have felt pressure to write work that conformed to the prevailing realist standards of satire in the nineteenth century, still prominent in many of the higher-paying magazine markets. Nevertheless, it is his early work, what one critic has described as his "orthographic" humor, where Lardner's most radical inventiveness and experimentation truly lie.[37] These stories, including the busher tales of Jack Keefe in *You Know Me Al* as well as *The Young Immigrunts* (1920) with its child writer/narrator, radically redefine the central modes of humor writing, using slang and vernacular language to transform the nineteenth-century conventions and forms of textual subjectivity that governed humorists like Twain and Dunne. Although Fitzgerald claimed the "boys' game" of baseball "kept out novelty," Lardner's early work operates as an experimental renovation of American humor writing.[38] Far from being purely "orthographic," as much of nineteenth-century humor was, Lardner's writings exemplify the vernacular modernist paradigm by exploiting the textuality of fiction, engaging questions of subjectivity and rejecting the assumptions of mimetic realism—all through the exploration of a deformed and transformed (s)language.

In many ways Lardner's career is the antithesis to that of the prototypical modernist. Fitzgerald's eulogy of him effectively points out all the ways in which Lardner's own history diverged from the master narrative of the Lost Generation. According to Fitzgerald, the successful writers of this group, "men of promise," "achieve[d] an adult education, if only in the school of war." While critics have long debunked the notion that experience in World War I somehow functioned as a prerequisite for modernist canonization, it is clear that Fitzgerald sees this particular form of "adult education" as an integral part of the maturation of artists of his generation and as something that Lardner lacked. Fitzgerald was at Princeton during World War I, but, as numerous Lost Generation histories document, a significant number of the other American figures associated with modernism (Dos Passos, Hemingway) were involved in the war, or, in the case of Faulkner, pretending to be involved. As opposed to the presumed "man's game" of war, "the text of Ring's schooling" was "a boy's game"; he spent his formative years as a sportswriter, covering the two very popular Chicago baseball teams, the White Sox and the Cubs. Not surprisingly, Fitzgerald's critique is misplaced: because Lardner was born in 1885, too early to achieve this education in the men's game of war, he could not become one of the "men of promise." Fitzgerald also conveniently omits Lardner's somewhat sardonic look at the war in two books, the journalistic *My Four Weeks in France* (1918) and Jack Keefe's extended adventures as a soldier in *Treat 'Em Rough* (1918). In these texts, Lardner maintains a significant distance from the masculinized ideals of the war that, when upended, underwrote the largely patriarchal assumptions of Lost Generation narratives. Lardner did not go to war only to find his ideals destroyed; an older and less impressionable satirist, he took few ideals with him in the first place.

Despite the somewhat dismissive language he uses in this eulogy of Lardner, Fitzgerald had an enormous amount of respect for the Chicago sportswriter and humorist. In the mid-1920s he lobbied to have Scribner's publish Lardner's work in a deluxe five-volume edition. But while Fitzgerald saw this work as something to be preserved, Lardner himself had not exactly engaged in a self-conscious preservation of his own literary legacy. Fitzgerald's eulogy notes in disbelief that Lardner had not kept copies of his manuscripts or publications and that "the material of *How to Write Short Stories* was obtained by photographing old issues in the public library!"[39] Given what Fitzgerald sees as Lardner's talent, he is shocked by the way in which Lardner treats his own material; this suggests that Lardner viewed his work as ephemeral and expendable, the absolute antithesis to literature, especially as understood by those constructing a self-conscious literary legacy in the modernist era. In his own mind, Lardner's work was meant not to last but to be consumed as entertainment.[40]

Lardner's perspective on the transience of his own work, one that nearly replicates James's criticism of the "natural gift" of the American—humor writing—finds a surprising contradiction in Gilbert Seldes's celebration of Lardner in *The Seven Lively Arts* (1924), where he claims that "it may shock Mr Lardner to know that he has done in little what Mr Joyce has done on the grand scale in *Ulysses*."[41] Seldes, the managing editor of the *Dial* when it published Eliot's *The Waste Land* in 1922, had modernist credentials to spare.[42] His connection between Lardner and Joyce, written at the moment when *Ulysses* dominated discussions of modernist fiction, might have seemed baffling to a writer like Fitzgerald, who saw Lardner as an exceptionally talented (and funny) sportswriter who never took his work that seriously. It is notable that Seldes made this particular comment at the height of Lardner's career; he was a very popular writer in 1924, and this comparison preceded the Scribner's deluxe reprint of Lardner's works. To laud Lardner in this way at this time meant to challenge existing literary and cultural hierarchies and—like Edmund Wilson's review of the same year—to hope for more ambitious work from the humorist.

Seldes was not the only major modernist to appreciate Lardner. Indeed, even Virginia Woolf commented favorably on Lardner's first collection, *You Know Me Al* (1916), in a 1925 review entitled "American Fiction." Her description of Lardner emphasizes his American-ness, his novelty, and his experimentation: "Mr. Lardner . . . provides something unique in its kind, something indigenous to the soul, which the traveller may carry off as a trophy to prove to the incredulous that he has actually been to America and found it a foreign land." Lardner, more than the other writers Woolf reviews in this essay (Sherwood Anderson and Sinclair Lewis), leads Woolf to a serious consideration of American literature in all its complexities: "French is simpler, English is simpler, all modern literatures are simpler to sum up and understand than this new American literature. A discord lies at the root of it; the natural bent of American is twisted at the start."[43] This notion of the "twisted" nature of American literature, particularly as exemplified by Lardner, offers one outsider's take on what I have called vernacular modernism. For Woolf, this language is not clear or transparent; it exhibits a "discord at the root" of its relationship to representation. Calling it "this *new* American literature," Woolf subtly identifies in this passage the degree to which Lardner's work demonstrates the complexities of modernist representation through the use of a vernacular and antirealist representational strategy, one that Richard Bridgman compares to Gertrude Stein's "monotonously revolving, slowly advancing style" and equates with the "surrealistic overturn of reason."[44]

Lardner's first collection, *You Know Me Al*, was published in book form in 1916, the same year that James Joyce published *A Portrait of the Artist as a Young Man*. Such a connection might appear as a perverse coincidence, but Gilbert Seldes's articulation of a link between Lardner and Joyce suggests this affiliation might have appeared to modernists themselves, as with the adjacency of Stein and "Slanguage" in *transition*'s "Revolution of the Word" issue, discussed in the introduction. The power and innovation of Joyce's debut novel derive from the careful inclusion of interior narration. The story of a developing mind, *Portrait* follows Stephen Dedalus as he grows into a self-conscious artist. The famous opening sections of the novel present Stephen as a child, through a child's consciousness. As the novel progresses, Stephen's understanding of the world becomes more sophisticated, and the textual representation of this understanding becomes more mature and self-consciously literary. This technique represents one of the major tenets of high modernism—the privileging of subjectivity—along with the understanding that these subjectivities are in constant flux, developing, changing, and evolving. Simultaneously, the novel posits that the language of realism should not necessarily be the default means of presenting these subjectivities. Instead, since language and subjectivity are inevitably intertwined, the proper means of demonstrating subjectivity is through the language available to that subject at the moment of experience.

Joyce's *Ulysses,* published six years later, begins to anticipate a crucial modernist question: What if the growth of this mind is redirected, and its endpoint is not the idealized artist figure, but something else? Lardner's *You Know Me Al,* had, in a sense, already put forth a provisional answer to this question. One of the major innovations of Lardner's early work is its continual privileging of the consciousness and subjectivity of the narrator through that narrator's own textual self-representation. Lardner's work lacks the mediating qualities that characterize the vast majority of nineteenth-century dialect realism through its emphasis on orality and reported speech, replacing this with a formally complex narrative voice riddled with slang and vernacular expressions; as Woolf notes in her review, Lardner "lets Jack Keefe the baseball player cut out his own outline, fill in his own depths, until the figure of the foolish, boastful, innocent athlete lives before us."[45] As with Joyce, Lardner's strategy is to let the character not only speak but write for himself (i.e., "cut out his own outline, fill in his own depths"), privileging that consciousness as it is, suggesting that the authentic experience of Jack Keefe may only become truly comprehensible though his own perception of it. In fact, it would not be a stretch to imagine the subtitle of *You Know Me Al* as *A Portrait of the Ballplayer as a Young Man.*

This choice of allowing his characters narrative control, typical of Lardner's work throughout his early career, immediately calls into question notions of representability and suggests the capacity of language to conceal as much as it reveals. Lardner does not attempt a *faux* ethnographic representation of some obscure class of American society from some privileged vantage point, as humorists before him had usually done. Likewise, he does not report speech from the perspective of the genteel editor. The textual and linguistic distance between the narrator and the figure of dialect humor was often vast in nineteenth-century humor, and writers in this genre exploited this gap by overwhelming readers with a transcribed dialect that was as much visual as audible. In many cases, as Merritt Moseley has noted, these writers "were not really writing a viable dialect, but rather distorting their language for an effect. Lardner, on the other hand, uses a narrator whose language is internally consistent, and whose knowledge and awareness are consistent with the sort of man his language shows him to be."[46] As technologies like sound recording allowed humorists to do away with the need for explicit framing and contexualizing nonstandard speech, Lardner's work began to push beyond the advanced dialect realism of Twain and Dunne. Instead of merely substituting incorrect grammatical and lexical forms for correct ones (as most nineteenth-century humorists did), Lardner allows a vernacular character to describe himself in the language to which he has access, a combination of baseball slang, common American vernacular, and empty clichés. Lardner achieves this impact by framing the book as a series of letters written by Keefe to his friend Al back in his small hometown of Bedford, Indiana. The comic fictional letter is one of the oldest forms of humor in America: Charles Farrar Browne's "Artemus Ward" letters, first published in 1858, are some of the best examples in the nineteenth century.[47] Like the dialect tales of the realist era, these examples of epistolary humor often relied on realist semiotics in which misspellings or phonetically-represented speech still communicated a set of ideas in a comprehensible way. Writers like Ward "write whole passages in which there is nothing incorrect about the prose except the spelling, and they use subordination in rather sophisticated ways," assuring the reader that a highly literate comedian is pulling the strings.[48]

Lardner's innovation involves the complete absence of any mediating or authorizing voice that assists in the interpretation of the letters. Instead, readers are left with a form of narration—a monologue akin to the recorded performances of Cal Stewart's "Uncle Josh"—that includes substantial gaps in time, unreliable and egocentric representations of events, and a constant use of language that does not adequately represent (i.e., clichés) or does not always seem accessible (i.e., specialized baseball argot). The act of reading a Lardner story like those in *You Know Me Al* does not demand merely an ability to replace misspelled words or obviously incorrect grammar with correct forms; instead, the entire plot must be reconstructed by the reader, who must not only read through the grammatical and orthographic mistakes, but also negotiate the narrative and logical gaps and complex persona of the narrator. Such linguistic and narrative strategies soon became quite celebrated in the American literary consciousness. A brief notice in *Writer's Digest*, for example, identified Lardner's work with its particular textual and linguistic strategies, claiming in 1929 that "Ring Lardner has been called the inventor of the American language. He made such idioms as 'could of' and 'base ball serious' a part of the tongue known as Lardner's Ringlish."[49] Lardner's association with Mencken's *American Language* (as important source and example) was already clear by the early 1920s, but the suggestion that Lardner has created his own literary language, in an article published in the year of *transition*'s "Revolution of the Word" issue, cements the connections between Lardner, Mencken, and modernist experimentation.

The narrative of *You Know Me Al*, originally published as a series of short stories in the *Saturday Evening Post* in 1914, follows Keefe, a "bush league" pitcher, as he tries to make it into major league baseball with the Chicago White Sox. Through fits and starts, he makes the team, gets married, and begins to raise a family while constantly deflecting any criticism of himself. In his letters to Al (who is termed "dear pal," "dear Al," and "friend Al" in various salutations), Keefe carries on a continual argument with the versions of events conveyed by others: sportswriters, coaches, and other players. Though these competing stories may technically be more "objective" and hence "realistic," the competing realities of other characters, Keefe's narration suggests, do not accurately represent Keefe's experience; his subjectivity reigns supreme. The entire book is an attempt at justification and self-aggrandizement via rewriting this realist experience from Keefe's own idiosyncratic and linguistically tangled perspective. The title, *You Know Me Al*, is Keefe's refrain: because Al knows him, he knows what can and cannot be true.

Readers of this text, on the other hand, are caught in a complex narrative bind; not knowing Keefe as Al supposedly does, his versions of the events seem anything but complete; they often appear to be downright lies processed through a twisted subjectivity. Keefe's description of his first professional meltdown, at the hands of a powerful Detroit Tigers team led by Ty Cobb, is one of the more explicit narrative interventions performed by Keefe:

> Cobb come up again to start the third and when Schalk signs me for a fast one I shakes my head. Then Schalk says All right pitch anything you want to. I pitched a spitter and Cobb bunts it right at me. I would of threw him out a block but I stubbed my toe in a rough place and fell down. This is the roughest ground I ever seen Al. Veach bunts and for a wonder Lord throws him out. Cobb goes to second and honest Al I forgot all about him being there and first thing I knowed he had stole third. Then Moriarty hits a fly ball to Bodie and Cobb scores though Bodie ought to of threw him out twenty feet.[50]

An understanding of Keefe's version of the events depends on a relatively sophisticated understanding of baseball terminology as well as a willingness to piece through the constant shifts in verb tense, the awkward verb conjugation, and the common misuse of words (like "of" for "have"). More than merely the use of malapropisms, Keefe's letters restructure the English language around his own agenda, supporting his self-image to the "boys back home." As he notes at the opening to this letter, he says "I am writing you this so as you will know the truth about the game and not get a bum steer from what you read in the papers."[51] In other words, Keefe's renarration operates as an explicit counterpoint to the narratives of journalistic realism.

In truth, Keefe's series of letters themselves serve as a "bum steer" for the reader, but this comic narrator sees nothing funny in his letters home. While he is the constant butt of jokes told by players, and especially by the assistant manager Kid Gleason, more often than not Keefe misapprehends the jokes, passing them on in a half-understood fashion to Al and to the readers: "Manager Callahan is a funny guy and I don't understand him sometimes. I can't figure out if he is kidding or in ernest." The narrator's deflection of or complete obliviousness to humor is characteristic of many of Lardner's stories, especially those that utilize the vernacular. As one character says in Lardner's later story "Harmony," "Never mind the comical stuff.... They ain't no joke about this!" Keefe's failure—both as a player and a narrator—is, in a sense, the result of taking himself too seriously. When Gleason tells him, "Rub some arnicky on your head to keep the swelling down and you may be a real pitcher yet," Keefe responds, "I ain't got no swell head. He [Gleason] says No. If I hated myself like you do I would be a moving picture actor."[52] That Keefe passes such details on to Al further complicates the narrative strategy. In general, when Keefe writes of his own experience on the field, he rewrites the events to absolve himself of any kind of failure, substituting subjective and textual reinvention for any form of realist representation. At other times, frequently off the field of play, he passes on less-than-flattering details that he does not completely understand, creating a text that, in its efforts to conceal the weaknesses of its narrator through linguistic obfuscation, finally reveals much more that the narrator realizes.

The act of reading *You Know Me Al*, ironically enough, makes readers into a slightly less "grim" and more amused version of what Richard Poirier has termed "grim readers." As in high modernist texts, in Lardner's humorous work, "We are met with inducements to tidy things up, to locate principles of order and structure beneath a fragmentary surface," but with a profoundly humorous—and far more accessible—twist than a high modernist text generally offers.[53] In his work, Lardner exploits the modernist obsession with fragmentary surfaces and creates one of the more complicated (and yet naïve) unreliable narrators in American literary history. It is the unreliability of this narration that sustains the humor; while reading *You Know Me Al*, readers come to know and expect Keefe's textual manipulation of the events as they occurred. Piecing together the "order and structure" of the events themselves and attempting to "tidy things up" result in a clearer picture of Keefe. *You Know Me Al* accomplishes this humorous transformation of Poirier's "grim reader" through its emphasis on the text itself, in particular the explicit difference between the realist world represented and the vernacular modernist text representing. This highlights the text's continual desire to deflect the real and to represent in its own subjective terms, eschewing grammatical norms and standard language for vernacular structures and innovative slang (Lardner's "Baseball-American" or "Lardner's Ringlish"). Lardner's hyperstylized first-person narration re-creates the world—not according to social or psychological principles, but according to internally consistent linguistic and textual ones.

Lardner biographer and editor Jonathan Yardley has suggested that "the real reason so many thousands responded with such joy to the early Jack Keefe stories was that they heard their own voices therein and were transfixed by what they heard." In contrast to what Yardley calls the "awkward pidgin English that readers could understand but with which they could not connect"—the standard, genteel language of middlebrow magazines of the era—Lardner's work signaled a massive shift toward the use of common language.[54] However, having always conceived of literature as a form written in this genteel "pidgin English," contemporary readers of Lardner must have been rather disconcerted in encountering something so unorthodox in the pages of the slick magazine and representative middlebrow publication the *Saturday Evening Post*. Yardley's notion that readers would have gravitated toward Lardner's work because of its innate familiarity ignores the degree to which his stories—particularly those in the vernacular—remain challenging both semantically and narratively. For example, Wood and Goddard's 1926 *Dictionary of American Slang* includes a four-page section on "Baseball Slang," suggesting the specialized terminology used in *You Know Me Al* remained in need of explanation to a broader audience, even after Lardner's work had received publication in a deluxe 1925 Scribner's set.[55] The shift to a vernacular language might make the stories at least superficially "easier" for an audience in the 1910s and 1920s to understand, but its consequent mangling of the representational standards of realism and even of the legacy of American humor made Lardner's vernacular fiction into a modernist puzzle, a narratological problem without a decisive answer.

The vernacular modernist puzzle of *You Know Me Al*, and a good deal of Lardner's other early work, turns on the protagonist's lack of knowledge about the humor of his/her own situation. The stories exploit conventions of reader identification: like the "Uncle Josh" recordings, Lardner's text locates both meaning and humor at the nexus between laughing *with* and laughing *at* the protagonist, a negotiation that the reader (or listener) must make. As with many major modernist texts, *You Know Me Al* is the story of the development of an individual; it is a type of bildungsroman masquerading as a picaresque. The problem with Keefe, however, is that he lacks any consistent internal development or personal growth and is ultimately the same psychological being at the end of the stories as he was at the beginning. However, this does not diminish the importance of subjectivity in the stories. In fact, the text's highly subjective narration—its most impressive formal innovation—serves as the engine of the humor. These narratives are clearly incomplete and borderline incoherent, but as with any modernist writer, readers must piece together the elements into some kind of narrative coherence. The only way such coherence can be achieved is through a sophisticated understanding of all the specialized linguistic elements Lardner employs in the stories: baseball slang, empty clichés, common vernacular phrases, and the strategic misuse of words to ensure the dominance of Keefe over his own particular narrative. Even then, the story is not "complete"; it remains fragmented.

Even more challenging than the stories of Jack Keefe, Lardner's quasi-autobiographical *The Young Immigrunts* operates as a nonsense book, a satire on the Lardner family, a parody of the popular book *The Young Visiters* (purportedly written by a nine-year-old British girl named Daisy Ashford), and an extension of the textual humor he developed in *You Know Me Al*.[56] *The Young Immigrunts* tells the story of the Lardner family's move from the Midwest to Greenwich, Connecticut, a move they actually made in the fall of 1919. Lardner's humor here begins on the title page, where Ring W. Lardner Jr. is credited as the author, "With a Preface by the Father." In its foreground of authorship and textuality the preface highlights some of the central concerns of comic vernacular modernism:

> The person whose name is signed to this novel was born on the nineteenth day of August, 1915, and was therefore four years and three months old when the manuscript was found, late in November, 1919. The narrative is substantially true, with the following exceptions:
>
> 1. "My Father," the leading character in the work, is depicted as a man of short temper, whereas the person from whom the character was drawn is in reality as pleasant a fellow as one would care to meet and seldom has a cross word for anyone, let alone women and children.
> 2. The witty speeches accredited to "My Father" have, possibly owing to the limitations of a child's memory, been so garbled and twisted that they do not look half so good in print as they sounded in the open air.
> 3. More stops for gas were made than are mentioned in the story.
>
> As the original manuscript was written on a typewriter with a rather frayed ribbon, and as certain words were marked out and others handwritten in, I have taken the liberty of copying the entire work with a fresh ribbon and the inclusion of the changes which the author indicated in pencil in the first draft. Otherwise the story is presented to the reader as it was first set down.[57]

While Lardner is parodying the convention of the "authorizing" preface, evoking both J. M. Barrie's preface for Daisy Ashford's book and Twain's "Explanatory" note in *Adventures of Huckleberry Finn*, his concerns center on vernacular modernist principles of textuality and subjectivity.[58] In fact, this preface might be read as a theorization of much of Lardner's early work. First, the narrator of this tale is, quite impossibly, Lardner's four-year-old son. Not only is he the narrator, however, he is also the author of the "manuscript." As in *You Know Me Al,* Lardner emphasizes the text as text; this is not the reported speech of a child (as in *Huckleberry Finn*) or ethnic caricature (as in Dunne's *Mr. Dooley*), but allegedly a written document created by a preliterate character. The final paragraph of the introduction heightens the absurdity, suggesting that Lardner Jr. has utilized a typewriter in the creation of the document (not to mention making marginal corrections to his own typescript).[59] Additionally, Lardner ("My Father") acknowledges his own mediation of the document, noting that it had already undergone revision ("certain words were marked out and others handwritten in") and needed retyping, which indicates a possible manipulation of the "author's intentions," calling into question the reliability of authorship in a modernist moment fascinated with authorial genius.[60]

While emphasizing the textual nature of the document, Lardner also points out its weaknesses. The "limitations of the child's memory" have corrupted particularly witty remarks and led to the misperception of the "father" (whom the preface-writing father naturally sees as "the leading character in the work"), resulting in a text not only mediated by language (the semiliterate writing of the "son" and the editorial interference of the "father"), but also told from such a subjective standpoint that its communication of the details themselves remains suspect. The hypersubjectivity of the child, also reminiscent of the opening pages of Joyce's *A Portrait of the Artist as a Young Man,* becomes a wry and satirical commentary on the trip, precisely because "Bill" (as Ring Jr. is known in the text) represents things as he experiences them, in text that approximates his aural and visual experience. Chapter titles like "Buffalo to Rochester 76.4" seem baffling at first, but the meaning of these titles become clear once the reader realizes that the numbers designate mileage. Likely seen on road signs, these titles are the representation of trip markers. The narrator Bill perceives these signs in the same way one might see a chapter title, signaling the need for a new beginning within the narrative. Additionally, Bill's self-conscious conclusion of chapters speaks to the artificiality of the text's fictional construction. In one case Bill notes, "Under those conditions I will not repete the conversation that transpired between Albany and Hudson but will end my chapter at the city limits of the last named settlemunt."[61]

Bill's mishearing (or mistransliteration) of the words his mother and father speak results not only in a series of malapropisms but also in a variety of clever textual mediations. Bride and groom become "bride and glum," the grand concourse becomes "the grand concorpse," a wrong turn leads to "a holycost of the first water," and the family eventually arrives in "the Bureau of Manhattan."[62] Many of these mistakes appear to be puns created by the "father" (i.e., Lardner himself), who lauds his own "witty speeches" in the preface. However, with Bill's other mistakes in both spelling and transliteration, there remains some doubt as to whether the puns themselves are intentional on the father's part or merely the fortunate—and transformative—result of Bill's lack of letters. The prefatory note only serves to obscure this, acknowledging textual revision and potential editorial interference with the initial text written by the narrator Bill.

Finally, *The Young Immigrunts* acknowledges its own narrative limits quite explicitly, when Bill falls asleep in the car in the chapter "Syracuse to Hudson 183.2": "Soon we past through Amsterdam and I guess I must of dosed off at lease I cant remember anything between there and Schenectady and I must apologize to my readers for my laps as I am unable to ether describe the scenery or report anything that may of been said between these 2 points."[63] Presumably, the correct spelling of Amsterdam and Schenectady results from signs on the road, though here Lardner as author pushes the already warped limits of plausibility. But plausibility, either in representation or in narration, is not what Lardner is after. This kind of textual and linguistic experimentation—used in this more centralized narrative—extends the possibilities of *You Know Me Al*, both in its humor and its vernacular modernist aesthetics.

These early works, including *You Know Me Al* and *The Young Immigrunts,* initially propelled Ring Lardner into the realm of literary celebrity, a reputation that was solidified with his move into darker and more conventional satire in the mid-1920s. While he would move away from his first-person vernacular tales, excluding most of them from the retrospective collection *Round Up* in 1929, this work was powerfully influential on a host of writers in the 1920s, ranging from humorists to crime-fiction writers, and from vernacular writers to high modernists. More than Lardner's dark satire, his vernacular tales of baseball players, precocious children, and "wise boobs" provided not only the basis for a revolution in American humor writing but also a model for vernacular aesthetic experimentation across popular genres in the early twentieth century. With Twain as his most important influence, Lardner's early work—lauded by Mencken in *The American Language*—proved that, through a sophisticated use of the vigorous and innovative American vernacular, popular writing could experiment with narration, subjectivity, and language in sophisticated ways that radically transformed its realist antecedents.

"Any Chance to Be Unrefined": Anita Loos, the Vernacular Modernist Diary, and Cinematic Narrative

> Please accept my envious congratulations on Dorothy—the way you did her through the intelligence of that elegant moron of a cornflower. . . . My God, it's charming. . . . Most of them will be completely unmoved—even your rather clumsy gags wont [sic] get them—and the others will only find it slight and humorous. The Andersons even mentioned Ring Lardner in talking to me about it. But perhaps that was what you were after, and you have builded better than you knew. But I wish I had thought of Dorothy first.
>
> —WILLIAM FAULKNER TO ANITA LOOS, FEBRUARY 1926

As Ring Lardner's star continued to rise throughout the mid-1920s, culminating in the 1925 Scribner's deluxe edition of his work, other humor writers were quick to exploit Lardner's formula, often with uneven results. A glance through the popular magazines of the era, including *Saturday Evening Post* competitors like *American Magazine, Colliers,* and others, reveals a variety of vernacular humorists emulating Lardner. Even pulp magazines like *Black Mask,* later known for its introduction of the hard-boiled crime narrative (discussed in chapter 4), would publish Lardneresque stories in its early issues. Of all of the humorists following Lardner's lead, the most successful of them was Anita Loos, who began her career as a scenarist for D. W. Griffith. Loos's first novel *Gentlemen Prefer Blondes* (1925) combines Lardner's flair for the vernacular with sophisticated elements of early film narratology. The result was a national bestseller, a cross-media phenomenon, and an example of how humor writing opens up the possibilities for literary experimentation that enable vernacular modernism to thrive.

In the thirty-year period after its initial publication, Anita Loos's most well-known novel, *Gentlemen Prefer Blondes,* lived more lives than perhaps any other text in American popular culture. Of twentieth-century texts, only L. Frank Baum's *The Wizard of Oz* (1900) could claim presence in as many forms of media to that point.[64] Initially a serialized tale in the slick fashion magazine *Harper's Bazar, Blondes* became, in turn, a novel between covers (1925), a stage play (1926–27), a film (1928), a Broadway musical (1948), and a Hollywood musical directed by Howard Hawks (1952).[65] It spawned a sequel, *But Gentlemen Marry Brunettes,* which made a similar transition from the pages of *Harper's Bazar* (1926) to the hardback market (1928) to the stage (as *The Social Register* [1932]) and to the silver screen (1934). The sequel was also resurrected as a Hollywood musical, in the 1955 film *Gentlemen Marry Brunettes*. This brief history of what literary critics generally understand as a novel—abstracted from other aesthetic forms—highlights the degree to which *Blondes* was embedded in a larger context of entertainment, particularly on Broadway and in Hollywood. In fact, Loos's fictional work in the latter half of the 1920s represented by far the minority of her creative output at that point in her career. Though she had published short fiction in *Vanity Fair* as early as 1916, most of her work up to the publication of *Blondes* had been in scenario writing (1912–23) and writing for Broadway (1923–24). After her serialized novel *The Better Things of Life* appeared in *Hearst's International-Cosmopolitan* in 1930 and 1931, Loos returned to Hollywood and spent a great deal of the rest of her career writing for talkies.

Despite this extensive and varied history, scholarship has only recently begun to explore the connections between two widely different versions of Anita Loos. One Loos is the influential scenarist in early American cinema and contributor to numerous D. W. Griffith films, friend to stars like Douglas Fairbanks and the Talmadge sisters, and gossipy memoirist of the young days of Hollywood.[66] The other Loos is the author of *Blondes*, a satire that literary critics frequently read as a scathing critique of gender roles in 1920s America.[67] Critics have struggled to bring these two versions of Anita Loos together, and their separation remains a cultural blind spot for the study of the 1920s. After all, she was the only major figure of this era to make the transition from writing for successful films to writing successful fiction; she even moved back into film after the nature of screenwriting had been altered by the coming of sound.[68] With only a couple of recent exceptions, scholarship has largely compartmentalized her work into mutually exclusive categories. Film scholars see her fiction as a mere break she took in the mid-1920s from the grinding work of Hollywood scenario writing. Literary critics often abstract Loos's one major novel from her extensive fictional output in slick magazines and from the innovations in film narrative that shaped her sensibilities. Both groups miss the fact that Loos's work, in film and in fiction, forms a coherent body highlighting her original ideas about narrative; indeed, Loos's sophisticated approach to her fiction suggests a strong relation to her modernist contemporaries, who struggled to find ways to incorporate the new visual aesthetic of cinema into their texts.

In her later fiction Loos does not reject her Hollywood past, when she was a young scenarist whose ideas were forged working with cinema giants like Griffith and Fairbanks. Rather, her subject matter and narrative style comment directly on film industry and cinematic narrative. Loos is in a unique position to demonstrate a new mode of thinking about the relation between American literary culture and Hollywood, between modernism and film. Most critical histories of this relation operate in one of two ways. The first trend charts the disaffection successful fiction writers felt as they became increasingly involved in writing screenplays during the 1930s. These writers (including F. Scott Fitzgerald, Nathanael West, and Budd Schulberg) exposed what Hortense Powdermaker called "the dream factory" as an artist's nightmare, most explicitly in West's *The Day of the Locust* (1939).[69] The second trend examines the ways in which modernist fiction attempts to re-create the experience of cinema through textual abstraction. Written primarily by authors who had experienced cinema principally as viewers, this fiction appropriates film's formal innovations and structures (e.g., the "Camera Eye" and "Newsreel" sections of John Dos Passos's *U.S.A.* trilogy [1930–36]) in an approximate way. Michael North's *Camera Works: Photography and the Twentieth-Century Word* (2007), for example, charts the "spectroscopic" elements—the "disorienting flicker" of narrative structure—in Fitzgerald's work.[70]

Loos, by contrast, was a successful film scenarist before she moved into serial fiction. In addition, she wrote one of the earliest texts demonstrating a theory of writing for film. Produced by someone emerging from the Hollywood system with a sophisticated theoretical framework for film narrative, Loos's fiction points to a new way of thinking about how film relates to modernist modes of fictional representation and structure. The aesthetic experience of cinema created new forms of narrative, forms that depended on fragmentation, reconstruction, elision, and the complex relation between the visual and the textual. More than merely "producing a new sensory culture," as Miriam Hansen has so influentially argued, film (particularly silent film) provided complex formal strategies of narrative and textuality.[71] These modernist themes and modes are themselves the basis for much of the grammar of film production. As a pioneer theorist of film narrative, Loos clarifies the degree to which the narrative structure of early film could import a modernist aesthetic into even popular fiction.

As a young scenarist whose ideas were forged working with cinema giants like D. W. Griffith and Douglas Fairbanks, Loos does not reject her Hollywood past in her fiction. Rather, her work combines the narratological specialties of silent film writing—especially the crafting of title-cards—with the comic experiments of Ring Lardner and the accompanying interest in subjectivity, the performance of identity, and textuality. *Gentlemen Prefer Blondes* is a profound example of vernacular modernist invention, incorporating the vernacular narrative voice with a new, and for a 1920s audience, decidedly vernacular form of storytelling: the popular film comedy. Like Lardner's Jack Keefe, Loos's blond narrator Lorelei Lee controls her own story, strategically allows (or refuses) access to her own thoughts, and textually frames the world around her to ensure her success. Into this Lardneresque environment, Loos introduces Dorothy, who, as Lorelei notes, "never overlooks any chance to be unrefined," disrupting Lorelei's coherent narration with a strategy derived from cinematic title-cards. In *Gentlemen Prefer Blondes,* Loos constructs a fascinating vernacular modernist text, one where competing strands of cinematic and literary vernacular narrative collide, building on Lardner's experiments with structure, narration, and subjectivity, and producing both aesthetically experimental and decidedly humorous results.

The New York Hat (1912), a two-reel melodrama directed by Griffith, was Loos's first screenwriting credit.[72] Her first eight years of scenario writing resulted in a number of successful films directed by Griffith, as well as ten comic films, released in 1916–17, that launched Douglas Fairbanks's career. This work crystallized her ideas about scenario writing, and Loos and her husband, John Emerson, assembled them in a scenario-writing manual published in 1920, five years before *Blondes*. The manual, *How to Write Photoplays,* is largely untapped by literary critics but is known to film scholars, for whom it provides an early framework for scenario writing in influential film studies texts like *The Classical Hollywood Cinema*.[73] In this slim and straightforward volume, Emerson's name precedes Loos's on the title page, though Loos probably wrote most of it.[74] Aside from the interest this book has for film scholars as an indication of an emerging theory of film, it provides a commentary on how Loos viewed writing for the screen as well as how she understood her audience. The book begins by cautioning the amateur scenarist not to get carried away with "jotting down that wonderful idea and sending it off in the same mail."[75] After this caveat, it purports to be a methodical instruction manual for the would-be writer, providing information on where to gather inspiration for stories, how to choose stories that will sell, how to use action, how to become a "continuity writer" (what Emerson and Loos call "a dramatist of the photoplay"), and how to write titles for a story (*Photoplays* 34).

Intertitles, the cinematic equivalent of prose exposition, were a contentious issue in early film criticism, opposed by multiple groups.[76] Popular audiences resented the screen time stolen from their favorite motion-picture stars by mere text. Early film critics saw the overuse of titles as a danger to the development of film as an art form. Critics like Vachel Lindsay, in the first edition of *The Art of the Moving Picture* (1915), celebrated film as a hieroglyphic medium, one that ought to be enshrined in our art museums beside visual-art masterpieces. Textual interludes, sometimes ornately stylized but more often plain white text, distracted cinephiles from the visual aesthetic of the film. However, title cards had come to narrative film to stay, and the question would be not if title cards would be a part of narrative film but how (and how often) the scenarists would employ them.

By 1917, only two years after Loos was exclusively contracted to write for Triangle–Fine Arts, she was described as "an expert subtitle writer," largely as a result of her collaborations with Emerson and Fairbanks in a series of films made in 1916 and 1917.[77] In the revised edition of *The Art of the Moving Picture* (1922), Lindsay singles Loos out as an innovator in title cards, both in theory and in practice. Though Lindsay still argues that "fewer words printed on the screen were better," he acknowledges that "'title writing' remains a commercial necessity. In this field there is but one person who has won distinction—Anita Loos."[78] Title cards were her specialty to such a degree that Griffith called on her just to compose them to provide narrative coherence to the disparate stories in his 1916 epic *Intolerance*.[79] Subtitles served a specific aesthetic and narratological purpose for Loos. As she and Emerson state in *How to Write Photoplays*: "Some photodramatists frown upon the use of many subtitles or of any printed matter on the screen. We have been particularly successful in using as many sub-titles as we wish. In this way, clever dialogue is carried over to the audience. There are some things which cannot be expressed in pantomime. For this reason we advise you to use explanatory sub-titles, with as clever and forceful wording as possible, whenever the action necessitates explanation" (*Photoplays* 37). Later they note that "sub-titles . . . should be more than a mere explanation—should contain a laugh or a bit of fine writing" (*Photoplays* 40).

In these brief comments, Emerson and Loos define the main functions of the title cards in silent cinema: explanation and dialogue. At another point in the book, they note that "the only place where the photodramatist may 'spread' himself in clever verbiage and literary style is in the subtitles, the inserts of printed matter flashed on the screen between photographed scenes. It is this matter of sub-titling which is winning the continuity specialist his place as an artist" (*Photoplays* 39). Here lies the crux of Loos's understanding of the art of writing in cinema. Titling serves as verbal commentary, often in the form of comic explanation or witty dialogue. "Artistry" for the scenarist has become associated with writing effective titles. In their study of the films of Loos and Fairbanks, John C.

Tibbetts and James M. Welsh describe the impact of a Loos title, which "meant the power of the editorial comment, the thrust of a personal satiric vision conveyed by the pungent slang of the wisecrack. In the subtitles, her films carried on a lively kind of monologue to the audience that ran a satirical counterpoint to the action on the screen."[80] As Loos herself told interviewer Karl Schmidt in 1917, "Often a script intended for drama has become comic by the invention of subtitles that 'kidded' the story."[81] The film historian Thomas Schatz identifies this as the "Anita Loos school" of scenario writing, singling out others who followed her model as having "a penchant for hyperbole, wisecracks, and double entendre."[82] For Loos and her "school," subtitles become modernist spaces where text can intentionally create conflicts of meaning with the images they accompany, and the artistry they represent is a function of the subversive power of "pungent slang" and vernacular language. These spaces isolate language as an object of aesthetic interest, straining its purely mimetic function while acknowledging its inability to capture every aspect of human experience. With a modernist bent, these titles undercut any sense of wholeness or completeness, highlighting the jagged edges of the narrative.

While Griffith recognized Loos's writing talent and brought her on as a salaried employee with the creation of Triangle–Fine Arts, Loos was still largely unknown to the industry.[83] A 16 June 1916 review of the Mae Marsh vehicle *A Wild Girl of the Sierras* (dir. Paul Powell, 1916) misspells Loos's name, as "Lees," and calls the film "one of the poorest features that the Triangle–Fine Arts Company has released in some time."[84] Around this time, however, Loos started winning over audiences with her writing in the Fairbanks pictures, which began with *His Picture in the Papers* (dir. Emerson, 1916). In this film, Loos displays her title-writing skill as she balances the lack of action early in the film with a heavy reliance on titles and then reduces the number of titles when the film's dramatic (and comic) action picks up. Pete Prindle (Fairbanks), the son of a vegetable magnate, must win back his father's good favor to marry the girl he loves. To do this, he must get his picture in newspapers to generate public awareness of Prindle's products and of a vegetarian lifestyle. As Loos's literary title cards tell the audience, however, "Pete prefers pugilism to pushing Prindle's Products." By contrast, they explicitly connect the vegetarianism of Melville, Pete's pathetic rival for the affections of Christine, to his symbolic impotence. The title cards become unambiguously instructive when Loos writes, "Melville says good-night, with a sanitary kiss. Note the kiss." The kiss the audience should "note" is absurd: Melville merely taps Christine on the cheek with his gloved fingers. This scene contrasts starkly to the one in which Pete bids Christine goodnight, a moment, the title cards articulate in a style reminiscent of ornate novelistic chapter titles, "wherein it is shown that beefsteak produces a different style of lovemaking from prunes." Other Loos scenarios poke similar fun at the tired conventions of romance; in Fairbanks's picture *The Matrimaniac* (dir. Powell, 1916), the title cards gloss a romantic moment with the dialogue, "Your eyes shine like—like—er—the scent of jasmine in a—er—in a lake of silver."[85] By the end of Loos's series of Fairbanks films, the trade papers mentioned her title writing nearly every time they discussed a film on which she had worked. In a review of *Hit-the-Trail Holliday* (dir. Marshall Neilan, 1918), *Variety* noted that her "titles cannot help but entertain," and in *Come On In* (dir. Emerson, 1918) her "captions have a large portion of the fun burden."[86] By the time the Constance Talmadge vehicle *A Temperamental Wife* (dir. David Kirkland, 1919) was released, reviewers could unequivocally say that "Miss Loos has written inserts that sparkle" or, in reviewing *A Virtuous Vamp* (dir. Kirkland, 1919), could nostalgically long for "the old light-hearted inspiration that formerly characterized the work of Anita Loos as a deviser of titles."[87] In just over three years, Loos had gone from the nearly invisible "Anita Lees" to a celebrity scenarist whose best work, reviewers feared, might be behind her. Still, in the early 1920s, as she became increasingly involved in writing for the stage, Loos's public persona in the entertainment industry was welded to her successes in matching (or humorously mismatching) word and image to great comic effect in major film successes of Douglas Fairbanks and Constance Talmadge. Her celebrated development and theorization of scenario writing provided an important background for her sophisticated narration in her fiction of the mid to late 1920s, itself a title-card-inspired modernism in the vernacular.

This foregrounding of vernacular modernist textuality emerges in Loos's most well-known work and first lengthy work of fiction, *Gentlemen Prefer Blondes,* a novel that uses a vernacular narrative to explore the text/image dichotomies that served as foundations for silent cinema. The plot has become almost universally known through the many forms the story has taken in popular media, but a summary will prove useful. The blonde protagonist, Lorelei Lee, is sent to Europe by her admirer Gus Eisman, "the button king," to receive an "education." She tackles London, Paris, Berlin, and Vienna, picking up many admirers along the way, whom she coaxes to spend vast amounts of money on her. She meets "Dr. Froyd," who cannot quite understand her, since she does not seem to repress anything. Finally, she returns to New York and marries the wealthy and religious Henry Spoffard, who spends much of his time "censuring" photoplays. At the conclusion of the novel, and in exchange for her hand in marriage, Lorelei has persuaded Henry to use his fortune to support the production of a film about "the sex life of Dolly Madison," in which she will play the lead.

In "The Biography of a Book," the preface Loos added to the 1963 reprint of *Blondes,* she details the biographical origins of the novel, providing later critics with the means for conceptualizing the text. She notes the importance of H. L. Mencken in the genesis of the novel, claiming to have written the novel as a satire of his preference for "a witless blonde" and as a way to gain his acceptance as a writer on a par with those he lauded in his influential 1919 study *The American Language*.[88] She also describes how Mencken turned down the story for his publication *American Mercury* because of its controversial treatment of sex and suggested she "send it to Harper's Bazaar, where it'll be lost among the ads and won't offend anybody" (*Blondes* xli).[89]

Loos's reconstruction of the moment that inspired *Blondes* reveals it as a novel steeped in Hollywood conventions. Her opening sets up the dynamics (articulated in her theoretical text) of textuality and visuality among the Hollywood crowd: "There was a time a number of years ago when I found myself on a train, the de luxe *Santa Fé Chief,* traveling from New York to Los Angeles. We were a party of co-workers in the movies, en route back to our studio after a cherished holiday in New York, for we belonged to the elite of the cinema which has never been fond of Hollywood." Among the group, which included Douglas Fairbanks and Loos's husband, was a blonde who, "although she towered above me . . . and was of rather a hearty type, was being waited on, catered to and cajoled by the entire male assemblage." Loos decided that there was a "radical difference" between the blonde and her because "she was a natural blonde and I was a brunette." This "palpably unjust" situation caused her to "reach for one of the large yellow pads on which I composed Doug's scenarios, and . . . [begin] to write down my thoughts; not bitterly, as I might have done had I been a real novelist, but with an amusement which was, on the whole, rather childish" (*Blondes* xxxvii–xxxviii).

Whether Loos's reconstruction of the events is accurate or not, it sheds light on how central Hollywood and the film industry are to the construction of *Blondes* and how Loos wants her readers to understand them. Rejecting the mantle of the "real novelist," Loos writes her thoughts on the pad used for her film scenarios. A diminutive brunette (of "ninety pounds"), she recedes into the world of text while the "hearty" blonde captures the male gaze (*Blondes* xxxvii).[90] Loos's action here is a metaphor for her larger role in Hollywood. As a scenarist specializing in titles, Loos inhabited the world of text—pads of yellow paper as opposed to the blonde locks of screen stars. Her writing, as she theorized in *How to Write Photoplays*, becomes an act of textual subversion, an attempt to use text to undermine the visual, thereby demystifying it and making it more complex, if not more comprehensible. This "biography" of *Blondes* emphasizes the novel's origins at a site of modernist friction, where conflict will produce a narrative in which images and text do not match and the reader must read deliberately to understand the text's narrative layers.

The novel itself is structured as a subversive act of writing. Subtitled *The Illuminating Diary of a Professional Lady*, *Blondes* is framed as a diary in which Lorelei records her thoughts and experiences. Critics have tended to overread Lorelei's act as a liberatory one.[91] Because Loos's depiction of Lorelei stems from her critique of the hearty blonde on the Hollywood-bound train, the dynamics that inform Lorelei's textual presentation of her own life and Loos's authorial manipulation of Lorelei are more complex than they initially seem. These complexities derive from that critical juxtaposition of the blonde as the object of the gaze in cinema and the scenarist who controls the text and therefore provides an ironic evaluation of this visual object. It is no coincidence, then, that Lorelei's diary is "illuminating," since cinema is the art of light and shadow. The diary's illumination is contentious: Lorelei uses her vernacular language alternately to conceal and to reveal, frequently glossing over critical moments while providing biting commentary at other times.[92] For Lorelei—as for Lardner and many other modernists—language is an untrustworthy medium for narration. But Lorelei's linguistic dodges are countered by Loos's cinema-inspired vernacular modernist strategies, which allow the story to unfold behind the language and force the reader to reconstruct essential elements of the narrative by reading through Lorelei's artifice, in a manner analogous to Lardner's baseball writings.

Near the opening of the novel, we begin to see the tension between words and images as Lorelei notes that she might become an "authoress" but that her second choice would be a "cinema star." Writing and the cinema are explicitly connected in Lorelei's dual ambitions, and among her earliest diary entries is a memory of her work on Griffith's film *Intolerance*, where she is one of the girls "falling off the tower" in the Babylonian crowd scene. Though Lorelei draws on this experience to suggest how to suppress "bolshevism" in the button factories (by applying the managerial skill she had seen Griffith demonstrate), it also establishes her ties to Hollywood (*Blondes* 8). Lorelei's role as an extra in *Intolerance* further points to Loos's connection to the character. Whereas Loos was called in for a specific textual job on Griffith's film—to write the title cards—Lorelei fulfills another specialized role, that of the visual spectacle.

Gus Eisman, however, has severed Lorelei's connection to the Hollywood world of the visual because, as Lorelei writes, his mother is "authrodox" (*Blondes* 6). He prefers that Lorelei emphasize her "brains" rather than focus on a life of visuality. Critics have noted that Lorelei's emphasis on brains and education suggests sexual metaphors that suppress the textual and intellectual associations of the terms. Susan Hegeman's nuanced reading of the complex levels of meaning embodied by the terms "brains" and "education" is particularly instructive in rejecting the earlier notions that there is a one-to-one correspondence between sex and "education" in the text.[93] In a sense, these terms operate as ambiguous modernist signifiers; it is clear that Lorelei is concealing something sexual about her intellectual relationships, but the power of her linguistic performance enables the complete and total elision of any final signified. Lorelei's obsession with porous and malleable terms like these helps to situate *Gentlemen Prefer Blondes* as a text critiquing the euphemistic (and "refined") language of nineteenth-century gentility, highlighting its hollowness in a twentieth-century world.

The gentlemen who profess a concern for her brains almost inevitably end up staying late into the night in Lorelei's rooms "educating" her; her continual displacement of any reference to sexuality is one of the novel's running jokes. Readings of the novel that stress the reader's fairly unmediated identification with Lorelei see this textual manipulation (through the double entendre "brains") as a form of empowerment, a demonstration of her ability to control her life and her text. However, given the inception of the novel as suggested in Loos's "biography," the value of this aesthetic strategy should be questioned at a more basic level. While Lorelei clearly manipulates men by appropriating their hollow language, her character should not necessarily appear triumphant in this act. Instead, the privileging of the brains of a character associated with the visual intersects with common cultural jokes about the brains (or lack thereof) of film stars, as well as with the negotiation of such humor in Loos's film theory.

After publishing *How to Write Photoplays,* Loos and Emerson followed it up with the less instructive *Breaking into the Movies* (1921). At its root, this text reads like a bit of commercial opportunism. Whereas *How to Write Photoplays* provides instruction, with examples, on how to approach the craft of scenario writing, *Breaking into the Movies* resembles an extended fan magazine, full of suggestions on how to reach stardom. Designed to appeal to people—like Lorelei or Merton Gill of Harry Leon Wilson's novel *Merton of the Movies* (1922)—who sought to end up on the screen as opposed to behind it, *Breaking into the Movies* does not provide the useful step-by-step methodology promoted in Loos and Emerson's first book. Instead, it reveals some of the contemporary thinking and cultural assumptions surrounding cinema stars in the silent era.

One of the more notable and relevant chapters in *Breaking into the Movies* is "Inside the Brain of a Movie Star." It begins humorously: "'But they have no brains!' someone is sure to say." The chapter goes on to dispel such an uncritical notion as "rather cheap cynicism," but the damage has been done.[94] By opening the chapter as they do, Loos and Emerson reiterate the cultural assumption that movie stars are brainless. As scenario writers, they clearly distance their intellectual work from standard thinking about Hollywood stardom. This dynamic is expanded by the fact that only one short chapter on scenario writing is included in *Breaking into the Movies*. The primary audience of the second book may think it is qualified to write scenarios, but the presence of such a brief chapter in a book filled with chapters like "Would You Film Well?," "Make-Up," "How to Dress for a Picture," and even "Salaries in the Movies" suggests another story.

If, as a result of this disjunction, we read Lorelei as a caricature of the reader of *Breaking into the Movies*, it becomes difficult to see her as a pure screen onto which Loos projects an ideological criticism of gender norms in the 1920s. Like the reader of *Breaking into the Movies*, Lorelei is clearly suited for an existence in front of the camera, and she does, after all, ostensibly give up her pretensions to be an "authoress" to become a "cinema star" at the book's conclusion. Her presence as a writer is thus thrown into question. Lorelei's manner of storytelling reflects on the surface the amateur scenario writer's impulse toward "jotting down that wonderful idea and sending it off in the same mail." Criticism of the novel tends to read this lack of sophistication as a linguistic performance, analogous to the powerful naïveté that leaves a trail of impoverished suitors at Lorelei's feet. Still, the significance of her reliance on this uncritical mode of storytelling must be considered.

Bourgeois and middlebrow concepts like sophistication and, more important for Lorelei, what she calls "reverance" (*Blondes* 52) form a semiotic matrix in which the book operates. Lorelei's use of these terms often seems confusing and contradictory; her level of linguistic obfuscation, clearly influenced by Lardner's early work, may be unparalleled in American fiction. According to her diary, her admirers are interested purely in her "brains." As a result, they want to "educate" her. When situations become too difficult for Lorelei to cover up with language, she glides over them. In the novel's first chapter, Lorelei describes her trip around the park with Gerry in a hansom cab. She writes, "I mean Gerry knows how to draw a girl out and I told him things that I really would not even put in my diary" (*Blondes* 11). Lorelei again says things she "would not even put in [her] diary" when she visits "Dr. Froyd" (*Blondes* 90). Her allusions to omissions from her diary provide a crucial context for understanding Lorelei's use of text. For her, text is a means of obfuscation, renarration, and revision. Like many experimental writers of the modernist era, Lorelei buries the narrative essentials. Instead of using literary references to challenge the reader, she conceals her story in an artificial and somewhat twisted language of propriety. Her diary, theoretically the location of all Lorelei's inmost thoughts, is merely a fictionalization of her real experience. Anything "unrefined," as Lorelei puts it, is left out (*Blondes* 96).

Placing *Blondes* in the context of this semiotics makes it possible to read some of Lorelei's catch phrases in the light of a matrix of meaning and representation derived from Loos's work in film narrative. If text in Lorelei's hands is always suspect, how are we to understand her favorite topics: her own "reverance" and her best friend Dorothy's habit of being "unrefined"? Clearly these are loaded terms, and Lorelei's insistence that her brains are her finest attribute and her unwillingness to allow her readers access to a deeper interiority make the terms suspect. Lorelei seems to reflect the dynamic between image and text in Loos's theory about silent films. With this in mind, we can connect Loos's experience as a title-card specialist, her biographical commentary on the book's inception, and the relationship between Lorelei and Dorothy.

If Lorelei is at least partially discredited through her misuse of text, Dorothy becomes a stand-in for Loos, who said in interviews that she modeled Dorothy on herself. Like Loos in the story she uses to preface the 1963 edition of *Blondes*, Dorothy is outside the circle of action. She is Lorelei's chaperone in Europe, and she follows a path separate from Lorelei's, choosing her boyfriends by her attraction to them, not by the size of their wallets. When Loos compares herself with Dorothy in a 1965 interview, she claims, "I have always been the brunette who lost out, and I've always gotten the wrong end of everything! I've gone through all my life without a single diamond!"[95] In the serialization of *But Gentlemen Marry Brunettes*, the second installment (June 1926), entitled "The Unrefinement of Dorothy," appears opposite a full-page portrait of Loos, its title, "This Is Anita Loos," underscoring the connection between the author and her fictional counterpart. However, the similarities run deeper. Like Loos, Dorothy is a master of language, one who uses it subversively as ironic commentary on Lorelei's world of visual pleasure.[96] This makes her, in Lorelei's words, "unrefined" and lacking in "reverance." It also makes her the novel's walking, talking title card.

Dorothy, then, is a convergent semiotic point in the novel. Evoking the biographical, the cinematic, and the "unrefined," Dorothy's initially marginal role in the narrative begins to make more sense as the text's unifying factor. Indeed, this reading may explain comments William Faulkner made in a letter to Loos: "Please accept my envious congratulations on Dorothy—the way you did her through the intelligence of that elegant moron of a cornflower.... I wish I had thought of Dorothy first."[97] Many admirers of the novel focused on the characterization of Lorelei, but Faulkner, developing a modernist narrative style of his own, saw Dorothy, a manipulator of words who forces her way into Lorelei's text, as the key to understanding the novel, perhaps even as a sign of the text's modernism. Faulkner is onto something. Dorothy offers a form of linguistic commentary that invades the veiled text of Lorelei's diary. Her running commentary lets a counternarrative emerge as a challenge to the artificial narrative surface. Her comments, examples of the power of vernacular language to destroy nineteenth-century propriety, break the narrative surface in ways analogous to Loos's title cards. Dorothy's words, like these cards, exhibit the same "penchant for hyperbole, wisecracks, and double entendre"—and even "pungent slang"—that identifies the "Anita Loos school" of scenarists.

Indeed, Dorothy's role expands as we make our way through the novel. Dorothy appears more often in Lorelei's narration, and her words are increasingly quoted rather than paraphrased. In the first chapter, "Gentlemen Prefer Blondes," Dorothy is practically nonexistent. We learn that she is to chaperone Lorelei in Europe and that she has a boyfriend she calls Coocoo. The conventional understanding of the composition of *Blondes* suggests that this chapter was written as a stand-alone story and that Loos continued it at the request of the publishers of *Harper's Bazar*. Accordingly, at the beginning of the second chapter (and second installment), Lorelei writes that Dorothy "does nothing but waste her time and yesterday, which was really the day before we sailed, she would not go to luncheon with Mr. Goldmark but she went to luncheon to meet a gentleman called Mr. Mencken from Baltimore who really only prints a green magazine which has not even got any pictures in it" (*Blondes* 19). At this juncture, authorized by Mencken in the same way Loos's original manuscript was authorized by him, Dorothy becomes a satiric force in the novel. Given the choice between the film producer Goldmark and the biting social commentator and author of *The American Language*, it is unsurprising that the witty and linguistically agile Dorothy chooses to dine with Mencken, despite the fact that his magazine lacks "pictures."

From this point on Dorothy's presence becomes more notable. Lorelei begins by chastising her for using so much "slang," continues by paraphrasing some of Dorothy's one-liners, and ends up ceding a significant portion of textual commentary to Dorothy (*Blondes* 22). By the end of the novel, Dorothy's revealing quips compete with Lorelei's concealing gaffes for the reader's attention. The most notorious of these "unrefined" moments occurs at the "Foley Bergere" in Paris, where Dorothy comments on the purported age of one of the performers in the production: "She is slipping it over on you Louie, because how could a girl get such dirty knees in only 18 years?" (*Blondes* 66). This, like Dorothy's earlier overuse of slang and multiple innuendos, is dismissed by Lorelei as "unrefined." This word (as well as Lorelei's fear of the corrupting power of Dorothy's slang) recalls nineteenth-century debates about class status and proper language, detailed in Kenneth Cmiel's study of American language, *Democratic Eloquence*. But Lorelei's constant invocation of obsolete cultural hierarchies also operates as a critique of "sophisticated" and "refined" realist fiction, demonstrating the emptiness of these categories by the mid-1920s. Ironically, though, as much as Lorelei rejects the "unrefinement of Dorothy," she increasingly includes her slang-laden comments in her diary, all while concealing Lorelei's own inmost thoughts. Because Dorothy's comments are suggestive (but not explicit) in the fashion of the "Anita Loos school," they are qualified for inclusion in Lorelei's narrative but always with some critical dismissal by Lorelei. As Lorelei notes, "Dorothy never overlooks any chance to be unrefined" (*Blondes* 100).

In a sense, Lorelei's concern with Dorothy is that of the misguided reformer. In one of her Paris entries, she notes, "I mean I really try to make Dorothy get educated and have reverance" (*Blondes* 52). In the end, however, Dorothy's "unrefined" comments become one of the means by which Lorelei negotiates the textual realities of the world. Pursued by the Lady Francis Beekman, whose husband has bought Lorelei a $7,500 diamond tiara, Lorelei relies on Dorothy to defuse the situation: "I mean I always encouradge Dorothy to talk quite a lot when we are talking to unrefined people like Lady Francis Beekman, because Dorothy speaks their own languadge to unrefined people better than a refined girl like I" (*Blondes* 59). Though Lorelei, as the object of the gaze, does not endorse Dorothy's "unrefined" and subversive "languadge," she depends on it not only to elude the aristocratic Lady Beekman but also to negotiate marriage with Henry Spoffard on her own terms.

Ultimately, *Blondes* ends up much where it began, in Hollywood, and Lorelei becomes a cinema star, not an authoress, returning to the world of the purely visual. Naturally, Dorothy comes along, but her place in Hollywood is appropriately situated somewhere between the visual and the textual. Lorelei notes, "Dorothy says that she was at the studio yesterday and she says that if the senarios those extra girls have written around themselves to tell Henry could only be screened and gotten past the sensors, the movies would move right up out of their infancy" (*Blondes* 122). Direct quotation of Dorothy's language has once again been suppressed, since Lorelei is on the verge of adopting a purely visual identity as a cinema star. Lorelei's flirtation with the textual is over, leaving Dorothy's quoted quips no room to break through. However, Dorothy's association with the "senarios" reinforces her links to textuality (and even to modernism) and takes us back to Loos, whose work—theoretical and practical—in scenarios and film narrative played a major part in helping movies "move right up out of their infancy."

The complex practice of negotiating the highly subjective and vernacular narrative of Lorelei and the running commentary of Dorothy places *Gentlemen Prefer Blondes* in the modernist realm of the "fragmented" narrative, requiring, like the work of Lardner, a smiling, but 'grim' reader who can put the elements of the story together, read both between the lines and past Lorelei's linguistic gaffes for the story behind the text. The narrative has not only enabled the film industry to "move right up out of [its] infancy," but it has also drawn explicit links between the "vernacular modernism" of silent film and the formally complex and slang-laden experiments in American humor. Loos expands on Lardner's model, complicating the single subjectivity that drives *You Know Me Al* and advancing the principles of vernacular modernism. Her text takes part in these major cultural tensions—between high- and lowbrow entertainment, between film and literature, and between text and image—in a modern world where the potential is emerging for text to be completely overrun by images.

Loos's later fictional work, including the sequel *But Gentlemen Marry Brunettes* and the serialized novel *The Better Things of Life* (1930–1931, heavily revised version published in 1963 as *No Mother to Guide Her*), continued to examine the friction between text and image and utilize the vernacular aesthetic that made *Blondes* so successful.[98] But *Blondes* remains monumental; its vernacular modernist aesthetics foreground the textuality of Lorelei's diary, and its complex incorporation of the narrative devices of silent film represent a sophisticated insider's take on cinematic storytelling, an alternative to other efforts by high modernists like Dos Passos and Joyce. Though less often placed in the broader network of experimental literary production by contemporary modernist critics, the novel was nonetheless a centerpiece of highbrow discussion in the 1920s. A favorite of Wharton, Faulkner, and Joyce, Loos even received a backhanded compliment from Wyndham Lewis, in which he compared the seemingly formless (though tightly woven) vernacular narration of Lorelei to the work of Gertrude Stein.[99]

Ultimately, though, Loos, like Lardner, constructs a brand of humor that is decidedly a work of twentieth-century vernacular modernism that stands in stark contrast to the dialect humor of the nineteenth century. Lardner and Loos demonstrate just how aesthetically experimental and complicated popular writing can be; these works are self-conscious textual artifacts, deeply invested in subjective forms of vernacular narration that reject both an aesthetics of realism and the realist mediation of nineteenth-century humor narratives. The fact that the earliest forms of vernacular modernism appear in humor writing is unsurprising; after all, humorists lack "reverance" for received forms, particularly forms that betray a pompous gentility. But the vernacular modernism they inaugurate is not always full of laughs. Still, their aesthetic innovations and focus on vernacular language carry over into the bittersweet and decidedly earnest tales of Jewish American ghetto life in the work of Anzia Yezierska and Michael Gold.

3 / "I Didn't Understand the Words, but My Voice Was Like Dynamite"

Anzia Yezierska, Mike Gold, and the Jewish American Break with Realism

> *It has taken the artists and poets to rediscover this life of the ghetto. The life in the ghetto was probably always more active and teeming than life outside. The ghetto made the Jews self-conscious. They lived on the fringe of two worlds: the ghetto world and the strange world beyond the ghetto gates.*
> —LOUIS WIRTH, THE GHETTO (1928)

> *It is in the immigrant development of the new America that the possibilities for a fundamental revolution of the word are inherent.*
> —EUGENE JOLAS, "THE KING'S ENGLISH IS DYING—LONG LIVE THE GREAT AMERICAN LANGUAGE" (1930)

Realism's political valences proved immensely important to immigrant writers in the late nineteenth and early twentieth centuries. While humor had begun to destabilize the objectivity and narrative situations inherent in dialect realism, immigrant writers continued to struggle with realism's conventions for a number of important reasons. Since the majority of realist texts posited cultural difference as visible linguistic difference in the text, immigrant writers—like the generation of African American writers in the 1890s—attempted to use the conventions of realism against these norms. On this influence, Thomas J. Ferraro has noted that "the ethnic writers of the teens and twenties had sharpened their imaginations in their late youth and early adulthood by reading Dreiser, Crane, Howells."[1] These realist conventions became a means of textually demonstrating both the humanity and the Americanness of immigrants. In other words, if realism depended on an objective narrator that defined genteel American language (and, by extension, American identity), the use of realism by immigrant writers—specifically Jewish American immigrants—became formative in showing the American reading public how similar this genteel public was to the poor, slum-dwelling immigrants that populated many of these books. While popular realist texts of the nineteenth century marked Jews as fundamentally different through the medium of dialect, the work of writers like Abraham Cahan and Mary Antin explicitly confronted the cultural hierarchies of many realist writers by showing their own characters speaking and thinking in the genteel language of realism.

The question of language and Jewish identity looms large in the late realist period. With the enormous influx of Eastern European Jews into the United States in the 1880s and 1890s, cultural depictions of these immigrants resembled, in both kind and degree, the stereotypes used to characterize African Americans during the same era. From sound recordings utilizing Jewish stereotypes to ethnographic depictions of Jewish neighborhoods for middle-American nickelodeon audiences, Jews found themselves constantly marked as different, exotic, and potentially subhuman.[2] Most importantly, however, these fears became bound up with concerns about language. Here, one need think only of Henry James's bewildered stroll through New York's Lower East Side, as depicted in his *The American Scene* (1907), as well as his anxieties about the devolution of the American language described in his lecture "The Question of Our Speech" (1905).[3] Jewish immigrants, residing largely in insulated, ghetto-like communities in large metropolitan areas like New York, posed explicit problems to projects of immigrant "Americanization" because of their unwillingness to relinquish markers of cultural difference. James's fear of the Yiddish-speaking hordes that surround him in the Lower East Side is one example of this, while the linguistic caricatures of Jewish figures in the realist fiction of the era served to further deemphasize the possibilities of assimilation.[4] The linguistic hybridity of these dialect characters—their jagged syntax, mispronounced words, and direct substitution of Yiddish for English—marked them as racialized others in a realist context that privileged objectivity and gentility through norms of narration. By the 1920s, however, this same linguistic hybridity was adopted and transformed by two writers of decidedly different political and aesthetic predilections. Drawing on and thematizing her own experiences as a writer, Anzia Yezierska developed a linguistic approach that foregrounded the defamiliarizing experience of cultural assimilation, while Michael Gold transformed his earlier experiences in avant-garde theater and fiction into an explicitly politicized and immigrant-inflected version of vernacular modernism.

"My Own Linguistic Psychology": Realism and Assimilation

> *Prosperity is prosaic.*
> —MARY ANTIN, *THE PROMISED LAND* (1912)

The first major Jewish American writer to grapple with the representational concerns of Jewish American immigrants in American fiction was Abraham Cahan, longtime editor of a Yiddish-language newspaper in the Lower East Side and ostensible cultural diplomat for the Jewish American population. When H. L. Mencken was investigating Yiddish words that had made their way into popular usage for the first edition of *The American Language,* he contacted Cahan, whom Mencken cited multiple times in the first edition of his work. Still, Cahan has become most well known for two novels he published in English: *Yekl* (1896) and *The Rise of David Levinsky* (1917). Cahan's work established some important paradigms for the work the followed it, adapting (especially in *The Rise of David Levinsky*) the Benjamin Franklin narrative to a mode of cultural assimilation, all while suggesting a nostalgia for an innocent past, both premodern and, in a sense, prepubescent.

Language, in these texts, operates according to the logic of dialect realism, where a genteel frame contains substantial dialect. In *Yekl,* Cahan employs a technique by which characters' Yiddish is rendered in a "fluent" English translation while uses of English are singled out (essentially marking this language as outside the realm of conventional usage). A footnote in *Yekl* reads, "English words incorporated in the Yiddish of the characters of this narrative are given in italics."[5] In addition, this text occasionally includes "translations" of particularly difficult English dialect in parentheses. To emphasize more strongly the difference between language as it is spoken and the genteel language of the realist narrator, Cahan italicizes and misspells English words that his characters grossly mispronounce, words that they drop into their Yiddish exchanges. The effect of this—the Yiddish sentences fluidly translated into English, interrupted by italicized English mispronunciation—is linguistic alienation much in line with the hierarchies of the dialect realism and humor writing of writers like Finley Peter Dunne and George Ade. Rather than give the impression that these characters share some relationship with the reader, Cahan lures the reader into some comfort with the language, only to short-circuit that relationship with a mark of dialect that the reader must almost pronounce aloud in order to discover its connection to the standard representation of the word. Thus, italics and phonetic spelling operate as markers of distinct ethnic, cultural, and, most importantly, linguistic difference. Lawrence Rosenwald has described Jake, the protagonist of *Yekl*, as a "linguistic traitor," whose close association with English (even in a form strongly marked by dialect) indicates both assimilation and unethical behavior.[6]

While this mode—in Cahan's first extended work of fiction in English—is complex, he smoothes over the rough edges of this dynamic in the bildungsroman that appeared two decades later. *The Rise of David Levinsky* uses a first-person narrator, a mode that disrupts conventional realist discourse. However, this nostalgic narrator is emblematic of the already assimilated immigrant. The text gradually uncovers the price of this assimilation—spiritual, creative, social, and romantic. However, the reader's experience of this text is from the reflective point of view of a character with whom s/he can linguistically identify. It matters little that the acquisition of an American identity for Levinsky entails both the loss of a rich and rewarding ethnic identity and the addition of a linguistic (and narrative) facility with English. From an aesthetic standpoint, Cahan has recognized the still politically and socially valuable strategy of realist representation. As one critic has noted of realist writers like Cahan, "For social power they sacrificed literary authority—that is, the prospect of passage into the community of self-proclaimed leaders of American letters."[7] For Cahan, acceptance in the eyes of a popular American audience was far more important than breaking down aesthetic boundaries. His work continues to be defined by the troubling standards of dialect realism, as his characters strive to narrate their own stories in an already assimilated language.

Following Cahan, Mary Antin's work—specifically, her loosely fictionalized memoir *The Promised Land* (1912)—also partakes in the discourse of realism. *The Promised Land* opens with a memorable description of assimilation:

> I was born, I have lived, and I have been made over. Is it not time to write my life's story? I am just as much out of the way as if I were dead, for I am absolutely other than the person whose story I have to tell. Physical continuity with my earlier self is no disadvantage. I could speak in the third person and not feel that I was masquerading. I can analyze my subject, I can reveal everything; for *she*, not *I*, is my real heroine. My life I have still to live; her life ended when mine began.[8]

Antin's insistence here on a narrative and discursive separation highlights the degree to which immigrant writers could reinscribe the realist relationship of genteel observer to object of study. Antin is writing about "*she*"; Antin can write "in the third person." Both of these signal a complete alienation from the preassimilated identity, along with a wholesale identification with newness, assimilation, Americanness, and "standard" English usage.

In the case of both Cahan and Antin, what is communicated by the language of the past and the language of the present may differ, but the necessity of transitioning between these two languages remains of the utmost importance. Antin's autobiographical persona can speak "as if I were dead," because the parallel projects of realism and Americanization have enabled her to turn her past into a "third person," something almost wholly unrelated to the person she is now. For Cahan, though this past may at some level be desirable, it remains unrecoverable for David Levinsky, a fact demonstrated through his performance of a mastery of English. As Levinsky learns English by questioning his coworkers, he meditates on the link between language, culture, and psychology: "It did not occur to him that people born to speak another language were guided by another language logic, so to say, and that in order to reach my understanding he would have to impart his ideas in terms of my own linguistic psychology."[9] Levinsky's performance of a nostalgic, fluent English throughout this novel suggests that he has done the inverse, transferred his own "linguistic psychology" and "language logic" to that of English. This loss (of language, culture, connection) is what haunts him at the text's conclusion, but, paradoxically, it is what enables him to tell the story. In a sense, *The Rise of David Levinsky* becomes a subtle critique of dialect realism, but—like Twain's work—one only possible from within realism's aesthetic and ideological boundaries.

The erasure of linguistic difference in the narrative voices of Antin and Cahan suggests that the Jewish American writers of the 1910s were struggling with the politics of representation that also became central among African American intellectuals in the mid-1920s (see chapter 5). Faced with both an increasingly virulent anti-Semitic nativism in political discourse and the resultant popular cultural productions that exoticized Jews as ethnic and racial others, Antin and Cahan worked to stress a *sameness* through the realist language of bourgeois gentility. Their aesthetic approach is somewhat understandable, given the tendency of many writers (both Jewish and not) of the era to exploit racial difference. In 1910 journalist Hutchins Hapgood, for example, suggested to writers that ethnic exoticism might be the solution to writers' block: "Instead of inventing your plots, if you are a novelist, you can take them from the lips of common people, provided you are interested enough in low life to put yourself in touch with the next best 'gorilla' or 'spieler' you may meet. You can take not only your plots from the lives of these people, but you can also derive the vigor and vitality, the figurative quality, of your style, from the slang and racy expressions of your lowly friends."[10] Certainly, the obsession with dialect and difference inspired many major writers to begin experimenting with language, as Michael North has charted in *The Dialect of Modernism*, but when ethnic writers themselves experimented with language and form, as Werner Sollors has argued, they tended to cling "to old-world languages and yet be more modern than their Americanized and American counterparts."[11]

Sollors's characterization is a valuable and trenchant description of the aesthetic environment that produced Cahan and Antin. By 1920 the immigrant narrative—taking its origin point in both Eastern and Western Europe—had become a valued cultural commodity. An excellent example of this is Netherlands-born editor Edward Bok's bestseller *The Americanization of Edward Bok* (1920). This text, part Franklinesque success story, part critique of America and the hollow nature of its success, was a bestseller and won the Pulitzer Prize in 1921. However, in the same year Edward Bok's celebrated autobiography appeared, it is possible to see the beginning of a fragmentation of the strategy of realist representation among immigrant writers in English.

In *Beyond Ethnicity*, Sollors suggests that "literary forms are not organically connected with ethnic groups; ethnicity and modernism form a false set of opposites; and the very desire to transcend ethnicity may lead writers back into the most familiar territory of ethnogenesis and typology."[12] While Anglo-American writers consistently mined the language and culture of ethnic others to achieve some kind of new form or aesthetic, for a couple of decades Jewish American writers in particular remained suspicious of how embracing hybrid linguistic forms could advance a new aesthetic practice, especially in the face of anti-immigrant rhetoric. However, with the rise of interest in the multiethnic and multilingual speech of the American streets, a language of which Mencken claimed that "no other tongue of modern times admits foreign words and phrases more readily," new possibilities emerged. These ethnic and political dynamics offered ways for Jewish American writers to advance the concerns of humorists and other vernacular modernists by exploring the potential for a radical aesthetic practice in the hybrid language of the Jewish immigrant.[13] This brand of vernacular modernism, as practiced in very different ways in the 1920s by writers like Anzia Yezierska and Michael

Gold, utilizes a previously ghettoized language as a means of creating a studied and self-conscious aesthetic distance, as opposed to creating social ostracization. To use the Yezierska metaphor that provides the title to this chapter, this vernacular modernist immigrant language served as a form of aesthetic dynamite that destroyed and completely reshaped the understanding of how a multilingual and multicultural subject might accurately describe experience.

"Slipping Back into the Vernacular": Anzia Yezierska and the Vernacular Modernism of Assimilation

> *"Poems of Poverty!"* cried Mother. *"Ain't it black enough to be poor, without yet making poems about it?"*
> —ANZIA YEZIERSKA, BREAD GIVERS (1925)

> *I jot down any fragment of a thought that I can get hold of. And then I gather these fragments, words, phrases, sentences, and I paste them together with my own blood.*
> —ANZIA YEZIERSKA, "MOSTLY ABOUT MYSELF" (1923)

During her 1923 trip to Europe, Anzia Yezierska made the appointed rounds of any serious American author of the early 1920s. According to her daughter and biographer, Louise Levitas Henriksen, Yezierska sought out George Bernard Shaw, Israel Zangwill, H. G. Wells, John Galsworthy, and Joseph Conrad to discover the secrets of their writing. The most interesting visit was with Gertrude Stein in Paris, where Stein gave her some typically Steinian advice: "Why worry? Nobody knows how writing is written, the writers least of all!"[14] The encounter between Yezierska and Stein has essentially gone unexamined in scholarship on these two writers, in part because they inhabit profoundly different spheres of the American literary canon. Despite the fact that they are both Jewish American women of roughly the same generation (Stein was born in 1874, Yezierska around 1880), they have come to represent very different things to scholars of American literature. Stein, firmly embedded in the modernist canon, has received less attention as an ethnic writer than she has as an avant-garde experimentalist; only a handful of critics—including Maria Damon, Barbara Will, and Priscilla Wald—have foregrounded her Jewish identity as central to their scholarship on Stein. Yezierska's rise in American literary studies, on the other hand, has been almost exclusively fueled by the interest in the subcanon of ethnic women's writing, with little attention to the formal structure and possible experimentation in her texts.[15] Yezierska's 1923 meeting with Stein certainly does not figure as the same kind of watershed moment in American modernism as Ernest Hemingway's arrival at 27 rue de Fleurus in the previous year. After all, Hemingway approached Stein as an apprentice and Yezierska's meeting occurred after she had already become a successful writer. However, the insistence that Stein remain an unqualified modernist writer and that Yezierska, at best, be labeled an *ethnic* modernist suggests that existing literary subcanons continue to struggle to deal adequately with the variety of modernist writing produced in this era.

Yezierska was all but invisible to scholars of American literature until the 1970s. Outside a brief mention in Allen Guttmann's 1971 study *The Jewish Writer in America,* Yezierska was even largely absent from the Jewish American literary canon, which was kinder to conventional realist and modernist figures such as Abraham Cahan, Mary Antin, and Henry Roth.[16] Yezierska's rediscovery by literary critics in the 1970s and 1980s (with the republication of *Bread Givers* [1925] in 1975, and the 1979 publication of the Yezierska collection *The Open Cage* and the 1985 edition of *Hungry Hearts* [1920]) came on the heels of an increasing interest in narratives of working women by feminist scholars.[17] Mary V. Dearborn exemplifies this when she notes that Yezierska's "fiction is welcomed, in short, because it provides valuable documentary evidence that ethnic women existed."[18] To both feminist and labor historians, such documentation was crucial to the expansion of labor histories to include more diverse voices in the understanding of twentieth-century labor.

Since Yezierska's rediscovery, the scholarship on her work has consistently emphasized ethnicity, gender, and class, placing her in subcanons that write out meetings like the one she had with Stein. Critics have recently gone so far as to include her in studies of Yiddish literature, even though—unlike Abraham Cahan—she never published in Yiddish.[19] Ethnic American writers such as Yezierska have been both blessed and cursed by the last forty years of American literary scholarship. With the emergence of ethnic studies, many American writers long forgotten by literary historians have reemerged in new editions and made their way into classrooms and scholarly journals. This new attention has certainly been a boon for writers like Zora Neale Hurston, whose work has become an indisputable part of the American and African American literary canons. While less canonical ethnic writers continue to inspire a significant amount of scholarship, the relationship of these writers to the rest of American literary history remains murky. In certain cases, such as Michael North's *The Dialect of Modernism* (1994), writers like Hurston and Claude McKay form a background for understanding the racial and linguistic appropriations of already canonized high modernists such as Stein, Eliot, and Pound. But in most literary histories, ethnic writers usually remain outside standard narratives, playing supporting roles, uninvolved in the major literary questions of a given moment. In part, this stems from an unwillingness of critics to confront these writers in the terms the writers themselves found most important. Instead, these figures are essentially seen as documentarians of a complex modernist "culture," recording the ethnic world around them: if not a world ignored, then one often exoticized, objectified, and aesthetically mined by canonical figures in a manner not unlike Hapgood's call to frustrated writers to get "in touch with the next best 'gorilla' or 'spieler' you may meet" and mine the ghetto's "low life" for literary inspiration. Central to the project of these critics is the construction of literary subcanons such as ethnic literature, a crucial step in rediscovering writers, but not necessarily an endpoint, as many of these writers considered themselves part of a larger literary landscape.

To designate a writer as ethnic suggests thematic, aesthetic, and ideological affinities with other writers sharing a similar background. This serves as an effective means of generating narratives of ethnic literary history, but often does a disservice to the writers themselves, many of whom neither published in exclusively ethnic literary journals nor explicitly targeted an ethnic audience (in fact, it was often a mainstream audience they sought). One need only think of the tensions surrounding Ralph Ellison's work (and his own admission of modernist influences) to see the complexity inherent in the construction of a "separate but equal" ethnic literary canon. Yezierska, for example, published her work alongside F. Scott Fitzgerald, Theodore Dreiser, Sherwood Anderson, Sinclair Lewis, Willa Cather, and Katherine Anne Porter in magazines like *Metropolitan* and *Century*. Her 1923 novel *Salome of the Tenements* was advertised by publisher Boni & Liveright in the international avant-garde magazine *Broom* just two months after the publisher had issued the American edition of Eliot's *The Waste Land* (1922).[20] And Wendy R. Katz has documented Yezierska's interest in figures from Walt Whitman to William Faulkner.[21] Still, Yezierska's writing is rarely—if ever—read by critics today without using the adjectival preface *ethnic*. The relationship Yezierska and similar writers held to modernism produces a convoluted story; ethnic writers were certainly aware of experimental writing in the 1910s and 1920s, but how did they respond?

With these concerns in mind, I argue that Yezierska's work certainly exemplifies what I have been calling "vernacular modernism." Unlike Henry Roth, whose mid-1930s work drew quite obviously on the modernist aesthetics of canonical figures such as James Joyce, Yezierska's vernacular modernism emerges in the shadow of popular writers such as Ring Lardner, who approached representation in more comic ways that stretched the function of language and emphasized a particularly intense subjectivity. Importantly, Yezierska's vernacular modernist style amounts to more than merely an "ethnic modernism," a term used by Werner Sollors and others; her work is a part of a larger, cross-ethnic body of work that takes as its inspirational source the colorful vernacular of the American language celebrated by Mencken in *The American Language*.[22]

Though a discussion of Yezierska has become practically de rigueur in monographs on Jewish American literature over the past two decades, her unconventional aesthetic—neither firmly realist nor recognizably modernist—has meant that she is rarely discussed in terms of style or form. Before Yezierska's ascendance, the writers most frequently assessed in studies of Jewish American literature conformed to relatively conventional literary models: Mary Antin and Abraham Cahan emerge from late nineteenth-century realism, while later writers Henry Roth, Saul Bellow, and Philip Roth exhibit strong affinities to commonly understood modernist aesthetics.[23] By conforming to the increasingly outdated modes of realism, early twentieth-century Jewish American writers (to varying degrees of self-consciousness) placed themselves outside the literary avant-garde. Interestingly, while Thomas J. Ferraro lumps Yezierska into the realist group of writers including Antin and Cahan, most literary histories leave Yezierska out of this group, precisely because her aesthetic is not sufficiently realist.[24] Unlike Antin and Cahan, who relied almost exclusively on realist models, and later writers like Henry Roth, who drew heavily on the models of European high modernism, Yezierska's ghetto fairy tales do not explicitly participate in either aesthetic discourse. In addition, the narration of her texts—particularly her short fiction—exhibits a reliance on Yiddish syntax, code switching, and elusive suggestion. Yezierska takes advantage of her own relationship to language to denaturalize the written word and destroy the naïve trust of language in realist writing and the troubling politics of dialect realism.

Yezierska's work mounts a strong critique against the gentility of realist writers Antin and Cahan, one that runs parallel to the critique of nineteenth-century gentility by high modernists. Yezierska brings to the inherited genre of the immigrant memoir a new kind of aesthetic practice, one that rejects the fundamental assumptions of realist writing and implicitly calls into question the political and social motives of the writers who preceded her. In opposition to the large number of popular culture productions that exoticized Jews as ethnic and racial others, Antin and Cahan worked to stress a sameness through realist language of bourgeois gentility within their narrators. Yezierska, on the other hand, rejected this form, preferring, especially in her early writing, the creation of an aesthetic distance (using the vernacular) that suggested the limits of realist language by foregrounding language as language, over and above its signifying operations.[25] Sally Ann Drucker argues that unlike Antin and Cahan, Yezierska "used [dialect] to show that her characters came from the culture of the ghetto, but without that culture denigrating or debasing them."[26] What Drucker calls dialect, I want to redefine as vernacular language, precisely because Yezierska rejects the hierarchies that dominate dialect realism in favor of an invented vernacular language that produces new hybrid forms. In other words, though Yezierska's characters may have experiences similar to the protagonists of Antin's and Cahan's work, their ability to describe that experience in a realist discourse breaks down and, frequently, this experience can only be rendered in the abstract, experimental vernacular of the immigrant. Yezierska's recognition that realist discourse fails in the wake of immigrant experience corresponds to Priscilla Wald's reading of Gertrude Stein's *The Making of Americans* (1925), where, Wald argues, "character and culture come together not in the fear of merging but in the fear of disappearing into incomprehensibility . . . with an immigrant divested of cultural narratives, and the familiar terms, that mark personhood."[27]

As with Antin and Cahan, Yezierska's central concerns involved the personal and spiritual prices of assimilation; her novels *Salome of the Tenements* and *Arrogant Beggar* (1927) both engage this question directly, even polemically, utilizing an aesthetic much closer to the realism of these earlier writers. Her more well-known works, the short-story collection *Hungry Hearts* and the novel *Bread Givers,* also weigh in on similar questions, but rather than present these questions in the objective narrative form of most realist writers, Yezierska foregrounds an immigrant consciousness constantly in development. While stories of assimilation are frequently narrated from a first-person perspective, they often emphasize the status of their narrators as already assimilated. Thus, in Antin's autobiographical *The Promised Land,* Cahan's fictional *The Rise of David Levinsky,* and other successful narratives of Americanization such as Edward Bok's bestselling *The Americanization of Edward Bok* and Ludwig Lewisohn's

Up Stream: An American Chronicle (1922), the storyteller stands above his or her life, on a par with the genteel reader. Yezierska's early fiction flies in the face of these conventions and demonstrates her peculiar aesthetics that aim to alienate readers from a language they should feel some affinity with, simultaneously complicating notions of linguistic purity and syntax in ways analogous to high modernists like Stein.

Critics have interrogated Yezierska's language from a variety of perspectives. Ruth Bienstock Anolik emphasizes how the female "bread givers" of Yezierska's most famous novel must occupy the assimilating linguistic space of Americanization, as the patriarch remains staunchly a scholar of Hebrew.[28] Others argue for the centrality of both linguistic and cultural hybridity not only to Yezierska's work, but also to her position within a modernist moment.[29] Delia Caparoso Konzett associates Yezierska with Zora Neale Hurston and Jean Rhys, calling their work "ethnic modernism" in a study that "raises the combined question of dislocation and ethnicity as a key feature of modernism, one that is still too-often dealt with in discreet separation."[30] While Konzett, Anolik, and others foreground gender and ethnicity as the determinants and signs of Yezierska's participation in a modernist culture, wedding these components to larger concerns of aesthetic choices strips the concept of modernism of its major signifying force, its aesthetic innovation. All of these critics have done important work in conceiving of Yezierska as a modernist, but their emphasis on gender and ethnicity as prerequisites for such attributions comes close to keeping Yezierska's writing within the proverbial literary ghetto, unable to assert its aesthetic value in a larger literary context. By drawing on the important work of these critics but recasting the linguistic experimentation in Yezierska under the rubric of vernacular modernism, it becomes possible to see her as engaged with a broader set of modernist aesthetics through both linguistic expatriation and cultural transformation.

A concern with the interstitial language of the American immigrant runs throughout Yezierska's work. Whereas Cahan and Antin adopted the assumptions of realism—the largely objective narrator, the classification of characters through linguistic difference, and so forth—Yezierska's work demonstrates an awareness of how language functions in the mouths of her characters as they undergo various forms of assimilation, some more successful than others. Indeed, what marks Yezierska as a vernacular modernist is her hyperawareness of how language constitutes her characters as they simultaneously constitute their language out of fragmentary snatches of English and Yiddish. The words in the mouths of her characters and narrators reject realist standards in favor of a vernacular form that disturbs the relationship between signifier and signified. Yezierska's modernism is not merely about subjectivity, but also about the process of assimilation and how an aesthetic of language can dramatize this process. Her characters, always striving to become American, find themselves drawn back to their Lower East Side, Jewish roots, even in the syntactical construction of their language.

The story that most clearly demonstrates Yezierska's self-conscious use of this aesthetic is "To the Stars," first published in *Century* magazine in May 1921 and included in her second, lesser-known 1923 collection *Children of Loneliness*. Sophie Sapinsky, the protagonist of "To the Stars" and an earlier story, "My Own People," dreams, as Yezierska did, of becoming a writer. The dean of her college and the creative writing professor both discourage her. The dean claims, "What chance is there for you, with your immigrant English? You could never get rid of your foreign idiom."[31] Undeterred by their lack of faith in her abilities and encouraged by an advertisement for a short-story contest, Sophie writes her story. Her determination is palpable: "Centuries of suppression, generations of illiterates clamored in her: 'Show them what's in you! If you can't write it in college English, write it "immigrant English!"'" (*HIFA* 164). Encouraged by the president of the college (a believer in "democracy in education" and a clear stand-in for John Dewey), Sophie takes her story to a creative writing class.[32] The president has told her: "There are things in life bigger than rules of grammar. The thing that makes art live and stand out throughout the ages is sincerity. Unfortunately, education robs many of us of the power to give spontaneously, as mother earth gives, as the child gives. You have poured out not a part, but the whole of yourself. That's why it can't be measured by any of the prescribed standards. It's uniquely you" (*HIFA* 171). The president's argument that "the power to give spontaneously" through art "can't be measured by any of the prescribed standards" echoes the concerns of modernist writers and critics, who were arguing much the same thing in the early 1920s. Existing forms and standards were mere fetters to be broken by new, more authentic and spontaneous expressions. But unlike the Deweyan college president, Sophie's creative writing class is by no means on the cutting edge of literary aesthetics.

Sophie's class savages her writing. The criticisms are notable: "'It's not a story; it has no plot'; 'feeling without form'; 'erotic, over-emotional'" (*HIFA* 172). In this multivalent moment, Yezierska accomplishes a number of things. First, it is clear that the standards of this creative writing class are those of the realism practiced by Cahan and Antin. Plot, formal construction, and emotional distance in narration all characterize this kind of writing. Through the suggestion that experimentation allows access to sincerity and spontaneity, Yezierska has subtly aligned Sophie (and herself) with high modernism, a mode of creation that faced some of the very same criticisms.[33] One need only recall the 1929 "Revolution of the Word" "Proclamation" from *transition* (discussed in the introduction)—and its claims that "narrative is not mere anecdote, but the projection of a metamorphosis of reality" and "the writer expresses, he does not communicate"—to see the ways that Yezierska's controversial aesthetics in "To the Stars" mirror those of the formally experimental writing of high modernism.[34] While modernists like Eugene Jolas of *transition* reached this revolution in aesthetics through a labored critique of nineteenth-century literature, Sophie and Yezierska have arrived at an analogous point through the inherent linguistic alienation in the immigrant experience. Undeterred by the class's criticism, Sophie sends off the story "for a judgment of a world free from rules of grammar," and, not so surprisingly, wins the first prize in the short-story contest (*HIFA* 172).[35]

Around the time Yezierska published "To the Stars," she entered an ongoing discussion in the *New York Times Book Review and Magazine* over Ludwig Lewisohn's memoir, *Up Stream*. Her letter—a response to Brander Matthews's negative review of Lewisohn's work—lays out a few important aesthetic principles against which Yezierska's own work should be read. She celebrates the multiethnic quality of American society and the value that immigrants bring to the linguistic identity of the United States: "Foreigners bring new color, new music, new beauty of expression to worn-out words. The foreign mind works on an old language like the surging leaven of youth. It rekindles and recreates our speech. Trite words, stale phrases, break up into new rhythms in the driving urge to express more vitally the rush of new experience, the fire of changing personality."[36] Her language here looks back to the work of the *Seven Arts* critics and Randolph Bourne's "Trans-National America"; her words are reminiscent of Van Wyck Brooks's claim that "slang has quite as much in store for so-called culture as culture has for slang."[37] It also echoes Mencken's claim in *The American Language* that "American thus shows its character in a constant experimentation, a wide hospitality to novelty, a steady reaching out for new and vivid forms. No other tongue of modern times admits foreign words and phrases more readily; none is more careless of precedents; none shows a greater fecundity and originality of fancy." The language of Yezierska's letter veers close to ethnic essentialism, but she notes that the "foreign mind . . . rekindles and recreates *our* speech," and that this leavening force, this experimental linguistic transformation allows all Americans—not just the foreigners she discusses—"to express more vitally the rush of new experience, the fire of changing personality." Like more easily identifiable modernists, Yezierska essentially argues that experimentation at the level of language is absolutely necessary to produce authentic, sincere, and vital representations of modern life: the immigrant language of the American streets is a language seemingly built for modernity.

In language analogous to the many modernist manifestos of the era, Yezierska's letter even describes a new "creative spirit" that "has arisen . . . in the form of a protest and a rebellion."[38] Her emphasis on the overhauling of language that the "foreign mind" enables even anticipates manifestos such as the 1929 "Proclamation" in Jolas's *transition*, which included points such as "the revolution in the English language is an accomplished fact" and the writer "has the right to use words of his own fashioning and to disregard existing grammatical and syntactical laws."[39] Jolas's later defense of the "Revolution of the Word" manifesto strongly echoes Yezierska's argument about immigrant language, boldly claiming that "it is in the immigrant development of the new America that the possibilities for a fundamental revolution of the word are inherent."[40] The ability of Sophie's "immigrant English" to shatter "trite words [and] stale phrases . . . into new rhythms in the driving urge to express more vitally the rush of new experience" parallels one of the central concerns of high modernist aesthetics. The "Proclamation" opens with a claim that the signees are "tired of the spectacle of short stories, novels, poems and plays still under the hegemony of the banal word, monotonous syntax, static psychology, [and] descriptive naturalism."[41] As Yezierska's defense of Lewisohn suggests, she was equally fed up with the legacy of realism and in hope of reinventing the language of her fiction and accessing something closer to the "real." In "To the Stars," the "sincerity" of Sophie's work, as the college president calls it, rises above the rules and regulations of language, a case in point of William Carlos Williams's call for "not 'realism,' but reality itself" in *Spring and All*, published in 1923, the same year as *Children of Loneliness*.[42]

Throughout her work Yezierska takes up the call of the "real" and the authentic in many guises.[43] This appears most explicitly in her use of first-person narration. While both Cahan and Antin use this narrative point of view, they do so in forms fully recognizable to early twentieth-century audiences. Though often dismissed as simple, Yezierska's use of the first person is more complex, and, in a way, more challenging than that of these earlier writers. Rather than translating her linguistic experience to something easily digestible for readers or using the trope of the dialect figure as in Cahan's *Yekl: A Tale of the New York Ghetto*, Yezierska occupies a third space, a liminal point both between these two options and outside them. This is most apparent in her earliest work, the story collection *Hungry Hearts*. Later in her career, Yezierska—like Lardner—gravitated toward more conventional forms, utilizing the third person in a novel of social critique, *Arrogant Beggar*. However, Yezierska always mixed first- and third-person narration, and the structure of *Hungry Hearts* demonstrates the kind of self-conscious use of these techniques later theorized in the story of Sophie Sapinsky.

The ten stories in *Hungry Hearts* are split evenly between first- and third-person narratives. The collection opens with three third-person pieces in the tradition of the realism of Cahan. The narrative voices of "Wings," "Hunger," and "The Lost 'Beautifulness'" approach the objective stance of the realist narrator, while the characters Shenah Pessah of "Wings" and "Hunger" and Hanneh Hayyeh of "The Lost 'Beautifulness'" speak like the unassimilated figures in Cahan's fiction. These three stories are followed by a block of four first-person narratives occupying the center of the book, one might say the "heart" of *Hungry Hearts*. In this block of stories, Yezierska's strategy—the aesthetic approach that will drive her most celebrated novel, *Bread Givers*—begins to emerge. This group of unconnected narratives thematizes cultural and linguistic assimilation through its use of vernacular language.

This block of stories begins with Yezierska's first published story, "The Free Vacation House," which originally appeared in the *Forum* in 1915. The unnamed narrator of this story opens the tale in quintessential Yezierska fashion: "How came it that I went to the free vacation house was like this."[44] The abruptness, the unconventional syntax, and the seeming substitution of Yiddish sentence structure for English immediately throw the reader into a realm in which the standard realist narrator is nowhere to be found, an absence that resembles the narrative experiments of Ring Lardner. The narrator of "The Free Vacation House" commands the reader's attention in a line that implies a particular intimacy, that of the occasional or informal storyteller, a radical move in a genre of literature where conventions generally demanded an aesthetic distance between the reader and the working-class characters. This break is more striking in that it directly follows three stories with a fairly conventional relationship to these standard narrative practices. Throughout "The Free Vacation House," the narrator remains in this vernacular register, making biting commentary about the

"Social Betterment Society" and its representatives along the way: "When she is gone I think to myself, I'd better knock out from my head this idea about the country. For so long I lived, I did n't know nothing about the charities. For why should I come down among the beggars now?" (*HH* 64). At certain points, "The Free Vacation House" inverts the conventions of realism, placing the vernacular figure in the narrator's position while having her accurately report the "standard" speech of the women from the charity office: "Before I could say something, she goes over to the baby and pulls out the rubber nipple from her mouth, and to me, she says, 'You must not get the child used to sucking this; it is very unsanitary'" (*HH* 62–63). The narrator's exact replication of the speech of these genteel charity workers implies an awareness and rejection of standard language in favor of something more appropriate—in spite of its grammatical irregularities—to the narrator's experience. This difference is clearly demarcated in "The Free Vacation House" when the narrator paraphrases (rather than reports) the barrage of questions she receives from the charity workers: "What is my first name? How old I am? From where come I? How long I'm already in this country? Do I keep any boarders? What is my husband's first name? How old he is? How much wages he gets for a week? How much money do I spend out for the rent?" (*HH* 63). This difference in reported speech and paraphrase highlights Yezierska's aesthetic strategy. It is not necessarily that her narrator cannot speak "college English" (to use Sophie's phrase); she has no problem imitating and reporting verbatim the language of the charity workers. But, to narrate her own story, the unnamed narrator needs "immigrant English"—that "vitally" expressive language appropriate to the modern experience.

The two stories in *Hungry Hearts* that follow "The Free Vacation House" continue the emphasis on linguistic development and cultural assimilation. These almost share a narrator; in "The Miracle," the first of these two stories, the narrator is Sara Reisel, while "Where Lovers Dream" is narrated by a character named only "Sara." The appearance of the same characters in multiple stories runs throughout *Hungry Hearts,* creating the impression of a fictional community larger than the individual stories and connecting the collection to modernist short-story sequences such as Sherwood Anderson's *Winesburg, Ohio* (1919) and Ernest Hemingway's *In Our Time* (1925). Indeed, when *Hungry Hearts* was turned into a film by MGM, elements of the stories were combined into a single narrative involving a protagonist named Sara and a love interest named David (based largely on "Where Lovers Dream").[45] Other characters make repeated appearances throughout Yezierska's fiction: Hanneh Hayyeh, the protagonist of the third-person-narrated "The Lost 'Beautifulness,'" has a minor role in "The Miracle," while the first two stories of the collection both involve Shenah Pessah.[46]

Insisting on the cross-textual importance of characterization might seem, at first glance, trivial. However, the fact that "The Miracle" and "Where Lovers Dream" both have a protagonist named Sara, coupled with their adjacent position in the collection, leads the reader to see these stories as not merely connected, but in some way continuous. Internal evidence, such as the personal histories of the characters and the location of each of Sara's parents, makes this direct continuity impossible, but their adjacency, combined with how the collection has already demonstrated cross-textual appearances of characters, closely links these two Saras. These two stories, located at the center of the volume (the fifth and sixth stories in a ten-story collection), create a crucial hinge on which the collection—and Yezierska's aesthetics—depends. While Sara Reisel (of "The Miracle") narrates her own experiences along the vernacular lines of "The Free Vacation House," Sara (of "Where Lovers Dream") moves somewhat closer to linguistic assimilation, a process completed in "Soap and Water," the last story in this four-story unit at the center of *Hungry Hearts*. The two stories that feature narrating Saras, however, suggest an ever-increasing awareness and sophistication in the use of English.

In both of these central stories, the narration already demonstrates a degree of linguistic assimilation beyond that of the narrator of "The Free Vacation House." In "The Miracle," Sara Reisel's family sends her to America to improve her marriage prospects. She tells her mother, "All I need is a chance. I can do a million times better than Hanneh Hayyeh. I got a head. I got brains. I feel I can marry myself to the greatest man in America" (*HH* 76). The story concludes with Sara realizing "the miracle of America come true" when her English teacher falls in love with her (*HH* 87).[47] Yezierska injects into this conventional romance plot a sense of linguistic malleability that occasionally arrives at moments of more recognizable modernist experimentation. Her description of the trip across the Atlantic, including her fantasy about meeting a great lover, demonstrates a host of experimental techniques that resemble familiar high modernist forms: the repetitive forms of Stein, the understatement of Hemingway, and the exploration of subjectivity that dominates modernist fiction.

> I did n't see the day. I did n't see the night. I did n't see the ocean. I did n't see the sky. I only saw my lover in America, coming nearer and nearer to me, till I could feel his eyes bending on me so near

that I got frightened and began to tremble. My heart ached so with the joy of his nearness that I quick drew back and turned away, and began to talk to the people that were pushing and crowding themselves on the deck.

Nu, I got to America. (*HH* 79)

Despite the use of relatively standard grammatical forms, this passage demonstrates how vernacular modernism can emerge at the level of syntax. The immigrant consciousness of this Sara echoes Stein with the insistent and repetitive "I did n't" form, and deflates emotion with the blunt statement, "Nu, I got to America." The repetition and syntactical inversions so characteristic of Stein's defamiliarizing style in *Three Lives* (1909) and *The Making of Americans* are rendered more natural—but no less modernist—in Yezierska's work. In fact, to read Yezierska closely is to be able to read Stein anew (as an "ethnic" writer and a modernist), since Stein's challenges to realist language often seem to mimic the invented vernacular of Yezierska's Yiddish-English hybrid. In instances like this, Yezierska's vernacular modernism veers close to Stein's high modernist style, while nevertheless transforming it through its insistent connection to her character's immigrant experience.

Immediately following "The Free Vacation House" and "The Miracle," Yezierska includes "Where Lovers Dream," another story that occupies this space between total linguistic assimilation and immigrant vernacular. With its lyric opening, the text seems to have veered more in the direction of Mary Antin's prose: "For years I was saying to myself—Just so you will act when you meet him. Just so will you stand. So will you look on him. These words will you say to him" (*HH* 88). This syntactically sophisticated opening soon gives way to another one of Yezierska's vernacular narrators, Sara, whose boyfriend David Novak is the male ideal and assimilating agent. David, says Sara, "was learning me how to throw off my greenhorn talk, and say out the words in the American" (*HH* 90). The contrast between the lyrical opening and the rest of the narration underscores how language, identity, memory, and narration are compounded in these stories at the center of *Hungry Hearts*.

In "When Lovers Dream," the questions of language and learning are intertwined in the concerns Sara has about her relationship with David. The opening frame of the story finds Sara trying to remain determined to uphold her dignity as she confronts the man who has jilted her: "I wanted to show him that what he had done to me could not down me; that his leaving me the way he left me, that his breaking my heart the way he broke it, did n't crush me; that his grand life and my pinched-in life, his having learning and my not having learning—that the difference did n't count so much like it seemed; that on the bottom I was the same like him" (*HH* 88). Sara contrasts David's "having learning" with her own "not having learning," a construction that recalls Stein's use of gerunds to emphasize states of being in *The Making of Americans*. Sara's determination fails her in this opening frame, though; she faints and must leave the party after David speaks to her. This experience triggers a flashback; Sara narrates this in a way that emphasizes the associative nature of memory: "Ah, I see again the time when we was lovers!" (*HH* 89). In the past, loving, learning, and language are connected in ways that emphasize Sara's inability to remake herself according to David's standards: "David was always trying to learn me how to make myself over for an American. Sometimes he would spend out fifteen cents to buy me the 'Ladies' Home Journal' to read about American life, and my whole head was put away on how to look neat and be up-to-date like the American girls" (*HH* 90). This attempt at self-refashioning through the genteel periodical the *Ladies' Home Journal* falls squarely in line with links between the tropes of fashion and consumerism and racial and ethnic identity across Yezierska's work.[48]

This Sara and her family remain unable to cross over into the "neat" and "up-to-date" world of "American girls." Marked by poverty and by language, Sara and her family are ultimately shunned by the young doctor David, whose wealthy uncle makes his financial support contingent on David's abandoning his greenhorn girlfriend. Though Sara studies English, she remains unable "to throw off [her] greenhorn talk," and her narration remains at the level of the vernacular, suggesting that Sara's experience, like that of the other narrators in *Hungry Hearts*, is more accurately and authentically rendered through this language. While "Where Lovers Dream" is set up like a story of transformation, that language insists that such a transformation does not—and perhaps cannot—occur. The final lines both document Sara's lack of change and suggest an emotional power that eludes standard narration: "For the little while when we was lovers I breathed the air from the high places where love comes from, and I can't no more come down" (*HH* 100). Though Yezierska's stories of self-remaking do not always end in emotional tragedy, even her most successful protagonists often remain unfulfilled.

"Soap and Water," the story that follows "Where Lovers Dream," signals a shift in narrative voice, a modification that dominates the latter half of the collection. This story features a fully assimilated narrator whose voice approaches the standard narration of "How I Found America," the well-known first-person narrative that concludes *Hungry Hearts*. "Soap and Water" is told from the perspective of an unnamed immigrant graduating from college with a teacher's certification. Like Sara Smolinksy of *Bread Givers*, this narrator demonstrates complete control over conventional language, a mark of her education as well as her assimilation. The story thematizes this assimilation; the narrator's inability to appear clean according to bourgeois standards (her lack of "soap and water") erases her education, itself indicated by the language in which the story is narrated. "Soap and Water," placed in the collection after a number of powerfully emotional stories told in varying degrees of vernacular, turns the conventions of realist language on its head, pointing toward the emptiness of the standard language that cannot, ultimately, help the narrator transcend her identity. The fear that the adoption of bourgeois American culture and realist language might not enable the narrative of success or create an emotionally and aesthetically challenging fiction lies underneath Yezierska's later work in the form of a muted, though still present, vernacular modernism.

Much of Yezierska's later fiction relied exclusively on third-person narration, rejecting the intense subjectivity of these stories in *Hungry Hearts*. Two of her novels of the 1920s, *Salome of the Tenements* and *Arrogant Beggar*, draw back into more conventional modes of melodrama and social critique. However, her most frequently studied work, *Bread Givers*, demonstrates an aesthetic between the hypersubjective first-person vernacular narrative and the language of the already fully assimilated character. In a way, *Bread Givers* provides an aesthetic missing link between the stories "When Lovers Dream" and "Soap and Water." Told by yet another Sara, this time Sara Smolinsky, *Bread Givers* articulates a harsh critique of traditional Jewish patriarchy, a trend in Yezierska's work noted by Thomas J. Ferraro and Magdalena J. Zaborowska.[49] As a young girl, Sara watches her religious father ruin the romantic prospects of her sisters by matching them with men who, in varying ways, make their lives miserable. Sara, determined to break the cycle of tradition and repression, strikes out on her own, with ambitions to become a schoolteacher.

As in "Soap and Water," the narration of *Bread Givers* emerges from the already-assimilated figure of Sara Smolinsky, one that has largely adopted a realist aesthetics. It is clear that Sara's complex impressions of the world around her at ten years old are not to be taken as a literal replication of a young girl's consciousness. The narration resembles that of Cahan's *The Rise of David Levinsky* in its reflective mode; however, reflection and nostalgia are not the only registers in which Sara's narrative voice expresses her history. Indeed, Sara's emotions often overwhelm the novel's mostly realist aesthetic modes. Such moments emerge in forms that resemble the Yiddish-English narration of the vernacular stories in *Hungry Hearts*. As Yezierska claims in the autobiographical piece "Mostly about Myself":

> I envy the writers who can sit down at their desks in the clear calm security of their vision and begin their story at the beginning and work it up logically, step by step, until they get to the end. With me, the end and the middle and the beginning of my story whirl before me in a mad blurr [sic]. And I can not sit still inside myself till the vision becomes clear and whole and sane in my brain. I'm too much on fire to wait till I understand what I see and feel. My hands rush out to seize a word from the end, a phrase from the middle, or a sentence from the beginning. I jot down any fragment of a thought that I can get hold of. And then I gather these fragments, words, phrases, sentences, and I paste them together with my own blood. (*HIFA* 132)

Yezierska's description of her working practice, in which "fragments, words, phrases, [and] sentences" are "paste[d] ... together with [her] own blood," echoes many of the central concerns for the high modernist artist, and even recalls T. S. Eliot's "these fragments I have shored against my ruins" in *The Waste Land*.[50] If the fragmentary nature of reality has become unavoidable in the modernist era, the modernist artist struggles to bring these disparate pieces of existence together in some coherent form, to "paste them together." In acknowledging both the fragments of individual consciousness of experience and the fragments of language that go into the literary means of capturing and communicating that experience, Yezierska's work not only parallels central formalist concerns of high modernist experimentation, it does so in a way that emphasizes the defining feature of linguistic and cultural hybridity.

Yezierska came to this particular understanding through second-language acquisition. When Yezierska's narrators speak in a fragmented form, they expose their own interstitial existence between languages. Yezierska's characters—and her narrators—use a hybrid combination of English words, Yiddish syntax, English translation of Yiddish expressions, and a number of untranslated Yiddish words. When she declares that she unites the fragments of language "with [her] own blood," Yezierska acknowledges the profound effect that ethnic heritage has, not just on the development of her characters (as in Cahan and Antin), but also on the very way in which she constructs language, word by word, phrase by phrase, sentence by sentence. As Sara in *Bread Givers* notes about her first intimate conversation with Hugo Selig, "After that, all differences dropped away. We talked one language. We had sprung from one soil."[51] The association of a particular creative practice with "blood" and "soil" has the potential to veer rather close to racial essentialism, as it does more clearly in Yezierska's *Salome of the Tenements;* in her other works, however, Yezierska emphasizes both the ability of her characters to become American and the important heritage that will always frame that Americanness. *Bread Givers* demonstrates this complex assimilation through its strategic placement of brief moments of vernacular modernist effusion, episodes in the text when Sara cannot rein in her emotion and remain reflective in her narration, and when an accurate representation of her modern life demands linguistic experimentation.

These moments appear more frequently in the early parts of the novel, which involve more dialogue—all of which Yezierska renders in the vernacular—and less of the dominant, reflective (and largely realist-inflected) voice that Sara begins to adopt near the novel's conclusion. In the opening moments, the juxtaposition of these voices immediately confronts the reader: "I was about ten years old then. But from always it was heavy on my heart the worries for the house as if I was mother" (*BG* 1). In these sentences the two narrative registers appear clearly. The matter-of-factly stated "I was about ten years old then" contrasts strongly with the sentence that follows it; the second sentence describes an emotional state that Sara finds difficult to render in standard syntax. At times, this explosion of vernacular language, the only means of communicating the consciousness of certain emotional experiences, even shifts tense to reflect time-specific thought patterns: "More and more I began to think inside myself. I don't want to sell herring for the rest of my days. I want to learn something. I want to do something. I want some day to make myself for a person and come among people" (*BG* 66). As Sara begins "to think inside" herself, to explore her own consciousness and subjectivity, her language becomes less wedded to standard forms. In this probing, Sara certainly feels what Yezierska called the "driving urge to express more vitally the rush of new experience, the fire of changing personality"; this results first in a series of repetitive forms reminiscent of "The Miracle": I don't want/I want/I want/I want. The Steinian "I want to learn something. I want to do something," is followed by one of Yezierska's characteristic syntactical inversions: "I want someday to make myself for a person." Here, Sara works to remake language in order to remake identity itself, "the fire of changing personality" recreated *through* vernacular modernist language.

Clearly, both Yezierska and Sara convert language into central metaphors of the immigrant experience. When Sara refuses to engage in the coarse humor of her classmates at college, she feels "shut out like a 'greenhorn' who didn't talk their language" (*BG* 180). When she asks someone about how he managed English words as a street vendor on his first day in America, he tells her, "To me it was only singing a song. I didn't understand the words, but my voice was like dynamite, thundering out into the air all that was in my young heart, alone in a big city" (*BG* 189). In a consideration of another Yezierska novel (*Salome of the Tenements*), Michael North notes the political valence of the link between dynamite and ethnicity, connecting this to cultural tropes of "political anarchy and violence" common in cultural representations of anti-immigrant nativism.[52] The fact that dynamite can also operate as a metaphor both for a dangerously emotional ethnicity and for the power of second-language learning confirms the intimate connection between ethnic identity, linguistic experimentation, and conventional notions about modernist threats to culture. For Yezierska, the experience of culture and of life is the experience of language, and life will always be consciously mediated by language and linguistic difference. While the narration in *Bread Givers* largely demonstrates a cultural and linguistic savviness over that of some narrators in *Hungry Hearts,* particularly in its more conventional style and syntax, Sara Smolinsky finds herself "slipping back into the vernacular" when emotionally overcome while teaching pronunciation to her Lower East Side students (*BG* 272).

In Yezierska's work, the vernacular lurks beneath her narrators' standard language, always ready to emerge in moments where realist representation cannot effectively capture the mental or emotional experience of her immigrant characters. Her vernacular modernism appears not merely as an essentialist marker of cultural or ethnic difference. Instead, her use of this language works at cross-purposes. On the one hand, it marks her characters—as did the dialect realism of Cahan. However, as her own theoretical writing suggests, it provides a critique of the "trite words [and] stale phrases" on which realist writing depended, and that Yezierska herself criticized in her defense of Lewisohn. Because her stories are about immigration and assimilation, Yezierska uses this strategy as a means of aestheticizing the process of assimilation, but in a manner that suggests the power of experimental language to communicate experience more "vitally." The unassimilated (and indeed the unrefined) elements of her characters are also signs of modernism; as much as the betterment societies and settlement houses strive to mold her characters into models of nineteenth-century bourgeois gentility, these characters remain hostile to these social and cultural codes, as well as to the genteel language of nineteenth-century dialect realism that operated as its own force of linguistic containment. As with so many high and vernacular modernists, Yezierska fights this stifling gentility with linguistic experimentation, the "immigrant development" that Eugene Jolas saw creating "the possibilities for a fundamental revolution of the word."

"The Broken Talk Came through the Airshaft Window": Michael Gold and Vernacular Expressionism

> *I will not deny the World Revolution provides a* Weltanschauung *that exfoliates a thousand bold new futurist thoughts in psychology, art, literature, economics, sex. It is a fresh world synthesis—the old one was killed in the war, and long live the new!*
> —MICHAEL GOLD, "LET IT BE REALLY NEW!" (1926)

While placing Yezierska and her vernacular first-person narratives in the orbit of vernacular modernism might seem relatively plausible (especially given her close association with John Dewey and her pilgrimage to Gertrude Stein's Paris apartment), doing the same with Michael Gold is anything but an easy task. Gold was well known for his relentless critiques of modernist writers and his promotion of working-class writing and realist aesthetics in his 1930s column "Change the World."[53] His notorious attack "Gertrude Stein: A Literary Idiot" took a clear stand on the kinds of literary modernism emanating from Paris. Gold called Stein's work "an example of the most extreme subjectivism of the contemporary bourgeois artist, and a reflection of the ideological anarchy into which the whole of bourgeois literature has fallen."[54] Modernists, Gold claimed, "destroyed the common use of language.... They went in for primitive emotions, primitive art. Blood, violent death, dope dreams, soul-writings, became the themes of their works" (*CTW* 25). While Gold admired Hemingway's style, he still characterized Hemingway's writing as the "heartless" work of "a white collar poet."[55]

Gold's positions on aesthetics and politics had become firmly entrenched during the 1930s, and his most vitriolic statements on modernism are, in large part, from this period. Earlier in his career, however, Gold was much more closely allied with experimental art forms. This included work with the aesthetically progressive Provincetown Players and New Playwrights Theatre, which led to productive associations with major figures in both theatrical and literary modernism, including Eugene O'Neill, Susan Glaspell, and John Dos Passos.[56] His most ambitious and experimental dramatic work, *Hoboken Blues* (published in 1927, performed by the New Playwrights Theater in 1928), attempts to grapple with the history of American racial injustice and capitalist exploitation in a form derived from Soviet constructivist theater. What remains lacking in criticism of Gold's work is any coherent picture of his career. How does one bring together communist polemics and experimental theater with Gold's most celebrated work, the fictionalized East Side memoir *Jews without Money* (1930)? Such disparate creative productions seem to emanate from altogether different writers—with completely different assumptions about the role of art in society. In a sense, Gold had investment in most of the major strands of literary production during the 1920s. His poetry rejects most received nineteenth-century forms but remains explicitly derivative of Walt Whitman. Gold's devotion to Whitman's aesthetic already puts him in an oppositional relationship to modernist poets like Ezra Pound, who sought to reject Whitman's influence in American poetry. Gold's short fiction vacillates between experimentation (in, for example, "Love on a Garbage Dump" and "Faster, America, Faster!") and polemical pieces in the tradition of literary naturalism. His plays can be decidedly naturalistic, clichéd, or experimental—sometimes all in the same text (as is the case with *Hoboken Blues*). And his one extended work, *Jews without Money,* is alternatively nostalgic and horrifying, naturalistic and lyrical.

Rather than ignoring Gold's experimental work and reading him exclusively as a proletarian memoirist or chalking up his varied output to political and aesthetic incoherence, it is useful to import two interlocking concepts into the study of Gold's work: vernacular language and expressionism. Gold's fascination with vernacular language and culture cuts across ethnic groups, appearing in *Jews without Money* as well as in the plays *Money* and *Hoboken Blues*. In addition, Gold's work across genres draws heavily on European expressionism, broadly conceived as a literary, dramatic, and artistic form that, according to Peter Nicholls, "veered between an often decadent preoccupation with types of spiritual 'sickness' and an attempt to harness liberated emotion to this project of social renewal."[57] For expressionist playwrights, Günther Berghaus writes, "strength of feeling and pathos of expression meant more . . . than mastery of form. . . . The unrestrained outpourings of the Expressionist actor showed a human being in a state of delirium seeking to reach his or her audience with a liberating, primeval cry."[58] With its roots in the development of American expressionism, Gold's work can be seen as a form of vernacular expressionism; Gold is profoundly interested in language, but he is also invested in dramatic and aesthetic techniques used in Europe (by figures like Bertolt Brecht and Vsevolod Meyerhold). In a sense, Gold's strange uses of dialect and vernacular language in his 1920s expressionist theater and of a hybrid, though muted, Lower East Side language in *Jews without Money* form a continuity around vernacular and expressionist incarnations of the grotesque. With an emphasis both in the expressionist grotesque and in reviving Whitman's street-level aesthetics, Gold's own approach seeks to negotiate the aesthetic threshold between realism and modernism, politics and literature, prose poetry and narrative. Rather than reading Gold's work through his programmatic and doctrinaire 1930s column "Change the World," considering his creative output and his statements on art in the 1920s enables a new reading of Gold, one that puts him more comfortably in the realm of the vernacular, the expressionist, and the modernist.

Gold's own positions on art throughout the 1920s are in more constant conflict than critics usually admit. During this period, a number of Gold's statements on aesthetics and politics form a trajectory from the self-described "mystic" manifesto "Towards Proletarian Art" (1921) through the nine-point proscriptive description of "Proletarian Realism" (1930) that codified his thinking at the beginning of the 1930s. Critics have tended to read these two texts as inherently related, even seeing the latter as "a rationalization and codification" of "Towards Proletarian Art" (*LA* 203). But articles and editorials published in *New Masses*, the radical literary magazine Gold edited beginning in 1926, present a more complex evolution of his thinking about the relationship between aesthetics and politics.

In "Towards Proletarian Art," Gold's first manifesto, he collapses a number of strands in early twentieth-century literary discourse. On the one hand, Gold opposes received forms, both of art and of artists, which he links to capitalist oppression: "The old moods, the old poetry, fiction, painting, philosophies, were the creations of proud and baffled solitaries. The tradition has arisen in a capitalist world that even its priests of art must be lonely beasts of prey—competitive and unsocial" (*LA* 65). While he notes this tendency of contemporary artists to see themselves as "the aristocrats of mankind," by linking this tendency to the past he emphasizes his desire to see proletarian art as a new form for a new world (*LA*

65). At the same time, Gold evokes the modernist moment, claiming in one of his more mystic flourishes that "it is the consciousness that in art Life is speaking out its heart at last, and that to censor the poor brute-murmurings would be sacrilege. Whatever they are, they are significant and precious, and to stifle the meanest of Life's moods taking form in the artist would be death" (*LA* 64).

Gold's faith in the artist's individual vision (those "poor brute-murmurings") and his insistence that the new artist be both social and socialized stand in partial conflict to one another, especially since Gold later maintained such hostility toward what might be characterized as the "brute-murmurings" of experimental modernists like Stein. But, more than anything else, it is Gold's own admitted "primitivism" that makes "Towards Proletarian Art" such a puzzling example of proletarian literary theory. While "intellectuals have become bored with the primitive monotony of Life—with the deep truths and instincts," Gold writes, "the masses are still primitive and clean, and artists must turn to them for strength again. The primitive sweetness, the primitive calm, the primitive ability to create simply and without fever or ambition, the primitive satisfaction and self-sufficiency—they must be found again" (*LA* 66). This equation of the working class (the "masses") with primitives remains one of Gold's stranger claims in this essay, particularly given the impetus in most proletarian writing of humanizing the masses (to counter their dehumanization by capitalist production). In effect, he is suggesting here that politically committed writers relinquish interest in other fetishistic forms of primitivism in bohemian literary culture and begin to write about some "real" primitives: the working-class (!). Gold's claims, then, create a strong bridge between his interests (in the primitivism of the masses) and larger concerns of primitivism in the work of modernists like Stein, Eliot, and others.[59]

While editing *New Masses,* Gold often saw parallels between the aesthetic and political avant-garde. The magazine routinely published work by John Dos Passos, and early issues sought to establish modernist credibility by featuring work by William Carlos Williams, D. H. Lawrence, Alfred Kreymborg, and even Ezra Pound. In "Let It Be Really New!," an editorial published in the magazine's second issue, Gold claimed that "the World Revolution provides a *Weltanschauung* that exfoliates a thousand bold new futurist thoughts in psychology, art, literature, economics, sex," and that he "would like the *New Masses* to be the bridge to this world for American artists and writers, which means it will not be a magazine of Communism, or Moscow, but a magazine of American experiment—only let's not experiment in the minor esthetic cults."⁶⁰ This contempt for what Gold calls "the minor esthetic cults" drives his later critique of modernist writers like Stein, but for much of the 1920s he praised modernist little magazines, singling out *transition* and the *Little Review* as positive examples of literary experimentation.⁶¹ Also during this period, Gold would praise such high modernists as Ernest Hemingway and James Joyce, calling *Ulysses* "one of the few masterpieces of our times."⁶²

These complex articulations, and *not* Gold's programmatic comments on "Proletarian Realism," inform the majority of his creative work, which largely dried up after this second manifesto was published in September of 1930.⁶³ During this creative period, Gold maintained an obsession with avant-garde elements in European theater; he constantly invoked terms like "futurism" and "constructivism," and in 1925 he published an essay in the *Nation* on Meyerhold's constructivist experiments in the Soviet Union, something Gold called "the neo-primitive stage."⁶⁴ Gold's "futurism" is certainly not the protofascist futurism of Marinetti, but another way of rendering the concept "avant-garde" (without the implication of "minor esthetic cults"). This obsession with avant-garde theater and the use of aesthetic estrangement for political effect has, in part, caused at least one critic to link Gold with Bertolt Brecht. Morris Dickstein, in an essay on the legacy of Gold's *Jews without Money*, suggests that "with his tough-guy manner and hard-boiled, telegraphic prose, Gold could have become an American Brecht, but he lacked the German playwright's instinct for survival and his canny ironic temperament, which complicated every proletarian pose into an avant-garde gesture."⁶⁵ Nevertheless, like Brecht, Gold saw the theater as a space to interrogate social and aesthetic assumptions under capitalism.

Though Gold's theatrical work has largely escaped the notice of critics, it establishes some important foundations for thinking about *Jews without Money* and demonstrates his interest in vernacular language as a central theme. His earliest surviving play, *Money*, was one of three Gold-authored one-act plays produced by the Provincetown Players in the late 1910s. The story of a group of Jewish American roommates and a bundle of missing savings, this play remains relatively realistic, but at least one linguistic element anticipates Henry Roth's modernist novel *Call It Sleep* (1934). When the roommates are talking among themselves, they speak fluently, but when a police officer arrives to investigate, Abram, the only English speaker in the group, speaks "in singsong, broken Ghetto English." The policeman speaks an equally thick urban vernacular, explaining his arrival: "Why, a feller just come up to me on my beat and told me there was a lot of Yits down here fighting like cats and dogs."⁶⁶ Gold's shift from the dignified fluency of the insulated community to the vernacular cacophony of the mixed social environment in *Money* parallels the linguistic and modernist differentiation between speech and internal monologue in Roth's more celebrated modernist novel.

But Gold's interest in language and the theater was not limited to stories of the Lower East Side. His most ambitious play, *Hoboken Blues,* explicitly attempts to combine the constructivist experiments of Meyerhold with a satire of American blackface minstrelsy. First published in the modernist anthology *The American Caravan* in 1927, the year that saw Al Jolson star in *The Jazz Singer,* Gold's play has escaped the attention of critics like Michael Rogin, whose study *Blackface, White Noise: Jewish Immigrants in the Hollywood Melting Pot* outlines the complex ways that Jewish performers related to blackface performance.⁶⁷ While *Hoboken Blues* tries to undercut the racist stereotypes associated with blackface, it is rather telling that one of the only critical essays published on *Hoboken Blues* to this point is subtitled "An Experiment That Failed."⁶⁸ Given the ideologically inflected stage directions (i.e., "NOTE: No white men appear in this play. Where white men are indicated, they are played by Negroes in white caricature masks"), Gold clearly wanted to write an advanced constructivist play about the nexus of racism and capitalism in the United States.⁶⁹ If anything, *Hoboken Blues* is Gold's most explicit avant-garde gesture, a text focused on the collision of constructivism and black dialect, of European and American forms of linguistic and aesthetic experimentation.

Part of the struggle evident in *Hoboken Blues* is Gold's attempt to wed the racist grotesquerie of the minstrel tradition to a constructivist aesthetic that he describes in detail in "Theater and Revolution": "Machinery has been made a character in the drama. City rhythms, the blare of modernism, the iron shouts of industrialism, these are actors. Paradox is an honored guest at the feast. Vitality and youth and courage are Three Graces. And futurism is the fantastic godmother of this swarm of new theaters in Russia; futurism, the cult of a few odd persons in New York."⁷⁰ The desire to unite the popular form of the minstrel show with constructivism, clearly seen as an elitist "cult of a few odd persons in New York" (perhaps even a "minor esthetic cult"), encounters further problems with Gold's insistence on presenting his vernacular characters as less sympathetic and more grotesque in the fashion of the German expressionist drama of the turn of the century. As Alan Wald writes, "Gold's clumsy efforts at Black dialect and his depiction of African American stereotypes in *Hoboken Blues* seem somewhat inexplicable in the context of Gold's militant antiracism.... What seems likely is that Gold was attempting to recreate Black urban culture with the same humor and earthiness with which he was depicting Jewish ghetto culture in his East Side novel; but the effort failed due to his lack of intimate familiarity with the materials and his primary focus on producing a Futurist spectacle."[71] Clearly, constructivism valued paradox, but Gold's literary talents were stretched beyond a breaking point in attempting to stuff all of these paradoxes into a single theatrical production.

With the contradictions of Gold's ambitious but failed constructivist-expressionist theatrical experiments in mind, the complexities of his most lasting work, *Jews without Money*, should become a bit more understandable. Often cited as one of the pioneering examples of the proletarian novel, *Jews without Money* resists many of the thematic conventions of this genre (strikes, conversion narratives, etc.), limiting its most explicit political engagement to the final pages. As a result, the text was lauded by notorious antileftist critic H. L. Mencken as "one of the most eloquent stories that the American press has disgorged in many a moon," and certain sections were published in Mencken's *American Mercury* (as well as in Gold's own *New Masses*) while Gold worked on the book through the 1920s.[72] In 1965 the book was even reprinted without the last half page, in which the fictional narrator "Michael" undergoes a political radicalization and praises the "workers' Revolution" as "the true Messiah."[73]

Michael's conversion at the book's conclusion has struck many critics as an afterthought to a narrative that nostalgically revels in the grotesquerie of the vernacular culture and language of New York's Lower East Side. Though the search for a messiah dominates the text and provides thematic coherence, the stylistic shift of this final chapter makes it, at least at the textual level, incongruous. While critics have characterized this novel as a "proletarian fictional autobiography" or a "ghetto or tenement pastoral," the strange, lingering nostalgia in Gold's text seems to push against any such cut-and-dried reading of the politics of the text.[74] With its endless delay of radicalization in favor of nostalgia, the text refuses an exclusively political reading; with its harsh and grotesque character types, it never quite seems as comfortably pastoral as critics suggest. *Jews without Money*, then, is stuck between the nostalgic memoir and the depiction of the brutalities of capitalism, never quite comfortable with either. It is for this reason that reading this text through Gold's earlier experiments—especially *Hoboken Blues*—can open up new avenues for understanding Gold's project.

Because one of Gold's primary aesthetic strategies throughout the 1920s was of a kind of European expressionism blended with the vernacular and dialect modes of the minstrel tradition (as in *Hoboken Blues*) and the immigrant experience (in *Money*), it is possible to see *Jews without Money* as an extension of this project, to see it, in effect, as an example of vernacular expressionism, rooted in the language and culture of the Lower East Side, drawing on the democratic cityscapes of Walt Whitman but with an emphasis on the grotesque that keeps the fictionalized memoir in a realm of aesthetics that seem frequently out of line with his later descriptions of "Proletarian Realism." *Jews without Money*, with its monstrous figures, its brutal and horrific descriptions of poverty, all accompanied by Howard Simon's expressionist woodcuts, takes a strange turn away from the mode of Yezierska (as well as from Cahan and Antin). If Yezierska's stories turn ghetto life into fairy tales of linguistic self-construction, Gold's major work moves in the opposite direction, emphasizing community languages over individuals and turning every experience into a grotesque, expressionist nightmare.

Most critical discussions of American expressionism focus exclusively on the theater of the late 1910s and 1920s; Gold's involvement in this movement is one of the unexplored aspects of his career. Mardi Valgemae's pioneering work on the emergence of the style emphasized its "objectification emphasized through distortion" and its "nightmarish visual images."[75] Gold's transition from expressionist theater to prose, while not unprecedented, was actually quite rare, and few critics have considered the stylistic influence across these genres. Sherrill E. Grace, in a study that charts expressionism's vacillation between poles of regression and apocalypse, argues that expressionist-influenced fiction (like Djuna Barnes's *Nightwood* [1936]) "presents intense personal emotion as well as social protest in forms that resist representation, that use distortion and varying degrees of abstraction, and that stress themes of degeneration, disintegration, and apocalypse."[76] The world of Gold's *Jews without Money* certainly exhibits many of these thematic characteristics: visions of a nightmarish world, abstract portraiture, and a social protest that becomes explicit in the novel's final pages. Gold's innovations in this text include his introduction of an almost Proustian nostalgia, his Whitmanesque lists, and his orientation toward the central importance of vernacular language, a "broken talk" that mirrors the expressionist abstraction of the novel.

Gold's characters, while not imbued with the same hybrid speech as those in Yezierska's work, still speak what the narrator calls "Jewish talk"

(*JWM* 113). In this way, he emphasizes the communal language of the East Side ghetto, an alternative to the individualist, assimilationist project that Yezierska demonstrates in so many of her texts. In many spots this social vernacular is implicit, though Gold does import some Yiddish expressions into the text. In one of *Jews without Money*'s most kaleidoscopic and Whitmanesque moments, Gold merges suffering, grotesquerie, and this "Jewish talk": "The whole tenement was talking and eating its supper. The broken talk came through the airshaft window. The profound bass of the East Side traffic lay under this talk. Talk. Talk. Rattle of supper dishes, whining of babies, yowling of cats; counterpoint of men, women and children talking as if their hearts would break. Talk. Jewish talk" (*JWM* 113). Later, this talk becomes more explicitly sutured to a long history of suffering; the talk itself assumes an immense, mythical proportion: "Then talk, talk, talk again. Jewish talk. Hot, sweaty, winey talk. A sweatshop holiday. Egypt's slaves around a campfire in the shadow of the pyramids. They drank wine even then. Thousands of years ago. And talked as now. The Bible records it. And their hearts were eased by it. And Moscowitz played the Babylonian harp" (*JWM* 116).

The "broken talk" of the Jewish community mingles with a cacophony of other broken sounds, but also speaks to a long legacy of Jewish social history.[77] This language, more often described than demonstrated, is to a certain degree like Woolf's description of Lardner's work, "twisted at the root." While earlier Jewish American novelists and memoirists emphasized the individual's struggle to adapt to the new American realities, often using language acquisition to thematize this transition, Gold's interest is not in the language learning of his central character but in the linguistic community he inhabits, the world of "Jewish talk." This "hot, sweaty, winey talk" becomes "a sweatshop holiday," highlighting the ways in which these figures' vernacular language is the only respite they have from the sufferings of capitalist oppression. That the community bands together, telling ancient stories in an ancient language implies a linguistic wholeness that eludes many of the vernacular modernists.

But Gold's emphasis on the "brokenness" of the language, as well as on the broken hearts the "Jewish talk" describes, complicates this notion of coherence; as with the characters of Yezierska and Cahan, the social protagonist of this scene in *Jews without Money* inhabits a space that is fundamentally shattered, fractured, and incoherent. The incomprehensible wailing (of men, women, children, and even animals) drifting in the window helps to politicize the vernacular language of the novel as it becomes the only means of expression in a world where the economic structures continue to close in on immigrant families. Whereas Yezierska's protagonists escape poverty through education and self-transformation, Gold's characters—for the majority of the novel, at least—can only emit a collective vernacular wail into the wilderness.

The broken nature of the language of *Jews without Money* provides a central means of understanding the novel's odd structure. Gold worked on this book through much of the late 1920s, routinely publishing excerpts subtitled "From a Book of East Side Memoirs" in *New Masses*. Though the first of these was titled "Jews without Money," this piece does not begin the book-length version. The excerpts function only partially as a serial (since they appeared every couple of months from June 1928 through the book's publication in 1930), but they operate according to a logic much more associative than serial or realist. Serial narratives imply continuity and plot-driven narration, while the memories published here operate in a more impressionistic manner. In *Jews without Money*, memories come back to the narrator in profound ways and are figured as impressions or theatrical set pieces rather than as parts of a highly structured realist narrative along the lines of Antin or Cahan's work. Indeed, the novel lacks a central storyline: memory after memory is piled up, and the narrator Michael's communist conversion at the novel's conclusion is the only example of a forward-moving narrative device.

More a collection of memories than a single narrative thread, Gold's text refuses the developmental mode of the bildungsroman—popular with both realists Cahan and Antin and vernacular modernist Yezierska—in favor of a set of associative memories organized around the poetic structures of remembrance. He foregrounds this strategy in lines such as, "I can see, in the newsreel of memory, the scene on our roof when I first heard this story" (*JWM* 84). His structures follow not the realist models of linear narration but a technique of impressionistic symbols reminiscent of Proust.[78] For example, Gold explicitly references seasons (summer/winter in chapters 4 and 19) while focusing on recursive moments and figures. The narrator Michael's friend Joey Cohen dies in a horrible streetcar accident early in the text but returns later on without any cue, signaling that the text is not following conventional narrative time. Like the "Jewish talk," the realist narrative assumptions of the Jewish American memoir have also been "broken" in *Jews without Money*.

But this brokenness assumes a new, poetic form in *Jews without Money*, as Gold alternates moments of realist narrative and modernist memory with the elevated language of Whitman's poetry. Throughout the text, Gold also inserts Whitmanesque lists to provide an accumulative impact of impressions. In the opening pages, he writes,

> People pushed and wrangled in the street. There were armies of howling pushcart peddlers. Women screamed, dogs barked and copulated. Babies cried.
> A parrot cursed. Ragged kids played under truck-horses. Fat housewives fought from stoop to stoop. A beggar sang.
> At the livery stable coach drivers lounged on a bench. They hee-hawed with laughter, they guzzled cans of beer.
> Pimps, gamblers and red-nosed bums; peanut politicians, pugilists in sweaters; tinhorn sports and tall longshoremen in overalls. An endless pageant of East Side life passed through the wicker doors of Jake Wolf's saloon. (*JWM* 13–14)

Here, individual images merge into an overall impression of poverty, emphasizing the dark, the grotesque, and the repulsive aspects of the environment while retaining a sense of nostalgia. This is not Whitman's colorful and dynamic humanism of the streets, but a grotesque vernacular, full of an "endless pageant" of hee-hawing and beer-guzzling. While other Jewish American writers emphasize the ability of their protagonists to emerge from the poverty of their surroundings, Gold revels in the grotesquerie of his childhood: not surprising, since he routinely listed Sherwood Anderson as one of the most important writers of the 1920s.

Still, Gold's interest in the grotesque does not always diminish the romance of his memories. At one point, again channeling Whitman, he writes an ode to the ugliness of his childhood home: "Shabby old ground, ripped like a battlefield by workers' picks and shovels, little garbage dump lying forgotten in the midst of tall tenements, O home of all the twisted junk, rusty baby carriages, lumber, bottles, boxes, moldy pants and dead cats of the neighborhood—every one spat and held the nostrils when passing you. But in my mind you still blaze in the halo of childish romance. No place will ever seem as wonderful again" (*JWM* 46). In Gold's text, the "home of all the twisted junk" is also the home of "childish romance"—the two are closely intertwined in ways that make the nostalgic grotesque and the grotesque nostalgic.[79] Unlike Yezierska, whose characters are frequently compelled to transform their domestic circumstances into some semblance of bourgeois propriety (see, for example, the obsession with "Soap and Water"), Gold's narrator revels in exposing every obscene and disturbing element of his childhood home. He understands the Lower

East Side "as a jungle, where wild beasts prowled, and toadstools grew in a poisoned soil—perverts, cokefiends, kidnapers, firebugs, Jack the Rippers," and as "a spectral place, a chamber of hell, hot and poisoned by hundreds of gas flames. It was suffocating with the stink of chemicals" (*JWM* 60, 306).

These descriptions, along with the dark and abstract woodcut illustrations by Howard Simon, help identify *Jews without Money* as an unabashedly expressionist text—one explicitly connected to Gold's avant-garde theater of the 1920s (including *Hoboken Blues*).[80] This expressionism, melded with the interest in vernacular language (the "hot, sweaty, winey talk" of his Jewish family and friends), situates Gold in an antirealist mode, one that distorts representation both linguistically and impressionistically and results in an example of vernacular expressionism. Certainly, Gold's Lower East Side upbringing contained many of these horrors, but Gold, with this peculiar almost antirealist aesthetic, deviates from the conventions of Jewish American memoir writing through the nightmarish abstraction and distortion of his descriptions. For example, Fyfka the Miser, a boarder in the narrator's family's apartment, becomes a "thing," "this yellow somnambulist, this nightmare bred of poverty; this maggot-yellow dark ape with twisted arm and bright, peering, melancholy eyes; human garbage can of horror" (*JWM* 76). Calling Fyfka a "thing," a "maggot-yellow dark ape," and a "human garbage can of horror" explicitly hearkens back to Gold's youthful injunction to discover the primitive not in the exotic but within the working class.[81] It also seems to contrast strongly with one of his later injunctions about "Proletarian Realism": "Away with drabness, the bourgeois notion that the Worker's life is sordid, the slummer's disgust and feeling of futility. There is horror and drabness in the Worker's life; and we will portray it; but we know this is not the last word; we know that this manure heap is the hope of the future" (*LA* 207).[82] There seems little hope for Fyfka or for any of the characters within Gold's text; for this reason the messianic ending has often been read as incongruous with the rest of *Jews without Money*.

Across Gold's varied output, it is possible to see a nexus of experimental European forms (constructivism and expressionism), vernacular language (minstrel dialect and "Jewish talk"), political commitment, and an increasing interest in the grotesque depiction of urban environments. Gold's literary career during the 1920s suggests something of a failed struggle to wrestle these competing forms into some kind of coherence. However, Gold's work demonstrates how wide the net for the representational mode of vernacular modernism might be extended. Gold's work is certainly a break with the realist traditions of Cahan and Antin, but his emphasis on the grotesque and violent separates him from Yezierska and places him far closer to another genre experiencing a vernacular modernist revolution in the 1920s: hard-boiled crime fiction, with its expressionistic mean streets, underworld slang, and cast of grotesque street figures.

4 / "Say It with Lead"

Carroll John Daly, Dashiell Hammett, and Modernism's Underworld Vernacular

It is very curious but the detective story which is you might say the only really modern novel form that has come into existence gets rid of human nature by having the man dead to begin with the hero is dead to begin with and so you have so to speak got rid of the event before the book begins.
—GERTRUDE STEIN, "WHAT ARE MASTER-PIECES AND WHY ARE THERE SO FEW OF THEM" (1935)

There are dives in New York's underworld where a language is spoken that an ordinary citizen, listening in, would find impossible to understand. It isn't English, French, German, or Yiddish; it is a language by itself.
—HENRY LEVERAGE, "DICTIONARY OF THE UNDERWORLD" (1925)

At the opening of his seminal essay on detective fiction, "The Simple Art of Murder" (1944), Raymond Chandler claims that "fiction in any form has always intended to be realistic."[1] His essay continues by articulating the distinction between the English school of detective fiction and the American, or hard-boiled, school. Joseph T. Shaw, influential editor of pulp magazine *Black Mask,* where the hard-boiled style first emerged, had much the same thing to say about hard-boiled fiction and realism in the introduction to his retrospective anthology *The Hard-Boiled Omnibus* (1946): "These writers observed the cardinal principle in creating the illusion of reality; they did not make their characters act and talk tough; they allowed them to. They gave the stories over to their characters, and kept themselves off the stage, as every writer of fiction should."[2] At some level, Chandler's and Shaw's point in these texts is to argue for the heightened realism (in content, at least) of hard-boiled detective writers. Chandler contrasts his (and Dashiell Hammett's) "realistic" fiction with that of the so-called Golden Age detective writers, whose work he feminizes as domestic and overly genteel.[3] In a sense, these claims to realism in hard-boiled fiction resemble those claims made by the realists of the late nineteenth century in America.

However, the distinctions Chandler, Shaw, and others have made about what constitutes realism rest on a number of assumptions about content rather than form. In his study *The Real Thing: Imitation and Authenticity in American Culture, 1880–1940* (1989), Miles Orvell has compellingly maintained that when realist writers argued for the depiction of "life not literature . . . what they in fact meant was blood, sex, money, grime, garbage, immigrants, and killing snowstorms—a recognition of experience previously excluded from polite literature."[4] But these new, harsher elements—transformed into expressionist grotesques by twentieth-century writers like Michael Gold—were just as stylized in the realist and naturalist writing of the nineteenth century. This peculiar definition of gritty reality also appears in Chandler's paean to Hammett: "Hammett took murder out of the Venetian vase and dropped it into the alley. . . . He wrote at first (and almost to the end) for people with a sharp, aggressive attitude to life. They were not afraid of the seamy side of things; they lived there. Violence did not dismay them; it was right down their street." Chandler's claims could extend to the entire hard-boiled school of writers, all of whom foregrounded the violence of the streets and "gave murder back to the kind of people who commit it for reasons, not just to provide a corpse."[5] For Chandler, as for the nineteenth-century American realists and naturalists, the presentation of the "seamy side of things" was a means of being "realistic." To a degree, if indeed "fiction in any form has always intended to be realistic," then the true test of realism, according to Chandler, is in that fiction's content more than in its style or aesthetic.

Given the concerns of *The Word on the Streets,* such a simple characterization of "realism" seems problematic. Is this an accurate term for what Hammett and other hard-boiled writers were attempting? Aesthetically speaking, the term seems misapplied. After all, there is little resemblance between the language and style of the hard-boiled writers and the work of William Dean Howells or Henry James; there is even a rather wide aesthetic gulf between hard-boiled fiction and the work of naturalists also interested in "the seamy side of things." Instead, writers like Dashiell Hammett and the hard-boiled pioneer Carroll John Daly forged a new mode of writing, one where language itself maintains a harsh aesthetic relationship to the world it describes, where signifiers and signifieds do not cleanly line up, and where genteel language becomes a sign of social corruption. Far from being an example of aesthetic realism, this hard-boiled vernacular modernism, full of underworld slang and grotesque swaths of violent imagery, exhibits important stylistic and narratological techniques that aggressively fragment the aesthetic and epistemological assumptions of both realism and classical detective fiction.[6]

"The Ensuing Crime, or Its Threat, Is Incidental": Detecting Modernism in *Black Mask*

> We have an idea that detective fiction as we view it has only commenced to be developed. As a matter of fact, we expect the greatest and most noteworthy development in this particular field of literature than will be seen in any other. All other fields have been worked and overworked. This, as we visualize it, has been barely scratched.
>
> —"THE AIM OF BLACK MASK" (1927)

Aficionados of detective fiction have no lack of histories of this genre, which is one of the best documented of all genres of popular fiction.[7] As a result, its history is a largely settled affair: beginning with the Dupin stories of Edgar Allan Poe, the genre moves through the work of Sir Arthur Conan Doyle, into the Golden Age writers of the early twentieth century, and finally arrives at the hard-boiled style of the 1920s and 1930s, first popularized in the pulp magazine *Black Mask*. The story of detective fiction is insulated; as a result, the genre exhibits a coherent and isolated developmental model. This well-established genealogy of detective fiction has—like the humor writing discussed in chapter 2—remained aloof and unconnected to broader historical narratives of American literature, in spite of the investment many canonical figures placed in both the reading and writing of detective and crime fiction. Although the genre virtually originates with the work of Poe, a major figure in the American literary canon, the histories of literary fiction and of detective fiction rarely cross paths. The fact is, however, that popular detective fiction constantly exerted an influence on fiction within the canon, and developments in canonical fiction themselves showed up in the work of mystery writers. From Mark Twain (*Pudd'nhead Wilson* [1894]) to Gertrude Stein (*Blood on the Dining-Room Floor* [1933]) to William Faulkner (*Intruder in the Dust* [1948] and *Knight's Gambit* [1949]), canonical writers regularly produced novels and stories that drew on the conventions of detective and crime writing. At the same time, many tropes present in the world of "literary" fiction appeared in popular detective fiction: Sherlock Holmes's *fin de siècle* decadence, Philo Vance's appreciation of psychoanalysis and modernist art, the "literary" poet and writer characters of Hammett's stories and novels.[8] Still, the high/low dichotomy separating highbrow fiction from genre fiction remained so strong that the most popular American detective novelist of the 1920s, the former literary editor and expert on modernist art Willard Huntington Wright (who wrote under the pseudonym

S. S. Van Dine), reflected on his popular success in a short autobiographical piece entitled *I Used to Be a Highbrow, But Look at Me Now* (1929).[9]

Van Dine's pithy title suggests an inability to "look at" the detective writer as anything but lowbrow, and this particular dichotomy retains some influence in the scholarship to this point. While critics generally conceive of "literary" fiction as exhibiting a particular genealogy that moves from romanticism through realism, naturalism, and modernism, historians of the detective and crime story see shifts of a different nature. Howard Haycraft's early construction of detective fiction history moves from the "Romantic Era" through the "Golden Age" and the "Moderns" (though at times his distinction between the Golden Age and the Moderns is difficult to discern). While Julian Symons's history is a bit more nuanced, his categories are much the same. John G. Cawelti collapses these distinctions into two competing strands: the classical detective story and the hard-boiled detective story. Yet none of these critics address the larger literary context—broader narratives of Anglo-American literary history—in which these writers were publishing. From the side-by-side magazine publication of writers like Van Dine and Sinclair Lewis in *Cosmopolitan* to the 1934 Modern Library publication of Hammett's *The Maltese Falcon* (1930), detective fiction has always demonstrated a strong affinity with the elite or "highbrow" world of literary fiction. When some connection is noted by critics, their tendency is to identify one or two of the most "literary" figures from the crime-fiction canon (for example, Hammett, Chandler, or James M. Cain) and elevate them to the realm of the literary, separating the proverbial wheat from the chaff much like Edmund Wilson did in his 1945 essay "Who Cares Who Killed Roger Ackroyd?"[10] To see a small handful of writers as exemplary and deserving of literary attention is also to miss some of the fundamental interrelationships between detective fiction and the larger trends of literary history.

At its very root, detective fiction is dependent on two competing nineteenth-century literary forms: realism and romanticism. For classical (or ratiocinative) detective fiction to function properly, the writer must insert a romantic individual into a realist world.[11] The protagonist is generally the exemplary model of reason, but (as in the case of Dupin, Holmes, and others in the same vein) the application of reason appears so highly idiosyncratic that its results remain difficult to replicate. This romantic figure (in Poe) becomes the figure of late Victorian decadence (in Doyle) and frequently retains her/his decadent sensibilities (though modifying them with modernist tastes) in the work of classical detective writers of the 1920s and beyond.[12] While the characterization is firmly romantic, the fictional world of the classical detective story exemplifies the emerging late nineteenth-century standards of American realism. In these stories the world is finally a legible environment, even if the reader may need the mediator of the amateur genius to demonstrate the legibility of this world and to prove that it is—in spite of any initial doubts—coherent, representable, and comprehensible.[13] William W. Stowe has called the classical detective's approach to detection a "practical semiotics," in which the crime provides a series of signifieds that must be properly decoded.[14] As a result detective and mystery writers in the classical mode have consistently obsessed over the notion of "fair play," a concept dependent on the ideas espoused by realism, producing any number of "rules" for writing detective fiction: the environment must be accurately described by a disinterested third party so that the reader will have an equal opportunity to solve the mystery.[15] Often, the classical detective writer uses a Watson character who functions as a stand-in for the reader and whose sensibilities (in contrast to the detective) are anything but exemplary; at other times, the stories are told in the third person to preserve a strict objectivity.[16]

The emergence of the hard-boiled detective story in the early 1920s, then, changes far more than just the subject matter (as Chandler argues). This new form throws the most basic elements of the classical detective story into doubt. Here, the detective does not complete his job by demonstrating a superior intellect. His (and it is almost always "his," especially in the genre's early years) manner of investigation is frequently predicated on a trial-and-error model. In looking at a number of these texts, it becomes clear why such an approach is necessary: the world is no longer legible according to the principles of realism. Networks and associations are not only better hidden, but they also extend far beyond the reaches of the locked room or English country house that provide the settings for so many classic mysteries. Crimes in the hard-boiled story are rarely isolated incidents of violence in a world of order. Rather, they often seem to be mere symptoms of a much larger social and economic disease of twentieth-century crime. Murders and other violent acts come and go, as do solutions. But the focus is less frequently on a symbolic restoration of order as it is on the survival of the detective in a continually hostile and unpredictable environment. Illuminating these distinctions, Stowe contrasts the "practical semiotics" of the classical detective story with the hard-boiled "hermeneutical interpreter," whose "interpretative process [is] a dialogic investigation rather than the application of a method."[17]

Far from exhibiting the facility with reason seen in figures like Dupin and Holmes, the hard-boiled detective's encounter with the world is usually physical and often violent. As Cawelti notes, in opposition to the privileged position of rational observer of realistic details that the classical detective inhabits, "the hard-boiled story ... typically implicates the detective in the crime from the very beginning," suggesting that the realist boundaries between subject and object have become unstable in this twentieth-century mode.[18] As the subjectivity of the detective gets closer and closer to the world he is investigating, the details of that world begin to appear more difficult to discern objectively, and the description of them frequently lapses into the grotesque. Paramount in the hard-boiled story is the detective's active engagement with the world, not only through his physical action but also through his linguistic and narratological control over how the story is experienced.

Detectives whose primary means of investigation involved action over cognition were not new to mystery fiction readers of the 1920s. While the late nineteenth-century detective is most frequently assumed to be cast in the same mold as Sherlock Holmes, one American detective made far more appearances than Holmes, beginning in 1886 (a year before Doyle created Holmes): Nick Carter, "Master Detective." Carter was a series character whose adventures were imagined by a host of in-house writers for dime-novel publishers Street & Smith.[19] Carter's exploits were far more like the melodramatic adventure tales that populated dime novels throughout the late nineteenth-century than the measured, ratiocinative tales of Holmes. A master of disguises known as "the little giant" to the underworld, Carter tracks criminals through late Victorian New York City in stories where he is frequently captured and escapes with an expert use of timing and violence.[20] Like the later hard-boiled figures, Carter infiltrates the criminal underworld, is occasionally knocked out while in action ("without any warning whatsoever, he received a violent blow on the head and sank senseless to the deck"), and fights his way out of trouble.[21] Still, Carter's relationship to crime is that of the incredibly talented amateur. Like Holmes and Dupin, Carter is consulted by the police after they have exhausted all possibilities in attempting to solve a particularly perplexing crime. His manner—when not in disguise—suggests all the refined sensibilities of a late Victorian gentleman, and, like a host of dime-novel protagonists, his speech exemplifies a natural aristocracy.[22] Nick Carter's city is certainly a dangerous one, but with the proper manipulation of costume, language, and violence, the detective will always solve the crime.

In transforming detective fiction from its ratiocinative coldness, the hard-boiled writers looked back to these action-packed adventure novels but began to subvert their realist assumptions with a variety of new strategies rooted in the experimental language of the streets. As with the other writers discussed in this study, many of the thematic and topical concerns were quite contemporary and in sync with critical discourse on modernist culture: the new sexual codes and gender roles of the Jazz Age; the increasing fascination with twentieth-century urban spaces; the emphasis on psychology; the complicated relationship to capitalism and other forms of power (gangsterism, fascism, etc.). However, as with other examples of vernacular modernism, the most important transformation in the hard-boiled story is not necessarily the story's content, but how it negotiates its content via narration and language. As Shaw noted in the introduction to *The Hard-Boiled Omnibus*, "The formula or pattern [of the hard-boiled story] emphasizes character and the problems inherent in human behavior over crime solution. In other words, in this new pattern, character conflict is the main theme; the ensuing crime, or its threat, is incidental."[23] Here, the crime is far less important than how the characters perceive, interact with, and ultimately represent that world. The hard-boiled detective story's relationship to the world is much like the work of the high modernists—as a form of self-conscious textual mediation of "reality."

A number of critics have gestured toward the idea that the hard-boiled detective story itself (particularly as exemplified by Dashiell Hammett and Raymond Chandler) resembles a form of modernism. In many cases, critics see the hard-boiled style as a watered-down version of the modernism of Ernest Hemingway.[24] Fortunately, recent criticism has acknowledged that the emergence of the hard-boiled style in the pages of *Black Mask* preceded Hemingway's earliest American publications by over two years, and that hard-boiled mainstays like Carroll John Daly and Dashiell Hammett had each published over twenty stories in *Black Mask* before Hemingway's first undeniably hard-boiled short story, "The Killers," appeared in *Scribner's* in March 1927. Ken Worpole, critic and historian of British working-class reading practices, has a much more nuanced consideration of this relationship, noting that "Hemingway's style itself had developed in a continuous relationship with the 'toughguy' school of thriller writing and could not be separated from it."[25] While Hemingway was earning his modernist credentials by typing Gertrude Stein's nearly thousand-page epic *The Making of Americans* (1925), the hard-boiled writers, like other writers in this study, were working through literary transformations in the American vernacular language as most clearly exemplified in the work of Ring Lardner.[26] And while Hemingway remained occupied with an obsession to write "one true sentence," the hard-boiled pulp writers sometimes churned out thousands of words a day—a practice that is tempting to think of as a commercial form of "automatic writing."[27] The approach was certainly different, but these comparisons have as much to do with their similarity in ideological outlook as they do with their minimalist prose style.

Critics utilizing a "culture of modernism" model have emphasized how the hostile urban environment (and the accompanying corruption and decay that provide the background for much of hard-boiled writing) replicates the dismal outlook of modernism itself. James Naremore, for example, has claimed that Hammett's *The Glass Key* is "better described as Hammett's *The Waste Land*," primarily because of its ideas about stability and identification in a modern environment, something Eysteinsson describes as a "pessimistic view of modern culture often associated with modernism (which its adversaries sometimes call 'wastelandism')," a worldview not limited to the modernists nor especially characteristic of all modernist writing.[28] Like Naremore, Jon Thompson sees Hammett as the exemplary hard-boiled modernist, not because of his style but because of "his skepticism toward bourgeois law and order, his philosophical and ideological relativism, the contradictory sexual politics of his fiction, and his rejection of rationality."[29] What Thompson describes might effectively be characterized as an antimodern or antirational response to modernity, though his argument largely ignores Hammett's aesthetic innovations.

Thompson's interest in "relativism" and the "rejection of rationality," however, points toward a more comprehensive means of thinking about the hard-boiled detective story as a form of modernism, rooted in the relationship between language and epistemology. The detective story has always depended on certain assumptions about what the characters actually know and how they understand the world around them. Indeed, for the ratiocinative detective, the acquisition of knowledge and proper interpretation of this knowledge are crucial in the solution of the crime. As in modernism, this ability to know (and, especially, to decode signs) breaks down in the hard-boiled detective story. Nothing in the world of Hammett, Chandler, or other hard-boiled writers is "elementary, my dear Watson." The detective in this genre occupies the epistemological position of a modernist subject; knowledge is always conditional, relative, and fragmentary, and the subject's function (like that of Poirier's "grim reader" of the high modernist text) must necessarily try to make sense of the incredibly incomplete and often inadequate set of information provided.

With knowledge fragmented and the world illegible by traditional methods of "semiotic" detection, the hard-boiled detective is frequently forced to "stir things up" (as Hammett's Continental Op self-consciously does in *Red Harvest*) in order to gain answers to his questions and move towards what ultimately becomes a provisional solution, at best. This involvement, often violent and usually illegal, breaks down the subject/object division that underscores the classical detective story, the conventions of realism, and the stable division between law and order. The classical detective story insists that the subject (whether narrator or detective) remains distant from the details of the crime; tampering with evidence, for example, to gain a conviction would be out of the realm of possibility in a Holmes story. In the hard-boiled detective story, such techniques are common. Because the crimes themselves are not neat and insular semiotic puzzles, the hard-boiled detective, like the modernist artist or reader, must remake the text of the world into something that resembles, if only fleetingly, coherence. In other words, the world is never completely comprehensible in objective terms in either the high modernist text or the hard-boiled detective story. In both cases some aesthetic intervention, whether a thick layer of classical allusions or the stylized violence of "stirring things up," remains necessary for any proper understanding of contemporary modernity.

In addition to having an active, "hermeneutic" engagement with the world, the hard-boiled detective also occupies the position of an aesthetic subject, the creator of the narrative text. While plenty of texts that preceded the 1920s used violence as a means of engaging the world, a fundamental change in narratological strategy characterizes this newly formed genre.[30] Rather than using a third-person narration or a removed first-person "Watson," these writers largely depend on the compromised subject position of the heavily invested—and often unreliable—first-person detective. Almost inevitably an unreliable narrator, the hard-boiled detective unfolds the clues (and the accompanying confusion) as he finds them; there is no objective authority or plot device that will reveal the criminal mastermind's nefarious plot at the story's conclusion. Instead, the highly subjective narration of the detective is the reader's only entrée to both the crime and the world in which it occurs. In such a narrative style, the reader *knows* that the information received through this narration is necessarily incomplete, but the epistemological assumptions of the genre—and, I might add, of broader characterizations of modernism—recognize that any story, told by anyone, is always incomplete, partial, and highly subjective. Only the hard-boiled detective—or the modernist artist—can, however briefly, bring the chaos of the early twentieth century into focus long enough for any pretense of aesthetic coherence.

This subjectivity is underscored by the stylistic narration of the hard-boiled detective. The major shift in the genre, the one that reveals it to be a form of vernacular modernism, is its insistence on utilizing characters that speak with a combination of bravado, thieves' cant, and professional argot. The language of the detective (or, occasionally, criminal) narrator is fundamentally compromised because he speaks or writes not in a language that insists on its objectivity, but rather in the corrupted language of the very figures he is investigating. This linguistic distinction is crucial; in effect, it rejects the divisions between subject and object that inform nineteenth-century realism's genteel hierarchies and casts off the ideological work they perform. As with other vernacular modernists, this language is not objectively descriptive and rather creates another world, a textual world that exists on its own terms. Hard-boiled figures invent their own phrases and adopt particularly inventive expressions from the underworld to describe the kinds of environments that standard realist aesthetics is incapable of handling. Even Chandler acknowledged this stylistic formalism in "The Simple Art of Murder," his ode to hard-boiled "realism":

> [Hammett] had a style, but his audience didn't know it, because it was in a language not supposed to be capable of such refinements.... All language begins with speech, but when it develops to the point of becoming a literary medium it only looks like speech. Hammett's style at its worst was as formalized as a page of Marius the Epicurean; at its best it could say almost anything. I believe this style, which does not belong to Hammett or to anybody, but is the American language (and not even exclusively that any more), can say things he did not know how to say or feel the need of saying.[31]

The "American language" of Hammett's fiction, Chandler writes (channeling Mencken), "only looks like speech," but is in fact a language that can communicate more than one realizes. In much the same way Yezierska and Jolas characterized immigrant language, Hammett's use of the vernacular transforms the language of the streets into something that "could say almost anything."

As with Jolas's publication of "Slanguage: 1929" in *transition*, the hard-boiled language of Hammett and others also grew out of a broader interest in the lexicographical interest in varieties of American vernacular language. While glossaries of criminal argot have a long history in the study of slang (they are among the first specialized dictionaries of slang), hard-boiled writing of the 1920s foregrounded this language as a particularly modern form of linguistic experimentation.[32] As detective fiction changed, the pulp magazines that were publishing the genre also saw the value of slang lexicography. *Flynn's*, which would publish Chandler, Hammett, and Carroll John Daly under its later title *Detective Fiction Weekly*, serialized Henry Leverage's "Dictionary of the Underworld" in 1925, noting in some installments that "here is another chunk of the vocabulary *Flynn's* is publishing weekly, both as a help to its readers in reading some of its underworld stories and as a matter of general interest."[33] The need for a textual apparatus for reading crime stories emphasized the experimental linguistic focus of the hard-boiled style. The first installment presented underworld slang as impenetrable and fluid:

> There are dives in New York's underworld where a language is spoken that the ordinary citizen, listening in, would find impossible to understand. It isn't English, French, German, or Yiddish; it is a language by itself.... *Flynn's* intends to present to you in successive issues a dictionary of this argot. We realize we are offering the vocabulary of a fluid, ever-changing tongue. By its very nature it must be incomplete. It will include words common to every-day slang. Every flapper uses some of these words. But they have been included because frequently they convey a different significance in underground channels. Then there are words that none but a crook or hobo would use or understand.[34]

Both Chandler's description of the hard-boiled style and *Flynn's* "Dictionary of the Underworld" present this "fluid, ever-changing" language as artful and self-conscious, in some cases opaque and in need of scholarly (or pseudoscholarly) paratextual apparatus.

Despite the celebration of innovative and experimental street language by both hard-boiled writers and pulp publishers, pulp literature has been closely aligned with the almost machinelike output of dime novels and thus seen as antithetical to the self-conscious aesthetics of literary modernism. Michael Denning and others have called the work of dime novelists "anonymous, 'unauthored' discourse," as if the demands of production themselves were so intense that writers were unable to put any stylistic stamp of individuality on their fiction; likewise, Erin A. Smith has compared pulp writers to "manufacturers, paid for making a product much as factory workers were."[35] Much the same could be said of many of the pulp magazines published in the first half of the twentieth century, but countering this trend was the nearly ubiquitous acknowledgement and celebration of authorship on magazine covers that began to dominate the pulps in the mid-1920s. Certainly, the consistent featuring of authors' and characters' names on pulp covers suggested that writers had developed a sense of personal craft and an identifiable style. The sign of authorship, almost a fetish among modernists, was in full effect in the pulps, and writers became known not only for the use of series characters but also for the employment of unique stylistic tropes. The promotion of authorship was especially prominent in the pages of *Black Mask*, the pulp magazine that saw the birth of the hard-boiled style and jump-started the careers of some of the best-known names in twentieth-century American detective and crime writing.

Founded in 1920 by H. L. Mencken and George Jean Nathan as a quick means to recoup their *Smart Set* losses, *Black Mask* spent its early years searching for an identity among the enormous number of pulp magazines on the marketplace. Of all these magazines, *Black Mask* has received the most attention from critics and scholars of detective fiction, in large part because it produced so many important genre writers.[36] Such criticism has generally focused on the individuals whose names graced the covers with regularity. But while individual writers became known for their own quirks, the magazine as a whole also began to move toward its own self-conscious deployment of style by the late 1920s, under the editorship of Joseph T. Shaw. To a great degree the critical attention on *Black Mask*, as opposed to many of its contemporaries, is warranted. While other pulp magazines specialized in genres—romance, Western, aviation, mystery, etc.—*Black Mask* took its specialization even more seriously. Over and above specializing in a single genre, *Black Mask* promoted a particular style of detective story, making it the only major pulp magazine to self-consciously address not just what content its stories contained, but *how* those stories would be told.

While this editorial transformation began to take shape when Shaw took over the editorship in November 1926, the most explicit statement of editorial principles appeared a few months later, in June 1927. "Black Mask has a definite purpose and a definite aim," begins the editorial "The Aim of Black Mask." The piece proceeds to delineate "our requirements of plausibility, of truthfulness in details, of realism in the picturing of thought, the portrayal of action and emotion. All stories submitted to Black Mask are judged and selected with these cardinal requirements in mind, together with the necessity for swift movement in starting and in the development of the plot." The ratiocinative school of detective fiction is the subtle target of the critique that follows: "The reader of today gets his impression quickly. He judges the character of a man by what he does and not, as formerly, by the author's description of his physical appearance."[37] Three major characteristics of the hard-boiled story are referenced here: the privileging of action over objective, realist description, and the emphasis on implied interiority in the phrase "realism in the picturing of thought." Although by the late 1940s, film noir had all but turned this interiority into a caricature with the man of action and a constant voice-over narration, by mid-1927, hardly more than six months into his editorship, Shaw had identified and articulated the direction that the emerging genre, and his magazine, would take.

By October 1929, after Shaw had spent nearly three years at the helm of *Black Mask,* the hardback publication of Hammett's work by Knopf made the editorial voice even clearer in its proclamation of a new era in detective fiction: "The day of the Sherlock Holmes type of story is practically ended. Despite the fact that the Fu Manchu and Philo Vance stories have been quite popular, the trend is all toward the serious and realistic presentation in fiction of crime, criminals, the underworld, and police and detective methods as they actually are in real life." Shaw's obsession with depicting the "real" in a magazine that sought to present a highly stylized world of crime should not confuse here; his push toward realism is a kinesthetic one, which rejects the static description of nineteenth-century writing for a "realism" of action and narration. Later in the same piece, he focuses on what particular elements of the "real" he sees as primary: "In few stories are the characters fantastic creations of the writer's imagination. Nearly always they are figures drawn from real life, thinking and speaking and acting as real men think and speak and act."[38] These three emphases, "thinking and speaking and acting," essentially define the world of the hard-boiled. Any encounter with the environment is inevitably mediated through a highly individualized thought, speech, or action, as the first-person narration of so many hard-boiled stories makes clear. Thinking and speaking precede acting and are the self-conscious medium through which the reader experiences the "realistic" action.

The new editorial emphasis on style upset more than a few *Black Mask* authors, including Erle Stanley Gardner, who complained in letters to Shaw and circulation manager Phillip C. Cody that they were trying to "Hammettize" the magazine.[39] Gardner claimed that Shaw had "gone arty" with the magazine, emphasizing "style" over content and alienating his pulp readership. "Personally I don't think the wood pulp reader cares so much for style," Gardner wrote to Shaw after the magazine had begun serializing the critically acclaimed *The Maltese Falcon*.[40] And though Gardner would freely admit to Shaw that "frankly, Hammett is an artist. I am a hack writer," he maintained that "if a reader wants Black Mask fiction he buys the black mask [sic]. If he wants Saturday Evening Post fiction he buys the Post. If he wants some of the Menken [sic] type he knows where to go for it."[41] Trade magazines saw a similar trend toward a particular kind of stylization: a *Writer's Digest* piece on *Black Mask* in 1930 advised potential authors, "Don't try to wish any mediocre stuff on this editor—you've got to be good! Simple, clipped style preferred to fine writing, so don't use any fancy language. Your detectives and gangsters, above all, must sound *authentic;* their dialogue *must ring the gong.* Study the magazine—*hard*—before you aim at it!"[42]

Gardner was largely correct with this characterization of Shaw's editorial practice; indeed, he had gone "arty" to a degree. Though Gardner continued to appear in the magazine, during much of Shaw's editorial tenure the writer's more fanciful (he would call them "romantic") tales of Ed Jenkins "the phantom crook" would not receive the same kind of publicity as the work of "Hammettized" writers like Frederick Nebel, Paul Cain, and ultimately Raymond Chandler. And though Shaw continued to emphasize "plausibility" as a concern, Gardner was right to point out the "arty" language and structures of *Black Mask*'s preferred writers. He later wrote to his friend (and *Black Mask* circulation manager) Phil Cody, "This grim, hard-boiled thing isn't realism because with all the private detectives I'v [sic] ever known I've never known one like those boys in B.M. used to write about, and no one I've talked to ever has either. Therefore, I say that stuff isn't realism. It's more fiction than the weirdest type of imaginative yarn."[43]

Though Shaw maintained a policy that stressed "plausibility," he would acknowledge the centrality of the character-driven elements of the hard-boiled style. In these texts, not only do we find that "character conflict is the main theme" and that "the ensuing crime, or its threat, is incidental," as Shaw would later write in *The Hard-Boiled Omnibus*, but we also see the characters themselves become mediators of the fictional reality, frequently implicated in the crimes they are purportedly working to solve.[44] Importantly, however, Shaw had clearly identified these changes by the end of the 1920s, at the moment when Hammett and others (such as Carroll John Daly and Raoul Whitfield) began to cross over into the hardback publishing market. The vision for what the detective story could become was itself a product of the 1920s, the decade most clearly associated with modernism.

As Ron Goulart writes in *The Dime Detectives*, "Although the twenties was a transition period, it was not the heyday of the hard-boiled private eye."[45] Goulart's history of the pulps spends the majority of its time on the 1930s, when the hard-boiled transformations of *Black Mask* began to be disseminated over the scores of other detective pulps on the market. Certainly, his estimation is correct; the 1920s were a period of experimentation in detective and crime writing (as well as in other pulp genres) rather than the moment of the full fruition of the hard-boiled style. This experimentation, however, lines up almost uncannily with other linguistic and formal experiments associated with high modernism. There is a great value in examining the detective stories of the early *Black Mask* stars in order to see exactly how this mode emerged both stylistically and epistemologically. The two most popular *Black Mask* writers in the 1920s were undoubtedly Daly and Hammett. In a 1924 readers' poll, the editors hesitated to announce a favorite: "Two authors ran such a close race in the voting that we will not tell which actually got first place. They are Carroll John Daly and Dashiell Hammett."[46] A close examination of the 1920s work of these two writers will provide a window into exactly how hard-boiled writers effected this watershed transformation of the detective genre through a self-conscious deployment of a real and invented underworld vernacular, exemplifying the genre's own "Revolution of the Word."

"A Halfway House between the Dicks and the Crooks": Destabilizing Realism in the Work of Carroll John Daly

> *I define a hack as a man who refuses as a matter of principle to improve the production apparatus.*
> —WALTER BENJAMIN, "THE AUTHOR AS PRODUCER" (1934)
>
> *There is nothing subtle about the methods of Race Williams.*
> —NEW YORK TIMES REVIEW OF *THE AMATEUR MURDERER* (1933)

If one figure complicates the purported highbrow aspirations of the hard-boiled detective story, it is Carroll John Daly. Had the style been pioneered by the more or less canonical Hammett, then the genre's history would become a great deal easier to see as somehow "literary." Daly, on the other hand, has been savaged by critics of the genre; few scholars have any positive things to say about him or his popular series character Race

Williams. One of the few scholarly publications on Daly sums up his career by calling him "a third-rate word-spinner who hatched a second-rate protagonist who did his thing in these fourth-rate productions best left on the broom-closet's top shelf in the back."[47] Philip Durham called him "a careless writer and a muddy thinker who created the hard-boiled detective, the prototype for numberless writers to follow."[48] And, in his seminal history of pulp detective fiction, Ron Goulart rightly notes that Daly "has been for most historians and critics of the hard-boiled detective field a somewhat embarrassing founding father. He's a key figure, the creator of an important character, but he was not a very good writer and, for a man said to have a sense of humor, he seemed completely unaware of how silly both he and Race Williams sometimes sounded."[49] Even longtime devotees of the hard-boiled such as E. R. Hagemann and Robert Weinberg have lamented Daly's subliterary output. In the important anthology *The Black Mask Boys*, editor William F. Nolan described Daly's first Race Williams novel *The Snarl of the Beast* thus: "The writing was impossibly crude, the plotting labored and ridiculous, and Race Williams emerged as a swaggering illiterate with the emotional instability of a gun-crazed vigilante."[50] While the presence of a Race Williams story in an issue of *Black Mask* reportedly boosted sales of the magazine by 15 percent during his editorial tenure, Joseph T. Shaw chose not to include Daly in his seminal anthology *The Hard-Boiled Omnibus*, the first attempt at creating a hard-boiled canon, virtually writing Daly out of the history of a form and style he helped originate.[51]

One of the reasons Daly has been so roundly maligned by the historians of the genre is the tendency to collapse author and narrator, a mistake seldom made in the study of "literary" fiction but often made in the realm of popular fiction. If Daly's character was "a swaggering illiterate," such an approach suggests, Daly himself must also be illiterate. In fact, editorials in *Black Mask* consciously played with and satirized this idea. In a letter about his first Race Williams story, "Knights of the Open Palm," Daly sends "even the best of wishes to H. C. North, the associate editor, who makes ungentlemanly remarcks [sic] about my spelling," prompting the editors to reply: "We are pleased that Mr. Daly is not offended at our *remarcks*."[52] In spite of this tongue-in-cheek banter, Daly's letter also emphasizes his attention to the craft of writing, especially in the revision of his stories, which he calls "the bread and butter of the fiction builder." He makes essentially the same claims in a 1927 article in the *Editor* about the revision process on his first novel, *The Snarl of the Beast*.[53] Daly's comments on revision may be a sort of posturing, but the work that precedes his hard-boiled writing suggests that his move to the vernacular style was a very self-conscious choice, grounded in his own understanding of narration and desire to find new genre forms. Regardless of attempts to dismiss Daly, he remains a force to be reckoned with in the history of the hard-boiled detective story. Erle Stanley Gardner, one of the most prolific *Black Mask* writers of the 1920s and 1930s, called Daly the "originator" of the style and modeled some of his own early characters (such as Ed Jenkins and Bob Larkin) on Daly's popular character Race Williams.[54] And the first identifiably hard-boiled story by Daly, "The False Burton Combs," appeared in the December 1922 issue of *Black Mask,* when Hammett was still trying to break through in more highbrow magazines like the *Smart Set*.[55]

While "The False Burton Combs" featured Daly's first hard-boiled narrator, his first publication in *Black Mask* was anything but hard-boiled. In October 1922 Daly published the psychological terror story "Dolly," a tale of murder and madness told by a borderline insane narrator. "Dolly" is an example of what Christopher Breu has termed "psychological *noir*," common in the early years of *Black Mask*.[56] After all, the original subtitle of the magazine was "An Illustrated Magazine of Detective Mystery, Adventure, Romance and Spiritualism"; the presence of the supernatural and psychotic loomed large in the early years of *Black Mask*. This kind of writing dominated the magazine in its first five years, as indicated by the numerous publications by Harold Ward under both his own name and the pseudonym Ward Sterling (forty-five stories and serial installments between the two names in the first forty issues of the magazine). Ward's specialty was the tale of psychological terror, and he clearly references his influences in "Under the Crimson Skull," when he details "a setting fit for the description of a Dante—a Poe—a De Maupassant."[57]

Daly's "Dolly," like the work of Harold Ward, draws heavily on the first-person style of Poe. In this story, the unnamed narrator, the son of "a well-known alienist," becomes morbidly obsessed with the throat of a woman named Dolly.[58] To obtain his father's consent to marry her, he hatches a plan to feign an insanity only cured by Dolly's presence, keeping a journal which he

> filled . . . day after day with thoughts of Dolly; weird, uncanny thoughts—thoughts that could only come from a disordered mind. It was mostly about her throat and the fascination which it held for me; that if Dolly was not for me she would be for no one else. For when my fingers played along that soft, white surface

came a desire—a desire which I knew I could not long control—to close my fingers tightly about that warm flesh, and crush forever the breath from that beautiful body.[59]

In a truly Poe-inspired conclusion, the narrator's initial performance of insanity overcomes his ability to reason, driving him to kill Dolly in a fit of actual insanity. In both content and style, Daly looks back to the work of Poe and to the contemporary work of H. P. Lovecraft, who began publishing "weird, uncanny" tales in amateur fiction magazines in 1916.

While the narration and subject of "Dolly" are anomalous among Daly's other publications in *Black Mask,* this piece helps to demonstrate both Daly's development as a writer and the emergence of the hard-boiled style in general. This is the last time that Daly would publish a *Black Mask* tale in this overwrought style, reminiscent of nineteenth-century gothic fiction. As in his later work, Daly consistently privileges the first-person, the primary component Christopher Breu uses to identify the elements of "psychological noir," a precursor to the hard-boiled that included stories "reflect[ing] the legacy of ... gothic true-crime and fiction narratives."[60] The introduction of a narrative subjectivity suggests the importance of the individual experience of the world, but this shift alone does not push Daly's work toward any stylistic experiments. In addition to the gothic narrator of "Dolly," Daly would also experiment with third-person narration (in his first novel, *The White Circle* [1926], for example), but the vast majority of his publications after "Dolly" demonstrated significant shifts in voice and tone. Gone from his fiction was the voice of the bourgeois narrator in the mode of psychological romanticism, rooted in late nineteenth-century notions about society and psychology. After "Dolly," his characters would be thrust into the twentieth century by their very explicit use of the American vernacular.

Leaving the style of "Dolly" behind, though, was not necessarily a commercial or an editorial choice on Daly's part. While editors used "Dolly" to premiere the short-lived "Daytime Stories" series ("not to be read at night by people with weak nerves"), readers praised the story for months afterward. Although the story was published in October 1922, the last reference to "Dolly" in the readers' column appeared in the 15 July 1923 issue, fifteen issues later.[61] In the meantime, Daly had published "The False Burton Combs" and debuted two new hard-boiled characters, "Three Gun" Terry Mack and Race Williams, who would become Daly's most famous *Black Mask* creation. If the readers' letters are any indication, their tastes in early 1923 remained conflicted: continuous praise of "Dolly" pointed to a preference for melodramatic, psychological nineteenth-century narration, while a letter published in the same issue as the debut of Terry Mack noted that "since the new editor has taken charge the magazine has greatly improved—masculine logic in choosing detective fiction beats feminine curiosity—no offense to the fair sex intended."[62] The reader's letter references the brief editorship of George W. Sutton Jr., whose editorial tenure ended in this issue, to be followed by Phillip C. Cody. Under Cody's editorship, the emphasis fell even more squarely on this "masculine logic," as Cody began publishing Daly, Hammett, and Erle Stanley Gardner with increasing frequency.

Daly's place in this transformation of the editorial policy of *Black Mask* is central, but one commonly repeated mistake suggests that Daly's work was so poor that even the pulps published him reluctantly. At one point, George Sutton reportedly told Daly, "I don't like these stories—but the readers do. I have never received so many letters about a single character before. Write them. I won't like them. But I'll buy them and I'll print them."[63] As the exclusion of Daly from the canonizing *Hard-Boiled Omnibus* implied, Joseph T. Shaw, editorial successor to Cody, also apparently disliked Daly's work. Still, Daly's name and his characters' names were almost always featured on the magazine's cover when his work appeared; Daly's stories routinely provided inspiration for the cover painting, as well. If the editors did not like Daly's work, readers certainly did, but this evaluative discrepancy serves to reinforce negative stereotypes about the readers of pulp magazines, a group *Vanity Fair* called "those who move their lips when they read."[64] Such strict cultural hierarchies in the interwar period might prove even more damning to Daly's reputation: if Daly was derided even by pulp editors, how could his work claim to engage in modernist experimentation?

What complicates this, however, is the fact that Daly was not published exclusively in the pulps in the early 1920s. Like Hammett, who published early work in the *Smart Set* before shifting to what he pejoratively called "blackmasking," Daly attempted and succeeded in publishing at least one story in the slick magazines.[65] In April 1923 Daly published "Paying an Old Debt" in the *American Magazine,* one of the more successful competitors with the *Saturday Evening Post* in the middlebrow marketplace. Unlike Hammett, however, Daly's pulp and slick writings were not fundamentally different in their style. This story, published four months after "The False Burton Combs" and a month before "Three Gun Terry," utilizes virtually the same vernacular narrator that all of Daly's pulp stories would use beginning in the next month. In "Paying an Old Debt," subtitled "A burglar's story," the narrator is a thief who reforms when taken on as a servant by a rich man. Thematically, this story differs from Daly's pulp work, where the righteous vigilante never regrets his use of violence, but like the semiliterate narrators Terry Mack and Race Williams, the unnamed narrator of "Paying an Old Debt" acknowledges his linguistic insufficiencies: "Why, if I was to write the way I talked no one could understand me."[66] The appearance of Daly's work in the *American Magazine* suggests the degree to which the vernacular narrator pioneered by Ring Lardner in the *Saturday Evening Post* had become part of the mainstream of American magazine fiction.

While Lardner exerted a vast influence on slick fiction in the early 1920s, not many stories with vernacular narration appear in the early years of *Black Mask*. Few stories were published using any kind of vernacular narrator, while the majority of them feature the gothic narrative style of "Dolly" or the third-person conventions of the action-packed melodrama. One exception to this was C. S. Montanye's "Looking Out for Orchid," published in the second issue of the magazine (May 1920). In both style and content, Montanye's piece is incongruous in this issue. Clearly derivative of Lardner, this story features narration by a "wardrobe mistress" who tries to protect a young female vaudevillian star from the advances of an admirer. The narrator utilizes slang and misspelling and even appropriates sports metaphors that echo Lardner's own technique: "They was more curves to her than they is to any big league pitcher livin', or them relics of the happy days of yestereen—corkscrews."[67] Not only an exception in the magazine, this story is a unique piece in the larger body of his *Black Mask* work; in his other publications in the magazine, Montanye produced detective stories, largely following classical models.

Lardner's influence looms even larger in Daly's own "Kiss-the-Canvas Crowley" (1 September 1923). Another obscure Daly story, this first-person narrative follows the brief career of a boxer whose fame stems from his ability to be knocked down in the ring. When his manager suggests he take on the nickname "Kiss-the-Canvas" Crowley to drum up publicity, he assents: "I'm a student and have read the books, so I took a leaf from one of the old proverbs: 'When in Rome do as the Italians do.' So I let 'em book me under the new moniker."[68] After his career is over, Crowley turns manager himself to get revenge on Billy Tiernan, the manager who ended his career. Crowley's discovery, a rural fighter he calls "Special Delivery Smitty" after Smitty knocks him out in a Pennsylvania roadhouse, turns out to be much weaker than Crowley thought. His plan to double-cross Tiernan by winning a fight he had agreed to lose is foiled, and Crowley gets paid by Tiernan, who knows that "Kiss-the-Canvas Crowley is honest to the core." As Tiernan and his winning fighter leave his office, Crowley muses, "Somethin' tells me that it ain't no time for speechmakin'. When they leave me I'm standin' there all alone and I do a smile. The old proverb is right. 'Honesty is the best insurance' after all."[69]

An oddly humorous outing for Daly in *Black Mask,* this story highlights the crucial connection between the vernacular humor of Lardner's sports stories and the hard-boiled narration on which Daly would begin to focus exclusively after this publication. Lardner's "Champion," a far more sinister boxing story that appeared in 1916, may have been part of the inspiration for Daly's work.[70] The narrator Crowley, though, exhibits many of the narrative attributes of both the Lardneresque humor figure and the Terry Mack/Race Williams character type that would dominate Daly's writing. The constant reference to and misquotation of proverbs recalls the humorous tradition of Lardner and Loos; the suggestion is that these clichéd phrases mean very little, which results in their frequent misuse or perversion via language. Clearly, Crowley (like Loos's Lorelei Lee) has heard these phrases and recognizes their importance, but ultimately his memory fails him and he provides colorfully inaccurate versions of the proverbs, suggesting a bankruptcy of meaning in overused language of this sort. At the same time, Crowley engages in obsessive self-questioning, a technique that would become a hallmark of the Race Williams stories: "What did I say? I didn't say nothin'. What did I do? I did a-plenty. I just took one clout at his ugly mug."[71]

While "Kiss-the-Canvas Crowley" provides a crucial link between the late-1910s humor writing of Lardner and Daly's own transformation of style, Daly's first few stories in the hard-boiled vernacular utilize this kind of language to different, though related, ends. It is here that the critique of the realist detective stories of the so-called Golden Age begins to develop. In Daly's stories, the use of the vernacular distances the words themselves from their referent, creating a synthetic, purely textual environment in which vernacular language strips away its realist relationship to the world. In the hard-boiled style, the language of violence and, in Daly's case, of masculine bravado, replaces the realist language of a disinterested spectator and expert reasoner. As the title of one Daly story would have it, the hard-boiled figure must "Say It with Lead," not with the overwrought and formulaic realist language of classical detective fiction.

The origins of the hard-boiled detective can be traced to Daly's second publication in *Black Mask,* "The False Burton Combs," published in December 1922, the year Michael North has called "the scene of the modern."[72] In this story, the unnamed narrator, "a gentleman adventurer," agrees to impersonate a reformed bootlegger who expects his silent and anonymous partners to make an attempt on his life. The story opens with a direct engagement of the narrator's class position: "I had an outside stateroom on the upper deck of the Fall River boat and ten minutes after I parked my bag there I knew that I was being watched." While the protagonist's social and economic identity—as both "gentleman adventurer" and the occupant of a stateroom—may recall the genteel amateur of Sherlock Holmes or Nick Carter, his narrative position and his choice of language indicate a very different genealogy, the man of the street. When the narrator senses that he's being followed, he notes, "There was nothing to be nervous about—my little trip was purely a pleasure one this time. But then a dick getting your smoke is not pleasant under the best of circumstances": not exactly the language of nineteenth-century gentility.[73] In this shift in language, so clearly distinct from the language of both adventure and detective fiction of the first two decades of the twentieth century, hard-boiled detective fiction begins to display its own brand of vernacular modernism. For, after all, what does the narrator mean when he speaks of "a dick getting your smoke"? Daly's 1922 readers, unaccustomed to reading this sort of language in any sort of fiction (and particularly in *Black Mask* fiction of the time), must have spent some time puzzling through this phrase on first encountering it. Even *Flynn's* 1925 "Dictionary of the Underworld" provides little help with the term "smoke," a repurposing of the term that Daly may have invented.[74] Daly pulls the language away from its normal referent, forcing his readers to become "grim readers" of vernacular modernism: to put together pieces of a broken and rearranged language that seems almost foreign in its streetwise inventiveness. Like the underworld slang gathered by Henry Leverage for *Flynn's*, Daly's vernacular "isn't English, French, German, or Yiddish; it is a language by itself."

"The False Burton Combs" is laced with a variety of contemporary slang terms, many of which have passed into the common vernacular through the immense popularity of crime fiction in the twentieth and twenty-first centuries. As with the examples in *transition*'s "Slanguage: 1929" and Mencken's "Declaration of Independence," others seem highly idiosyncratic and dated: "If things got melodramatic why I guess I could shoot as good as any bootlegger that ever robbed a church. They're hard guys, yes, but then I ain't exactly a cake-eater myself."[75] As with Lardner's humor, the language of Daly's character works to reshape the world through text; language is important as a marker of class, but it also suggests a profound difference between text and the world. Unlike the realist detective stories of the late nineteenth and early twentieth centuries, "The False Burton Combs" is not a text in which language provides a transparent means of engaging reality. Instead, the entirety of the experience of the world is heavily mediated and aestheticized through the slang-inflected narration.

What emerges in a nascent form in "The False Burton Combs" becomes far more explicit in stories featuring Daly's most popular series character, Race Williams. Appearing first in June 1923, Williams would ultimately be featured in fifty-four stories in *Black Mask;* nearly half of these became the basis for seven novels published between 1927 and 1935. After leaving *Black Mask* in 1934, Daly continued to publish Race Williams stories through the 1950s in other pulps, including *Dime Detective, Thrilling Detective, Popular Detective,* and *Smashing Detective Stories.* The first decade's worth of these stories, however, all published in *Black Mask,* demonstrate the vast changes that the genre was undergoing in its shift toward the hard-boiled. As the few scholars who have discussed Daly's work have shown, his Race Williams stories are fascinating in the ways in which they engage, whether centrally or tangentially, a number of 1920s obsessions: the Ku Klux Klan ("Knights of the Open Palm"), trade union corruption ("Three Thousand to the Good"), live radio broadcasting ("I'll Tell the World"), the swindling of Native Americans out of oil revenues ("Half-Breed"), and other contemporary social issues.[76]

While critics like Sean McCann have convincingly argued for the importance of social engagement found in the Williams stories, an even more crucial legacy of these stories in crime and detective fiction is the wholesale transformation of narrative form and choice of language. In the opening of "Knights of the Open Palm," Williams makes the famous claim that he would repeat in some form in almost every story he narrated:

> As for my business, I'm what you might call a middleman—just a halfway house between the dicks and the crooks. Oh, there ain't no doubt that both the cops and the crooks take me for a gun, but I ain't—not rightly speaking. I do a little honest shooting once in a while—just in the way of business. But my conscience is clear; I never bumped off a guy what didn't need it. And I can put it over the crooks every time—why, I know more about crooks than what they know about themselves. Yep, Race Williams, Private Investigator, that's me.[77]

By the time Daly published "I'll Tell the World" in 1925, Williams would insist on being called a "confidential agent" (as opposed to "Private Investigator") to avoid any association with detectives, though he would later return to calling himself an "investigator." The distinction here is a crucial one. At one level it suggests an affinity with pulp adventure fiction (and a continuity with the "gentleman adventurer" of "The False Burton Combs"), as opposed to the ratiocinative detective story, what Race likes to call the "detective of fiction."[78] At the same time, it privileges an individual agency in the action of the character. Rather than merely detecting or investigating, an agent actually acts within her/his world. As "a halfway house between the dicks and the crooks," Williams begins to destabilize the assumptions of the realist detective story by problematizing the binary between the law breaker and the law enforcer, and by doing so in a language that also sits between these two binaries and questions their fundamental differences.

In the classical detective story, "the dicks and the crooks" are in general quite easily identifiable.[79] While a uniformed police officer (such as the Prefect in Poe's Dupin tales) might have some difficulty understanding the differences between the two, the amateur detective (frequently in the employ of the police) will lend his talents to the legal authority and resolve any confusion in these identities. Nick Carter, on the other hand, might be quite adept at using disguises to infiltrate criminal gangs, but his identity as a detective is never compromised in these adventures. Race Williams, however, demonstrates an identity that does not necessarily presuppose two separate and opposed positions: this is not a disguise he can remove and return to bourgeois gentility.

By positing the existence of a "halfway house" between the two opposing groups that effectively define the genre of crime fiction, Daly begins to tear down the realist framework and epistemological structures of the classical detective story. The creation of a liminal space, simultaneously inside and outside the law, also undermines the distinction between subject and object that is so crucial to both realism and the detective story. Williams's narration initiates a fundamental distrust in the figure of the detective/narrator, whose complicity in violent acts and whose use of vernacular language make a mockery of the objectivity necessary in both realism and the ratiocinative detective story. No longer is the language of the narrator a transparent conduit for representation of a "reality." Instead, the slang-filled stories of Daly create a textual environment that bears little resemblance to the world of nineteenth-century realism. As a result, Race Williams, the violent "confidential agent," creates a story in which the compromised vernacular narration calls into question the very accuracy of its contents. As Williams says at the opening of the first novel in which he appears, "It's the point of view in life that counts," and Race's point of view, replete with slang and action, began to dominate the pages of *Black Mask* in the late 1920s.[80]

While many critics have been eager to dismiss Daly as a hack, the equivalent of an awkward growing pain that would be sloughed off with the emergence of Hammett as the dominant influence, a close look at Walter Benjamin's definition of a hack as "someone who refuses as a matter of principle to improve the production apparatus" might complicate this general understanding of Daly's work.[81] Daly did not necessarily improve the means of production for pulp writers; in an economic sense, the magazines were much the same before and after he published in them. Still, if "production apparatus" is understood in an aesthetic sense, Daly did promote drastic changes to the way the genre of detective fiction operated. Far from replicating the hegemonic standards of the classical detective story or the tale of the gentleman adventurer, Daly sought a third way, a twentieth-century "halfway house" in which binary oppositions between "the dicks and the crooks" came under question, and the means and narration of the detective assumed an aesthetic primacy over the "solution" to any mystery. While Daly's work is at times formulaic and repetitive, the formulas he established were indeed a new vernacular "production apparatus," one that launched the hard-boiled style and led to the more celebrated careers of writers like Dashiell Hammett.

"What's the Use of Getting Poetic about It?": Muckers and Modernism in Dashiell Hammett's Fiction

> THE CLEANSING OF POISONVILLE *is not a serial, but in reality is a series of adventures of the Continental detective who is drawn into a fight for life with the crooked bosses of a city, who have gone mad with the power of their own corruption. Outside of their gripping interest, these stories are remarkable if only for the fact that* their manner of telling points the way to a new type of detective fiction, *which in* BLACK MASK *is coming to take the place of the old, worn-out formula sort of gruesome-murder-and-clever-solution detective story.*
> —ADVERTISEMENT FOR THE SERIALIZATION OF HAMMETT'S RED HARVEST IN BLACK MASK, NOVEMBER 1927 (EMPHASIS ADDED)

> I'm one of the few—if there are any more—people moderately literate who take the detective story seriously. I don't mean that I necessarily take my

> *own or anybody else's seriously—but the detective story as a form. Some day somebody's going to make "literature" of it . . . and I'm selfish enough to have my hopes, however slight the evident justification might be.*
> —DASHIELL HAMMETT TO BLANCHE KNOPF, 20 MARCH 1928

While Carroll John Daly first utilized the hard-boiled style in his detective fiction, Dashiell Hammett more often appears in genre histories as the style's progenitor, an influence on countless writers who followed, in the pages of *Black Mask* and elsewhere. Hammett's engagement with the dichotomy of high and low culture has been of frequent interest to scholars of both the detective story and of modern American writing. Critics struggle with how properly to understand Hammett's relationship to canonical literature. His novels were praised by reviewers of the time and published by Knopf, one of the leading publishers of modernist fiction. His celebrated novel *The Maltese Falcon* (1930) was reprinted in a Modern Library edition in 1934, the same year the company published the first official American edition of James Joyce's *Ulysses*. If any American detective writer before World War II enjoyed literary credibility by association, it was Hammett.

Hammett's success in the realm of highbrow publishing, however, was not merely the result of a few publishers and critics enjoyably slumming in genre fiction. His work was taken quite seriously by the writers of far more canonical texts, most notably Gertrude Stein. When Stein returned to the United States in 1934 for the first time in over thirty years, she wanted to meet two cultural celebrities: Charlie Chaplin and Dashiell Hammett. Stein's literary celebrity had risen after the publication of *The Autobiography of Alice B. Toklas* (1932), prompting the publication of a reduction of her *The Making of Americans: Being a History of a Family's Progress* (1925) by Harcourt Brace as *The Making of Americans: The Hersland Family* (1934), as well as the 1934 New York production of her play *Four Saints in Three Acts*, a play first published in *transition*'s "Revolution of the Word" issue. As Stein describes their meeting in *Everybody's Autobiography* (1937), the host of the dinner was not quite sure who Hammett was: "She said yes what is his name. Dashiell Hammett said Miss Toklas. And how do you spell it. Alice Toklas spelt it. . . . Ah yes said Mrs. Ehrman now what is he. Dashiell Hammett you know The Thin Man said Alice Toklas. Oh yes said Mrs. Ehrman yes and they both hung up."[82] At the dinner, Stein and Hammett discussed writing. In Stein's version, she asks Hammett why it is that in the twentieth century, men all write about themselves, they are always themselves as strong or weak or mysterious or passionate or drunk or controlled but always themselves as the women used to do in the nineteenth century.... He said it's simple. In the nineteenth century men were confident, the women were not but in the twentieth century the men have no confidence and so they have to make themselves as you say more beautiful more intriguing more everything and they cannot make any other man because they have to hold on to themselves not having any confidence.[83]

It should come as no surprise that Hammett and Stein discussed the differences between nineteenth- and twentieth-century writing; after all, these figures are two of the most important influences on twentieth century writing in their respective circles. In a lecture given the following year, Stein would even call the detective novel "the only really modern novel form that has come into existence," and she worked through a significant period of writers' block in 1934 by penning her own enigmatic and challenging detective story, *Blood on the Dining-Room Floor*.[84] While Stein thought about the relationship of detective fiction to ideas of the "modern," Hammett would often use self-consciously "high" literary figures in his work, sometimes as pretentious buffoons ("The Girl with the Silver Eyes" [1924]), sometimes as megalomaniacal killers (as in *The Dain Curse* [1929]), and sometimes as detective stand-ins (Robin Thin, the poet-detective, in "The Nails in Mr. Cayterer" [1926]).[85]

This engagement with the literary has prompted critics to experiment with ways of allying Hammett's work with modernism. Stephen Marcus's seminal appreciation of Hammett in *Partisan Review* called him a modernist in all but name: "What Hammett has done ... is to include as part of the contingent and dramatic consciousness of his narrative the circumstance that the work of the detective is itself a fiction-making activity, a discovery or creation by fabrication of something new in the world, or hidden, latent, potential, or as yet undeveloped within it."[86] James Naremore called Hammett's prose "closer to the spirit of literary modernism" than Raymond Chandler's, and even went so far as to call *The Glass Key* (1930) "Hammett's *The Waste Land*."[87] Also emphasizing Hammett's thematic concerns, Jon Thompson "explore[s] the ways in which the combination of a number of ideological elements—Hammett's individualism, his skepticism toward bourgeois law and order, his philosophical and ideological relativism, the contradictory sexual politics of his fiction, and his rejection of rationality—produced the hard-boiled modernism found in *The Glass Key* and Hammett's other fiction."[88] Indicative of more recent shifts in modernist studies, Christopher T. Raczkowski suggests that the work of Hammett engages "modernist concerns about (or sense of crisis in) vision and epistemology; especially as visual practices and ideologies impact society through the legal and criminal apparatuses of the state that vie for explanatory authority around the genre's many corpses."[89] Along a different set of lines in contemporary modernist criticism, David M. Earle has seen Hammett and other pulp writers as part of a Foucauldian "subjugated knowledge" of modernism, a strain he calls "pulp modernism."[90]

While these critics all explore possible means by which Hammett might be included in a broader definition of modernism, the only work to engage Hammett's obsession with the idea of the "literary" directly is Mark McGurl's *The Novel Art: Elevations of American Fiction after Henry James*. Examining Hammett's letter to Blanche Knopf where he betrayed a desire to "make 'literature'" out of detective fiction, McGurl calls Hammett a "low modernist," a combination of terms that simultaneously rejects and embraces existing modernist hierarchies.[91] This insistence on seeing him as "low" comes, in large part, from the inability of Hammett's work to match up with his optimistic plans, laid out in that same letter, where Hammett says, "I want to try adapting this stream-of-consciousness method, conveniently modified, to a detective story, carrying the reader along with the detective, showing him everything as it is found, giving him the detective's conclusions as they are reached, letting the solution break on both of them together." Certainly, Hammett's awareness of stream-of-consciousness fiction and desire to emulate its method suggest that he had clear ideas of what he thought literary fiction was, and if he was going to "make 'literature'" out of detective fiction, he would have to move in this direction. Ultimately, he never wrote his stream-of-consciousness detective novel; later work like *The Glass Key* and *The Maltese Falcon* utilized different narrative strategies, eliminating all access to the characters' thoughts. While he calls this new method "something altogether different from the method employed in 'Poisonville,'" his Continental Op stories and novels (including *Red Harvest*, the novel "Poisonville" would become) come the closest to realizing this goal of a stream-of-consciousness detective fiction immersed in the vernacular language of the streets.[92]

It would be a mistake, however, to assume that Hammett had only begun to think about the concept of "literature" when the possibility of publishing *Red Harvest* with a reputable publisher like Knopf arose in 1928. Hammett's writing career in the 1920s had its own complex relationship to the idea of literature. Initially, Hammett attempted to publish in Mencken and Nathan's the *Smart Set* with very little success. Still, Hammett's first publication, "The Parthian Shot," finally appeared in this magazine in October 1922 (the same month Daly published his first *Black Mask* tale "Dolly"). Shortly thereafter Hammett began publishing in the pulps, placing his first story in *Black Mask* in December 1922, quite possibly at the suggestion of Mencken, whose ownership of and editing interest in *Black Mask* had ended about a year earlier.

Hammett's shift to the pulps was not an eager one. When he began what he would later decry as "blackmasking," he used the pseudonym Peter Collinson, presumably to differentiate his "serious" work in the *Smart Set* from his more commercial fare in *Black Mask* and another pulp, *Brief Stories*.[93] Hammett's literary ambitions were to be a part of "the smart set," but his work found a more comfortable home in the pulps, and after publishing two stories in the 15 October 1923 issue of *Black Mask* (one as Hammett, the other as Collinson), the Collinson pseudonym disappeared and Hammett put his own name to the rest of his pulp work. Unable to break into the world of literary fiction, Hammett resigned himself to working as an ad man by day and a writer of pulp stories by night. Like many other pulp writers who harbored secret desires of literary success, though, Hammett would not stop thinking about what constituted literature. Instead, in articles devoted to the art of writing ad copy, he would theorize about the nature of the "literary," while exploring the practice of literature in the pulps.

While Hammett's later comments on his pulp writing have often dismissed the idea that he harbored literary pretensions in his detective stories, in the late 1920s Hammett's own definition of literature was rather permeable. In the 1928 letter to Blanche Knopf, he considered the possibility of "making literature" out of detective fiction, turning pulp fiction into high art. Nearly two years earlier, after the publication of "The Creeping Siamese" in March 1926, Hammett had practically given up writing fiction entirely because of a disagreement with *Black Mask* editor Phil Cody. For almost a year Hammett stopped writing for the magazine. In the interim, Joseph T. Shaw took over the editorial duties and begged Hammett to return to the pages of the magazine. At this time, however, Hammett was working hard on his other career, his day job as a writer of advertising copy for the Samuels Jewelry Agency. Hammett's ad copy was creative and well received, and critics have suggested important links between his work in advertising and his detective fiction writing.[94]

While writing ad copy, Hammett was also theorizing about the nature of advertising in a series of articles published between October 1926 and March 1928 in *Western Advertising,* one of the more prominent trade journals on the west coast. The first of these, published during Hammett's absence from the pages of *Black Mask,* shows that even when not publishing fiction Hammett was thinking about the concept of "literature." Titled "The Advertisement IS Literature," this piece provides a fascinating glimpse into Hammett's reading practices in the mid-1920s, as well as into his own idea of what writers he perceived as sufficiently "literary" and what critics were reasonable judges of this quality. "The test by which advertising copy must stand or fall," Hammett writes, "is the test by which we evaluate every branch of literature. Goethe, Carlyle, Croce, Spingarn, Mencken are a few of the many who have put it into words. 'What has he tried to do? How well has he succeeded?'"[95] By concluding this list of critics with Mencken, Hammett not only alludes to his earlier desire to be published in the *Smart Set,* but also sets up the remainder of the article, which argues that the language of advertising (as well as literature) should be clear, but necessarily stylized.

"The Advertisement IS Literature" also suggests some familiarity with the *American Language* and the work of Ring Lardner. Hammett writes, "The language of the man in the street is seldom either clear or simple. If you think I exaggerate, have your stenographer eavesdrop a bit with notebook and pencil. You will find this common language, divorced from gesture and facial expression, not only excessively complicated and repetitious, but almost purposeless in its lack of coherence."[96] The aestheticization of this complicated and incoherent "language of the man in the street" stands as one of the central concerns of Hammett's *Black Mask* fiction, and is a hallmark of the "style" attributed to Hammett by Raymond Chandler in "The Simple Art of Murder." In Hammett's stories, how people speak is generally more important than what they actually say; on top of this, the Continental Op's slang-laden narration, while less abrasive than that of Race Williams, still suggests heavy mediation through the intricacies of a twentieth-century American vernacular. Hammett goes on to write, "You may read tons of books and magazines without finding, even in fiction dialogue, any attempt faithfully to reproduce common speech. There are writers who try to do it, but they seldom see print. Even such a specialist as Ring Lardner gets his effect of naturalness by skillfully editing, distorting, simplifying, coloring the national tongue, and not by reporting it verbatim."[97]

Implicit in Hammett's comments here about the literary potential of ad writing lies a subtle critique of realism. The work of Lardner, for example, does not present a mimetic representation of everyday speech, but creates an "effect of naturalness" through a stylistic mediation. Hammett suggests that even Lardner's work, so frequently lauded for its accuracy in recording American speech patterns, has undergone "editing, distorting, simplifying, [and] coloring." If anything, what Hammett maps out here is not just a methodology for excellent ad writing, but also a kind of manifesto for the literary aspirations of his own detective writing. Any form of textual representation necessitates stylization; there can be no unmediated representation of reality. When this assumption about the textual mediation of vernacular language is considered alongside the heightened subjectivity of Hammett's Continental Op stories, the self-consciousness of his vernacular modernism is clear.

Two stories published early in Hammett's career illuminate his subtle critique of realism and of the classical detective model and the epistemological assumptions of the ratiocinative approach. The first, "Slippery Fingers," appeared in the 15 October 1923 issue of *Black Mask* and was Hammett's last publication under the Peter Collinson pseudonym.[98] While this early story does feature Hammett's signature *Black Mask* character, the Continental Op, it does not yet display the mature vernacular style that would emerge later in the 1920s. However, it takes up the question of representation quite explicitly through its focus on fingerprints as a signifier. Fingerprints have been a convention in crime fiction since at least Mark Twain's *Pudd'nhead Wilson* (1894), where the title character uses his interest in what he calls the "physiological autograph" to clear up the mystery of a murder as well as a case of infants switched at birth.[99] Following the appearance of fingerprinting in Twain, the physical marks themselves act as an emblem of the scientific and semiotic nature of classical detective fiction. If one looks closely enough at a fingerprint (i.e., if one reads its details carefully), both its uniqueness and its authorship become clear. As in the criminal world the detective investigates, the fingerprint offers decodable details that allow for firm and coherent solutions. The fingerprint, then, serves as a microcosmic embodiment of the realist assumptions of classical detective fiction.

The fingerprints left by the murderer in "Slippery Fingers" are, quite literally, slippery. While the prints themselves are stable indicators of identity, the murderer doctors his fingers with gelatin during the questioning and fingerprinting by the police, producing a set of fake prints. To a certain degree, this story operates as a fictional extension of part of Hammett's epigrammatic piece "From the Memoirs of a Private Detective," published in the *Smart Set* in March 1923: "Even where the criminal makes no attempt to efface the prints of his fingers, but leaves them all over the scene of the crime, the chances are about one in ten of finding a print that is sufficiently clear to be of any value" (*CS* 908). Hammett's focus in the *Smart Set* piece is, appropriately enough, the debunking of popular notions about what being a detective means. In "Slippery Fingers," fingerprints do work as signs, but the mimetic quality of the sign as signature has become compromised though artifice and mediation. Such easily interpreted signifiers simply do not exist in the world of the hard-boiled private detective.

If "Slippery Fingers" calls into question how much a detective can rely on the traditional signifiers of classical detective fiction, an even lesser-known story reveals the artificiality of genteel language present in these texts. "Itchy," an obscure Hammett tale published in *Brief Stories* in January 1924, tells the story of Floyd "Itchy" Maker, whose criminal exploits are romanticized in the newspapers, which call him "a man of culture and refinement."[100] Itchy's vernacular language is anything but refined; it is clear that the newspapers have merely attempted to transform a routine burglary into the work of a "gentleman crook" to sell more issues. Nevertheless, Itchy begins to take the characterization seriously and to let it inform his own criminal identity. Soon, all the newspaper reports agree: "He was a gentleman crook, a brother to those suave dandies of fiction who so easily confound the best policing brains of the several continents," and Itchy begins visiting a local bookstore to buy and study the stories of gentlemen crooks, (mis)using textual models to craft his own refinement, much like Lorelei Lee of *Gentlemen Prefer Blondes* or Tom Sawyer in Twain's work.[101] Itchy's engagement with these texts evolves into a performative language that stresses the artificiality of figures like the genteel crook:

> He read aloud to himself in his room at night, and felt that his language was being improved thereby. Every day or two he visited the bookstore, ostensibly to inquire for new books, but actually for the sake of the saleswoman's conversation. The books could give him the right words and the correct combinations, but they didn't give him the right pronunciations. The saleswoman could, however, and not only the pronunciations but the right sort of accent . . . After he had returned to his room he would repeat everything she had said, painstakingly aping each trick of enunciation.[102]

This encounter stresses the class difference between Itchy and the saleswoman at the bookstore, as evidenced by "not only the pronunciations but the right sort of accent." The words themselves are not enough; Itchy must master "each trick of enunciation" to become a plausible version of an implausible (and fictionalized) gentleman crook.

Ultimately, Itchy makes great strides in his attempts at self-transformation, thrilling victims "addicted" to gentleman crook stories, but these ludicrous changes finally help identify and capture him. Hammett emphasizes the ridiculousness of Itchy's situation: "His grammar had improved by now until the double negative was rare, though tenses still puzzled him, and his accents were worth all the imitative labors they had cost him." Finally apprehended because he is one of only three men wearing dress clothes on the streets of San Francisco, Itchy delivers a line that he has long held in reserve: "I'm tired of you. . . . You weary me. You bore me. You exasperate me. You—you're a big slob!"[103] The first part of these closing lines are drawn largely verbatim from a story Itchy has read, but his addition of "you're a big slob" reveals the ultimate failure of his linguistic transformation and the veneer of the gentleman crook vanishes at the last moment as an impoverished concept that belongs only in genteel crime fiction.

While "Slippery Fingers" posits a world that is no longer legible under the traditional methods of realism, "Itchy" begins to emphasize the importance of language as a defining thematic concern of Hammett's hardboiled work. As in Daly's fiction, Hammett's work often featured a host of underworld slang terms like those featured in *Flynn's* 1925 "Dictionary of the Underworld." Hammett even kept a list entitled "Jargon of the Underworld," something he may have prepared for publication in 1931, though it remained unpublished.[104] Hammett's work under editor Joseph T. Shaw began to increasingly demonstrate the ways in which language could be used as an artificial form of representation, one subject to experimental innovations. After he took time off from publishing in *Black Mask* and began theorizing about advertising in the trade magazines, Shaw lured him back to his "blackmasking," and Hammett published his most ambitious works to that point, the novella "The Big Knock-Over" (February 1927) and its sequel "$106,000 Blood Money" (May 1927). These stories deal with the daring daylight robbery of a downtown San Francisco bank by a veritable "*Who's Who in Crookdom*" and the subsequent investigation and destruction (rather than capture) of the masterminds behind the crime (*CS* 555).

When the Op instigates a melee at Larrouy's bar in an attempt to break the case open, Hammett's narration begins to take on a decidedly modernist style, evoking the stream-of-consciousness mode that he would reference in the letter to Blanche Knopf just over a year later.

> A bottle came through and found my forehead. My hat saved me some, but the crack didn't do me any good. I swayed and broke a nose where I should have smashed a skull. The room seemed stuffy, poorly ventilated. Somebody ought to tell Larrouy about it. How do you like that lead-and-leather pat on the temple, blondy? The rat to my left is getting too close. I'll draw him in by bending to the right to poke the mulatto, and then I'll lean back into him and let him have it. Not bad! But I can't keep this up all night. Where are Red and Jack? Standing off watching me? (CS 570)

Here, in a moment of extreme violence, the vernacular modernism latent in Hammett's earlier work solidly breaks through. The first three sentences here operate as relatively standard narration for a bar fight in a hard-boiled detective novel; however, the minute the total change in the atmosphere becomes apparent (the "stuffy, poorly ventilated" room), things begin to transform. The Op acknowledges the air quality in the room because the lights have been shut off; suddenly sensory information becomes distorted. The sense of smell trumps the sounds of fists and gunfire that surround the Op in a dilated temporal moment. What follows is a series of questions, comments, and reflections directed at a variety of people. The Op is clearly talking to himself, but doing so in the present tense, placing the reader inside his experience of the barroom brawl. Rather than presenting a mimetic representation of the fight—impossible, since it is happening in the dark—Hammett presents a psychological impression of the Op's thoughts, rendered in the vernacular, as he encounters his antagonists. The shifts in time (past, present, future), the shifts in audience (the Op himself, "blondy," and the reader), and the shifts between placing the reader in an external reality and in the head of the Op all represent vernacular modernist efforts in experimenting with unstable point of view.

Importantly, "The Big Knock-Over" is also the first story in which the Op clearly fails at the story's conclusion. Of course, this operates as a narrative strategy to set up the sequel, but it also calls into question one of the central assumptions of the ratiocinative detective story. In the classic form, the master narrative involves, as Cawelti notes, "restoring the serenity of middle-class social order."[105] Daly, Hammett, and the hard-boiled writers that followed not only introduced the detective of action over reason, but they also complicated the notion that readers read detective stories for the satisfying conclusion of a "solution." The end of "The Big Knock-Over" does feature a solution to the question of who masterminded the heist, but the Op only realizes this in hindsight. The diminutive old man, Papadopoulos, fools the Op with his feeble appearance and the Op lets him go: "I had been putty in his hands, his accomplices had been putty. He had slipped the cross over on them as they had helped him slip it over on the others—and I had sent him safely away" (CS 591). The Op's naïve reliance on "realist" appearances fails him in the end.

This dichotomy between the realist and the hard-boiled or vernacular modernist sensibility is set up as one of the themes in both stories and is emphasized in the sequel, "$106,000 Blood Money." The Op's partner in both stories is the young Jack Counihan,

> a tall, slender lad of twenty-three or four who had drifted into the Continental's employ a few months before. It was the first job he'd ever had, and he wouldn't have had it if his father hadn't insisted that if sonny wanted to keep his fingers in the family till he'd have to get over the notion that squeezing through a college graduation was enough work for one lifetime. So Jack came to the Agency. He thought gum-shoeing would be fun.... A likeable youngster, well-muscled for all his slimness, smooth-haired, with a gentleman's face and a gentleman's manner, nervy, quick with head and hands, full of the don't-give-a-damn gaiety that belonged to his youthfulness. (CS 548–49)

Hammett's characterization of the "gentleman" Counihan evokes the world of Fitzgeraldian romance, and Counihan himself seems like a character out of *This Side of Paradise* (1920).[106] This characterization becomes increasingly important in "$106,000 Blood Money," where Counihan is easily corrupted by the money Papadopoulos offers him for protection. The Op, already aware of Counihan's part in the conspiracy, has him dress the part in "evening duds ... everything but the high hat" in an attempt to expose his flawed nineteenth-century romantic notions about crime (CS 618).

In the story's final showdown, Counihan gives a speech directly out of a classic detective story, ending it with "that, my dear Sherlock, about concludes the confession." The Op counters, though, exposing the truth behind Counihan's fiction. "You met the girl and were too soft to turn her in. But your vanity—your pride in looking at yourself as a pretty cold proposition—wouldn't let you admit it even to yourself. You had to have a hard-boiled front. So you were meat to Papadopoulos' grinder. He gave you a part you could play to yourself—a super-gentleman crook, a master-mind, a desperate suave villain, and all that kind of romantic garbage" (*CS* 631). The Op's indictment of Counihan is simultaneously an articulation and a critique of the conventions of the classical detective story and (as in "Itchy") of the fiction of the "gentleman crook." Counihan has been taken in by the Sherlockian fictions of Conan Doyle—he addresses the Op as "my dear Sherlock"—and acts accordingly. The Op's response ("romantic garbage") is, in effect, the hard-boiled twentieth-century answer to the amalgamation of realism and romanticism in the nineteenth-century classical detective tradition. Counihan is no Professor Moriarty, and the notion that a "super-gentleman crook" could exist is downright ludicrous in the world of Hammett's fiction.

Hammett's repudiation of the super-detective/super-criminal dichotomy also represents a move away from Daly's adventure-oriented tales. While Race Williams, like other Daly characters, is certainly no super-detective ("a halfway house between the dicks and the crooks"), he constantly battles criminal masterminds who provide the titles for many of Daly's novels (the title characters in *The Snarl of the Beast, The Hidden Hand, Man in the Shadows*, etc.). In Hammett's universe, virtually every character occupies Williams's "halfway house"; there are no moral absolutes, and the characters' drift between crime and crime prevention is often seamless and natural.

In a sense, however, Counihan's corruption is almost predetermined due to his particular use of language. A child of the wealthy, the cleanness and standardization of his speech suggests a dangerous artifice; at the very least, it signals the fact that he does not belong in the world of the Op. Identification and relative integrity are often demonstrated via one's language in Hammett's work. The tougher one talks, the more trustworthy one generally is. The Op, though his actions occasionally cross the boundary into the morally questionable, performs his integrity through both his narration and his awareness of the power language has to alter reality through aesthetic manipulation.

As Hammett's career developed, the narrative stylization in his Continental Op stories intensified, culminating in one of the most expressionistic detective novels of the twentieth century, *Red Harvest*. Serialized in *Black Mask* from November 1927 through February 1928 under the title "Poisonville," and published in a revised form by Alfred A. Knopf in 1929, *Red Harvest* operates as a total renunciation of nineteenth-century conventions of realism in the detective story.[107] On the surface, this novel seems rather "pulpy": stitched together from four related stories that editors in *Black Mask* claimed were "not a serial, but in reality . . . a series of adventures," the Op never learns what his original job in the mining town of Personville was and discovers the murderer of his original employer about a quarter of the way through the novel.[108] What follows is a barrage of gang violence and political power plays that expose the ruthless capitalist underpinnings of the town's corruption and ultimately decimate the town, causing the National Guard to arrive at the novel's conclusion.[109] Certainly the Op "solves" a variety of mysteries at various points during the novel, but the details of these mysteries recede into the background when juxtaposed with the wide swaths of expressionist violence that dominate the action of *Red Harvest*.

Central to the novel is the ability of language to make and remake reality. The novel's celebrated opening paragraph demonstrates how Hammett intends to thematize speech, language, and narration throughout *Red Harvest*: "I first heard Personville called Poisonville by a red-haired mucker named Hickey Dewey in the Big Ship in Butte. He also called his shirt a shoit. I didn't think anything of what he had done to the city's name. Later I heard men who could manage their r's give it the same pronunciation. I still didn't see anything in it but the meaningless sort of humor that used to make richardsnary the thieves' word for dictionary. A few years later I went to Personville and learned better."[110] This passage foregrounds subjectivity through the use of the initial "I" as well as the emphasis on memory, interpretation, and an epistemological relationship to the world. More important, however, are questions about the representational function of language. The Op recognizes the limitations of his own perception and the differences in regional and class pronunciation that make for a Menckenian "American language," and he suggests how these subtle differences can create wholly new meanings. At first, the Op thinks of this as purely a case of localized mispronunciation (like Itchy's lower-class "accents"); however, sometimes the way words are distorted by speech actually does have meaning (it is not just "meaningless humor"). Perhaps this "mucker"—"a course, vulgar person," according to Wood and Goddard's 1926 *Dictionary of American Slang*—knows more than the Op is initially willing to admit.[111] Language can be molded and transformed to more accurately describe a reality; this vernacular modernist innovation produces a veritable "richardsnary" of street language, that constantly innovative vocabulary that defines the hard-boiled world. A naïve view of language (i.e., one with realist antecedents) would not fundamentally question the ability of received language to accurately represent.[112] In a realist universe—or even in a classical detective story—Personville would be Personville, plain and simple. In the world of the hard-boiled, the power of vernacular language actually transforms Personville into Poisonville (not just linguistically, but phenomenologically). But the Op does not take language at face value; he has "learned better" by peeling back the layers of linguistic artifice to find a vernacular "richardsnary" underneath the realist dictionary.

In contrasting this passage with the openings of novels by Agatha Christie and Raymond Chandler, Dennis Porter argues that "the fact that Hammett forces the reader to pay attention to his medium suggests immediately that we are in the presence of a *texte de plaisir.*"[113] More than merely an example of Barthes's *jouissance,* Hammett's opening points toward one of the central concerns of *Red Harvest:* the ways in which the stylization and manipulation of language can actually alter and redefine the world it describes. As a result, characters that speak in an inflated, genteel language (such as the lawyer Charles Proctor Dawn) are examples of pure artifice, while "muckers" tend to speak something closer to the truth, even if their language revels in a vernacular artfulness. The "brittle" language of the hard-boiled narrator acknowledges that language is by nature a mediating force, and it also serves as a baseline for the judgment of other characters' integrity. To a degree Hammett extends this idea in the follow-up to *Red Harvest, The Dain Curse* (serialized in *Black Mask,* November 1928–February 1929; published between covers, 1929), in which the highbrow writer Owen Fitzstephan is discovered to be orchestrating his own melodramatic plot of murder. His facility with literary language is a key to his own corruption; when Fitzstephan asks the Op why he did not take copies of his literary works, the Op replies, "I was afraid I'd read them and understand them . . . and then you'd have felt insulted" (*CN* 207). Like the elite cultural characters in *Red Harvest,* Fitzstephan's literary abuse of language compromises his integrity and links directly to his homicidal plotting.

Similarly, in *Red Harvest* the Op short-circuits the intentional obfuscation used by mine owner Elihu Willsson, who wants the town of Poisonville cleaned up. Willsson says, "I want a man to clean this pig-sty of a Poisonville for me, to smoke out the rats, little and big. It's a man's job. Are you a man?" Willsson's strategy here is two-fold; he is eager for the "crooks and grafters" to be run out of Poisonville, one way or another; his use of metaphor is both a nod to the overblown language of the dime novel and a means of protecting himself from liability, since what he requests from the Op will most likely involve murder. The Op's response is typically debunking, bringing the language back to the level of the vernacular and away from Willsson's melodramatic metaphors: "What's the use of getting poetic about it? . . . If you've got a fairly honest piece of work to be done in my line, and you want to pay a decent price, maybe I'll take it on. But a lot of foolishness about smoking rats and pig-pens doesn't mean anything to me" (*CN* 38). When capitalist villains appropriate the language of the hard-boiled it is, the Op makes clear, painfully obvious.

Once the Op concludes the case in *Red Harvest,* he must come to terms with how to remain a loyal company man and simultaneously save himself from reprimand for his significant deviations from company policy. As he says, "I spent most of my week in Ogden trying to fix up my reports so they would not read as if I had broken as many Agency rules, state laws and human bones as I had" (*CN* 186). At some level this is a metatextual commentary on *Red Harvest* itself. To a degree, the novel functions as a vernacular modernist parallel to the Op's "report," complete with linguistic manipulation—a "broken" vernacular language—that never allows the reader to experience Poisonville outside of the Op's consciousness and highly stylized narration of the events. The Op's literary work, however, is all for naught as he claims in the novel's final sentences: "I might just as well have saved the labor and sweat I had put into trying to make my reports harmless. They didn't fool the Old Man. He gave me merry hell" (*CN* 187). As with the more ambitious aesthetic experiments of high modernism, textual obfuscation can work, but not with a trained, sophisticated reader, and the Op's vernacular narration in *Red Harvest*—complete with gaps and biases—emerges as the more accurate rendering of the Poisonville operation, an experience for which the hard-boiled vernacular is the best and only representational form.

Hammett's later work, like that of other vernacular modernists, drifted in different aesthetic directions. In *The Maltese Falcon* and *The Glass Key,* texts that have already received attention as potentially "modernist" novels, he modifies the vernacular narration utilized in the Op stories, turning it into an almost antisubjective narrative form. Here, the reader is allowed absolutely no access to the consciousness of any of the characters. The wholesale rejection of the subjective suggests the opposite end of the modernist spectrum: the distanced poetics of Eliot and Pound, the emotionless narratives of Wyndham Lewis, and Roland Barthes's conception of "degree zero" writing. The narration, however, remains clipped and brittle, an objective transformation of the vernacular style Hammett developed in the Op stories.

While the emotionally distanced mode of *The Maltese Falcon* and *The Glass Key* was certainly influential, it was the vernacular modernism of his Continental Op stories that had the most profound effect on the genre of detective fiction, inspiring writers like Chandler, Ross Macdonald, Walter

Mosley, and others. In works like "The Big Knock-Over" and *Red Harvest*, the foregrounding of language as part of an epistemological artifice, one that often conceals as much as it reveals, is at the heart of the hard-boiled. As writers like Daly and Hammett realized, the world, read through an individual's subjectivity, is not the objectively legible, realist environment of the classical detective story. Instead, it is filtered through one's consciousness and again mediated by the language used to narrate one's experience in that world. Not only do these writers suggest "the possibilities for writing in a modernist mode using the language of the streets" (as Jon Thompson has argued), they also use the language of the streets to imply the necessary limits of all linguistic and literary expression.[114] This complex attitude toward the "language of the streets," an attitude that invests the language of working-class figures with a self-conscious aesthetic sensibility and critiques the artificiality of the genteel, is a powerful element of vernacular modernism, an argument that also makes its way into the treacherous debate surrounding the politics of linguistic representation in African American fiction of the 1920s.

5 / "The Necromancy of Language"

Realist Uplift and the Urban Vernacular in Rudolph Fisher and Claude McKay

> *Maybe these Nordics at last have tuned in on our wave-length. Maybe they are at last learning to speak our language.*
> —RUDOLPH FISHER, "THE CAUCASIAN STORMS HARLEM" (1927)

> *If we are to believe the majority of writers of Negro dialect and the burnt-cork artists, Negro speech is a weird thing, full of "ams" and "Ises." Fortunately we don't have to believe them. We may go directly to the Negro and let him speak for himself.*
> —ZORA NEALE HURSTON, "CHARACTERISTICS OF NEGRO EXPRESSION" (1934)

In his decades-long work on *The American Language,* one of H. L. Mencken's most profound oversights was his willful ignorance of African American vernacular. While the second (1921) and third (1923) editions of *The American Language* highlight a variety of "non-English dialects," Mencken has little to say about African American vernacular speech, restricting his discussion to a handful of "negro . . . loan-words" and devoting not a single word to African American slang (*AL* 1:44, *AL* 2:54, *AL* 3:56). It was not until his second supplement (1948) that Mencken finally included one African American authority on black vernacular. In a brief discussion of slang, he cites Zora Neale Hurston's "Story in Harlem Slang," published in 1942 in the *American Mercury,* the magazine Mencken started eighteen years earlier but had long since ceased to edit. By the time Mencken's second supplement appeared, Melville Herskovits's groundbreaking 1941 study *The Myth of the Negro Past* had begun to dispel the rumor that African American culture was without roots and, by extension, without a linguistic self-consciousness. Herskovits and Hurston were both students of Franz Boas, and the influence of Boasian cultural anthropology on the study of American and African American vernacular speech and culture had become widespread by the late 1930s.

Mencken's willful ignorance about African American language was certainly not unique, however. In fact, his implication that African Americans merely spoke a degraded dialect form of English had been dominant since the nineteenth century and continued to inform language study in the 1920s. In one of the earliest issues of the *American Mercury* in 1924, Mencken published George Philip Krapp's "The English of the Negro," which argued that "the Negro speaks English of the same kind and, class for class, of the same degree as the English of the most authentic descendants of the first settlers at Jamestown and Plymouth."[1] Krapp, a professor of English at Columbia University, was one of Mencken's major sources in his writing of *The American Language* and was long at work on his own *magnum opus, The English Language in America,* which would appear in 1925. Mencken and Krapp often cited each other, so there is no clear line of influence here; rather, the two represented a broader phenomenon in which African American language was considered, at best, a small handful of "loan words" to the broader American vernacular, and, at worst, a linguistic atavism full of antiquated pronunciations, "because," as Krapp writes, "the Negro, being socially backward, has held on to many habits which the white world has left behind."[2]

Essentially, both Mencken and Krapp were participating in a long-standing tradition that saw African American language as necessarily a dialect that marked difference and inferiority. Krapp's article, for example, cites a host of nineteenth- and twentieth-century dialect writers as evidence of "Negro English." Perhaps the most notorious predecessor of this hegemonic understanding of African American language is James A. Harrison's notorious 1884 essay "Negro English," which argued that "much of his talk is baby-talk, of an exceedingly attractive sort to those to the manner born; he deals in hyperbole, in rhythm, in picture-words, like the poet; the slang which is an ingrained part of his being as deep-dyed as his skin, is, with him, not mere word-distortion; it is his verbal breath of life caught from his surroundings and wrought up by him into the wonderful figure-speech specimens of which will be given later under the head of Negroisms." While Harrison compares "Negro English" favorably to the language of poetry, only about half of his examples are innovative "Negroisms"; the remainder are actually "word-distortions" drawn from, as he admits, the dialect writing of white southerners "J. C. Harris, J. A. Macon, Sherwood Bonner, and others."[3] Scholars of African American language and literature have responded in different ways to this foundational essay. Henry Louis Gates Jr. highlights "its valorization of the figurative in black discourse," but influential linguist Geneva Smitherman cites Harrison's article as an example of how "white scholars . . . considered 'speaking Negro' pathological."[4]

While Mencken and Krapp were content rehashing old arguments about African American language as merely a malformed or underdeveloped version of standard English, African American writers of the 1920s began to return to nonstandard language in an effort to demonstrate the complex innovation of the black vernacular. Of course, this raised a host of issues in a climate dominated by debates about the proper subject matter for African American writers, the politics of black representation, and the potential negative repercussions from representing working-class African American culture to a largely white readership. The novels of Rudolph Fisher and Claude McKay contributed to this debate by initiating an African American form of vernacular modernism. In their fiction, Fisher and McKay reject the gentility of realist representation as well as the bourgeois environments and perspectives it implies; in its place they promote an aesthetic that values the creative potential of street slang. Countering the "uplift" tradition in African American literature that centered its narratives on virtuous, middle-class characters, both Fisher and McKay emphasize working-class characters, class conflicts, and language of what James Weldon Johnson called "black Manhattan." Their appropriation, transformation, and elevation of African American street language position these two writers as vernacular modernists, suggesting a framework for understanding the experimental language in both poetry and prose of African American writers in the context of larger literary developments in the United States and beyond.

"Shapin Words": The Politics of African American Language in the Harlem Renaissance

> When the artist, black or white, portrays Negro characters is he under any obligations or limitations as to the sort of character he will portray?
> —"THE NEGRO IN ART: HOW SHALL HE BE PORTRAYED" (1926)

Like so many protagonists of high modernist texts, the central figure in part three of Jean Toomer's fragmented modernist masterpiece *Cane* (1923) is a frustrated writer. Ralph Kabnis articulates concerns about his own creative process when he notes that "dreams are faces with large eyes and weak chins and broad brows that get smashed by the fists of square faces. The body of the world is bull-necked. A dream is a soft face that fits uncertainly upon it. . . . God, if I could develop that in words."[5] At the beginning of "Kabnis," the title character desires to develop these images into powerful metaphors that resemble the modernist language of the first two parts of Toomer's *Cane*. Later, Kabnis, stripped of his teaching position, drunk, and in the "Hole" where Fred Halsey "spices up the life of the small town," returns to the problem he faces with words.[6] This time, however, his language is decidedly different: "I've been shapin words after a design that branded here. Know whats here? M soul," Kabnis raves.

> "Ever heard o that? Th hell y have. Been shapin words t fit m soul. Never told y that before, did I? Thought I couldnt talk. I'll tell y. I've been shapin words; ah, but sometimes theyre beautiful an golden an have a taste that makes them fine t roll over with y tongue.... Th form thats burned int my soul is some twisted awful thing that crept in from a dream, a godam nightmare, an wont stay still unless I feed it. An it lives on words. Not beautiful words. God Almighty no. Misshapen, split-gut, tortured, twisted words."[7]

The concern of the writer and poet remains, but the terms of Kabnis's creative dilemma are nearly unrecognizable as they have changed from the elevated modernist metaphors of *Cane*'s first two sections to the "misshapen, split-gut, tortured, twisted" Southern dialect of rural Georgia. Introduced as a teacher and figure of Northern African American uplift, Kabnis's language is utterly transformed by his encounter with the South; he remains tormented about the ability for words to describe his language and experience, because, he exclaims, "they wont fit int th mold thats branded on m soul."

Kabnis's linguistic transformation represents not only an endorsement of dialect; it also makes clear his rejection of the bourgeois ideology of African American uplift, represented by the school president Hanby, who self-importantly claims that "the progress of the Negro race is jeopardized whenever the personal habits and examples set by its guides and mentors fall below the acknowledged and hard-won standard of its average member." Only after Kabnis rejects Hanby, who "affects the manners of a wealthy white planter" and "delivers his words with a full consciousness of his moral superiority," does he begins to speak in dialect and ponder the inability of language to "fit int the mold thats branded on m soul."[8] Kabnis's adoption of dialect in "The Hole" demonstrates a descent into racial identity, what Werner Sollors has called "hereditary qualities, liabilities, and entitlements."[9] But as Kabnis describes his "shapin words," he does so not in the high modernist metaphors that dominate *Cane* but in the nonstandard dialect of rural Georgia. Language fails him not because he has begun speaking in dialect; his shift to this language is part of his attempt at "shapin words" most appropriate to the experience he seeks to describe.

Ralph Kabnis is an unusual character in the early years of the Harlem Renaissance; in resorting to dialect to describe his experience, he runs counter to the dominant ideas about the use of dialect by African American writers. In 1922, the year before *Cane* appeared, James Weldon Johnson opened *The Book of American Negro Poetry* with a preface that attempted to shut the door on African American dialect writing, arguing that current African American writers "are trying to break away from, not Negro dialect itself, but the limitations on Negro dialect imposed by the fixing effects of long convention."[10] He follows by arguing for a racialized language that can still reject the baggage that dialect carries with it:

> What the colored poet in the United States needs to do is something like what Synge did for the Irish; he needs to find a form that will express the racial spirit by symbols from within rather than by symbols from without, such as the mere mutilation of English spelling and pronunciation. He needs a form that is freer and larger than dialect, but which will still hold the racial flavor; a form expressing the imagery, the idioms, the peculiar turns of thought, and the distinctive humor and pathos, too, of the Negro, but which will also be capable of voicing the deepest and highest emotions and aspirations, and allow of the widest range of subjects and the widest scope of treatment.
>
> Negro dialect is at present a medium that is not capable of giving expression to the varied conditions of Negro life in America, and much less is it capable of giving the fullest interpretation of Negro character and psychology.[11]

Johnson's preface embodies the central aesthetic problems of 1920s African American literature: how to "hold the racial flavor" without recourse to the dehumanizing hierarchies of dialect realism ("the mere mutilation of English spelling and punctuation"). Johnson's search for "a form that will express the racial spirit" is most clearly realized in his own 1927 poetry collection *God's Trombones,* where he boldly claims in the introduction that "*traditional* Negro dialect as a form for Aframerican poets is absolutely dead."[12]

Johnson and others were acutely aware of the politics of linguistic hierarchy; the use of dialect ran counter to what Madhu Dubey has called the "uplift" paradigm of African American literature, viewing literature as an ideological battleground over representation.[13] American literary history is littered with texts that used dialect to emphasize African American inferiority, and the aesthetic debates of the Harlem Renaissance often centered on questions of realism, dialect, and gentility. As with other marginalized groups (such as the Jewish American writers discussed in chapter 3), literary texts became the location where African American writers strove to demonstrate a common humanity through language; keeping in mind the potential and likelihood of a substantial white readership, these writers spun tales of a black middle-class existence that emphasized a similarity with the lives of many white readers.[14] This meant that African American writers were initially reluctant to embrace the nexus of dialect and modernist experimentation that Jean Toomer's *Cane* demonstrated. Realism and not modernism, critics argue, provided the most effective means of launching a racial critique of America. As George Hutchinson notes, "Adopting and adapting the tools that were most available, appropriate, and powerful in the context of the cultural fray, [Harlem Renaissance writers] affiliated primarily with a type of literature that critiqued, in a 'realistic' mode, the forms of American social hierarchy."[15] The prevailing notion, then, among these writers was that the mode of realism provided a window into images of racial injustice, unclouded by stylistic or formal obstacles, while modernism's emphasis on form over content jeopardized these same critiques.

Opponents of this relatively rigid position included writers associated with the short-lived journal *Fire!!* (1926), as well as other writers associated with the younger generation of the Renaissance, including Rudolph Fisher and Claude McKay. The denial of dialect and other folk forms, these opponents argued, amounted to a denial of "blackness" itself; in ridding African American literature of dialect and other elements of black vernacular culture, writers were turning their work "white." Langston Hughes's well-known essay "The Negro Artist and the Racial Mountain" (1926) stands as the most famous articulation of this position, but other writers in this camp made similar claims. In a 1927 essay entitled "Negro Artists and the Negro," Wallace Thurman set Hughes's poetry in opposition to works by Jessie Fauset and Walter White, who he claims wrote "just the sort of literary works both Negroes and sentimental whites desired Negroes to write."[16] In introducing the concept of sentimentality, Thurman evokes the "matricidal" modernist critique of nineteenth-century American sentimental culture.[17] Younger African American writers sought to represent a wider swath of African American life, including facets previously excluded from "polite" fiction. Shane Vogel calls this the "Cabaret School" of writers, which "was not all that interested in literary realism. It instead actively worked to undermine the politics of representation that governed the Harlem Renaissance."[18] Although some early histories of African American literature equate the depiction of controversial urban subjects (what Robert Bone calls the "low-life milieu") with realism, many of these figures challenged realism's standards of genteel conduct and mimetic representation.[19] Importantly, these writers strove not only to represent new elements but also to find in these subjects new means of representation, experimental forms that rejected the assumptions of realism. At the center of these debates lies one of the most important discussions of the role and responsibility of progressive artists with respect to racial representation during this period.

In 1926 the *Crisis,* the W. E. B. Du Bois–edited journal of the NAACP, published a symposium entitled "The Negro in Art: How Shall He Be Portrayed."[20] Running on an almost monthly basis from March through November, the magazine asked prominent American authors and publishers a series of seven questions dealing with the sorts of "obligations or limitations" an artist might face in representing African American characters.[21] Respondents included a number of white authors who had published texts about black culture, including Carl Van Vechten (the very first contributor to the symposium), Du Bose Heyward, Vachel Lindsay, Sherwood Anderson, Haldane McFall, and Julia Peterkin. Important white social critics such as H. L. Mencken and Sinclair Lewis also contributed, and influential publisher Alfred A. Knopf submitted a brief response. Major figures in the NAACP, the *Crisis,* and the Harlem Renaissance were also featured: these included Mary W. Ovington, J. E. Spingarn, Walter White, Langston Hughes, Jessie Fauset, Benjamin Brawley, and Countee Cullen. The narrative created by these responses is strange in its near universal agreement that, as Julia Peterkin put it, "for the most part I have small sympathy with propagandists of any kind or color. In my opinion, the minute any one becomes an advocate he ceases to be an artist."[22] Though some disagreed on particular issues—for example, that "the continual portrayal of the sordid, foolish and criminal among Negroes [was] convincing the world that this and this alone is really and essentially Negroid" or that there was "a real danger that young colored writers will be tempted to follow the popular trend in portraying Negro character in the underworld rather than seeking to paint the truth about themselves and their own social class"—the freedom of the artist from any obligation or limitation still took precedence in virtually all of the responses. As Miriam Thaggert has argued, "The *Crisis* symposium can be credited with raising the issue of black representation in a public and accessible forum and with disseminating the terms and positions that would shape future discussions of the Harlem Renaissance."[23]

It is in the context of this symposium that W. E. B. Du Bois's well-known polemic "Criteria of Negro Art" should rightly be understood.[24] Though not officially a part of the symposium, "Criteria of Negro Art" appeared in the October 1926 issue of the *Crisis*, the month immediately following the issue that contained Peterkin's response. After six months of the symposium (no responses appeared in July), there was very little disagreement among the contributors, excepting Haldane McFall's vitriolic response to a negative review he had received in the *Crisis*. Perhaps the leading questions in the symposium's questionnaire had not prompted the kinds of responses for which Du Bois, as editor of the *Crisis*, had hoped. Du Bois's essay famously declares, "Thus all Art is propaganda and ever must be, despite the wailing of the purists. I stand in utter shamelessness and say that whatever art I have for writing has been used always for propaganda for gaining the right of black folk to love and enjoy. I do not care a damn for any art that is not used for propaganda. But I do care when propaganda is confined to one side while the other is stripped and silent."[25] Du Bois's language here, including the use of the term "propaganda" four times in four consecutive sentences, responds, quite explicitly, to Peterkin's symposium contribution, where she claims to have "small sympathy with propagandists." Peterkin and the other black and white contributors to the symposium who deviated from the leading propagandistic questionnaire are certainly the "wailing . . . purists" Du Bois calls out here.[26] For Du Bois, the terms art and advocacy—seen as mutually exclusive by Peterkin—are crucially interrelated in the conceptualization of African American representation.

Though Du Bois's use of the term "propaganda" in "Criteria of Negro Art" has all but defined the essay's position on aesthetics, this overlooks another term that he uses repeatedly throughout the piece: truth. "I am one who tells the truth and exposes evil and seeks with Beauty and for Beauty to set the world right," Du Bois writes.[27] For Du Bois, "Negro Art" should exist at the nexus of truth, beauty, and propaganda, three terms that he links to the aesthetic impulses of racial uplift. This emphasis on truth hearkens back to Du Bois's earlier work in sociology, particularly in his 1899 study *The Philadelphia Negro*. In the opening chapter of this, Du Bois's first book publication, he writes, "We must study, we must investigate, we must attempt to solve; and the utmost that the world can demand is, not lack of human interest and moral conviction, but the near-quality of fairness, and an earnest desire for truth despite its possible unpleasantness."[28] Du Bois's emphasis on truth in *The Philadelphia Negro*, however, is dependent on certain normalizing structures; according to Shane Vogel, "Du Bois's statistical data and historical context produced both an economic norm—the black middle class—and a moral (sexual and gender) norm."[29] As Kevin K. Gaines has argued, although "Du Bois pursued [in *The Philadelphia Negro*] a vision of scientific truth that might undermine racist representations," his emphasis on middle-class patriarchal norms skews the standards of truth—and of what might be called Du Bois's moral realism—toward representations of bourgeois gentility.[30] "In many respects it is right and proper to judge a people by its best classes rather than by its worst classes or middle ranks," Du Bois wrote in *The Philadelphia Negro;* and the pursuit of a truth colored by what Gaines calls "the self-serving, class-bound assumptions of racial uplift ideology" characterizes Du Bois's approach to sociological truths.[31]

In this way Du Bois's 1920s aesthetics and his 1890s sociology derive from the same realist impulse: to represent the truth, but with a responsibility to uplift the race. For Du Bois, uplift and realism are inseparable and interdependent concepts: to represent the truth necessarily means to uplift the race, because, as he writes in "Criteria," "we can afford the Truth. White folk today cannot."[32] Any claim of the "purists" in favor of art for art's sake is met with a strong sense of the responsibilities of realist representation and its connection to racial uplift. In other words, just as Du Bois's sociological study emphasized the "better class," so must "Negro Art" orient itself to the "Truth" of this better class; the artist and the sociologist have a responsibility to position that "better class" as the normalizing force in the representation of African American life. In the name of "Truth," the "worst classes [and] middle ranks" are, in Du Bois's uplift project, relegated to the margins, much like the dialect figures of realist fiction. "The apostle of Beauty," he writes in "Criteria," "thus becomes the apostle of Truth and Right not by choice but by inner and outer compulsion."[33] This "inner and outer compulsion" suggests both psychological and sociological responsibilities of the artist, echoing Howells's statements about realism and the responsibility of the writer throughout the 1880s.

Although Du Bois's essay did not technically end the "Negro in Art" symposium (Charles W. Chesnutt's response would appear in November), its title and tone exude a finality, stopping discussion and attempting to make a definitive statement on the connections between realist representation and uplift. However, in the December 1926 issue of the *Crisis,* the symposium's narrative continued outside the bounds of the questionnaire. With a scathing review of Carl Van Vechten's *Nigger Heaven,* Du Bois brings the discussion full circle: Van Vechten's response in the symposium was the first published in the March issue, and Du Bois's review of *Nigger Heaven* sees the novel as a betrayal, claiming that "Harlem is no such place as that, and no one knows this better than Carl Van Vechten."[34] Other African American intellectuals would have more moderate opinions about the novel. In *Opportunity,* James Weldon Johnson defended the novel, claiming in interesting terms that "Mr. Van Vechten is a modernist. In literature he is the child of his age. In NIGGER HEAVEN he has written a modern novel in every sense. He has written about the most modern aspects of Negro life, and he has done it in the most modern manner; for he has completely discarded and scrapped the old formula and machinery for a Negro novel."[35]

Johnson's choice of words here, calling the novel "modern" and Van Vechten "modernist," is compelling; clearly, the term has traveled quite far in critical circles since this 1926 review. While this positive review of *Nigger Heaven* suggests all the ways in which its subject and approach are new, Du Bois saw the text as politically reprehensible and retrograde in its representation of African American life. In truth, the novel sits somewhere in between. Its representations are neither as old-fashioned and racist as Du Bois imagines nor as experimental as Johnson sees them. The fact that Van Vechten was the first person to write a "serious" and popular text that examined the underbelly of black urban life meant that the novel became a Rorschach test for the politics of African American representation in the mid-1920s. What is striking, though, is the degree to which *Nigger Heaven* actually follows the models established in other African American fiction through 1926. While Johnson saw Van Vechten as a "modernist," the narrative and structural approach of the novel did not pose any significant challenge to the forms and models of realism; instead, it confirmed them. However, Van Vechten's novel—which Du Bois called "neither truthful nor artistic"—provides an important link between the politics of representation and the study of African American language.[36]

As debates raged about the proper representation of African Americans, white and black writers and linguists began approaching African American language in new ways that sought to mark this language not, as George Philip Krapp did, as "socially backward," but as inventive and imaginative, a product of urban modernity. Probably the most famous example of this is Zora Neale Hurston's 1942 "Story in Harlem Slang," where the narrative is merely an excuse for Hurston to provide a glossary of 124 slang terms current in early 1940s Harlem. Hurston's glossary itself is a kind of modernist textual apparatus, analogous to footnotes, guides, and glossaries commonly associated with high modernist texts; in fact, her story is nearly unreadable without the help of the glossary. Hurston's longstanding interest in the ethnographic recording of language and cultural habits drew on her undergraduate work with Franz Boas, and "Story in Harlem Slang," like much of her fiction and nonfiction, revels in the interior logic of a culture without establishing a hierarchal relationship to some normalized standard. For example, she defines "Go when the wagon comes" as "another way of saying, 'You may be acting biggity now, but you'll cool down when enough power gets behind you.'"[37] The text of Hurston's story actually resembles Mencken's "Declaration of Independence" in its attempt to overload the page with nearly impenetrable expressions.

Hurston's glossary is the first example of African American slang cited by Mencken; it is generally one of the first examples of an African American glossary cited by historians of African American Vernacular English. As such, it is among the first recognized lexicons of African American language that does not present African American English primarily as malformed dialect, in the tradition of James A. Harrison. But the genealogy of the "glossary" of African American slang has a longer history than many historians acknowledge, and its roots lay in Harlem Renaissance debates about linguistic and cultural propriety. Hurston's "Story in Harlem Slang" follows close on the heels of Cab Calloway's music-oriented *Hepster's Dictionary* (1938); prior to that the most detailed documentation of African American slang appeared in the journal *American Speech*, which routinely gathered glossaries of terms in question. Julie Coleman's otherwise comprehensive *History of Cant and Slang Dictionaries* omits Hurston's influential (if unorthodox) glossary, but presents a series of late 1930s articles and glossaries in *American Speech*—including Norman E. Eliason's "Some Negro Terms" (1938) and Ruth Banks's "Idioms of the Present-Day American Negro" (1938)—as the earliest examples of African American lexicographies. While the presence of these glossaries charted an increase in the diversity of American speech forms that followed both Mencken's *The American Language* and a general Boasian turn in the study of culture in the late 1920s and 1930s, efforts to categorize African American slang and represent it as a fundamental part of the inventive and modern nature of African American culture has its roots in Harlem Renaissance aesthetics.

In fact, the first detailed description of "Harlem slang" actually appeared in Carl Van Vechten's notorious *Nigger Heaven*, the text that brought debates about black representation to a boiling point. Van Vechten's two-page "Glossary of Negro Words and Phrases" includes fifty definitions of contemporary Harlem slang, including four terms that show up later in Hurston's "Glossary of Harlem Slang." As opposed to Hurston's dynamic definitions, Van Vechten's glossary is rather staid; Van Vechten only becomes playful when he cross-references the sexualized terms "boody" and "hootchie-pap" without actually defining them, suggesting that—despite the reputation of his novel as an immoral depiction of Harlem—a sense of bourgeois propriety governs his list making.[38] It is clear, however, that Van Vechten took his glossary seriously; while working on the novel, he kept detailed notes on expressions and phrases he encountered in Harlem, some of which never made it into the published glossary.[39] Additionally, he solicited feedback on the manuscript of the novel from James Weldon Johnson and Rudolph Fisher, and Fisher provided specific feedback on a couple of terms in the glossary.[40]

It is not surprising that Fisher took specific interest in Van Vechten's glossary, since his 1928 novel *The Walls of Jericho* (discussed in detail below) follows Van Vechten with its own eleven-page "An Introduction to Contemporary Harlemese, Expurgated and Abridged," which features 110 different terms. Fisher's "Introduction" is quite playful, from its qualification as "Expurgated and Abridged" to its layers of cross-references, using multiple terms of "Harlemese" in sentences designed to show a particular word in context. In addition, Fisher's "Introduction," which features ten terms that show up in Hurston's glossary, does not shy away from more salacious and humorous entries. For example, "Haul It" is defined as "*Haul hiney. Depart in great haste. Catch air. It*, without an obvious antecedent, usually has pelvic significance."[41] Fisher's Harlem lexicon is, almost certainly, the first glossary of African American slang published by an African American. It predates Hurston's "Story in Harlem Slang" by fourteen years and presents an African American language of the streets as an example of truly modernist experimentation.

Glossaries like Van Vechten's and Fisher's form the earliest attempts at describing the language of the streets of Harlem. These terms are not malformed versions of dialect but rather new and vibrant examples of "shapin words" to fit modern African American experience. The discipline of linguistics also began to take notice of African American language around this time, and, perhaps most notably, the journal *American Speech* published Nathan Van Patten's "The Vocabulary of the American Negro as Set Forth in Contemporary Literature" in 1931. Anticipating Zora Neale Hurston's 1934 critique that "If we are to believe the majority of writers of Negro dialect and the burnt-cork artists, Negro speech is a weird thing, full of 'ams' and 'Ises,'"[42] Van Patten, a librarian at Stanford University, writes that "for seventy-five years, we have been gaining a false impression as to the speech of the Negro in America. Hundreds of novels and countless short stories have been written by authors with no first-hand knowledge of how a Negro speaks and without either a desire to present a correct record or any realization of why such a presentation is desirable.... No other race has ever been so consistently misrepresented in dramatic, musical, and literary forms as has the Negro."[43] Van Patten seeks to correct this disservice by compiling a glossary of terms drawn from four novels of the late 1920s: Claude McKay's *Home to Harlem*, Carl Van Vechten's *Nigger Heaven*, Eric Walrond's *Tropic Death* (1926), and R. Emmet Kennedy's *Gritny People* (1927). While his selection conflates the urban slang of McKay and Van Vechten's work with the West Indian dialects of Walrond and the Louisiana languages of Kennedy, he nonetheless sees the novels of this particular period as ushering in a new emphasis on African American language in literature.

The emergence of an African American slang as a literary strategy in texts by Fisher and McKay explicitly challenges the genteel realism championed by an older generation of African American writers and intellectuals. Fisher's "Harlemese" and what McKay calls "the necromancy of language" in his novel *Banjo* demonstrate how embracing African American vernacular language of the 1920s could be the most effective means of critiquing an overly cautious aesthetic practice that governed aesthetic ideologies represented by "The Negro in Art" symposium and Du Bois's decidedly realist aesthetic principles.[44] Long before Hurston's "Story in Harlem Slang" and the explosion of interest in African American Vernacular English that emerged after World War II, the writings of Fisher and McKay both cataloged and celebrated the vibrant language of the Harlem streets; McKay's work translates the experimental power of the Harlem vernacular across the Atlantic, giving it a diasporic resonance as it migrates to Marseilles in *Banjo* (1929). In *The Walls of Jericho* (1928) and *Home to Harlem* (1928), Rudolph Fisher and Claude McKay demonstrate a particular brand of vernacular modernism, attuned to the specific conventions of the African American novelistic traditions and to the politics of representation in the Harlem Renaissance. In their work of the late 1920s, Fisher and McKay seek to equate a black vernacular language with aesthetic experimentation and directly engage the anxieties surrounding racial representation that drove the *Crisis* symposium.

In doing so, Fisher and McKay both challenge the dominant narrative forms of uplift that characterized the early Harlem Renaissance, as well as the conventions of African American fiction since the mid-nineteenth century. Rather than focusing on an exemplary character that represents the possibilities of uplift in the black community, Fisher's novel *The Walls of Jericho* disperses narrative centrality, deemphasizing (and harshly parodying) the middle-class strivers while equating their experience with—and even subordinating it to that of—working-class figures. Claude McKay's *Home to Harlem* and its quasi-sequel *Banjo* provide an even more radical critique of these conventions, allowing the wandering vernacular figures of Jake and Banjo to dominate their narratives, while hermetically sealing the normally representative intellectual figure's experience inside the stories of these working-class characters in settings both domestic and diasporic. In both cases, these writers deploy a vernacular modernist aesthetics to revolutionize the possibilities for representing race.

"Any Language You Had the Ingenuity to Devise": Dickties and Rats in Rudolph Fisher's Fiction

> *Despite the objections of the dickties, who prefer to ignore the existence of so-called rats, it is of interest to consider Henry Patmore's Pool Parlor on Fifth Avenue in New York.*
> —RUDOLPH FISHER, THE WALLS OF JERICHO (1928)

Of all the major figures of the Harlem Renaissance, Rudolph Fisher remains one of the most enigmatic and least discussed. Like Wallace Thurman, Fisher died prematurely, but unlike Thurman, whose successes included the short-lived journal *Fire!!* (1926), the play *Harlem: A Melodrama of Negro Life* (1929), and the novels *The Blacker the Berry* (1929) and *Infants of the Spring* (1932), Fisher did not ever produce a major text that his contemporaries found fully representative of his talents. As a result, memories of him are tinted with a bit of regret as they suggest a writer who never had the opportunity to live up to his potential. In his first memoir, *The Big Sea* (1940), Langston Hughes eulogized Fisher in precisely this fashion: "The wittiest of these New Negroes of Harlem, whose tongue was flavored with the sharpest and saltiest humor, was Rudolph Fisher, whose stories appeared in the *Atlantic Monthly*. His novel, *Walls of Jericho*, captures but slightly the raciness of his own conversation. He was a young medical doctor and X-ray specialist, who always frightened me a little, because he could think of the most incisively clever things to say—and I could never think of anything to answer."[45] Hughes's evaluation of Fisher's work here is telling: Fisher was well known for his lively banter (frequently in "swift and punning innuendo") that could never quite be translated into literary discourse.[46] In effect, the case of Fisher exemplifies the difficulty in the mid-1920s for African American writers to recreate the vernacular language of everyday urban experience in fiction.

Outside of Hughes's memory of his quick wit, Fisher is probably best known for a set of small contributions to the history of the Harlem Renaissance. His short fiction and nonfiction, especially the story "The City of Refuge" (1925) and the essay "The Caucasian Storms Harlem" (published in the Mencken-edited *American Mercury* in 1927), frequently find their way into anthologies of Harlem Renaissance writing, and his second novel, *The Conjure-Man Dies* (1932), recently anthologized by the Library of America, is the only example of a Harlem Renaissance detective novel. While the novelty of *The Conjure-Man Dies* has led to a small amount of criticism on this novel, Fisher's first novel, *The Walls of Jericho* (1928), has effectively disappeared from the critical radar. This omission is disappointing, given the text's interest in setting itself within the debates around African American linguistic representation and its radical restructuring of the conventional bourgeois narrative of its contemporary models.

The critical invisibility of *The Walls of Jericho* appears to have a number of sources. First, Fisher had the unlucky fate of publishing his first novel in the same year that Du Bois's *The Dark Princess*, McKay's *Home to Harlem*, and Larsen's *Quicksand* appeared. This was by far the most productive year in the publishing of novels to that point in the Harlem Renaissance, only matched in 1929 by published output.[47] In the literary historiography, Fisher's debut novel gets lost in the mix with McKay's and Larsen's debuts, as well as with Du Bois's strange and ambitious internationalist novel. In fact, most critics merely group *The Walls of Jericho* with McKay's *Home to Harlem*, citing the second as the more interesting of the two books.[48] Actually published a few months after McKay's novel, Fisher's has become lost in the shuffle.

A second reason that *The Walls of Jericho* has vanished is its reception by contemporary critics. The novel did raise the ire of some conservative black critics, who saw its emphasis on the working-class environment and questionable language of "Jinx" Jenkins and "Bubber" Brown as retrograde.[49] However, Fisher tempered these comic characters with a variety of middle-class strivers and bourgeois "dickties," moderating the viewpoint of W. E. B. Du Bois, whose review in the *Crisis* claimed that "if the background were as sincere as the main picture, the novel would be a masterpiece."[50] While Du Bois found the comic characters of Jinx and Bubber "only moderately funny, a little smutty and certainly not humanly convincing," and considered "the main story of a piano mover and a housemaid . . . a well done and sincere bit of psychology," other reviewers had a completely different response. An unsigned review in the *New York Times* called the central romance plot of "Shine," the piano mover, and

Linda Young, the housemaid, "a rehash of regular late nineteenth-century stock melodrama," but praised the representations of the working-class, noting that "his piano movers, poolroom hangers-on, gamblers, bootleggers, 'kitchen mechanics' and other colored persons who are still permitted to talk their native dialect—however mixed with the special lingo of Harlem—have authentic quality and carry conviction."[51] The divisive issue of language is important here: for Du Bois, such language is merely "smutty," while the *New York Times* reviewer found "the special lingo of Harlem" to be "authentic" and to "carry conviction." Like Lardner, Yezierska, and other vernacular modernists, Fisher simply "permit[s]" his characters "to talk their native dialect," allowing these figures to experiment with language on their own, outside of genteel restrictions.

These competing reviews speak directly to the anxieties around racial representation that characterized "The Negro in Art: How Shall He Be Represented" in 1926. The problem with both these reviews lies in their insistence on seeing *The Walls of Jericho* as a text with a clear foregrounded narrative and a background full of "local color." Such formal constructions were commonplace in African American fiction from the 1890s onward. The central narrative of the striving, upwardly mobile figure dominated novels by Frances E. W. Harper, Pauline Hopkins, Chesnutt, Johnson, White, and Fauset. If working-class or dialect-speaking characters appeared in these novels, they almost always remained peripheral to the workings of the narrative itself and were certainly not figures meant for reader identification. For all its controversial depictions of working-class life in Harlem, even Van Vechten's *Nigger Heaven* utilized central characters that were representative of upward social and economic mobility. In all these cases, the restrained aesthetics and thematics of the texts themselves are closely bound to their reluctance to venture outside the black bourgeoisie for central characters. As long as nonstandard language is considered "dialect," it remains outside the center of narrative, always subordinate, always degraded. The narrative form, then, reinscribes certain linguistic hierarchies.

Fisher's fiction provided a significant alternative to these models from the very beginning. In his first published short story, "The City of Refuge," which appeared in the *Atlantic Monthly* in 1925, Fisher depicts Harlem as composed of a variety of interconnected classes, each speaking its own vernacular, and tells the story from the perspective of someone not "above" or outside of these connections but fully integrated within them. In this story the central character, King Solomon Gillis, is a refugee from the South, where he "shot a white man and, with aid of a prayer and an automobile, probably escaped a lynching."[52] While figures of the Great Migration would become central to the later work of African American writers, especially those associated with modernism (Hurston, James Baldwin, Richard Wright, and Ralph Ellison, to name a few), the use of Gillis as the protagonist of this story is a radical choice for Fisher. Southern and uneducated, the refugee Gillis with his accompanying Southern language is the antithesis of black protagonists in the realist uplift fiction published by African American writers through the mid-1920s.[53] In addition, Fisher does not exert much effort to justify Gillis's killing of the Southern white man; as a result, the story lacks the polemic of, for example, Walter White's *Fire in the Flint* (1924). Both White's novel and Jessie Fauset's *There Is Confusion* (1924) strive to make their central figures "representative" members of the black middle class, fully in line with Du Bois's uplift aesthetics. Even Jean Toomer's *Cane*, frequently considered one of the great exceptions of the period, mostly utilizes the standardized voice of the light-skinned, highly educated Northern visitor in the exotic and culturally "other" rural South.[54]

Gillis, however, is no leader and no symbol of African American uplift. In fact, he is easily led astray by Mouse Uggam, another migrant from Gillis's hometown in North Carolina. Uggam, also a vernacular character, exploits Gillis's lack of streetwise sensibility and has him unwittingly become a distributor for narcotics. As Uggam tells his boss, the cabaret owner Tom Edwards, Gillis is "a baby jess in from the land o'cotton and so dumb he thinks ante bellum's an old woman."[55] Fisher's story, then, presents a wide swath of African Americans: the green newcomer Gillis, the streetwise Uggam, Edwards, and, perhaps most importantly, the "cullud policemans" that astonish Gillis. Rather than merely telling the story of an exceptional middle-class figure surrounded by a dialect-speaking "folk," Fisher's story examines the ways in which the city reformulates identities and creates a diverse community—socially, economically, and linguistically. "The City of Refuge" does not depend on a central, educated figure, designed for reader identification and surrounded by dialect characters that this protagonist must understand, control, or reform. Instead, migration to Harlem has created a new community with its own unique and malleable vernacular language and culture. The Harlem of Fisher's stories is not characterized by the social hierarchy of realist uplift that privileges middle-class figures over working-class migrants. At its most radical Fisher's fiction tilts, as it does in "The City of Refuge," toward the working class and its vibrant vernacular language. In his most ambitious work, though, Fisher creates a narrative structure that eschews a foreground/background dichotomy and equalizes the representation of vernacular figures like Gillis and the educated protagonists that dominated African American fiction into the mid-1920s.

Whereas Carroll John Daly insisted that his innovative hard-boiled detective inhabited "a halfway house between the dicks and the crooks," Fisher's debut novel *The Walls of Jericho* creates a narrative that sits halfway between the "dickties" and the "rats," contemporary Harlem slang for self-important middle-class and poor African Americans, respectively.[56] As a result, the novel follows several different storylines. Most central is the romance between Joshua Jones, a piano mover known as "Shine," and Linda Young, a "k.m." (i.e., "kitchen mechanic," or maid) with aspirations toward becoming a secretary. Shine's friends and coworkers "Jinx" Jenkins and "Bubber" Brown provide comic commentary throughout the text and have an ongoing rivalry that reinforces a deep homosocial bond. The "racial conflict" narrative involves Fred Merrit, a light-skinned lawyer and typical uplift figure (his name is "Merrit" after all), who moves into a house on an all-white street near Harlem. Also figuring prominently are a host of bourgeois black and white characters including Agatha Cramp, a cold and unfeeling white devotee of "Service" (*WOJ* 59). The novel's conclusion finds Shine and Linda together after the destruction of Merrit's house, not by fearful whites but by Henry Patmore, the black owner of a Harlem pool hall who has long held an old grudge against Merrit. In *The Walls of Jericho*, Fisher weaves a complex tapestry of life in Harlem, refusing to focus on a single group because of class or education and instead pushing a narrative multiplicity that argues for a more representative treatment of all facets of life in Harlem.

While the novel largely classifies its characters as either "dickties" or "rats," Fisher himself is skeptical of these characterizations and plays with their implications at multiple points in the text. Still, the novel opens with a nod toward the class division in Harlem: "Despite the objections of the dickties, who prefer to ignore the existence of so-called rats, it is of interest to consider Henry Patmore's Pool Parlor on Fifth Avenue in New York" (*WOJ* 3). Fisher's invocation of middle-class objections to the depiction of "so-called rats" serves as an indictment of the unwillingness of African American writers and intellectuals of the period to examine the working-class culture of Harlem, and it takes another stab at Du Bois's anxieties over racial representation. These "dickties," presumably including many of the published African American novelists of the early 1920s, effectively ignored the life and language of this vernacular culture. This invisibility is also a function of geography: while "there are proud streets in Harlem: Seventh Avenue of a Sunday afternoon, Strivers' Row, and The Hill," Fifth Avenue contains "bargain-stores, babble, and kids, dinginess, odors, thick speech" (*WOJ* 4, 3).

The "thick speech" of Fifth Avenue is one of Fisher's central preoccupations in this text, as evidenced by the novel's appendix: "An Introduction to Contemporary Harlemese, Expurgated and Abridged" (*WOJ* 295–307). To utilize one of Henry Louis Gates Jr.'s signature theoretical constructs, by highlighting "formal revision, or intertextuality, within the Afro-American literary tradition" along with "repetition and revision, or repetition with a signal difference," Fisher is "signifyin(g)" heavily in this appendix.[57] The primary target of this signifyin(g) act is Van Vechten, whose *Nigger Heaven* concludes with a somewhat staid two-page "Glossary of Negro Words and Phrases." Fisher's much longer "Introduction" also points to the increasing interest in African American vernacular in linguistic and philological studies, expressly following Mencken's glaring exclusion of African American influences on English in *The American Language*.[58] Reviewers saw the glossary as an integral part of the text itself; in the *New York Times*, an unsigned review noted that Harlem "speaks a language of its own so different from any spoken by either whites or blacks elsewhere in the country that the present author has appended a glossary to make his narrative easier reading. The combination of narrative and glossary provides a considerably informing picture of negro life as it has developed in the urban jungle of our standardized tenements."[59] Fisher's "Introduction" provides a playful and interpretive paratextual "key" to the reading of the narrative, forming its own vernacular modernist critical apparatus.

Unlike Van Vechten's rather formal definitions in the glossary of *Nigger Heaven*, Fisher uses his "Expurgated and Abridged" glossary to emphasize the slipperiness of meaning in what he humorously terms "Contemporary Harlemese." For example, Fisher defines "ask for" as "challenge to a battle in terms that don't mean maybe," and explains "bring mud" as "to fall below expectations, disappoint. He who escorts a homely *sheba* to a *dickty shout brings mud*" (*WOJ* 297, emphasis in original). In this "introduction" to the language of Harlem, Fisher is only slightly interested in familiarizing the reader with a "foreign" language (in the way that Van Vechten's literal definitions certainly do). Rather, Fisher sends his reader looking back and forth in the glossary, since terms are frequently defined by other terms, as the definition for "bring mud" does with the words "sheba," "dickty," and "shout." In certain cases, terms are not defined elsewhere in the glossary. The search for a final, ultimate signifier can become a maze of linguistic referentiality.[60] At the same time, this suggests that the vernacular of Harlem does not exhibit a one-to-one correspondence with a "standard" language, indicating its own brand of inventiveness. The text of the novel itself emphasizes the modernist malleability of the vernacular. In Henry Patmore's pool room on Fifth Avenue, for example, "you could play for any stake and use any language you had the ingenuity to devise" (*WOJ* 5). "Harlemese" is, because of its innovative and modernist qualities as a language of the streets, a moving target that can only be roughly sketched—not completely contained—by a single glossary.

Fisher's text remains insistent that the language of "Harlemese" is self-consciously devised, rather than merely some kind of transplant of Southern dialect. Indeed, this is Fisher's own version of vernacular modernism, most expressly presented in the exchanges between Jinx and Bubber, whose narrative opens the novel and provides a parallel plot that suggests more than a mere background "subplot." Jinx and Bubber, friends and rivals, engage in a variety of verbal battles throughout the text, including what may be the first explicit literary representation of playing (or "slipping" as Fisher terms it) the "dozens" (*WOJ* 9). One exchange between Jinx and Bubber in particular makes clear these characters' own self-consciousness about both the malleability of language and its migratory transformation in the geographically (and linguistically) diverse urban environment of Harlem.

An argument begins over the proper usage of the verb "smite" in the past participle form when Bubber notes that it appears that Shine "has been smote sho' 'nuff, though, don' it." Jinx insists the form is "smit," and the discussion develops over two pages. Bubber asks, "What you know 'bout language?" and Jinx responds "Mo' 'n you. Don' nobody talk language down yo' home in South Ca'lina." Instead, they "don' talk 'tall. Jes' grunt," and Jinx finally tells Bubber that the "fact is, ev'y time you forgit you up nawth, you start gruntin' in yo' native language" (*WOJ* 89). One of the funnier exchanges in the novel, Jinx and Bubber's conversation about Northern and Southern languages works on multiple levels. In part, this represents exactly the sort of characterization that both disturbed Du Bois and fascinated white reviewers of the novel, giving extended voice to African American characters who are not explicitly part of an uplift tradition but who nonetheless have complex and interesting linguistic lives. At the same time, this exchange flies in the face of notions that these characters are not highly self-aware; instead, they seem fully conscious of how their language operates to the point of debating its proper grammatical formulation, as well as its regional variants. That one of these positions is technically "correct" is beside the point, since Fisher's goal in the novel is to highlight the vibrant flexibility of this Harlem vernacular. Far from the mere "gruntin'" of the "native language" of the South, the linguistic experimentation of Jinx and Bubber emphasizes the modernist invention of "any language you had the ingenuity to devise."

While Jinx and Bubber form the core of the linguistic humor of the novel, Fisher contrasts their inventive and entertaining exchanges with the ridiculous and clichéd language of the middle-class dickties in the novel. Originally introduced as members of an informal club "superiorly self-named the Litter Rats," both a play on their own literary pretensions and a suggestion that the "rats" of Fifth Avenue (like Jinx and Bubber) are anything but literate, the novel's middle-class African American figures are ruthlessly satirized throughout the text (*WOJ* 35). In contrast to the language of Jinx and Bubber, which self-consciously emphasizes its own inventiveness, the language of the dickties is ridden with clichés taken directly from bourgeois white culture. The first utterance of one of these figures is the exclamation "Preposterous!"—a sign of the preposterous and ridiculous nature of these characters and their language (*WOJ* 35). This explicit linguistic poaching appears most clearly during the General Improvement Association's ball, when the "Litter Rats," occupying the box of Noel Dunn, "the Nordic editor of an anti-Nordic journal," watch the spectacle of the largely working-class characters on the dance floor. Dunn and Litter Rat member J. Pennington Potter exchange empty exclamations ("Marvelous!" "Wonderful!") during this scene (*WOJ* 102). Later, when a fight nearly breaks out between Shine and Patmore, Dunn repeats, "Marvelous," "and after a moment, 'Marvelous!' cried J. Pennington Potter, like one who at lasts sees the light" (*WOJ* 132).

Potter may not literally have seen the light, but he has certainly heard and copied the flaccid language of the *white* figures that surround him. The larger suggestion in this scene is that Potter himself has little "ingenuity to devise" any kind of inventive or original relationship to language. Instead, the dickties of the novel are largely content repeating both linguistic and cultural tropes of the white middle-class, a practice that echoes critique made by a number of African American writers of the era, including Langston Hughes in his well-known essay "The Negro Artist and the Racial Mountain," published in the *Nation* during the same summer that featured the *Crisis*'s symposium on racial representation in art. Hughes ends his influential essay in manifesto-like fashion, claiming that "we younger Negro artists who create now intend to express our individual dark-skinned selves without fear or shame. If white people are pleased we are glad. If they are not, it doesn't matter. We know we are beautiful. And ugly too. The tom-tom cries and the tom-tom laughs. If colored people are pleased we are glad. If they are not, their displeasure doesn't matter either. We build our temples for tomorrow, strong as we know how, and we stand on top of the mountain, free within ourselves."[61] Hughes's statement about the need for African American artists to embrace their own experiences is manifested in the linguistic exuberance of the working class-characters in Fisher's novel, providing a bold contrast to the presentation of dickties like Potter in *The Walls of Jericho*.

In a sense, the General Improvement Association's Annual Costume Ball, in the section of *The Walls of Jericho* titled "Uplift," creates a running commentary on the debates and anxieties surrounding "proper" representation of African American culture. The G.I.A., a satire of an amalgamation of uplift organizations, holds the only ball in Harlem in which all sectors of society mingle. It also includes a significant number of whites, represented by Agatha Cramp, the cold figure of charity; editor Noel Dunn; Tony Nyle, the young and flirtatious first-time visitor; Conrad White, "a writer of stories about Negroes" (*WOJ* 115); and White's fiancée Betty Brown. These white figures are mingled among linguistically indistinguishable dicky African Americans in two boxes: one contains the more straight-laced members of the "Litter Rats" while the other is full of white aesthetes seeking thrills in Harlem, clearly suggested as decadent in contrast to Potter's group. An exchange between Betty Brown and her host, the flamboyant and "beautifully Ethiopian" Cornelia Bond, demonstrates Fisher's own hyperawareness of the politics of racial representation in the late 1920s (*WOJ* 116).

After the white writer Conrad White (almost certainly a fictionalized version of Carl Van Vechten) claims that "downtown I'm only passing. These . . . are my people," Betty and Cornelia discuss the writing of novels about African American life (*WOJ* 117). Betty says, "I'm going to write a novel much better than anything else Con has ever done . . . and present it as the work of a Negro." Conrad responds that two things will assuredly come of this. First, "You can be sure some critic will call it the best thing ever done by a Negro," a comment to which Cornelia responds, "As if that's paying you a hell of a compliment" (*WOJ* 118). Second, Conrad notes that "you can be sure that some fay will insist that it should have been more African." Cornelia glosses this comment by suggesting that "the critic's name . . . will probably be Rabinowitch" (*WOJ* 119).

The exchange here demonstrates the complex negotiations among black and white writers, African American critics, and the popular white taste for the representation of an "African" primitivism. Betty's proposed novel, itself an enactment of minstrel traditions ("I'm going to ... present it as the work of a Negro"), could be hailed both for its authenticity of representation (as Van Vechten's *Nigger Heaven* was in certain circles) and simultaneously criticized for being insufficiently "African." When Cornelia singles out a Jewish critic (Rabinowitch) as the most likely person to see such a novel as inauthentic, she speaks to the anxieties around both racial and ethnic representations of African Americans in other art forms, as well. The drive for an authentic black representation helped to obscure the ways in which Jewish Americans were already on the boundaries of whiteness.[62] By emphasizing a primitive Africanness in a work about African Americans, the Jewish critic might deflect social concerns about her/his own marginal status as a "fay."[63] Thus, Fisher is negotiating a host of competing perspectives here. On the one hand, the "Litter Rats" merely parrot the bourgeois language of the whites involved in uplift organizations. Simultaneously, though, this decadent group of writers and artists represent a parody of the white fascination with exoticism that many critics have seen as defining the Harlem Renaissance. The latter group, including Conrad White, troubles the idea of authenticity by suggesting that the public debates around the very notion of racial authenticity (in the white press, at least) have no grounding whatsoever. When white (or in this case, explicitly Jewish) critics become arbiters of black "authenticity," the very term is, as Potter might say, preposterous.

Importantly, though, this discussion occurs in the upper echelons of the Manhattan Casino while the dance continues below. As Fisher writes, "Ordinary Negroes and rats below, dickties and fays above, the floor beneath the feet of the one constituting the roof over the heads of the other. Somehow, undeniably, a predominance of darker skins below, and, just as undeniably, of fairer skins above. Between them, stairways to climb. One might have read in that distribution a complete philosophy of skin-color, and from it deduced the past, present, and future of this people" (*WOJ* 74). The debates occurring in the boxes above have, for all intents and purposes, little to do with the "ordinary Negroes and rats below," and it is significant that the novel's narrative primarily concerns the figures on the dance floor: Shine, Linda, Jinx, and Bubber. Of the bourgeois figures in the boxes, only the fair-skinned lawyer Fred Merrit plays any major role in the development of the novel.

In the context of most African American novels published before 1928, Merrit would most certainly be the central figure of the narrative. A light-skinned lawyer determined to move into an all-white street near Harlem, Merrit has all the trappings of a protagonist in a text by Chesnutt,

White, Fauset, or Johnson. Even the novel's title, *The Walls of Jericho*, suggests the destruction of physical walls of separation and racial segregation. As his other works (including the stories "The City of Refuge," "Ezekiel," and "The Promised Land") suggest, Fisher was fond of titles with biblical allusions. But, importantly, the reference to Jericho here is a bit of a ruse on Fisher's part. Instead of using the battle as a metaphor for interracial strife, the "walls" become psychologized and refer directly to the development of the piano mover Shine, whose real name is, appropriately enough, Joshua Jones.[64] Shine's own internal battle is itself a search for an individual authenticity; Linda recognizes that his tough attitude is primarily a performance and encourages him to plumb the depths of his own personality and tear down the walls that prevent him from experiencing life directly.

At its conclusion, *The Walls of Jericho* is the story of Shine's personal transformation from a member of a group of "rats" to an individual not wholly defined by his social circumstances; at the same time, it is an economic transformation from employee to manager of the piano moving company, though such a transformation does not alter Shine's language, which remains far closer to Jinx and Bubber than to the bourgeois figures in the text. Many walls come down at the novel's conclusion: Merrit's house is burned to the ground, not by racist whites, but by the resentful African American pool hall owner Henry Patmore. Shine's disdain for the dickty Merrit cools, and Merrit partners with Shine in running the moving company. Only by equating multiple narratives, characterized by a variety of linguistic performances, is Fisher able to achieve this kind of multilayered conclusion. The various walls—themselves all surfaces—must come "tumblin' down," as the novel's epigraph declares. Simultaneously, Fisher's text seeks to bring down the walls of representation entrenched in African American literary discourse. Through the elevation of not only Shine but of Jinx and Bubber as well, the highly self-conscious "devisers" of the vernacular language of "Harlemese," Fisher's text points the way for other kinds of linguistic experimentation in African American fiction.

"This Heah Language Is Most Different from How They Talk It": Claude McKay's "Rich Reservoir" of Vernacular Modernist Language

> But he admired the black boys' unconscious artistic capacity for eliminating the rotten-dead stock words of the proletariat and replacing them with startling new ones. There were no dots and dashes in their conversation—

> nothing that could not be frankly said and therefore decently—no act or fact of life for which they could not find a simple passable word. He gained from them finer nuances of the necromancy of language and the wisdom that any word may be right and magical in its proper setting.
> —CLAUDE MCKAY, BANJO (1929)

With the interest in literary and cultural studies of the African diaspora consistently rising following the 1993 publication of Paul Gilroy's *The Black Atlantic: Modernity and Double-Consciousness,* scholarly interest in Claude McKay has increased exponentially. McKay's career is one of the most visibly international of all the writers associated with the Harlem Renaissance: born in Jamaica, he spent formative years in Harlem, traveled widely in Europe and North Africa, and made political visits to the Soviet Union. His literary output is also widely varied: he produced Jamaican dialect poetry; highly formal poetry in standard English; fiction that centered on working-class and poor communities in Harlem, Marseilles, and Jamaica; literary and political essays; and an important memoir documenting his travels. As a result, placing McKay in a largely domestic tradition I have termed American vernacular modernism seems to go against the grain of contemporary studies of McKay. By doing this, however, I do not seek to challenge the idea that McKay was an internationalist (he certainly was), but to explore his heavy investment in the aesthetic and linguistic transformation of popular American writing during the 1920s. McKay's formative experience in Harlem and his acute understanding of the politics of representation in African American literary culture allowed him to see the experimental potential of what he termed "the necromancy of language" and to explore the vernacular modernist possibilities in the language on the streets of Harlem and of the diasporic "Ditch" of Marseilles.

McKay's career began with a peculiar relationship to language. As Michael North has argued in *The Dialect of Modernism,* McKay's work constitutes a series of "linguistic expatriations," from the artificial donning of Jamaican dialect in his early poetry, to rejection of that dialect for the "generalized language of empire," to a later interest in dialect in his fiction.[65] The bulk of McKay's work is itself a testament to the artificiality of language, its adoption and rejection, and, finally, its inadequacy for representation. In contrast to the dominant trend in African American literary studies, North's work situates McKay in the pantheon of Anglo-American modernists like Stein, Pound, and Eliot. Other critics of McKay see his work as primarily invested in a latent romanticism or in the popular standards of 1920s realism.[66] In certain cases, such as his 1925 Russian collection *Trial by Lynching*, McKay's work operates as a curious example of early proletarian literature, designed to radicalize the reader through clear depictions of social and economic injustice under capitalism.[67]

To a degree McKay's fiction has elements of all these things—modernist, romantic, realist, and proletarian—and when his poetry is factored in, the equation becomes even more complex. For example, Gary Edward Holcomb has recently suggested that critical understandings of McKay fail to properly account for all of McKay's tendencies, using the phrase "Queer Black Marxism" in an attempt to correct these compartmentalized misreadings.[68] Rather than trying to account for all of McKay's work, my interest here is in coming to terms with how and why McKay shifted from the highly formal, almost Victorian language of his early 1920s poetry to the "earthy" prose of his later fiction. He destroyed his first novel, *Color Scheme*, after failing to find a publisher around 1925. Relatively little is known about the contents of this novel beyond the notorious and memorable comment McKay made in a letter to Arthur Schomburg: "I make my Negro characters yarn and backbite and fuck like people the world over."[69] Drawing on references in McKay's letters, McKay's biographer and posthumous editor Wayne F. Cooper has claimed that the novel was "a satire in 'black and white' that ignored the genteel traditions that had previously constrained earlier black novelists," and that American publishers rejected it because it was "uneven in quality and much too explicit in its sexual frankness and language to be published."[70] In retrospect, McKay likened the conception of *Color Scheme* to Van Vechten's *Nigger Heaven*, writing to Langston Hughes that "it was written around the type of people in Van Vechten's 'Nigger Heaven.' You had told me that Van Vechten was doing Harlem for material for a book & I knew then it would be no 'nice' little book to please the exquisite taste of the Negro intelligentsia. So I was trying to beat Van Vechten to it."[71]

Many of the same criticisms were leveled at McKay's first published novel, *Home to Harlem*, despite the fact that it departed quite radically from Van Vechten's emphasis on bourgeois figures like Byron Kasson and Mary Love. Comparisons with Van Vechten were, however, inevitable. While white critics saw value in *Home to Harlem*'s more authentic rewriting of Carl Van Vechten's controversial 1926 novel *Nigger Heaven*, many black critics derided it for the exact same reason. Unlike the major Harlem Renaissance novelists that preceded him—White and Fauset—McKay chooses a central protagonist who is not a member of the "Talented Tenth," Du Bois's celebrated agents of uplift. Jake Brown is a working-class Harlemite who sets off for the prototypical modernist experience, the Great War. He soon discovers that African American soldiers are given menial duty, and he spends the majority of his time "toting planks and getting into rows with his white comrades."[72] Like the major modernist figures of the era (such as Dos Passos and Hemingway), Jake becomes disillusioned with the war. However, Jake's feelings about the war are profoundly different from the white enlisted men who see their ideals crushed on the killing fields. Because of his race, he never sees those battlefields; soon after his arrival in Europe he deserts the army and returns to manual labor in England by way of Le Havre. As he contemplates his return to Harlem, he asks, "Why did I ever enlist and come over here? . . . Why did I want to mix mahself up in a white folks' war?" (*HTH* 8).

Critics have never been quite sure what to do with *Home to Harlem* and McKay's second novel, *Banjo*, in part because these novels run up against the standards of realism that supposedly form the foundations of their narrative technique. *Home to Harlem* has been called a "picaresque" by a number of critics, but it lacks the larger narrative drive and ideological orientation of the picaresque genre. In fact, it operates more as a series of sketches with Jake Brown at the center: Jake's return to Harlem, Jake's friend Zeddy, Jake's friendship with Ray, Jake's recovery from syphilis, and so on.[73] The only thing that ties the novel together is the centrality of Jake to each of these sequences. In response to the difficulty of the novel's formal construction, much scholarship has shied away from the discussion of Jake, whose largely unchanging character refuses most readings, in part because he is drawn in a way that privileges performance and surface over attempts at psychological depth. Instead, critics have seized upon the character of Ray, the Haitian intellectual who appears in both *Home to Harlem* and *Banjo* and serves as a thinly veiled stand-in for McKay himself. However, McKay's narrative strategy ultimately posits Ray as an outsider in both of these texts; his presence—especially in *Home to Harlem*—is fleeting.

Some critics have seen the narrative of *Home to Harlem* as "framed by an 'intellectual' perspective"; however, the explicit framing device of the narrative is anything but intellectual.[74] African American fiction through the mid-1920s was almost always framed by intellectual discourse, whether that be a third-person realist narrator containing the voices—both elite and vernacular—or a first-person collector of stories (for example, Chesnutt's *The Conjure Woman* [1899] or James D. Corrothers's *The Black Cat Club* [1902]), whose educated narration both interpreted and mediated the experience of folk culture. The politics of this discursive relationship are themselves the uplift politics of dialect realist representation; this practice serves to mediate and marginalize—or at the very least contain and control—dialect characters in relationship to the standardized language of the narrator.

In radical fashion *Home to Harlem* turns this framework on its head. In three parts, the novel devotes the first and third sections exclusively to Jake, dedicating the second section (and the middle of the text) to the relationship between Jake and Ray as it develops during their employment on the Pennsylvania Railroad. Ray's presence in part 2 is actually further condensed when Jake contracts syphilis and the narrative shifts to his recovery in Harlem while Ray is still working as a porter on the train. The literal and formal frame of the novel, then, is not intellectual but vernacular. Instead of reading Jake's experience through the intellectual lens of Ray (the standard mode of dialect realism and regionalist fiction), the text asks its readers to consider Ray through the vernacular narrative frame provided by Jake. McKay has moved beyond Fisher's work, which puts these two worlds on equal ground; here the formerly marginalized vernacular figure dominates the narrative, giving relatively brief space to an intellectual who is increasingly troubled by his status as a representative of "uplift."

As a result, Ray occupies the simultaneously centralized and marginalized position commonly occupied by the dialect storyteller in realist and regionalist fiction. Ray's position is clearly important; it is analogous to Uncle Julius in Charles W. Chesnutt's "conjure tales." However, in being contained by Jake's story and experience (and by that of the title character in *Banjo*), Ray's language and character become objectified, set apart from the normalized world of the frame. An outsider, Ray's comments shed light on the narrative, but do not drive it. Indeed, Ray's comments about Jake's life provide an important window into understanding the value of Jake's character. Still, the use of Jake (and not Ray) as the guiding character in the novel separates *Home to Harlem* from the majority of African American fiction published in the 1920s. Even Van Vechten's *Nigger Heaven*, an important precursor to *Home to Harlem*, allows Mary Love and Byron Kasson, two clear representatives of the black bourgeoisie, to dominate its narrative.[75] The vernacular culture in Van Vechten's text is always filtered through the experience of these figures of the Talented Tenth, replicating the standard realist hierarchies in its representation of this strange and objectified environment.

Ray's position as the objectified intellectual in *Home to Harlem* and

Banjo means that what he says and does are crucial, but readers must always understand these in terms of the vernacular world that frames them. As a result, his literary aspirations and intellectual *ennui* have importance, but only insomuch as they reflect on or relate to Jake's world. Near the middle of *Home to Harlem,* for example, Ray rehearses the history of literary styles as a history of personal growth into an adult literary figure, a bildungsroman in miniature. Ray's childhood reading of mid-nineteenth-century romance ("*Les Misérables, Nana, Uncle Tom's Cabin, David Copperfield, Nicholas Nickleby, Oliver Twist*") gives way to "free-thought pamphlets" and "the great scintillating satirists of the age," including many turn-of-the-century experimental writers (*HTH* 225). But the changing world—including both "the great mass carnage in Europe and the great mass revolution in Russia"—has altered the very way literary representation works (*HTH* 225–26). Ray has "lived over the end of an era," and he seeks some new form of writing: modernism (*HTH* 226).

Though Ray does not use the term modernism, the examples he gives make it clear that he dreams of writing in the style of the high modernist writers of the late 1910s and early 1920s:

> Dreams of patterns of words achieving form. What would he ever do with the words he had acquired? Were they adequate to tell the thoughts he felt, describe the impressions that reached him vividly? What were men making of words now? During the war he had been startled by James Joyce in *The Little Review*. Sherwood Anderson had reached him with *Winesburg, Ohio*. He had read, fascinated, all that D. H. Lawrence published. . . . And literature, story-telling, had little interest for him now if thought and feeling did not wrestle and sprawl with appetite and dark desire all over the pages. (*HTH* 228)

Ray's—and presumably McKay's—desire to create modernist literature out of his experience speaks to a running theme in literature about the black artist in 1920s African American fiction. In particular, Ray resembles Ralph Kabnis of Jean Toomer's *Cane,* who mutters, "God, if I could develop that in words," after working through his own set of vivid images and metaphors near the beginning of that text's third section. In *Home to Harlem,* McKay takes this further, however, explicitly aligning the desire to create "dreams of patterns of words achieving form" with the experiments of Joyce, Anderson, and Lawrence, all major modernist figures. While the struggling artist appears across a host of fictional texts by African Americans during the 1920s, no text puts the desire to create so clearly inside the modernist pantheon as *Home to Harlem* does with the character of Ray.

The tormented artist, struggling to cope with the world through an inadequate language, stands in stark contrast to Jake, whose facility with language is naturally impressive. On first meeting Ray and examining Ray's French edition of Alphonse Daudet's *Sappho* (1884), Jake comments that "this heah language is most different from how they talk it," suggesting that Jake recognizes the artificiality of literary language and values the authenticity of vernacular social discourse in ways analogous to Twain's dyad of Huck/Tom (*HTH* 129). The levels of translation—crucial to the transnational McKay—are multiplied: Daudet's novel translates the themes of Sappho's works from Greek to French; and while Ray (a native French speaker) reads with facility, Jake, who has learned French in his brief stint during the war, reads and compares Daudet's text to his own experience learning the language as a social phenomenon. Literary language, language "how they talk it," and translation are all closely intertwined as Ray and Jake examine this novel.

When he distances himself from the artificiality of literary language, Jake simultaneously acknowledges the malleability of his own language in his daily life in Harlem, a phenomenon that McKay links directly to this fictional consideration of Sappho's poetry. Directly preceding his comment about "this heah language," Jake exclaims, "Bumbole!" Immediately, McKay explicates the importance of the word: "'Bumbole' was now a popular expletive for Jake, replacing such expressions as 'Bull,' 'bawls,' 'walnuts,' and 'blimey.' Ever since the night at the Congo when he heard the fighting West Indian girl cry, 'I'll slap you bumbole,' he had always used the word. When his friends asked him what it meant, he grinned and said, 'Ask the monks'" (*HTH* 130). As in Fisher's "Introduction to Contemporary Harlemese," Jake defines one slang term with another. In this case, Van Vechten's glossary is helpful: "monk" is short for "monkey-chaser," "a Negro from the British West Indies."[76] Jake's original response during this fight suggests a relatively sophisticated engagement with the linguistic: the West Indian women are fighting "in a language all their own," a phrase that also characterizes the language of Fisher's "rats" in *The Walls of Jericho* (*HTH* 97). The cross-cultural appropriation of a linguistic signifier (first the British "blimey," then the West Indian "bumbole"), the wholesale transformation of its signified, and its reformulation of meaning all point toward a specifically modernist relationship to language. The diasporic streets of Harlem have provided a host of vernacular terms with shifting meanings that both require and soon outstrip the textual apparatus of the Harlem lexicon. However, Ray's search for a language that can accurately depict a world where "thought and feeling ... wrestle and sprawl with appetite and dark desire all over the pages" fails in *Home to Harlem*, in part because he remains unable to recognize and value the vibrancy of Jake's street language. The answers to Ray's questions about language and experimental representation, though, are obvious and all over the text. In framing the narrative with Jake's experience, McKay make it clear that Ray's search for a language that can adequately represent modern experience will not be found in the works of the European literati but in the social discourse on the streets of Harlem.

Accordingly, the formally experimental moments in McKay's *Home to Harlem*—the novel's identifiably modernist representational techniques—appear when Ray directly engages the elements of Jake's world. These include Ray's experimentation with cocaine and his experience of jazz in a juke joint in Philadelphia.[77] In the chapter "Snowstorm in Pittsburgh," unable to sleep and terribly depressed about being "black and impotent" in a racist society, Ray takes the "neatly-folded white papers" containing cocaine out of Jake's coat pocket, thinking they will help him sleep (*HTH* 154, 157). What results is a page of kaleidoscopic, stream-of-consciousness prose rendered in free indirect discourse. His mind moves from visions of his home in Haiti to his experience at Howard University, "a prison with white warders," to a fantasy of African royalty. He imagines himself as "a gay humming-bird," "an owl flying by day," "a young shining chief in a marble palace," "a blue bird in flight," and "a blue lizard in love" (*HTH* 157–58). Ray's intoxicated visions, where "taboos and terrors and penalties were transformed into new pagan delights," replicate some of the stream-of-consciousness techniques used by the major modernist figures Ray idolizes later in the text (*HTH* 158). Likewise, Ray's experience of jazz at the sporting house in Philadelphia creates a similar experience, in which he is

> lost in some sensual dream of his own. No tortures, banal shrieks and agonies. Tum-tum ... tum-tum ... tum-tum ... tum-tum.... The notes were naked acute alert. Like black youth burning naked in the bush. Love in the deep heart of the jungle.... The sharp spring of a leopard from a leafy limb, the snarl of a jackal, green lizards in amorous play, the flight of a plumed bird, and the sudden laughter of mischievous monkeys in their green homes. Tum-tum ... tum ... tum-tum ... tum-tum.... Simple-clear and quiv-

ering. Like a primitive dance of war or of love ... the marshaling of spears or the sacred frenzy of phallic celebration. (*HTH* 196–97)

This modernist-primitivist fantasy emerges after the "piano-player had wandered off into some dim, far-away, ancestral source of music" (*HTH* 196). Grammatical structures and realist language fall away here in the face of the modernized primitive music of the pianist. The use of music as a means to open up representational norms emerged in African American literature in the mid- to late-1920s. Langston Hughes's poetry, in *The Weary Blues* (1926) and *Fine Clothes to the Jew* (1927), used musical metaphors to ground experimental verse, and Zora Neale Hurston's "How It Feels to Be Colored Me" (1928) describes a jazz orchestra "break[ing] through to the jungle beyond."[78] In the same year that *Home to Harlem* was published, Helga Crane, the protagonist of Nella Larsen's *Quicksand*, experiences a similar modernist-primitivist moment when lost in the throes of musical passion.

The cumulative impact of these moments suggests a solution to Ray's question, "What were men making of words now?" The problem that Ray has with coming into his own as a writer stems, in large part, from his inability to see the aesthetic value in Jake's language and culture. McKay's decision to frame the narrative with Jake makes this clear, and Ray's constant desire to, as he says, "lose myself in some savage culture in the jungles of Africa" speaks to his own need to distance himself from his identity as an intellectual (*HTH* 274). If Ray cannot discover how to become a modernist writer in *Home to Harlem*, McKay certainly can. Only by having his alienated intellectual character experience the unmediated culture of Jake can McKay begin to move his own writing into the realm of vernacular modernism. These experiential moments of the culture of a vernacular character like Jake provide the possibility not only for Ray to escape his own feelings of inadequacy and impotence but for McKay to experiment with language and representation. In effect, these moments are analogous to Jake's seamless adoption and transformation of the word "bumbole," as well as his constant use of a dynamic and elastic vernacular throughout the novel.

Ray's recognition of the value and modernist aesthetic of black vernacular language coincides with his first successes as a poet in McKay's "sequel" to *Home to Harlem*, *Banjo*, published in 1929. *Banjo*'s narrative is heavily fragmented and even less coherent than *Home to Harlem*; the subtitle of *Banjo* is appropriately "a story without a plot." Its central figure is Lincoln Agrippa Daily, alias Banjo, "a child of the Cotton Belt."[79] Banjo lives in a cosmopolitan Marseilles and carouses with a diasporic group of black expatriates from the United States, the West Indies, and Africa. As with *Home to Harlem*, the Haitian intellectual Ray enters the narrative in part 2, but this time he remains in the text until it ends. Ray's presence through the novel's conclusion is possible, in large part, because he comes to realize that his desire to become a modernist artist depends on his experience of the vernacular language and culture of the black expatriate community. Like Ralph Kabnis of the final section of Jean Toomer's *Cane*, Ray abandons his efforts to conform to a modernist elitism in favor of a "descent" into the working-class vernacular modernism of the "black boys" in the Ditch.

The consequence of this realization is Ray's most explicit statement of his appreciation of and indebtedness to the vernacular language of Banjo and Jake. For Ray, "Close association with the Jakes and Banjoes had been like participating in a common primitive birthright" (*B* 321). While this statement identifies the vernacular experience with two very distinct characters, McKay's emphasis on the social and communal nature of language and culture (a "common primitive birthright") acknowledges an alternative genealogy of modernism, one that emphasizes the collaborative over the radically individualist. Following these comments about "birthright," McKay's text makes clear the connection between Ray's new knowledge of the "making" of words and the vernacular language of "the Jakes and Banjoes": "He admired the black boys' unconscious artistic capacity for eliminating the rotten-dead stock words of the proletariat and replacing them with startling new ones. There were no dots and dashes in their conversation—nothing that could not be frankly said and therefore decently—no act or fact of life for which they could not find a simple passable word. He gained from them finer nuances of the necromancy of language and the wisdom that any word may be right and magical in its proper setting" (*B* 321). These "finer nuances of the necromancy of language" are, in effect, the lessons of vernacular modernism. Rejecting "the rotten-dead stock words"—akin to Eugene Jolas's rejection of "the hegemony of the banal word [and] monotonous syntax"—"the Jakes and Banjoes" exhibit a relationship to language reminiscent of Anzia Yezierska's claims that "the foreign mind works on an old language like the surging leaven of youth. It rekindles and recreates our speech. Trite words, stale phrases, break up into new rhythms in the driving urge to express more vitally the rush of new experience, the fire of changing personality."[80] If neither Ray nor McKay has emerged fully as a modernist artist at the end of these two novels, it is because it takes them both until the final pages of *Banjo* to see the powerful relationship between the experimental nature of vernacular language and that of vernacular modernist forms of representation.

In *The Dialect of Modernism,* Michael North has argued that modernist writers display "a realization that language exists and grows by inclusion, that it is most accurately placed not within land boundaries but somewhere on the high seas, in keeping of travelers and linguisters. Language itself is in a condition of spiritual truancy, a condition that has been most apparent, in this century at least, to those who have been truants themselves."[81] In this study, North includes McKay in an elite group of high modernists, a practice becoming increasingly more common in the study of American and black diasporic literature. Seeing McKay purely as an expatriate, and equating his expatriate experience with that of Anglo-American writers who found their styles abroad, threatens to reinscribe the central hierarchies of modernist canonization, privileging the continental European experience of internationalists. The reasoning follows that because McKay traveled widely in Europe during the 1920s (and experienced what North calls "spiritual truancy" and what Lukács might term "transcendental homelessness"), he must be a modernist.[82]

By contrast, this reconsideration argues that McKay's modernism was both vernacular and diasporic. Acknowledging McKay's investments in the broader linguistic concerns of American popular literature and of Harlem Renaissance debates about racial representation enables a reading of McKay's work as part of the broad and complex vernacular modernist experimentation of the 1910s and 1920s. McKay's most explicit interests were first and foremost with the American publishing scene, as his experience in 1925 with the aborted *Color Scheme* manuscript demonstrated. His desire to shock American audiences with a frank depiction of black vernacular culture ("I make my Negro characters yarn and backbite and fuck like people the world over") failed when this manuscript was rejected. By 1925 experimental vernacular language had become mainstream in a number of genres, including comedy and memoir, and it was beginning to dominate the pages of pulp crime magazines. In African American fiction, however, the relationship to vernacular language had more significant obstacles to overcome, such as the continuing use of dialect to reinforce racial hierarchies and pernicious stereotypes in the work of popular white magazine writers like Octavus Roy Cohen. After a number of scandalous 1926 publications, including the journal *Fire!!* and Van Vechten's *Nigger Heaven* (the book to which *Home to Harlem* was most frequently compared), the American popular readership was a great deal more amenable to (and even significantly titillated by) challenging depictions of black urban culture. McKay's texts operate in dialogue with Van Vechten's novel, removing the intellectual framework and suggesting the powerful modernist representational strategies in vernacular language.

What *Home to Harlem* and *Banjo* accomplish, however, is both to break free from the realist uplift tradition that dominated African American fiction of the period *and* to challenge the racist depictions of popular white writers by imbuing working-class characters with a textual and linguistic self-consciousness all their own. Rather than borrowing models from the international crowd of white expatriate modernists, McKay derives his modernist experimentation from the black vernacular of Harlem, and in *Banjo* he translates the experimental practice and outlook of a broadly cross-class and cross-ethnic American vernacular modernism into the international and diasporic space of the Ditch in Marseilles. While white, high modernist writers were struggling to rid themselves of "the rotten-dead stock words" of realist language, Ray, McKay's stand-in in these texts, recognizes that the inventive black vernacular of the international cast of working-class characters that surround him has already done this modernist work. In this sense, McKay's work, like the work of Rudolph Fisher, elevates African American slang as a truly modern (and modernist) form of linguistic encounter with the world; it does not hearken back to a romanticized past imbued with dialect. For McKay and Fisher, the "necromancy of language" is the vanguard of a black vernacular modernism that sees aesthetic and linguistic value in "any language [they] had the ingenuity to devise." Ultimately, these writers issue a call for their own "Revolution of the Word" that becomes more present in subsequent African American fiction of the 1930s and beyond.

Conclusion

Modernism's Familial Relations

The repurposing of Theodore Irwin's "Slanguage: 1929" in *transition*'s "Revolution of the Word" issue marks not only an acknowledgment of the aesthetics of vernacular modernism, but also an early sign of its incorporation by high modernism. Largely confined to the popular realm during the 1910s and 1920s, by 1929 the Mencken-influenced strain of vernacular modernism would begin to cross-pollinate the work of its high modernist relatives. This was the beginning of what Michael Denning has called "the 'proletarianization' of American culture, the increased influence on and participation of working-class Americans in the world of culture and the arts": and it marked not only a politicized entrance of working-class Americans "into the world of culture," but also the attention by the producers of culture to the lives, conditions, and subjectivities of working-class individuals.[1] For example, in 1934 Philip Rahv and Wallace Phelps, editors of the *Partisan Review*, attempted to articulate a political aesthetic that could draw on both proletarian realism and modernist narrative forms, arguing that "the measure of a revolutionary writer's success lies not only in his sensitiveness to proletarian material, but also in his ability to create new landmarks in the perception of reality."[2] While politically committed writers on the Left were imbibing modernist aesthetics, high modernists were increasingly drawn toward proletarian subjectivities and the vernacular language that accompanied them. Following a decade and a half of focus on working-class readers and language, vernacular modernism provided a model for writers in the 1930s.

Writers and critics of the period explicitly acknowledged this debt to their vernacular modernist predecessors. Take, for example, John Dos Passos's celebrated *U.S.A.* trilogy (1930, 1932, 1936). When he collected the three volumes in 1937, Dos Passos added an introductory section, titled "U.S.A.," that included the evocative phrase, "But mostly U.S.A. is the speech of the people."³ Dos Passos's attention to vernacular language throughout the three novels is one of the more notable achievements of *U.S.A.*, and this did not go unnoticed by critics of the time. In a 1930 review of *The 42nd Parallel,* the first novel in the trilogy, Edmund Wilson writes, "For the method of *The 42nd Parallel,* Dos Passos has perhaps gone to school to Ring Lardner and Anita Loos; he is, at any rate, the first of our writers—with the possible exception of Mark Twain—who has successfully used colloquial American for a novel of the highest artistic seriousness.... He still has moments of allowing his people to contract into two-dimensional caricatures of qualities or forces he hates; but, in general, we live their lives, we look at the world through their eyes."⁴ What is striking about Wilson's comment here is that he effectively sees Dos Passos as an extension of the "unfulfilled" promise of Lardner, whose failure to translate his talent into more ambitious works frustrated Wilson, Fitzgerald, and others, as I outlined in chapter 2. Still, Wilson, who had been working on his canonizing modernist history *Axel's Castle* since at least 1928, clearly had the experimental principles of modernist aesthetics in mind when he reviewed *The 42nd Parallel.*⁵ Additionally, Wilson's language here ("we live their lives, we look at the world through their eyes") echoes Virginia Woolf's review of Lardner's *You Know Me Al* as well as her theoretical writing on modernism. What Woolf had seen in Lardner's 1916 humor novel about a semiliterate baseball player, Wilson sees in Dos Passos's "novel of the highest artistic seriousness." Twenty-first-century critics of modernism might find the link between Lardner and Dos Passos obscure and unconventional, but for Wilson, whose formation of one of the earliest modernist canons has continued to exert influence on thinking about the boundaries of modernism, Dos Passos's work was a direct outgrowth of a vernacular modernist line running through Twain, Lardner, and Loos, and *The 42nd Parallel* all but fulfilled the promise of Lardner's vernacular aesthetics.

In addition to Dos Passos's completion of *The 42nd Parallel* (published in early 1930), the year 1929 includes not only Irwin's "Slanguage," but also a number of other instances of what might be called vernacular modernist crossover. This is the year that Ring Lardner's collection *Round Up* was published by Scribner's and the year Dashiell Hammett's *Red Harvest* appeared to great acclaim from Knopf. It was also the year of Michael Gold's first book of sketches, *120 Million*, and of Claude McKay's second novel, *Banjo*. Clearly, the success of vernacular modernism at the end of the 1920s was setting the stage for its 1930s adoption by high modernist figures like Henry Roth, whose *Call It Sleep* (1934) more obviously recycles Joycean aesthetic paradigms and fuses them with a Yiddish-inflected English reminiscent of Anzia Yezierska. Zora Neale Hurston's work (begun in the mid-1920s, but more fully realized in the 1930s) extends Fisher and McKay's experiments with language, narration, and propriety into what Henry Louis Gates Jr. has called a "speakerly text."[6] Ultimately, a host of writers of the 1930s, some instantly canonized, others adopted more recently into discussions of modernism, began experimenting in earnest with variations on what H. L. Mencken called the "American Language" and its modernistic "steady reaching out for new and vivid forms." Even Mencken revisited his *magnum opus* for a final 1936 edition of *The American Language*, largely rewritten and with a considerably expanded section on "American Slang" and a much more diverse appendix of "Non-English Dialects in America." But despite the many prominent signs of vernacular modernism across the American literary landscape, perhaps the most explicit example of this symbolic integration of vernacular and high modernist form is found in the fiction of William Faulkner.

Faulkner has always represented an anomaly in American modernism. While figures like Eliot, Pound, Hemingway, Dos Passos, and Stein, with their continental associations, are easily incorporated into larger narratives about transatlantic and transnational modernism, Faulkner remains resolutely provincial—a writer who never expatriated himself from the United States, who wrote from an explicitly regional perspective in a region that was much farther from European and transnational sensibilities than, for example, William Carlos Williams's New Jersey.[7] In this way, Faulkner has long stood as the most specifically "American" of the American modernists, and as a chronicler of the U.S. South with roots in Southwestern humor, he too has been linked quite explicitly to Twain and the traditions of American literature from some of the earliest critical considerations of his work.[8] Faulkner himself acknowledged his debt to Twain in a 1955 interview, where he called Twain "the first truly American writer, and all of us since are his heirs, we descended from him."[9]

Like many of the writers considered in *The Word on the Streets*—and many of the canonical figures of the period as well—Faulkner straddled the line between high and popular, and his engagement with popular culture is already the subject of a significant amount of criticism.[10] He wrote a great deal of genre fiction, including the detective novel *Intruder in the*

Dust (1948); detective stories published in the collection *Knight's Gambit* (1949); the sensational crime novel *Sanctuary* (1931), which he called "a cheap idea ... deliberately conceived to make money"; *Pylon* (1935), a text seemingly in dialogue with the early 1930s explosion of aviation pulps; and *If I Forget the Jerusalem* (1939), which features a character who writes for the romance pulps.[11] Even Faulkner's more celebrated texts exhibit traces of popular influence; Christopher Breu, for example, has even outlined the importance of the pulp construction of masculinity to *Light in August* (1932).[12] Critics have also noted how easily Faulkner's work was appropriated by mid-twentieth-century popular culture. Indeed, a number of Faulkner's novels of the 1930s ended up in pulp paperback editions on drugstore racks in the 1940s and 1950s alongside the works of Jim Thompson and Raymond Chandler.[13]

But Faulkner's engagement with popular fiction goes beyond the mere recycling of genre formulas as literary fodder; his work is emblematic of the interconnectedness of experimental vernacular and high modernist modes. Beginning with the Lardneresque letters in his first novel *Soldier's Pay* (1926), Faulkner's work attends to the complexities and experimental possibilities of vernacular language. As with the high modernists of *transition*, Faulkner seemed acutely aware of how the vernacular voice and the modernist voice together create the interlaced complexities of American modernism. Indeed, Faulkner's linguistic approach often makes the stylistic and syntactical boundaries between narration, interior monologue, and dialogue quite permeable. While later works would explore in more depth the complexities of history and narration, Faulkner's celebrated novel *The Sound and the Fury*, which appeared only a few months after *transition*'s publication of "Slanguage: 1929," demonstrates the interrelated modes of American modernism, suggesting that high and vernacular modernism have an interdependent relationship and that the story of American modernism remains incomplete without the explicit acknowledgment a plurality of modernistic voices.

Modernism's various interrelated strands appear in *The Sound and the Fury*'s narrative structure, one of its most influential features. Told in four different voices, *The Sound and the Fury* moves from the most difficult and subjective narration (of Benjy Compson) toward a more comprehensible and objective, but perhaps less "truthful," third-person narration. The two central sections of the novel are narrated by the brothers Quentin and Jason, whose narrative styles and situations could not be more different. Quentin's sensitive and introspective nature contrasts strongly with Jason's brash and angry misogyny. However, these two central sections, in effect, form the "heart" of *The Sound and the Fury* and posit the stylistic adjacency of the high modernist subject with the vernacular modernist subject. Quentin and Jason, therefore, form two sides of the coin of American modernism: Quentin's Joycean stream-of-consciousness sits beside Jason's slangy, hard-boiled narration, suggesting not merely the interdependence of these two modes, but also the familial connection between high modernist and vernacular modernist aesthetics.

Quentin's narration has long been connected to the work of Joyce and other transatlantic modernists, but Jason's status as a modernist narrative lens is less clear. However, the rubric of vernacular modernism allows for a more nuanced understanding of Jason's narrative, which draws on the conventions and language of the hard-boiled crime story (and, to a slightly lesser degree, the comic "Ringlish" of Lardner). Jason's section operates as a kind of ineffectual detective story in which he attempts to thwart his niece's plans. Its memorably misogynist opening—"Once a bitch always a bitch, what I say"—sets the stage for Jason's failed quest to curb his niece's sexual escapades.[14] Read in isolation, this opening would seem to support Faulkner's connection to the colloquial tradition of Twain. However, it also strongly resembles the opening to hard-boiled pioneer Carroll John Daly's 1923 slick magazine cross-over "Paying an Old Debt" (briefly discussed in chapter 4), where the reformed criminal narrator opens with a suspiciously similar phrase: "Once a criminal always a criminal, there's them that say that."[15] Daly's pulp writing is rife with these sorts of idiomatic vernacular expressions, and when Jason echoes them, he has, for all intents and purposes, walked out of the pages of a pulp magazine and into one of the most celebrated novels of American modernism.

This is not to suggest that Faulkner somehow had read and intentionally quoted the largely forgotten Carroll John Daly, even if he would become friends with *Black Mask* writer Dashiell Hammett a couple of years after the publication of *The Sound and the Fury*. Instead, it opens up the possibility of thinking about Faulkner—and, by extension, the rest of American high modernism—as fully aware of the experimental possibilities offered by the vernacular language of the street. These two parallel passages demonstrate an interconnectedness that has largely been ignored; with this in mind, Faulkner's praise of Anita Loos, Gilbert Seldes's and Virginia Woolf's admiration for Ring Lardner, and Gertrude Stein's fascination with Dashiell Hammett all make a great deal more sense. These writers were not slumming in genre fiction or mining popular culture for transformable ideas; instead, they saw a world where the "slanguage" of contemporary America—Mencken's "lush and vigorous thing called American slang" — was a part of the larger modernistic "revolution of the word."

Like the "Slanguage" feature in *transition, The Sound and the Fury* brings high modernism into direct (and in this case, familial) contact with its vernacular parallel. As Jason's narration follows Quentin's in *The Sound and the Fury*, so is Irwin's "Slanguage: 1929" surrounded in *transition* by Gertrude Stein's "Four Saints in Three Acts" and Stuart Gilbert's commentary on Joyce. The ultimate conceit of Faulkner's novel is that the "story" of the Compson family remains incomplete without these varied voices. Although Jason's chapter might be easier to follow than Quentin's, Faulkner's placing of these two chapters together emphasizes that *both* are aesthetic constructions, formal and linguistic experiments, and that Jason's vernacular language demonstrates an equal disdain for the staid conventions of realism. While these brothers and their two parallel forms of experimentation would have to be compartmentalized in 1929, the American cultural drive toward becoming both vernacular and modernist would subtly unite these strands by the mid-1930s.

This brief consideration of the novel Faulkner regarded as his best should not be seen solely as a way to justify the readings of the noncanonical texts that occupy the majority of *The Word on the Streets*. Instead, *The Sound and the Fury* suggests that the interconnected nature of "vernacular" and "modernist" was a very present part of modernist literary culture in the United States, particularly in the years following 1929. As critics of modernism, we must not read popular texts merely as a way to ground our readings of the well-established and occasionally overemphasized canon; rather, we must think about reconstructing a literary matrix in which Faulkner and Daly, Roth and Yezierska, Hurston and Fisher, Dos Passos and Lardner can exist side by side, each offering versions of a self-consciously modernist literary production. That some of these writers courted a popular audience should not exclude them from discussions of modernism. Instead, with new attention on modernism's complex relationship to the marketplace, the rubric of vernacular modernism allows for sophisticated and nuanced formal readings of the popular texts that were as comfortably placed in the mainstream reading consciousness as they were in the libraries and writings of high modernist heavyweights. Simultaneously, with its emphasis on the modernist touchstone of language and the influential popular linguistics of H. L. Mencken, vernacular modernism acknowledges the experimental qualities of American slang and the powerful influence it exerted on popular writing in the modernist era. Ultimately, this study hopes to contribute to ongoing discussions of the relationship between high and low culture, between modernism and the popular, in ways that challenge the traditional elitism of the modernist canon and acknowledge the formal and thematic complexities of popular texts themselves. Such an understanding of broad literary experimentation makes possible a dismantling of persistent boundaries around modernist writing as well as new understanding of American modernism—its writers, its modes, and its readers—defined not by its emphasis on exclusion but by cross-racial, cross-ethnic, and cross-class experiments in vernacular language.

Notes

Introduction

1. McMillan, *Transition*, 1.
2. [Jolas], "Proclamation," 13.
3. Crosby, "The New Word," 30. Another piece in this section, Eugene Jolas's own "Logos," develops these ideas even further. In a staunch critique of realism, Jolas notes that "the photographic conception of the word can no longer interest us. We desire a nomenclature that evokes an immediacy and the essence of an abstraction." See Jolas, "Logos," 29.
4. Irwin, "Slanguage: 1929," 32–34.
5. Ibid., 32–33.
6. Jolas, "King's English," 146–47.
7. Freeman, *American Testament*, 17.
8. [Jolas], "Proclamation," 13.
9. Bradbury, "Modernisms/Postmodernisms," 316.
10. Nicholls, *Modernisms*, vii.
11. Levenson, *Modernism*, 8. For an earlier consideration of the formal transformations of modernist experimentation, see Levenson, *Genealogy of Modernism*.
12. Eagleton, *Against the Grain*, 140.
13. Singal, "Towards a Definition," 7.
14. See Potter and Trotter, "Low Modernism"; Juan Antonio Suárez, *Pop Modernism: Noise and the Invention of the Everyday* (Urbana: University of Illinois Press, 2007); Sollors, *Ethnic Modernism*; Keresztesi, *Strangers at Home*; de Jongh, *Vicious Modernism*; Douglas Mao and Rebecca L. Walkowitz, eds., *Bad Modernisms* (Durham: Duke University Press, 2006); Earle, *Re-Covering Modernism*; Rabinowitz, *Black & White & Noir*; Sarah Wilson, *Melting-Pot Modernism* (Ithaca: Cornell University Press, 2010); Lisi Schoenbach, *Pragmatic Modernism* (New York: Oxford University Press, 2012); Entin,

Sensational Modernism; Katherine Biers, *Virtual Modernism: Writing and Technology in the Progressive Era* (Minneapolis: University of Minnesota Press, 2013); etc.

15. On the vagaries of canon expansion, see Guillory, *Cultural Capital*.

16. Eysteinsson, *Concept of Modernism*, 38.

17. Marjorie Levinson, "What Is New Formalism?," 560.

18. Eysteinsson, *Concept of Modernism*, 187.

19. Ezra Pound would write the following to Margaret Anderson, editor of the *Little Review*: "I may reserve my opinion that literature is not a commodity, that literature emphatically does not lie on a cou[n]ter where it can be snatched up at once by a straw-hatted young man in a hurry." See Scott and Friedman, eds. *Pound/The Little Review*, 157.

20. Randolph Bourne, "Trans-National America," *Atlantic Monthly*, June 1916, 86–97.

21. Denning, *Cultural Front*.

22. Connolly explicitly links these vernacular writers—especially "the outstanding writer of the new vernacular" Hemingway—to sound film: "The talking picture popularised the vocabulary with which Hemingway wrote and enabled him to use slang words in the knowledge that they were getting every day less obscure, he surf-rode into fame on the wave of American popular culture." *Enemies of Promise*, 63. For other examples of film as "vernacular modernism," see Hansen, "Mass Production of the Senses," 59–77; Miriam Bratu Hansen, "Fallen Women, Rising Stars, New Horizons: Shanghai Silent Film as Vernacular Modernism," *Film Quarterly* 54.1 (2000): 10–22; and Frost, *Problem with Pleasure*, 209–35. For visual art, see Paula Rabinowitz, "Great Lady Painters, Inc.: Icons of Feminism, Modernism, and the Nation," in *Modernism, Inc.: Body, Memory, Capital*, ed. Jani Scandura and Michael Thurston (New York: NYU Press, 2001), 193–218.

23. Cowley, "Middle American Style," 3.

24. Ibid., 14.

25. For his general propositions on the development of the colloquial style, see Bridgman, *Colloquial Style*, 12.

26. For a thorough discussion of the role of dialect literature in late nineteenth century America, see Jones, *Strange Talk*.

27. Bridgman, *Colloquial Style*, 23.

28. Joshua L. Miller's *Accented America* makes a convincing argument that the monolingual fantasy of early twentieth-century America was perpetuated by a variety of political and academic strategies, including popular linguistics.

29. One of the first major musicological texts to create this distinction was Hitchcock, *Music in the United States*.

30. Bohlman, "Vernacular Music."

31. Terms like "high modernism," "highbrow," "lowbrow," and "literary" (in the sense of "high literature") will appear extensively throughout *The Word on the Streets*. Occasionally, when context warrants, they will be explicitly enclosed in quotation marks. However, even when used without "scare quotes," they should be seen as exactly what they are: problematic constructions with a host of historical and cultural connotations.

32. Vološinov, *Marxism*, 23.

33. Denning, *Mechanic Accents*, 83–84.

34. For an influential reading on the multiple modes of conceptualizing Conrad's work, see Jameson, *Political Unconscious*, 206–80.

35. One of the ideas I stress here is that the discussion of aesthetics is never apolitical,

and the study of ideology is never without recourse to aesthetics. Criticism has often been too willing to compartmentalize these two elements of texts (hence the emphasis on ideology in the New Modernist studies), but the shunning of aesthetics for ideology marks a specific political and ideological valuation.

36. Strychacz, *Modernism*, 7.

37. McGurl, *Novel Art*, 6, 8.

38. Graham, *Great American Songbooks*, 27; Huyssen, *After the Great Divide*, viii.

39. North, *Dialect of Modernism*; Chinitz, *T. S. Eliot*; Morrisson, *Public Face*; Graham, *Great American Songbooks*.

40. Denning, *Mechanic Accents*, 24; Cheng, *Astounding Wonder*, 26; Strychacz, *Modernism*, 20.

41. Woolf, "Character in Fiction," in *Essays*, 3:426.

42. Erich Auerbach's major work *Mimesis* even includes a chapter on Virginia Woolf and Marcel Proust, arguing for their modernist writing as an extension of realist tendencies. For a discussion of the modernist desire to create a more realistic depiction of existence than the realists, see Orvell, *The Real Thing*, 240–86.

43. Loeb, *Way It Was*, 224.

44. Vials, *Realism for the Masses*. See also Entin's *Sensational Modernism* for a slightly different take on the representational strategies of 1930s documentarians.

45. Both critics of and advocates for modernism seized on this distinction. Georg Lukács, for example, consistently argued against modernism's tendency toward fragmentation, as its "immediacy" and "abstraction" fundamentally obscured images of social and economic "totality." But realist totalities, as critics of Lukács pointed out, may themselves be illusions, and the totalities of American realism and naturalism, while presenting dense and complex social structures, work to reinforce—not undermine—social and ethnic difference, largely through the dynamics of dialect language. "Realism in the Balance," 32, 38. For Lukács's other arguments against "Expressionism" and modernism, see *Essays on Realism* (Cambridge: MIT Press, 1981); and Georg Lukács, *Realism in Our Time: Literature and Class Struggle* (New York: Harper and Row, 1964). For a discussion of Lukács's critics, see Eysteinsson, *Concept of Modernism*, 179–206.

46. Bakhtin, *Dialogic Imagination*, 262.

47. Howard, *Form and History*, 105.

48. Bridgman, *Colloquial Style*, 54.

49. In another classic of the period, George Washington Cable's *The Grandissimes* (1880), dialect characters are objects of pity, while figures with standard accents provide narrative identification.

50. Jones, *Strange Talk*, 45–46.

51. See Kaplan, *Social Construction*, and Castronovo, *Beautiful Democracy*.

52. See James, *Question of Our Speech*.

53. Glazener, *Reading for Realism*, 12, 20.

54. For June Howard this distancing makes naturalism complicit with the politics of "progressive reform" (*Form and History*, 127–41).

55. Cmiel, *Democratic Eloquence*.

56. Howells, "Editor's Study," 155.

57. Jones, *Strange Talk*, 10.

58. Cmiel, *Democratic Eloquence*, 132. On feminization, see Douglas, *Feminization of American Culture*.

59. Glazener, *Reading for Realism*, 13, 229–55.
60. Santayana, *Genteel Tradition*, 40.
61. Parrington, *Main Currents*, 435.
62. Cowley, "Revolt against Gentility," 192.
63. Ibid., 194, 205.
64. Ibid., 199, 202.

65. For a more nuanced consideration of the meaning of the "genteel tradition" and its valuation of culture in nineteenth-century literary study, see John Tomish, *A Genteel Endeavor: American Culture and Politics in the Gilded Age* (Stanford: Stanford University Press, 1971); Douglas, *Feminization of American Culture*; Carol Klimick Cyganowski, *Magazine Editors and Professional Authors in Nineteenth-Century America: The Genteel Tradition and the American Dream* (New York: Garland, 1988); and Mark J. Noonan, *Reading* The Century Illustrated Monthly Magazine: *American Literature and Culture, 1870–1893* (Kent, OH: Kent State University Press, 2010).

66. Coleman, *Cant and Slang Dictionaries*, 3:168. Coleman does not regard John Russell Bartlett's 1848 *Dictionary of Americanisms: A Glossary of Words and Phrases Usually Regarded as Particular to the United States* as the earliest in this regard, in part because some of his material seems to be derived from other sources. See Coleman, *Cant and Slang Dictionaries*, 2:245–46.

67. Wood and Goddard, *Dictionary of American Slang*, 10, 61.

68. Coleman lists four American slang dictionaries published between 1859 and 1921. She lists eighteen that appeared between 1922 and 1936. Coleman, *Cant and Slang Dictionaries*, 3:ix.

69. Miller, *Accented America*, 107. Pound is quoted in Eble, introduction to *American Speech*, 227–28.

70. Algeo, *Origins and Development*, 196. See also Eble.

71. Miller's account leaves little room for writers—especially popular or noncanonical writers—to challenge (self-consciously or not) the hegemony of English in the United States of the early twentieth century. While he celebrates the ability of some canonical figures (like Gertrude Stein, Nella Larsen, John Dos Passos, and Jean Toomer) to do what he calls "syncopate" (18) the language through a process of defamiliarization, the vernacular modernists I discuss in *The Word on the Streets* represent examples of vernacular (i.e., popular) writers who sought to redefine their relationship to the American langauge just as they sought to redefine the language itself, a task they undertook and documented self-consciously.

72. Miller, *Accented America*, 108, 109. On the influence of Boas and Sapir on the study of American culture, see Hegeman, *Patterns for America*.

73. Braddock, *Collecting as Modernist Practice*, 3.

74. Sonne, "Crime and Detective Story," 18ff; *Hot Dog*, "Can You Write 'The American Language?'" Advertisement. *Writer's Digest*, January 1925, 55.

75. In addition to Eliot's famous "notes" to *The Waste Land*, I am thinking of the timeline, genealogy, and map from Faulkner's *Absalom, Absalom!* (1936); the maps and genealogies in *The Portable Faulkner* (1946, edited by Malcolm Cowley); Stuart Gilbert's *James Joyce's "Ulysses": A Study* (1930) and running commentary on *Finnegans Wake* (a.k.a. *Work in Progress*) in *transition;* and Joseph Campbell and Henry Morton Robinson's *A Skeleton's Key to Finnegans Wake* (1944), among others.

76. Genette, *Paratexts*, 2.

77. Ibid., 327. Genette acknowledges that his *Paratexts* is not a history of the phenomenon. Such a history would no doubt single out the early twentieth century as a moment when paratexts began to shift in their function.
78. Yezierska, "Mr. Lewisohn's 'Up Stream,'" 22.
79. Huyssen, *After the Great Divide.*
80. Rainey, *Institutions of Modernism*, 6.
81. Poirier, "Difficulties of Modernism," 135; Strychacz, *Modernism*, 27. See also Rainey, *Institutions of Modernism.*
82. Frost, *Problem with Pleasure*, 3.
83. James F. English, "Cultural Capital," 371.
84. Bourdieu, *Rules of Art*, 105–9, 285–312.
85. Quoted in Duffield, "The Pulps," 26.
86. Bürger, *Theory of the Avant-Garde*, liii.
87. Bourdieu, *Field of Cultural Production*, 41.
88. Loos, *Gentlemen Prefer Blondes*, xli.
89. Mott, *History of American Magazines*, 389. Mott also describes *Harper's Bazar* during the 1920s: "It had been losing money for a good many years when the International Magazine Company, William Randolph Hearst, president, purchased it in 1913. It immediately became more sophisticated, gay and 'smart.' The fact is that, although the magazine had been designed for well-to-do homes, it had always inclined to hark back to the Methodistic Harper Brothers: it had been Harperish, but now it became Hearstian. . . . Under Sell it contained many pages of the latest designs in styles, and on the literary side it printed Compton Mackenzie and Laurids Bruun serials, with John V. A. Weaver and Mildred Cram, and such English writers as Arnold Bennett, W. L. George, and Robert Hichens" (390).
90. James Wood, *Magazines in the United States*, 129.
91. Audit Bureau of Circulations, *A.B.C. Blue Book: Publishers Statements for Period Ending December 31, 1925.*
92. There are some exceptions. Notably, the British *Harper's Bazaar* published Gertrude Stein's "Why I Like Detective Stories" in 1937: not Stein's most challenging piece, but certainly an example of editors trying to take advantage of the cultural capital surrounding Stein in the mid-1930s after her success with *The Autobiography of Alice B. Toklas* (1932).
93. Loos, *Gentlemen Prefer Blondes*, 19.
94. The *Little Review*, for example, cost seventy-five cents a copy in 1925.
95. Loos, *Gentlemen Prefer Blondes*, xli.
96. Munson, *Awakening Twenties*, 139.
97. McGann, *Textual Condition*, 13. For an excellent application of McGann's bibliographical codes to traditional modernist subjects, see Bornstein, *Material Modernism.*
98. In an earlier essay McGann calls this a text's "dialectical life" or "critical history." See McGann, "Keats and the Historical Method," 993.
99. Guillory, *Cultural Capital*, 68.
100. Bourdieu, *Field of Cultural Production*, 50–51.
101. For some examples of studies that come out of these relationships, see the plethora of 1990s volumes that pair a canonical figure's name with "and popular culture": Kershner, *Joyce and Popular Culture;* Fowler and Abadie, *Faulkner and Popular Culture*; etc.
102. Of course, this does not even begin to scratch the surface of the traces of popular

culture in modernist texts, especially those of poets. For example, T. S. Eliot's *The Waste Land* includes references to the popular Tin Pan Alley song "The Shakesperian Rag" and to Bram Stoker's *Dracula*, a text so popular he didn't feel the need to cite it in his notes. For more on Eliot and popular culture, see Chinitz, *T. S. Eliot*.

103. Scholes, *Paradoxy of Modernism*, 200.

104. Brodhead, *Cultures of Letters*, 115.

105. Hughes, *The Big Sea*, 223–233.

106. It is also clear that the other writers in this study, writers working in more identifiable "genres," benefited from an increased literary access as well. Ring Lardner's baseball stories depended on the emergence of the sport as a "national pastime" (indeed, a popular phenomenon constructed by sportswriters like Lardner himself); Daly's and Hammett's crime writing directly engaged Prohibition and the popular fascination with gangsters and bootleggers in the late 1920s.

107. Mencken, *The American Language: A Preliminary Inquiry*, 26.

108. Kenner, *The Counterfeiters*; North, *Machine-Age Comedy*.

1 / "The Steady Reaching Out for New and Vivid Forms"

1. Jolas, "King's English," 146.

2. Ibid.

3. Josephson, "Toward a Professional Prose," 59.

4. Mencken, "Final Estimate," Smart Set *Criticism*, 183.

5. Mencken, *The American Language: A Preliminary Inquiry*, 17; Mencken, *The American Language: An Inquiry into the Development*, 2nd ed., 20; Mencken, *The American Language*, 3rd ed., 21. References to Mencken's four editions (1919, 1921, 1923, and 1936) of *The American Language* will henceforth be cited in text as *AL* 1, *AL* 2, *AL* 3, and *AL* 4 (specific page numbers follow a colon).

6. Mencken, "Our One Authentic Giant," Smart Set *Criticism*, 179; Mencken, "Final Estimate," Smart Set *Criticism*, 188.

7. Hemingway, *Green Hills of Africa*, 22.

8. Mencken, "Our One Authentic Giant," Smart Set *Criticism*, 180.

9. Henry Nash Smith, *Virgin Land*, 2.

10. Sewell argues that "Twain's relation to the colloquial or vernacular language was ambivalent throughout his life—even during the composition of *Huckleberry Finn*, the novel in which rules come under the heaviest attack." *Twain's Languages*, 16.

11. See, for example, ibid.; and Mitchell, "Verbally *Roughing It*," 67–92.

12. Mencken, *Prejudices: Third Series*, 13–14.

13. Ibid., 16.

14. Arac, "Babel and Vernacular," 9.

15. Jones, *Strange Talk*, 1.

16. Nettles, *Language, Race, and Class*, 69.

17. Jones, *Strange Talk*, 51.

18. Mencken, "Twain and Howells," Smart Set *Criticism*, 178–79.

19. See Mitchell, "Verbally *Roughing It*."

20. Jones, "Twain, Language, and the Southern Humorists," 128.

21. Twain, *Roughing It*, 7; hereafter cited as *RI*.

22. Burns, "Fabrication and Faultline," 252.

23. The phrasing here recalls at least two of the points made in Jolas's "Revolution of the Word" "Proclamation": "The literary creator has the right to disintegrate the primal matter of words imposed on him by text-books and dictionaries"; and "He has the right to use words of his own fashioning and to disregard existing grammatical and syntactical laws" (13).

24. Sewell, *Twain's Languages*, 132.

25. Twain, *Adventures of Huckleberry Finn*, xxxvi; hereafter cited as *AHF*.

26. In the most thorough argument of this sort, David Carkeet identifies "nine distinct dialects" (321), and arrives at seven only after ignoring a vast number of inconsistencies in Huck's dialect and rejecting identified dialects that appeared in the novel's earliest composed sections. "Dialects in *Huckleberry Finn*," 315–32.

27. Bakhtin, *Dialogic Imagination* 345.

28. Twain, *Gilded Age*, 645, 741.

29. "A Note on the Text," *AHF* 554.

30. Lee Clark Mitchell points to Huck's concluding remarks (where he speaks of "what trouble it was to make a book") and to the misspelling of "sivilized" to argue that the text is unambiguously *written* by Huck. "'Nobody but Our Gang,'" 94–95.

31. Blakemore, "Huck Finn's Written World," 28.

32. Sewell, *Twain's Languages*, 135.

33. Twain, *Gilded Age*, 712.

34. Mencken, "Popularity Index," Smart Set *Criticism*, 177–78.

35. Mencken, *Second Mencken Chrestomathy*, 222.

36. Ibid., 223. See also Orvell, *The Real Thing*.

37. Mencken, "Criticism of Criticism of Criticism," 143; Mencken on *Ulysses* quoted in Teachout, *The Skeptic*, 114.

38. "So many young men get their likes and dislikes from Mencken," narrator Jake Barnes laments in Hemingway's *The Sun Also Rises* (1927), 49.

39. Wilson, "H. L. Mencken," 13.

40. I say this not to get into yet another debate about who is the most representative modernist. (On this, see, for example, Perloff, "Pound/Stevens.") Rather, I see Mencken as yet another nexus of creativity; as editor, he published many of the most challenging of the popular writers in the United States (as well as many writers based in Europe). As critic, he influenced an entire generation of disaffected young men and women in the wake of World War I.

41. Allen, *Only Yesterday*, 195–211.

42. Ibid., 199. See Hoffman, *The Twenties*, esp. 344–55. Other approaches to Mencken frequently focus on a single element of his thought (such as his opinion of the American South, as in Hobson's *Serpent in Eden*) as emblematic of his worldview.

43. Alternatively, when studies do include *The American Language*, such as Fecher's *Mencken*, his philological work is sequestered into its own category and seen as largely independent of his work as "critic" or "philosopher."

44. Others include Waldo Frank's *Our America* (1919), George Santayana's *Character and Opinion in the United States* (1920), Harold Stearns's *Civilization in the United States* (1922), D. H. Lawrence's *Studies in Classic American Literature* (1923), William Carlos Williams's *In the American Grain* (1925), Charles and Mary Beard's *The Rise of*

American Civilization (1927), Vernon Parrington's *Main Currents in American Thought* (1927–1930), and Constance Rourke's *American Humor* (1931).

45. Nelson, "Babylonian Frolics," 668.

46. For example, in Terry Teachout's acclaimed 2002 biography of Mencken, *The Skeptic*, he devotes more time to Mencken's influential review of Dreiser's 1910 novel *Jennie Gerhardt* than he does to *The American Language* (all four editions and two supplemental volumes) in its entirety.

47. Hackett, "Living Speech," 55.

48. Miller, *Accented America*, 12, 79.

49. Ibid., 9, 38.

50. Mencken, *Prejudices: Third Series*, 58.

51. Mencken, "Two Englishes," 6.

52. Mencken, "Spoken American," 6.

53. Mencken, *Mencken's America*, 38–39.

54. Mencken, "Nothing Dead," back page.

55. Ibid.

56. In a review of the fourth edition of *AL*, William Carlos Williams seemed to prefer the "certain crudities contained in the earlier editions," noting that "the often unsupported surmises, the ill-assorted jumble of some of the matter in the earlier editions had an instinctive justness about them, sometimes, which added zest to the whole. I miss them. They left a jagged edge but so does the American language." Williams, "An Incredible Neglect Redefined," *Selected Essays*, 170–71.

57. This passage was cut from the third edition of *AL*.

58. Miller sees Mencken's American language as "a standard vernacular connoting racial whiteness" and is in a sense correct that Mencken's version of American emphasizes the language's ability to "swallow . . . other languages whole" and "limitlessly assimilate new words, accents, and slang forms." However, the ability of Mencken's American language to cut across boundaries of race, ethnicity, and class stands in stark contrast to the conservative English-only movement of the early twentieth century. This multiracial component of Mencken's language is one of the principal differences between "American" and English. *Accented America*, 82, 85.

59. On the emphasis of privilege and refinement in the *Atlantic Monthly*, see Glazener, *Reading for Realism*.

60. Aldington, "Young American Poet," 22–25.

61. Aldington, "English and American," 96.

62. Ibid., 97.

63. Mencken, *Mencken's America*, 36.

64. Hughes, "Our Statish Language," 846, 849.

65. If Mencken had one serious blind spot in his discussion of the American vulgate, it is his lack of interest in African American language. However, Mencken is not unique in this: in the early editions of *The American Language*, he challenges philologists that attempt to attribute culturally specific words like "banjo" and "breakdown" to French instead of to "negro slaves" (*AL* 2:54, *AL* 3:56–57). By the time he published the second supplement (1948), he would devote a number of pages to "jive" ("an amalgam of Negro slang from Harlem and the argots of drug addicts and the pettier sort of criminals, with occasional additions from the Broadway gossip columns and the high-school campus") and cite Zora Neale Hurston's "Story in Harlem Slang" (published in 1942 in the *Ameri-*

can Mercury). Hurston's story is discussed in more depth in chapter 5. See Mencken, *The American Language, Supplement II*, 706–10.

2 / "Never Mind the Comical Stuff.... They Ain't No Joke about This!"

1. James, *Hawthorne*, 43.
2. In addition to Twain, the work of Charles Farrar Browne, writing as Artemus Ward, might also be a reference point for James in this quote. Browne's writing, like Twain's, turned on the relative illiteracy of his literary persona in such works as *Artemus Ward: His Book* (1862).
3. See, for example, Pound's "Credo" and 1918 essay "Henry James." *Literary Essays*, 9, 295–338. See also Kenner, *The Pound Era*, 3–23.
4. On Twain's "black" speech, see Fishkin, *Was Huck Black?*
5. Rourke, *American Humor*.
6. Compare, for example, Reynolds's *Beneath the American Renaissance*.
7. Rourke, *American Humor*, 209–36.
8. See, for example, Twain's first published sketch "The Dandy Frightening the Squatter" (1852). *Collected Tales*, 1–2.
9. On the connections between Southwestern humor and realism, see Martin, *Frontier Roots*.
10. His focus on the work of Browne/Ward suggests that at least this one writer emphasized a particular kind of social and political satire of the moral failures of the Civil War era. Brom Weber, "The Misspellers," 128. Walter Blair distinguishes between "the misspellers" (or the "literary humorists") and the "rural humorists." The misspellers created texts—often letters or other ostensibly written documents—purported to originate from the pens of pseudonymous alter egos. The works of pseudonymous authors Artemus Ward (Charles Farrar Browne), Josh Billings (Henry W. Shaw), Petroleum V. Nasby (David Ross Locke), and Bill Arp (Charles Henry Smith) exemplify this tradition. For brief histories of both groups, see Blair, *Native American Humor*, 102–24.
11. Not discussed here (but certainly important to these questions of dialect, humor, and Chicago writing) is James D. Corrothers, whose *The Black Cat Club* (1902) is briefly discussed in chapter 4.
12. Dunne, *Mr. Dooley*, vii.
13. On the quarantining of dialect, see Bridgman, *Colloquial Style*, 23.
14. Dunne, *Mr. Dooley*, 1.
15. A similar effect would appear to readers encountering "Dooley's" articles in the newspaper, surrounded by other articles in standard journalist prose.
16. Dunne, *Mr. Dooley*, x.
17. Mencken, *Prejudices: A Selection*, 14.
18. E. F. Bleiler argues that "the slang element in them is small. They are really written in the vernacular, in the colloquial tradition." Introduction to Ade, *Fables in Slang*, vii. Blieler actually compares Ade with Josh Billings, Bill Nye, and "Mr. Dooley." Bleiler's conflation of the humor styles of Billings, Nye, and Dunne is problematic. Unlike Billings and Dooley in particular, Ade does not exploit the conventions of dialect to their fullest extent.
19. Ade, *Fables in Slang*, 52.
20. For an influential discussion of the phenomenological importance of these new technologies, see Kittler, *Gramophone, Film, Typewriter*.

21. For a thorough history of ethnic comedy on cylinders and discs, particularly performers that predate "Uncle Josh," see Feaster, "'The Following Record,'" 391–416.

22. Jenkins, *What Made Pistachio Nuts?*, 75.

23. Feaster, "Framing the Mechanical Voice," 59.

24. As Feaster notes, "Conventionalized spoken cues were used to guide listeners in their experience of commercial phonograms, contextualizing entire performances or parts of more elaborate programs such as the 'minstrel first part.'" "Framing the Mechanical Voice," 91.

25. Katz, "Sound Recording," 13.

26. Feaster, "Framing the Mechanical Voice," 58–59, 91.

27. Katz, "Sound Recording," 16. Mark Katz's focus—like nearly all of the historical discussions of sound recording—is on early music. Only Patrick Feaster's work has sought to encompass the entirety of recorded output.

28. Camlot, "Early Talking Books," 164–65.

29. Jacob Smith, "Frenzy of the Audible," 33. While there was a certain parallel between the listener's successful negotiation of modernity (in the phonograph) and Uncle Josh's similar failures, the difficulties of identification persist.

30. Gunning, "Cinema of Attractions," 57. See also Kenner, *The Counterfeiters* and North, *Machine-Age Comedy*.

31. Bowser, *Transformation of Cinema*, 179.

32. Geismar, *Lardner Reader*, xxix. For another example of this characterization of Lardner's output, see Patrick, *Ring Lardner*, xxix.

33. Fitzgerald, *The Crack-Up*, 36.

34. Wilson, "Ring Lardner's American Characters," in *Shores of Light*, 97.

35. Bridgman, *Colloquial Style*, 151.

36. "Three Stories a Year Are Enough for a Writer," *New York Times* March 25, 1917, SM8.

37. Moseley, "Ring Lardner," 54. There is no shortage of examples of experimental writers and artists producing their most experimental work early in their careers and softening their experimentation later in their careers.

38. Fitzgerald, *The Crack-Up*, 36.

39. Ibid, 38.

40. Lardner parodies this in the pseudonymous foreword to his burlesque autobiography, *The Story of a Wonder Man* (1927): "The publication of this autobiography is entirely without the late Master's sanction. He wrote it as a pastime and burnt up each chapter as soon as it was written; the salvaging was accomplished by ghouls who haunted the Lardners' ash bbl. during my whole tenure of office as night nurse to their dromedary" (v). For a discussion of this, see Keough, *Punchlines*, 86.

41. Seldes, *The 7 Lively Arts*, 117.

42. For an excellent discussion of Seldes, the *Dial*, and *The 7 Lively Arts*, see North, *Reading 1922*, 140–72.

43. Woolf, "American Fiction," in *Essays*, 4:276.

44. Bridgman, *Colloquial Style*, 148, 151. In an essay on Woolf and Lardner, Todd Avery takes for granted the "aesthetic affinity between this pair of innovative modernist fiction writers" and explores their similar interests in the politics of sport. "Girls in Europe," 45.

45. Woolf, "American Fiction," in *Essays*, 4:276.

46. Moseley, "Ring Lardner," 55.

47. An earlier example of this mode of writing, Caroline Kirkland's *A New Home, Who'll Follow?* (1839), does not explicitly use the epistolary form, but retains its discursive function.

48. Moseley, "Ring Lardner," 57.

49. *Writer's Digest* June 1929, 27. On "Lardner's Ringlish," see also Randolph Adams et al., *Literary History*, 755.

50. Lardner, *Selected Stories*, 15. One of the other interesting characteristics of these stories is the use of real players from the 1914 baseball season: from the White Sox, catcher Ray Schalk, third baseman Harry Lord, and outfielder Ping Bodie; from the Detroit Tigers, outfielder Ty Cobb, outfielder Bobby Veach, and third baseman George Moriarty.

51. Ibid., 14.

52. Ibid., 7, 237, 21.

53. Poirier, "Difficulties of Modernism," 130.

54. Jonathan Yardley, introduction to Lardner, *Selected Stories*, xiii.

55. Wood and Goddard, *Dictionary of American Slang*, 61–64.

56. On the reference to *The Young Visiters*, see Yardley, *Ring*, 222–23. See also Ashford, *The Young Visiters*.

57. Lardner, *The Young Immigrunts*, ix–x.

58. Interestingly, this kind of preface in a child's book reinforces the notion that similar practices in African American autobiography (especially slave narratives) serve the function of infantilizing these authors.

59. This is, once again, a reference to the Ashford book, where a facsimile of the first page of the book—in her own handwriting—appears opposite the first page of chapter 1.

60. Although it had not appeared yet, and its editorial history was not well known until much later, it is tempting to link this textual strategy to T. S. Eliot's *The Waste Land*, a text that underwent significant revision at the hands of an interested editor, Ezra Pound.

61. Lardner, *The Young Immigrunts*, 62.

62. Ibid., 34, 78, 44, 76.

63. Ibid., 61.

64. Of course, Harriet Beecher Stowe's *Uncle Tom's Cabin* (1851) inspired a veritable industry of adaptations, which ran well into the 1920s.

65. Until 1929 the magazine later known as *Harper's Bazaar* was titled with the odd spelling *Harper's Bazar*. Since this essay deals with fiction published prior to the name change, the magazine will be consistently referred to as *Harper's Bazar* (with one exception—a quote by Loos herself).

66. Loos published as many memoirs as novels. These include *A Girl Like I* (1966), *Kiss Hollywood Good-by* (1974), *Cast of Thousands* (1977), and *The Talmadge Girls: A Memoir* (1978). Other biographical material appeared in the posthumous *Fate Keeps On Happening: Adventures of Lorelei Lee and Other Writings* (1984). Gary Carey's biography *Anita Loos* emphasizes the "gossipy" side of Loos scholarship as does the recent *Anita Loos Rediscovered: Film Treatments and Fiction by Anita Loos*, edited by Cari Beauchamp and Mary Anita Loos. Neither of these latter two books contains an incredibly helpful scholarly apparatus or, importantly, a bibliography of Loos's short fiction.

67. Early scholarship on *Gentlemen Prefer Blondes* certainly fits this model. For examples, see Blom, "Loos and Sexual Economics"; Hegeman, "Taking *Blondes* Seriously"; John T. Matthews, "Gentlemen Defer Blondes: Faulkner, Anita Loos, and Mass Culture,"

in *Faulkner, His Contemporaries, and His Posterity* (Tubingen: Francke, 1993), 207–21; Jonathan Silverman, "Lorelei's Doomed Performance: Anita Loos and the American Dream," *Prospects* 27 (2002): 547–68. Mark McGurl reads *Blondes* as a Menckenian critique of "cultural leveling." *The Novel Art*, 109.

68. The African American writer-director-producer Oscar Micheaux also worked in all these forms. Unlike Loos, however, he began as a novelist and made films under substantially different economic and industrial conditions in the specialized world of African American independent film.

69. Powdermaker, *Hollywood*. See also Ian Hamilton, *Writers in Hollywood, 1915–1951* (New York: Harper & Row, 1990); and Tom Cerasulo, *Authors out Here: Fitzgerald, West, Parker, and Schulberg in Hollywood* (Columbia: University of South Carolina Press, 2010).

70. North, *Camera Works*, 122.

71. Hansen, "Mass Production of the Senses," 70.

72. Loos, *Girl Like I*, 56.

73. Bordwell, Staiger, and Thompson, *Classical Hollywood Cinema*, 26, 186.

74. According to Carey, an ostensible commitment to dual authorship was a convention of all Loos's early film work. Biographical data about the couple, however, suggests that Loos was the primary writer of the photoplays and of *How to Write Photoplays*. For background on the gendered division of intellectual labor in early Hollywood, see Morey, "'Would You Be'"; and Beauchamp, *Without Lying Down*. In *Popcorn Venus*, Marjorie Rosen provides an early feminist history of Hollywood.

75. Emerson and Loos, *How To Write Photoplays*, 4; hereafter cited as *Photoplays*.

76. While writers during the silent era used "subtitles," "titles," "title cards," and "intertitles" interchangeably, recent writing on silent film primarily uses "intertitles" or "title cards," because the meaning of "subtitles" and "titles" has widened since then.

77. Schmidt, "Handwriting on the Screen," 622. For a more detailed discussion of the Loos and Fairbanks films, see chapter 6 of Tibbetts and Welsh, *His Majesty the American*.

78. Lindsay, *Art of the Moving Picture*, rev. ed., xxix.

79. Tucker reconstructs the making of *Intolerance* through interviews with contributors still living in 1980, including Loos.

80. Tibbetts and Welsh, *His Majesty the American*, 91.

81. Schmidt, "Handwriting on the Screen," 623.

82. Schatz, *Genius of the System*, 53.

83. Carey, *Anita Loos*, 32.

84. Fred, review of *A Wild Girl of the Sierras*, 26.

85. *Wild and Woolly* (dir. Emerson, 1916), a film dominated by relatively conventional dialogue title cards, ends with a title-card metacommentary on the film's conclusion: "But wait a minute, this will never do! WE can't end a Western romance without a wedding. Yet—after they're married where shall they live? For Nell likes the East, And Jeff likes the West, So where are the twain to meet?"

86. Jolo, review of *Hit-the-Trail Holliday*, 29; Dime, review of *Come On In*, 44.

87. Lood, review of *A Temperamental Wife*, 54; Lood, review of *A Virtuous Vamp*, 55.

88. Loos, *Gentlemen Prefer Blondes*, xxxviii; hereafter, the novel will be cited as *Blondes*. The importance of Mencken's approval of *Blondes* to Loos is laid out in Schrader's "'But Gentlemen Marry Brunettes.'"

89. The serial installments were literally buried deep in the pages of *Harper's Bazar*,

a fashion magazine in the 1920s in which the table of contents routinely appeared after fifty or more pages of advertisements. Mencken's suggestion forms the centerpiece for Sarah Churchwell's essay "'Lost among the Ads.'" Churchwell reads the intertextuality present in the original magazine publication of the novel, emphasizing the ways in which the visual representations of Lorelei in the *Harper's Bazar* illustrations seem linked to the visuality of the ads. For another reading that focuses on the emerging "discourse of expertise" in cosmetics and fashion, see Lutes, "Authoring *Gentlemen*."

90. Interestingly, these contrasting images of the tiny, bookish brunette and the "hearty" blonde recapitulate discourses surrounding race and ethnicity in the late 1910s and early 1920s. In particular, these images are reminiscent of the ideas of Lothrop Stoddard and, most specifically, Madison Grant, whose delineation of the Caucasian types—Nordic, Mediterranean, and Alpine—in his *The Passing of the Great Race* emphasizes the size and strength of blond Nordics while viewing the other Caucasian types as smaller and, importantly for this discussion, brunette. Grant argues that the fundamental "influences [of racial superiority] are so deeply rooted in everyday consciousness that the average novelist or playwright would not fail to make his hero a tall, blond, honest, and somewhat stupid youth, or his villain a small, dark, and exceptionally intelligent individual of warped moral character" (229). The fact that *Blondes* emerges in a cultural moment when these discourses maintained some dominance in American society is a noteworthy and, thus far, unexplored topic in Loos scholarship. I am in debt to Adam McKible's unpublished lecture "Lothrop Stoddard and Racial Pseudoscience in the 1920s" for the summaries of Stoddard's and Grant's ideas.

91. For a compelling argument that sees Lorelei's performance as liberatory, see Cella, "Narrative 'Confidence Games.'"

92. Lorelei's use of language at times approximates the language used by title card writers struggling to avoid the censors. Text, in many cases, can suggest in ways that images cannot, and Lorelei's diary frequently operates at this level.

93. See Hegeman, "Taking *Blondes* Seriously." For the earlier correspondences, see Blom, "Loos and Sexual Economics."

94. Emerson and Loos, *Breaking Into Movies*, 33.

95. Kobal, *People Will Talk*, 179.

96. For Laura Frost, Dorothy becomes "the voice of overt irony, modernism's signature rhetoric." See *Problem with Pleasure*, 230.

97. Faulkner, *Selected Letters*, 32.

98. For a longer discussion of Loos's investment in cinematic narrative in both *Blondes* and *But Gentlemen Marry Brunettes*, see Hefner, "'Any Chance to Be Unrefined.'"

99. Wyndham Lewis, *Time and Western Man*, 69–81. For a discussion of Loos and Stein, see Hammill, *Women, Celebrity*, 55–75; and Frost, *Problem with Pleasure*, 232.

3 / "I Didn't Understand the Words, but My Voice Was Like Dynamite"

1. Ferraro, "Avant-Garde Ethnics," 3–4.

2. For early recordings, see the recent compilation of wax cylinder recordings *Jewface* (Reboot Stereophonic, 2006). The Edison Company produced two well-known films documenting New York's East Side Jewish community: *Move On* (1903), depicting a Jewish merchant being accosted by a policeman; and *New York City Ghetto Fish Market* (1903), showing a panorama of an Essex Street market.

3. Amanda Adams's talk at the 2007 Modern Language Association's Annual Meeting was particularly instructive on this latter point. *Performing Authorship*, 113–40.

4. For more information, see Jones, *Strange Talk*.

5. Cahan, *Yekl*, 3.

6. Rosenwald, *Multilingual America*, 94. See also Wirth-Nesher, *Call It English*, 32–51.

7. Ferraro, "Avant-Garde Ethnics," 3.

8. Antin, *The Promised Land*, 1.

9. Cahan, *Rise of David Levinsky*, 134.

10. Hapgood, *Types from City Streets*, 22.

11. Sollors, *Beyond Ethnicity*, 247. Sollors follows with a fascinating discussion of Yiddish language modernism.

12. Ibid., 258.

13. For a broader consideration of transnational diasporic modernism in Yiddish and Hebrew, see Schachter, *Diasporic Modernism*.

14. Henricksen, *Anzia Yezierska*, 195.

15. See chapter 5 of Maria Damon's *Dark End of the Street* for her examination of Gertrude Stein as a Jewish writer; and see her essay "Gertrude Stein's Jewishness" for a reading that foregrounds the anxieties that result from contextualizing Stein as a Jew. Barbara Will draws on this early work of Damon's to see ethnicity as central to Stein's work. Werner Sollors alludes to Stein as an ethnic modernist in *Beyond Ethnicity*, 255–56. For a related consideration of Stein's *The Making of Americans* as an immigrant narrative (without an explicit focus on Stein's Jewishness), see Priscilla Wald, *Constituting Americans*, 237–98.

16. Historians of Jewish American literature have remained ambivalent about Yezierska. Marcus Klein's and Hana Wirth-Nesher's surveys both ignore Yezierska, while Julian Levinson incorporates her in a study of "tales of reclamation" of Jewish heritage among American Jews (*Exiles on Main Street* 6) and Donald Weber discusses the function of hunger in Yezierska as "a genealogy of Jewish affect" (*Haunted in the New World* 4). Strangely enough, Yezierska is more commonly seen alongside names such as Zora Neale Hurston, Mourning Dove, Sui Sin Far, and Jean Rhys in comparative studies of multiethnic writers rather than as a defining figure in the Jewish American canon. For examples of these juxtapositions, see Harrison-Kahan, "No Slaves"; Lori Jirousek, "Ethnics and Ethnographers: Zora Neale Hurston and Anzia Yezierska," *Journal of Modern Literature* 29.2 (2006): 19–32; and Charlotte J. Rich, *Transcending the New Woman: Multiethnic Narratives in the Progressive Era* (Columbia: University of Missouri Press, 2009).

17. A number of other texts of working women's experience appeared at this moment as well: Agnes Smedley's *Daughter of Earth* (1929, repr. 1973); Tillie Olsen's *Yonnondio: From the Thirties* (written in the 1930s, published in 1974); and Meridel Le Sueur's *The Girl* (published as stories 1935–45, as a novel 1978).

18. Dearborn, "Anzia Yezierska," 108.

19. Judith Sanders sees Yezierska as "a transitional figure between Yiddish and American literature." "Her Literary Dowry," 7.

20. The advertisement highlighted "January Publications." Boni & Liveright, which also published Loos's *Gentlemen Prefer Blondes* and is discussed in the introduction, was one of most radical publishers of the modernist era. Though Boni & Liveright advertised in many contexts, from the avant-garde to the mainstream, the appearance of an ad for

Salome of the Tenements in the pages of this journal of American writers abroad—in the same year Yezierska met Stein—indicates more than mere coincidence.

21. Wendy Katz, "Untying the Immigrant Tongue," 158.

22. Sollors's *Ethnic Modernism* describes the innovations of many American writers working in languages other than English while simultaneously celebrating English-language texts with a canonical pedigree: Jean Toomer's *Cane* (1923) and Henry Roth's *Call It Sleep* (1934). See also Sollors, *Beyond Ethnicity,* 237–58; Keresztesi, *Strangers at Home*; and Konzett, *Ethnic Modernisms*.

23. Describing literary experimentation in Yiddish during this era, Sollors claims that "at a time when Jewish-American writing in English showed few traces of modernist influences . . . Henry Roth's *Call It Sleep* marked the full breakthrough of high modernism only in 1934." *Beyond Ethnity*, 248.

24. Ferraro, "Avant-Garde Ethnics." Steven J. Belluscio also calls Yezierska's work an example of "immigrant social realism." *To Be Suddenly White*, 191.

25. A contemporary essay in Mencken's *American Mercury* dismissively called Yezierska's language "Yidgin," suggesting that the incorporation of Yiddish words and phrases (both in Yiddish and in translation) was not "aesthetically pertinent": "All they contribute is a sense of indulgent recognition to the Jewish reader, who feels 'in on it,' and a vague sense of outlandishness to the Gentile." Brody, "Yiddish in American Fiction," 207.

26. Drucker, "Yiddish, Yidgin, and Yezierska," 99.

27. Priscilla Wald, *Constituting Americans*, 239.

28. Anolik, "All Words."

29. See Harrison-Kahan, "'Drunk with the Fiery Rhythms'"; and Codde, "Willing Embrace."

30. Konzett, *Ethnic Modernisms*, 4.

31. Yezierska, *How I Found America*, 162. ("To the Stars" was republished in *How I Found America*, hereafter cited as *HIFA*.)

32. Many critics have discussed the importance of the Yezierska-Dewey relationship. See, for example, Dearborn, *Love in the Promised Land*.

33. Julian Levinson reads Yezierska's work "as Romantic, subversive, and 'visionary,' rather than 'ethnic,' documentary and realist—terms that are frequently associated with her." *Exiles on Main Street*, 102. The class's critique of Sophie's writing certainly suggests an affinity with Romanticism, but it is important to remember how closely modernism was linked to the Romantics in early texts.

34. [Jolas], "Proclamation," 13.

35. Also in Jolas's manifesto: "[The literary creator] has the right to use words of his own fashioning and to disregard existing grammatical and syntactical laws." Ibid.

36. Yezierska, "Mr. Lewisohn," 22. Elsewhere Yezierska makes similar claims about "ignorant people," claiming that "ignorant people have a much richer language and a more intense expression than educated people, because educated people use conventional, handed-down phrases that have no vitality; and the ignorant create their own phrases." See Henry Harrison, "Anzia Yezierska," 11.

37. Van Wyck Brooks, *America's Coming-of-Age*, 29.

38. Yezierska, "Mr. Lewisohn," 22.

39. [Jolas], "Proclamation," 13.

40. Jolas, "King's English," 146.

41. [Jolas], "Proclamation," 13; Jolas, "King's English," 146.

42. Williams, *Spring and All,* 45.

43. For a discussion of the centrality of the "real" to modernist writers, see Orvell, *The Real Thing,* 240–86.

44. Yezierska, *Hungry Hearts,* 62; hereafter cited as *HH.*

45. For discussions of the film adaptation, see Konzett, *Ethnic Modernisms,* 56–58; and Lisa Botshon, "Anzia Yezierska and the Marketing of the Jewish Immigrant in 1920s Hollywood," in *Middlebrow Moderns: Popular American Women Writers of the 1920s,* ed. Lisa Botshon and Meredith Goldsmith (Boston: Northeastern University Press, 2003), 203–24.

46. Some characters not only cross boundaries within the collection but also pass into other books entirely, suggesting that Yezierska's fictional version of the Lower East Side is—like Faulkner's Yoknapatawpha County, Hurston's Eatonville, or Anderson's Winesburg—larger than any individual work.

47. This often-romantic obsession with the teacher/philanthropist figure (and master of language) dominates much of Yezierska's fiction and has its roots in her own brief and tortured relationship with philosopher John Dewey. See Dearborn, *Love in the Promised Land.*

48. For competing debates on the relationship between consumerism and race in Yezierska's work, see Harrison-Kahan, "'Drunk with the Fiery Rhythms'"; and Tyrone R. Simpson II, "'The Love of Colour in Me': Anzia Yezierska's *Bread Givers* and the Space of White Racial Manufacture," *MELUS* 34.3 (2009): 93–114. Yezierska's novel *Salome of the Tenements* directly engages fashion culture, and much of the criticism of this novel emphasizes this. See North, *Reading 1922;* and Harrison-Kahan, "No Slaves to Fashion."

49. Importantly, this critique turns in on itself in what Magdalena J. Zaborowska calls the "Hollywood-style reward featuring love and reconciliation with Sara's ailing and widowed father." *How We Found America,* 149. Thomas Ferraro notes, "What is most provocative about Yezierska's interrogation is not that she identifies a psychologically operative patriarchy, but that she shows how a specifically Jewish and feminine socialization allows patriarchy to catch up with even the most rebellious of daughters." *Ethnic Passages,* 83.

50. Eliot, *The Waste Land,* 20.

51. Yezierska, *Bread Givers,* 278; hereafter cited as *BG.*

52. North, *Reading 1922,* 99.

53. See Murphy, *Proletarian Moment,* 55–81; and Rideout, *Radical Novel.* To a degree, *New Masses* advanced something analogous to the official Soviet mode of "socialist realism" in its aesthetic forms. See Edwin Seaver, "Socialist Realism," *New Masses* 22 October 1935, 23–24. A certain hostility toward aestheticism characterized Gold's early 1920s editorship of the *Liberator* as well. For an interesting discussion of this, see McKible, "'Life Is Real and Life Is Earnest.'"

54. Gold, *Change the World!,* 23; hereafter cited as *CTW.*

55. Gold, *Mike Gold: A Literary Anthology,* 160; hereafter cited as *LA.*

56. The Provincetown Players produced three one-act plays early in his career—*Ivan's Homecoming* and *Down the Airshaft* (both 1917) as well as *Money* (1920, anthologized in 1929). Gold also had *La Fiesta: A Comedy of the Mexican Revolution in Three Acts and a Prologue* produced by a substantially different version of the Provincetown Players in 1929, after the play was banned in Boston. *Ivan's Homecoming* and *Down the Airshaft* are

lost, though Alan Wald refers to a Yale University doctoral dissertation (by Robert Sarlos) that provides plot summaries of them. See Wald, *Exiles from a Future Time*, 345n45. *Money* has seen two publications (both under Gold's name, even though the play was performed under the name Irwin Granich). One is a Samuel French edition; the other is in Barrett H. Clark and Thomas R. Cook's 1929 volume *One-Act Plays*. *La Fiesta* is held (in two typescript versions) at the New York Public Library for the Performing Arts.

57. Nicholls, *Modernisms*, 142.
58. Berghaus, *Theater, Performance*, 59–62.
59. See North, *Dialect of Modernism*.
60. Gold, "Let It Be Really New!," 20, 26.
61. See Gold, "3 Schools of U.S. Writing," 13–14; and Gold, "Notes on Art," 10–12.
62. Gold, "Floyd Dell Resigns," 10.
63. Gold, "Notes of the Month," 3–5.
64. Gold, "Theater and Revolution," 536. For a discussion of constructivism, a mode that "purged the theatre of its naturalistic clutter and aesthetic ornaments," see Berghaus, *Theater, Performance*, 193.
65. Dickstein, "Hallucinating the Past," 158.
66. Gold, *Money*, 227–28.
67. Rogin, *Blackface, White Noise*. Absolutely essential to any understanding of the phenomenon of blackface minstrelsy is Eric Lott's *Love and Theft*. The table of contents of this edition of *The American Caravan* includes, in addition to a number of names that have disappeared from most literary histories, an enormous number of major American modernist writers of the era, including Ernest Hemingway, Malcolm Cowley, William Carlos Williams, Edmund Wilson, John Dos Passos, Yvor Winters, Gertrude Stein, Louise Bogan, Allen Tate, Robert Penn Warren, Hart Crane, and Eugene O'Neill.
68. Richard Tuerk's "Michael Gold's *Hoboken Blues*" contains an excellent history of the (failed) production of Gold's drama in 1928. For more production history, see also Valgemae, *Accelerated Grimace*, 88.
69. Gold, *Hoboken Blues*, 549. This particular stage direction was not followed in the New Playwrights Theatre production of *Hoboken Blues*, and white actors played black characters in blackface, which some critics cite as a reason the play fared so poorly. In *New Masses*, John Dos Passos (whose *Airways, Inc.* appeared in the same season), wrote of *Hoboken Blues* that "nobody would take for granted the rather childish but unpretentious blackface minstrelshow method of presentation." Dos Passos, "Did the New Playwrights Theatre Fail?," 13.
70. Gold, "Theater and Revolution," 536.
71. Alan Wald, *Exiles from a Future Time*, 53–54.
72. Mencken, "Life of the Poor," 381.
73. Gold, *Jews without Money*, 309; hereafter cited as *JWM*.
74. On the "proletarian fictional autobiography," see Foley, *Radical Representations*, 284–320. On "ghetto or tenement pastoral," see Denning, *The Cultural Front*, 230–58.
75. Valgemae, *Accelerated Grimace*, 2.
76. Grace, *Regression and Apocalypse*, 142.
77. The notion of "broken talk" also connects quite strongly to the concerns of African American writers during the 1920s in the debates over the politics of dialect writing. See chapter 5 for a discussion of these debates.
78. This connection of Gold's nostalgic mode to Proust is a rather perverse one, con-

sidering that Gold called Proust the "master-masturbator of the bourgeois literature" in his 1930 manifesto "Proletarian Realism" (*LA* 206). But Proust had not always been treated so hostilely by Gold and the *New Masses*. In fact, the *New Masses* review of Gold's first collection of fiction and poetry, *120 Million*, appeared on the same page of the March 1929 issue as a review of a translation of Proust's *Swann's Way*.

79. Of course, this image recalls other modernist images of decay and destruction such as Eliot's *The Waste Land* and the valley of ashes in Fitzgerald's *The Great Gatsby* (1925).

80. Even the excerpts of Gold's novel published in *New Masses* were accompanied by expressionist-inspired artwork. Howard Simon's woodcuts for *Jews without Money* evoke the expressionist work of German artist Kathe Kollwitz and act as direct references to the woodcuts in Louis Wirth's 1928 sociological study *The Ghetto*. In *The Ghetto* the woodcuts by Todros Geller work as modernist compositions (particularly "Holy Emissary" and "Street Musicians"), but they also serve to elevate their subject with a degree of dignity. Simon's woodcuts work with Gold's text against any kind of sentimental description of poverty. In two of the woodcuts, women figure prominently in the foreground, but in a grotesque fashion. One of these (opposite page 57) seems linked to the short descriptive paragraph: "In the maelstrom of wagons, men, pushcarts, street cars, dogs and East Side garbage, the mothers calmly wheeled baby carriages. They stopped in the shade of the Elevated trains, to suckle their babies with big sweaty breasts" (*JWM* 57). In another woodcut (opposite page 176), Simon foregrounds a woman being groped from behind by a grim-looking man while a child looks on in shock. Commercial transactions occur in the background among figures apparently unconcerned with the behavior of the couple in the foreground. Though this image appears opposite Gold's description of the appearance of gypsies on the East Side, the image itself does not seem to have any direct reference to a passage in Gold's text. The grotesque sexuality here enhances the suggestions of the added strangeness that the gypsies bring to the neighborhood.

81. Grace's "regression" follows a tradition of characterizing German expressionist writing as invested in "primitivism" (Wilhelm Worringer, Michael Patterson). See Grace, *Regression and Apocalypse*, 30–34.

82. Of course, the majority of characters in *Jews without Money* are *not* workers in any traditional Marxian sense; they are much closer to the *lumpenproletariat*. Still, Gold's categories do not ever seem to be as fast and loose as this (especially as concerns his upbringing on the East Side), so the "messiah" of communism is seen as not only salvation for conventional workers but also for the denizens of this neighborhood.

4 / "Say It with Lead"

1. Chandler, *Later Novels*, 977.

2. Shaw, introduction to *Hard-Boiled Omnibus*, viii.

3. Chandler, *Later Novels*, 979. In her study *Hard-Boiled*, Erin A. Smith has noted how Chandler's argument works to gender the Golden Age writers (frequently British) as feminine against the American "man ... who is himself not mean" with which Chandler's essay culminates (36–42). For another compelling look at the masculine gendering of the detective story in the 1920s, see Breu, *Hard-Boiled Masculinities*.

4. Orvell, *The Real Thing*, 240. Clearly, Orvell's description has as much to do with naturalism as it does with realism. However, it is important to remember that the theory

behind naturalism emphasized the stronger power that social forces exerted in the lives of the poor.

5. Chandler, *Later Novels*, 988–89.

6. Of course, as with other literary genres, including "high" literature, earlier aesthetic modes continued to appear, and the success of S. S. Van Dine's and Ellery Queen's "classic" work through the 1920s and beyond speaks to the ways in which an older mode is never clearly or cleanly supplanted by a new one.

7. Major examples of these include Haycraft, *Murder for Pleasure*; and Symons, *Mortal Consequences*; as well as broader studies like Cawelti's *Adventure, Mystery*.

8. Even Joyce's *Ulysses* appeared as a topic of discussion in hard-boiled writer Raoul Whitfield's 1932 novel *The Virgin Kills*. For a discussion of this phenomenon, see McCann, "Roughneck Reaching."

9. Van Dine, *I Used to Be a Highbrow*. For more on Van Dine's tormented relationship and brow anxieties, see Hefner, "'I Used to Be a Highbrow.'"

10. As a case in point, the Library of America has produced two-volume editions of the work of both Hammett (1999 and 2001) and Chandler (1995), an effective canonization by one of the major cultural institutions in American literary studies. In addition, Chandler's story "Red Wind" first appears in the seventh edition of *The Norton Anthology of American Literature*.

11. For an excellent description of the classical detective story, see Cawelti, *Adventure, Mystery*, 80–138.

12. Van Dine's Philo Vance serves as an excellent example of what happens to decadence with the onset of modernism. Vance, the amateur psychoanalyst and collector of modernist art, has tastes that seem evolved from the late nineteenth-century sensibilities of Holmes. His affected manner of speech (dropping his g's and utilizing slang at inappropriate moments) points toward modernism (or at least toward a modern sensibility). But, if modernist at all, Vance seems to be a modernist character trapped in a series of rigorously realist novels.

13. Arguably, the environment Dupin occupies is (appropriately) one of romanticism. From the dark parlor rooms where he and the narrator talk during the day to the cacophony of voices that confuse and disturb in "Murders in the Rue Morgue," Dupin's Paris is only truly legible to Dupin, whose uncanny ability to get inside the criminal mind of his antagonist (as in "The Purloined Letter") speaks to the romantic spirit of his works.

14. Stowe, "Semiotics to Hermeneutics," 367.

15. For an example of rules for classical detective stories, see Van Dine, "S. S. Van Dine Sets Down Twenty Rules for Detective Stories," in *I Used to Be a Highbrow*, 31–36. For one example of a purely romantic detective story, see Charles Brockden Brown's *Edgar Huntly: or, Memoirs of a Sleep-Walker* (1799), in which the title character's investigation into the death of his close friend goes completely awry because the romantic environment is almost totally illegible and incomprehensible.

16. Franco Moretti, in a structuralist/Marxist study of the genre, sees Watson as far less intelligent than the reader: "Although we will never be as clever as the detective, we could never be as stupid as Watson. Detective fiction thus assigns the reader an intermediary role between the extremes of *passive reading* (Watson automatically records events that he does not understand) and of *writing* (Holmes, who narrates the *fabula*, emerges as the true author of the work: Poe affirmed that in writing short stories, one must always start from the solution)." See Moretti, *Signs Taken for Wonders*, 148.

17. Stowe, "Semiotics to Hermeneutics," 378, 380.

18. Cawelti, *Adventure, Mystery*, 146.

19. Although Nick Carter was the most enduring of these characters, late nineteenth-century dime novels featured a host of other detective series characters, including Old Sleuth, Old King Brady, Old Cap. Collier, and even Allen Pinkerton. On this history, see Pamela Bedore, *Dime Novels and the Roots of American Detective Fiction* (New York: Palgrave Macmillan, 2013).

20. One of the more direct descendants of Carter in the pulps is Erle Stanley Gardner's Ed Jenkins, "The Phantom Crook," who appeared in nearly seventy-five stories in *Black Mask*. While Jenkins is not technically a detective (though he often masqueraded as one), he is a master of disguise along the lines of Carter. Of course, Sherlock Holmes also frequently employed disguises in his cases.

21. Celebrated Author, "Nick Carter, Detective," 6. Compare this to Chandler's Philip Marlowe, who consistently sinks into a "black hole" when slugged from behind.

22. For a discussion of how dime novels use disguise and disinheritance as ways of masking (and then unmasking) the natural nobility of working-class characters, see Denning, *Mechanic Accents*, esp. 167–200.

23. Shaw, introduction to *Hard-Boiled Omnibus*, vii.

24. For an example of this, see Grebstein, "Tough Hemingway."

25. Worpole, *Dockers and Detectives*, 35. Worpole's consideration of what he calls "the masculine style in popular fiction" anticipates the work of Erin Smith in *Hard-Boiled* and Christopher Breu in *Hard-Boiled Masculinities*.

26. Hemingway probably did not encounter the hard-boiled writers in their original pulp context, though he later had an interesting relationship with the pulps. However, he certainly read Hammett's work, something he mentions in *Death in the Afternoon*: "So we were very careful about death for a while. My eyes were too bad to read and my wife was reading Dashiell Hammett's bloodiest to date, *The Dain Curse*, out loud and every time that Mr. Hammett would kill a character or a set of characters she would substitute the word umpty-umped for the words killed, cut the throat of, blew the brains out of, spattered around the room, and so on" (228).

27. Hemingway, *A Moveable Feast*, 12. The economic conditions of production under which the pulp authors worked are most clearly articulated in two memoirs of the era: Gruber, *The Pulp Jungle* and Hersey, *The Pulpwood Editor*. For a discussion of how these conditions impacted both aesthetics and ideology of writers in *Black Mask*, see McCann, "Roughneck Reaching." These conditions have their roots in the dime novels of the late nineteenth century. For a discussion of one related genre of dime novels and the conditions of dime-novel writers, see Bold, *Selling the Wild West*, 1–36; and Denning, *Mechanic Accents*, 17–26.

28. Naremore, "Dashiell Hammett," 67; Eysteinsson, *Concept of Modernism*, 30.

29. Thompson, *Fiction, Crime, and Empire*, 135. See also Raczkowski, "Modernity's Detection."

30. From the city mysteries of the 1840s to the adventure tales published in pulp magazines in the decades that preceded the emergence of the hard-boiled, characters often acted on the violent, crime-ridden world around them. The connection between violence and detection and the hard-boiled detective story's debt to the Western is discussed in Ruehlmann, *Saint with a Gun*; and Slotkin, *Gunfighter Nation*, 217–28. For Slotkin's discussion of city mysteries, see *The Fatal Environment*, 151–58.

31. Chandler, *Later Novels*, 989.

32. The first example of a slang dictionary in Britain was Thomas Harman's *Caveat or Warening for Commen Curtesors* (1567), "a short glossary of beggars' language" that was designed "to clear England of its undeserving poor by revealing their tricks and disguises." See Coleman, *Cant and Slang Dictionaries*, 1:1.

33. Leverage, "Dictionary of the Underworld," 17 January 1925, 1056. Aspiring crime-fiction writers could also find resources to prevent "the indiscriminate use of the underworld vernacular" (18) in glossaries like Owen E. Sonne's "Crime and Detective Story."

34. Leverage, "Dictionary of the Underworld," 3 January 1925, 690.

35. Denning, *Mechanic Accents*, 24; Erin Smith, *Hard-Boiled*, 21. See also John Cheng's discussion of the "industrial production" of pulp writing in *Astounding Wonder*, 26; as well as contemporaneous critiques of pulp writing such as Robinson, "Wood-Pulp Racket," 64–67.

36. See, for example, McCann, *Gumshoe America*; Erin Smith, *Hard-Boiled*; Breu, *Hard-Boiled Masculinities*; and Earle, *Re-covering Modernism*.

37. "The Aim of Black Mask," *Black Mask*, June 1927, iii.

38. *Black Mask*, October 1929, vi.

39. Erle Stanley Gardner to Phil Cody, 22 March 1930, Erle Stanley Gardner Papers, Harry Ransom Center, University of Texas at Austin; hereafter cited as ESGP.

40. Gardner to Joseph T. Shaw, 11 November 1929, ESGP.

41. Gardner to Shaw, 7 April 1930, ESGP.

42. Lichtblau, "NEW Gangster Story," 57.

43. Gardner to Cody, 10 May 1937, ESGP.

44. Shaw, introduction to *Hard-Boiled Omnibus*, vii.

45. Goulart, *The Dime Detectives*, 20.

46. *Black Mask*, October 1924, 40.

47. Barson, "There's No Sex in Crime," 110.

48. Durham, "*Black Mask* School," 58.

49. Goulart, *The Dime Detectives*, 32.

50. Nolan, *Black Mask Boys*, 35.

51. Ibid., 39.

52. Daly, "From the Author," 127.

53. Daly, "Putting Over," 167–69.

54. Gardner, "Getting Away with Murder," 72.

55. This December 1922 issue of *Black Mask* did contain Hammett's debut in the magazine, a short international adventure story called "The Road Home" (published under the pseudonym Peter Collinson), which contained nothing of the hard-boiled style that would appear later in his Continental Op stories.

56. Breu, *Hard-Boiled Masculinities*, 46–55. This style would return to *Black Mask*, in a slightly more hard-boiled fashion, under the editorship of Fanny Ellsworth (December 1936–April 1940) in the work of writers like Cornell Woolrich.

57. Ward, "Under the Crimson Skull," 29.

58. The psychoanalytic undertones of the story are made explicit here, as the narrator's father is, in fact, a practitioner of the medical precursor to psychology.

59. Daly, "Dolly," 57, 59.

60. Breu, *Hard-Boiled Masculinities*, 47.

61. "Something New for You," *Black Mask*, October 1922, 65. In the interim, the mag-

azine shifted from a monthly to a bimonthly publication schedule, beginning in February 1923.

62. C.P.O., "We Interest Him Strangely," *Black Mask*, 15 May 1923, 127.

63. Daly, "The Ambulating Lady," 21.

64. Duffield, "The Pulps," 26.

65. Hammett, *Selected Letters*, 37.

66. Daly, "Paying an Old Debt," 15.

67. Montanye, "Looking Out for Orchid," 105. Since Mencken was highly involved with the selection of manuscripts in the first year of *Black Mask*, it is unsurprising that this Lardneresque piece made it into the pages of the magazine, in spite of its incongruity with much of the rest of the issue's contents.

68. Daly, "Kiss-the-Canvas Crowley," 50.

69. Ibid., 61.

70. Because of its close relationship to gambling and corruption and its own poetry of violence, boxing is the sport most frequently included in hard-boiled stories. Two notable instances are in Hammett's *Red Harvest* and Raoul Whitfield's "Murder in the Ring" (*Black Mask*, December 1930).

71. Daly, "Kiss-the Canvas Crowley," 61.

72. North, *Reading 1922*.

73. Daly, "False Burton Combs," 3.

74. Leverage's "Dictionary of the Underworld" has only one definition for "smoke": "To talk (too much)." "Dictionary of the Underworld," 4 April 1925, 819.

75. Ibid., 9–10. "Cake-eater" does not show up in Leverage's "Dictionary of the Underworld," but it makes a clever appearance in Wood and Goddard's *Dictionary of American Slang* (1926), discussed in the introduction.

76. Sean McCann has written an excellent analysis of Daly's "Knights of the Open Palm" and its ideological critique of the Klan in the context of *Black Mask*'s notorious Klan issue (1 June 1923). See *Gumshoe America*, 39–86. For another consideration of this, see Zhang, "Behind *Black Mask*," 105–51.

77. Daly, "Knights of the Open Palm," 18.

78. Daly, *The Tag Murders*, 80.

79. In his essay on crime fiction, "Raffles and Miss Blandish," George Orwell lauds the moral sensibility of earlier crime fiction over the equivocation of mid-twentieth-century pulp fiction.

80. Daly, *Snarl of the Beast*, 1.

81. Benjamin, *Understanding Brecht*, 94.

82. Stein, *Everybody's Autobiography*, 2–3.

83. Ibid., 3–4.

84. Stein, *Writings, 1932–1946*, 358.

85. In addition, "Tulip," the unfinished manuscript Hammett left at his death, concerns the struggles of a writer late in his career.

86. Marcus, "Dashiell Hammett," 371.

87. Naremore, "Dashiell Hammett," 61, 67.

88. Thompson, *Fiction, Crime*, 135.

89. Raczkowski, "Modernity's Detection," 651.

90. Earle, *Re-covering Modernism*, 103. Paula Rabinowitz uses the same term in *Black*

& *White & Noir*, but her interests involve how the cinematic style of film noir actively engages both leftist and populist politics as well as ideas of race and gender in American history. For another take on Hammett as a modernist, see Gray, "Jimmying the Back Door."

91. Hammett, *Selected Letters*, 47; McGurl, *The Novel Art*, 175.

92. Hammett, *Selected Letters*, 46.

93. Probably the most well-known example of a writer using a pseudonym in the pulps was Frederick Faust, who published poetry under his own name and became the "king of the pulps" under the pseudonym Max Brand.

94. For one example of this, see Marling, *American Roman Noir*, 93–147.

95. Hammett, "Advertisement IS Literature," 35.

96. Ibid., 36. The connection to Stein's repetitious style here is obvious.

97. Ibid.

98. I will be using the texts of Hammett's stories reprinted in *Crime Stories and Other Writings*. Hereafter, stories will be cited with the notation *CS*.

99. Twain, *Pudd'nhead Wilson*, 114.

100. Hammett, *Lost Stories*, 186.

101. Ibid., 189.

102. Ibid., 192–93.

103. Ibid., 194, 195, 196.

104. The opening of the typescript suggests intended publication: "This list has been re-arranged from one received by one of our writers from San Quentin Prison. A few corrections in spelling and grammar have been made—in the meaning, not the vocabulary." Hammett, "Jargon of the Underworld," Dashiell Hammett Papers, Harry Ransom Center, University of Texas at Austin. Hammett's list shares a number of terms with Leverage's "Dictionary of the Underworld"; however, it does not appear to derive from Elisha K. Kane's "The Jargon of the Underworld." Other hard-boiled writers often collected lists of this kind. See, for example, Raymond Chandler's lists of "Railroad Slang," "Slang and Hard Talk," "Hollywood Slang," "Narcotic Squad Slang," "San Quentin Prison Slang," and "Pickpocket Lingo" in McShane, *Notebooks of Raymond Chandler*, 53–54, 57–58, 62–63.

105. Cawelti, *Adventure, Mystery*, 96.

106. Counihan's untrustworthy smoothness also resembles what William Marling calls "the clash of the rough and the smooth in the domain of popular style" in an essay on *The Maltese Falcon*. "Style and Ideology," 42–43.

107. For a discussion of the changes Hammett made to the text of *Red Harvest* between its publication as a serial and as a hardback, see Hagemann, "'Cleansing of Poisonville.'"

108. *Black Mask*, December 1927, 33.

109. A great deal of criticism, including Michael Denning's *The Cultural Front*, has already attempted to fit *Red Harvest* into the paradigm of the proletarian novel. Like Gold's work, discussed in chapter 3, Hammett's aesthetic is absorbed in the violence and corruption of the environment, and *Red Harvest* offers even less of a proletarian hope at its conclusion. Still, *Red Harvest* clearly demonstrates some element of Hammett's political thinking that might be usefully connected to the vernacular expressionism of Gold and the work of other proletarian writers.

110. Hammett, *Complete Novels*, 5; hereafter cited as *CN*.

111. Wood and Goddard, *Dictionary of American Slang*, 34. Leverage's "Dictionary of the Underworld" does not include "mucker," but it defines "muck" as "offensive talk." 28 February 1925, 1151.

112. In James, language is rarely the problem; it is the characters who fail the language, not the other way around.

113. Porter, *Pursuit of Crime*, 137.

114. Thompson, *Fiction, Crime*, 146.

5 / "The Necromancy of Language"

1. Krapp, "English of the Negro," 190.

2. Ibid., 191. It is worth noting that the logic of Krapp's argument bears some similarity to George S. Schuyler's "The Negro-Art Hokum," *Nation* (1926), in that it attempts to demolish racial essentialism, but it still remains ignorant of the practice of African American vernacular.

3. James Harrison, "Negro English," 233, 279.

4. Gates, *Figures in Black*, 173; Smitherman, *Word from the Mother*, 9.

5. Toomer, *Cane*, 81.

6. Ibid., 97.

7. Ibid., 109.

8. Ibid., 93.

9. Sollors, *Beyond Ethnicity*, 6. See also Gates, *Figures in Black*, 167–95, where he presents the descent into dialect in a decidedly more romantic fashion.

10. Johnson, preface to *Book of American Negro Poetry*, xl.

11. Ibid., xl–xli.

12. Johnson, *Complete Poems*, 9. See also Thaggert, *Images of Black Modernism*, 29–64.

13. Dubey, *Signs and Cities*, 6.

14. The political use of bourgeois forms of representation permeates much of the fiction of the era, but the early 1920s works of Walter White and Jessie Fauset are perhaps the most obvious examples of this trend, which continues through the late 1920s in the work of writers like Nella Larsen.

15. Hutchinson, *Harlem Renaissance*, 117.

16. Thurman, "Negro Artists," 38. Another example of this position can be seen in Hurston's "Characteristics of Negro Expression" (1934) in *Folklore, Memoirs*, 830–46.

17. For comparison, see Ann Douglas's discussion of modernism's "matricidal" inclinations in *Terrible Honesty*.

18. Vogel, *Scene of Harlem Cabaret*, 27.

19. Bone, *Negro Novel*, 65. Benjamin Brawley calls this group, for example, "the new realists." See *The Negro Genius*, 231–68. Sterling Brown writes that "Rudolph Fisher portrays Harlem with a jaunty realism." *Negro in American Fiction*, 135. Bone's history acknowledges the importance of linguistic innovation in writings by what he terms the "Harlem School": "Beginning with the Harlem School, the linguistic texture of the Negro novel has been greatly influenced by the rhythms and inflections of Negro speech, and especially by jive, the colorful argot of the urban Negro." *Negro Novel*, 66.

20. For another recent consideration of this symposium, see Thaggart, *Images of Black Modernism*, 11–16.

21. "Negro in Art," *Crisis* 31.5 (March 1926): 219.

22. "Negro in Art," *Crisis* 32.4 (September 1926): 238.
23. Thaggert, *Images of Black Modernism*, 15.
24. For an additional discussion of this essay and its contexts, see David Levering Lewis, *W. E. B. Du Bois*, 176–82.
25. Du Bois, "Criteria of Negro Art," 296.
26. As if to underscore his point, Du Bois's essay is set opposite a special feature of the *Crisis* called "Pictures of 500 Children," a multipage project full of both candid and studio photographs of African American children looking, for the most part, directly into the camera. The layout, with Du Bois's text and the photos on facing pages, suggests that the propagandistic art that Du Bois describes is, in fact, necessary for these children to have "the right . . . to love and enjoy" any aspect of their adult lives. Daylanne English sees the *Crisis*'s emphasis on family photos as connected to eugenic discourses. See "W. E. B. Du Bois's Family *Crisis*."
27. Du Bois, "Criteria of Negro Art," 292.
28. Du Bois, *The Philadelphia Negro*, 3.
29. Vogel, *Scene of Harlem Cabaret*, 139.
30. Gaines, *Uplifting the Race*, 159.
31. Du Bois, *The Philadelphia Negro*, 316; Gaines, *Uplifting the Race*, 175.
32. Du Bois, "Criteria of Negro Art," 297.
33. Ibid., 296.
34. Du Bois, "Books," 81.
35. Johnson, "Romance and Tragedy," 316. Wallace Thurman also praised the novel, suggesting that he "would not be surprised should some of our uplift organizations and neighborhood clubs plan to erect a latter-day abolitionist statue to Carl Van Vechten on the corner of 135th Street and Seventh Avenue for the author has been most fair, and most sympathetic in his treatment of a long mistreated group of subjects." "Stranger at the Gates," 279. Thurman's comments on the novel continue in the only issue of *Fire!!* See "Fire Burns," 47–48.
36. Du Bois, "Review of Nigger Heaven," 81.
37. Hurston, "Story in Harlem Slang," 95.
38. Van Vechten, *Nigger Heaven*, 285–86.
39. Van Vechten, "Notes for *Nigger Heaven*, chiefly typewritten," Carl Van Vechten Papers, Yale Collection of American Literature, Beinecke Rare Book and Manuscript Library.
40. "Notes and Suggestions Made by Various Authors Concerning Carl Van Vechten's *Nigger Heaven*," Carl Van Vechten Papers, Yale Collection of American Literature, Beinecke Rare Book and Manuscript Library.
41. Fisher, *Walls of Jericho*, 300; hereafter cited as *WOJ*.
42. Hurston, *Folklore, Memoirs*, 845–46.
43. Van Patten, "Vocabulary of the American Negro," 24.
44. The self-conscious deployment of African American slang in the work of Fisher and McKay challenge Gates's claim that "only Jean Toomer's *Cane*, Langston Hughes's first two volumes of poetry, and Sterling Brown's *Southern Road* demonstrated the use of this black poetic diction, precisely because these poets were the point of consciousness of their language." Gates, *Figures in Black*, 187.
45. Hughes, *The Big Sea*, 240.
46. Ibid.

47. For a discussion of the publishing history of the Harlem Reniassance, see Wintz, *Black Culture*, 154–89.

48. Contemporary reviewers frequently made this comparison. In a review of Larsen's *Passing* in *Opportunity*, Mary Fleming Labaree lamented, "The pity of it!—if 'Walls of Jericho' and 'Home to Harlem' perched upon our bookshelves with 'Plum Bun' and 'Passing' nowhere to be seen." See Labaree, "Our Book Shelf," 255.

49. Jinx and Bubber also appear as supporting characters in *The Conjure-Man Dies* and the story "One Month's Wages," unpublished until after Fisher's death.

50. Du Bois, "The Browsing Reader," 374.

51. "'The Walls of Jericho' and Other New Works of Fiction," *New York Times*, 5 August, 1928.

52. Fisher, *Collected Stories*, 3.

53. The only real exception to this is Paul Laurence Dunbar's fascinating 1902 novel *The Sport of the Gods*.

54. The move in *Cane*, from South to North to South again, suggests a model more like *Home to Harlem*, where the bourgeois experience is somehow contained within the vernacular experience. However, the perspective of the poems and sketches in the first section, as well as "Kabnis," the dramatic poem of the last section, is most certainly that of the outsider, seeing the experience of Southern African Americans as both romantic and grotesque (in the sense of Sherwood Anderson's *Winesburg, Ohio*). The trajectory of the text as a whole even implies that its perspective comes from figures like Kabnis and Lewis, both Northern "outsiders" in the Southern black community in that final section.

55. Fisher, *Collected Stories*, 6.

56. Fisher defines these terms in his "Introduction to Contemporary Harlemese": dicty is a "high-toned person" and rat is defined as the "antithesis of *dickty*" (*WOJ* 298, 304).

57. Gates, *The Signifying Monkey*, xxi, xxiv.

58. See, for example, Van Patten, "Vocabulary of the American Negro." It was only after the publication of Zora Neale Hurston's "Story in Harlem Slang" in the *American Mercury* in 1942 that Mencken finally acknowledged the importance of African American contributions to the American language. See Mencken, *The American Language*, Supplement II, 263–70, 710.

59. See, for example, "'The Walls of Jericho' and Other New Works of Fiction," *New York Times*, 5 August 1928.

60. This kind of referentiality is also present in Wood and Goddard's *Dictionary of American Slang*, and the emphasis on the glossary as an often baffling source of "answers," should also be seen as a form of signifying on modernist paratexts like T. S. Eliot's notorious notes to *The Waste Land* (1922).

61. Hughes, "Negro Artist," 694. During this period, Hughes was undergoing his own transformation, from a more moderate poetic aesthetic in *The Weary Blues* (1926) to the aggressive vernacular forms of *Fine Clothes to the Jew* (1927).

62. The cultural politics of Jewish performers enacting an African American identity through minstrelsy on both stage and screen has been discussed in Michael Rogin's *Blackface, White Noise*.

63. Notably, in the year before Fisher's novel was published, well-known Jewish stage performer Al Jolson performed in blackface in the first widely successful sound-synchronized film, *The Jazz Singer* (dir. Crosland, 1927).

64. The novel's epigraph is from a spiritual: "Joshua fit d' battle ob Jericho/And d' walls come tumblin' down—"

65. North, *Dialect of Modernism*, 110–23, 112.

66. Brawley includes McKay in his group of "new realists." For a reading that emphasizes McKay's romanticism (especially in his poetry), see Gosciak, *Claude McKay*.

67. In a letter to James Weldon Johnson, McKay wrote of *Home to Harlem*, "I consider the book a real proletarian novel, but I don't expect the nice radicals to see that it is, because they know very little about proletarian life and what they want of proletarian art is not proletarian life, truthfully, realistically, and artistically portrayed, but their own false, soft-headed and wine-watered notions of the proletariat." McKay to Johnson, 30 April 1928, James Weldon Johnson and Grace Nail Johnson Papers, Yale Collection of American Literature, Beinecke Rare Book and Manuscript Library.

68. Holcomb, *Claude McKay*.

69. Cited in Cooper, *Passion of Claude McKay*, 26.

70. Cooper, foreword to the 1987 edition of McKay, *Home to Harlem*, xvi.

71. Claude McKay to Langston Hughes, 3 April [1928], Langston Hughes Papers, James Weldon Johnson Collection in the Yale Collection of American Literature, Beinecke Rare Book and Manuscript Library.

72. McKay, *Home to Harlem*, 4; hereafter cited as *HTH*.

73. The picaresque, at least in its most formative instantiations, involves adventures of a lower-class figure that ultimately achieves some sort of success or redemption. At the same time, this genre mounts a critique of existing socioeconomic realities: not surprising, as the genre emerged near the end of feudalism and leveled charges of hypocrisy at the church and aristocracy. Critics who have called the novel "picaresque" include Tillery, *Claude McKay*, 85.

74. Smethurst, *New Red Negro*, 10.

75. It seems like Van Vechten wanted to create a similar vernacular frame in *Nigger Heaven*, particularly in the prologue that deals with Anatole Longfellow, "alias the Scarlet Creeper." Ultimately, however, this framing device is jettisoned for a more conventional narrative form. See *Nigger Heaven*, 3.

76. Ibid., 286.

77. In this sense, Ray's experience is much like that of the hard-boiled figures of Dashiell Hammett and Raymond Chandler, whose most intensely subjective experiences emerge as a result of drugs or violence. See chapter 4 for a description of Hammett's "The Big Knock-Over."

78. Hurston, *Folklore, Memoirs*, 828.

79. McKay, *Banjo*, 11; hereafter cited as *B*.

80. Yezierska, "Mr. Lewisohn's 'Up Stream,'" 22.

81. North, *Dialect of Modernism*, 123.

82. Lukács, *Theory of the Novel*, 41.

Conclusion

1. Denning, *The Cultural Front*, xvii.
2. Phelps and Rahv, "Problems and Perspective," 9.
3. Dos Passos, *U.S.A.*, 3.
4. Wilson, "Dahlberg, Dos Passos and Wilder," in *Shores of Light*, 447.

5. Wilson published earlier versions of the chapters from *Axel's Castle* in the *New Republic* from 1928–30.

6. Gates, *The Signifying Monkey*, 170–216.

7. Cleanth Brooks's early and influential study identifies Faulkner's provincialism as "a vantage point from which to criticize, directly or perhaps merely by implication, the powerful metropolitan culture." *William Faulkner*, 1.

8. See, for example, Ellison, "Twentieth-Century Fiction and the Black Mask of Humanity," in *Collected Essays*, 81–99.

9. Qtd. in Blotner, *Faulkner*, 1554.

10. See, for example, Fowler and Abadie, *Faulkner and Popular Culture*.

11. Faulkner, *Novels, 1930–1935*, 1029. See also Wenska, "There's a Man with a Gun"; and Forter, *Murdering Masculinities*, 85–125. On *Pylon* and aviation pulps, see Earle, *Re-Covering Modernism*, 198–201. Faulkner also called his 1938 novel *The Unvanquished* (made up of stories published in the *Saturday Evening Post* and *Scribner's*) "trash" and "a pulp series." Faulkner to Morton Goldman, Oxford, MS, August 1934, in Faulkner, *Selected Letters*, 84.

12. Breu, *Hard-Boiled Masculinities*, 115–41.

13. See Earle, *Re-Covering Modernism*, 154, 169–96, and "Faulkner and the Paperback Trade."

14. Faulkner, *Novels, 1926–1929*, 1015.

15. Daly, "Paying an Old Debt," 13.

Bibliography

Adams, Amanda. *Performing Authorship in the Nineteenth-Century Transatlantic Lecture Tour.* Burlington, VT: Ashgate, 2014.
Adams, Randolph G., et al. *Literary History of the United States.* New York: Macmillan, 1948.
Ade, George. *Fables in Slang and More Fables in Slang.* Introduction by E. F. Bleiler. New York: Dover, 1960.
"The Aim of Black Mask." *Black Mask,* June 1927, iii.
Aldington, Richard. "English and American." *Poetry* 16.2 (May 1920): 94–98.
——. "A Young American Poet." *Little Review* 2.1 (1915): 22–25.
Algeo, John. *The Origins and Development of the English Language.* 6th ed. Boston: Cengage, 2010.
Allen, Frederick Lewis. *Only Yesterday: An Informal History of the 1920s.* 1931. Reprint, New York: Perennial Classics, 2000.
Anolik, Ruth Bienstock. "'All Words, Words, about Words': Linguistic Journey and the Transformation in Anzia Yezierska's *The Bread-Givers.*" *Studies in American Jewish Literature* 21 (2002): 12–23.
Antin, Mary. *The Promised Land.* 1912. Reprint, New York: Penguin, 1997.
Arac, Jonathan. "Babel and Vernacular in an Empire of Immigrants: Howells and the Languages of American Fiction." *boundary 2* 34.2 (2007): 1–20.
Ashford, Daisy. *The Young Visiters.* London: Chatto & Windus, 1919.
Auerbach, Erich. *Mimesis: The Representation of Reality in Western Literature.* Princeton: Princeton University Press, 1953.
Avery, Todd. "'The Girls in Europe Is Nuts over Ball Players': Ring Lardner and Virginia Woolf." *Nine: A Journal of Baseball History and Culture* 13.2 (Spring 2005): 31–53.

Bakhtin, M. M. *The Dialogic Imagination: Four Essays.* Edited by Michael Holquist, translated by Caryl Emerson and Michael Holquist. Austin: University of Texas Press, 1981.

Barson, Michael S. "'There's No Sex in Crime': The Two-Fisted Homilies of Race Williams." *Clues: A Journal of Detection* 2.2 (Fall–Winter 1981): 103–12.

Beard, Charles A., and Mary R. Beard. *The Rise of American Civilization.* New York: Macmillan, 1930.

Beauchamp, Cari. *Without Lying Down: Frances Marion and the Powerful Women of Early Hollywood.* New York: Scribner, 1997.

Beauchamp, Cari, and Mary Anita Loos, eds. *Anita Loos Rediscovered: Film Treatments and Fiction by Anita Loos.* Berkeley: University of California Press, 2003.

Belluscio, Steven J. *To Be Suddenly White: Literary Realism and Racial Passing.* Columbia: University of Missouri Press, 2006.

Benjamin, Walter. *Understanding Brecht.* London: New Left Books, 1973.

Benstock, Shari. *Women of the Left Bank: Paris, 1900–1940.* Austin: University of Texas Press, 1987.

Berghaus, Günther. *Theater, Performance, and the Historical Avant-Garde.* New York: Palgrave Macmillan, 2005.

Blair, Walter. *Native American Humor.* San Francisco: Chandler Publishing, 1960.

Blakemore, Steven. "Huck Finn's Written World." *American Literary Realism* 20.2 (Winter 1988): 21–29.

Blom, T. E. "Anita Loos and Sexual Economics: *Gentlemen Prefer Blondes.*" *Canadian Review of American Studies* 7 (1976): 39–47.

Blotner, Joseph. *Faulkner: A Biography.* New York: Random House, 1974.

Bohlman, Philip V. "Vernacular Music." *Grove Music Online.* http://www.oxfordmusiconline.com/public/book/omo_gmo.

Bold, Christine. *Selling the Wild West: Popular Western Fiction, 1860 to 1960.* Bloomington: Indiana University Press, 1987.

Bone, Robert. *The Negro Novel in America.* New Haven, CT: Yale University Press, 1965.

Bordwell, David, Janet Staiger, and Kristen Thompson. *The Classical Hollywood Cinema: Film Style and Mode of Production to 1960.* New York: Columbia University Press, 1985.

Bornstein, George. *Material Modernism: The Politics of the Page.* Cambridge, UK: Cambridge University Press, 2001.

Bourdieu, Pierre. *The Field of Cultural Production.* New York: Columbia University Press, 1993.

———. *The Rules of Art: Genesis and Structure of the Literary Field.* Translated by Susan Emanuel. Stanford, CA: Stanford University Press, 1995.

Bourne, Randolph. "Trans-National America." *Atlantic Monthly,* June 1916, 86–97.

Bowser, Eileen. *The Transformation of Cinema, 1907 to 1915.* New York: Scribner, 1990.

Bradbury, Malcolm. "Modernisms/Postmodernisms." In *Innovation/Renovation,*

edited by Ihab Hassan and Sally Hassan, 311–27. Madison: University of Wisconsin Press, 1983.
Braddock, Jeremy. *Collecting as Modernist Practice*. Baltimore: Johns Hopkins University Press, 2012.
Brawley, Benjamin. *The Negro Genius*. New York: Dodd, Mead, 1940.
Breu, Christopher. *Hard-Boiled Masculinities*. Minneapolis: University of Minnesota Press, 2006.
Bridgman, Richard. *The Colloquial Style in America*. New York: Oxford University Press, 1966.
Brodhead, Richard H. *Cultures of Letters: Scenes of Reading and Writing in Nineteenth-Century America*. Chicago: University of Chicago Press, 1993.
Brody, Alter. "Yiddish in American Fiction." *American Mercury*, February 1926, 205–7.
Brooks, Cleanth. *William Faulkner: The Yoknapatawpha Country*. New Haven, CT: Yale University Press, 1966.
Brooks, Van Wyck. *America's Coming-of-Age*. New York: B. W. Huebsch, 1915.
Brown, Sterling. *The Negro in American Fiction*. 1937. Reprint, Port Washington, NY: Kennikat Press, 1968.
Bürger, Peter. *Theory of the Avant-Garde*. Minneapolis: University of Minnesota Press, 1984.
Burns, Philip. "Fabrication and Faultline: Language as Experience in *Roughing It*." *Midwest Quarterly* 29.2 (Winter 1988): 249–63.
Cahan, Abraham. *The Rise of David Levinsky*. 1917. Reprint, New York: Penguin, 1993.
———. *Yekl: A Tale of the New York Ghetto*. New York: D. Appleton, 1896.
Camlot, Jason. "Early Talking Books: Spoken Recording and Recitation Anthologies, 1880–1920." *Book History* 6 (2003): 147–73.
Carey, Gary. *Anita Loos: A Biography*. New York: Knopf, 1988.
Carkeet, David. "The Dialects in *Huckleberry Finn*." *American Literature* 51.3 (1979): 315–32.
Castronovo, Russ. *Beautiful Democracy: Aesthetics and Anarchy in a Global Era*. Chicago: University of Chicago Press, 2007.
Cawelti, John G. *Adventure, Mystery, and Romance: Formula Stories as Art and Popular Culture*. Chicago: University of Chicago Press, 1976.
Celebrated Author. "Nick Carter, Detective." *Nick Carter Detective Library* 1 (8 August 1891).
Cella, Laurie J. C. "Narrative 'Confidence Games': Framing the Blonde Spectacle in *Gentlemen Prefer Blondes* (1925) and *Nights at the Circus* (1984)." *Frontiers* 25.3 (2004): 47–62.
Chandler, Raymond. *Later Novels and Other Writings*. New York: Library of America, 1995.
Cheng, John. *Astounding Wonder: Imagining Science and Science Fiction in Interwar America*. Philadelphia: University of Pennsylvania Press, 2012.

Chinitz, David. *T. S. Eliot and the Cultural Divide*. Chicago: University of Chicago Press, 2003.
Churchwell, Sarah. "'Lost among the Ads': *Gentlemen Prefer Blondes* and the Politics of Imitation." In *Middlebrow Moderns: Popular American Women Writers of the 1920s*, edited by Lisa Botschon and Meredith Goldsmith, 135–66. Boston: Northeastern University Press, 2003.
Cmiel, Kenneth. *Democratic Eloquence: The Fight over Popular Speech in Nineteenth-Century America*. New York: William Morrow, 1990.
Codde, Philippe. "'A Willing Embrace of the Shadow': Cultural and Textual Hybridity in Anzia Yezierska's *Bread Givers*." In *"Lost on the Map of the World": Jewish-American Women's Quest for Home in Essays and Memoirs, 1890–Present*, edited by Phillipa Kafka, 7–24. New York: Peter Lang, 2001.
Coleman, Julie. *A History of Cant and Slang Dictionaries, Volume 1: 1567–1784*. New York: Oxford University Press, 2004.
———. *A History of Cant and Slang Dictionaries, Volume 2: 1785–1858*. New York: Oxford University Press, 2004.
———. *A History of Cant and Slang Dictionaries, Volume 3: 1859–1936*. New York: Oxford University Press, 2009.
Connolly, Cyril. *Enemies of Promise*. New York: Macmillan, 1948.
Cooper, Wayne F. Foreword to the 1987 edition of *Home to Harlem*, by Claude McKay, ix–xxvi. 1928. Reprint, Boston: Northeastern University Press, 1987.
———, ed. *The Passion of Claude McKay: Selected Poetry and Prose, 1912–1948*. New York: Schocken Books, 1973.
Corrothers, James D. *The Black Cat Club: Negro Humor and Folklore*. New York: Funk & Wagnalls, 1902.
Cowley, Malcolm. "The Middle American Style: D. Crockett to E. Hemingway." *New York Times Review of Books*, 15 July 1945, 3, 14.
———. "The Revolt against Gentility." In *The Portable Malcolm Cowley*, edited by Donald W. Faulkner, 191–206. New York: Viking, 1990.
Cowlishaw, Brian T. "The Reader's Role in Ring Lardner's Rhetoric." *Studies in Short Fiction* 31 (1994): 207–16.
C.P.O. "We Interest Him Strangely." *Black Mask*, 15 May 1923, 127.
Crosby, Harry. "The New Word." *transition* 16/17 (June 1929): 30.
Daly, Carroll John. "The Ambulating Lady." *Writer's Digest*, April 1947, 19–24.
———. "Dolly." *Black Mask*, October 1922, 57–65.
———. "The False Burton Combs." In *The Hard-Boiled Detective: Stories from Black Mask Magazine, 1920–1951*, edited by Herbert Ruhm, 3–30. New York: Vintage, 1977.
———. "From the Author of Knights of the Open Palm." *Black Mask*, 1 June 1923, 127.
———. "Kiss-the-Canvas Crowley." *Black Mask*, 1 September 1923, 49–61.
———. "Knights of the Open Palm." In *The Great American Detective*, edited by William Kittredge and Steven M. Krauzer, 17–38. New York: Mentor, 1978.

———. "Paying an Old Debt." *American Magazine*, April 1923, 13–15, 132–33, 135.
———. "Putting Over a Detective Novel." *Editor*, 10 December 1927, 167–69.
———. *The Snarl of the Beast*. 1927. Reprint, New York: HarperPerennial, 1992.
———. *The Tag Murders*. New York: E. J. Clode, 1930.
Damon, Maria. *The Dark End of the Street*. Minneapolis: University of Minnesota Press, 1993.
———. "Gertrude Stein's Jewishness, Jewish Social Scientists, and the 'Jewish Question.'" *Modern Fiction Studies* 42.3 (1996): 489–506.
Dearborn, Mary V. "Anzia Yezierska and the Making of an Ethnic American Self." In *The Invention of Ethnicity*, edited by Werner Sollors, 105–23. New York: Oxford University Press, 1989.
———. *Love in the Promised Land: The Story of Anzia Yezierska and John Dewey*. New York: Free Press, 1988.
de Jongh, James. *Vicious Modernism: Black Harlem and the Literary Imagination*. New York: Cambridge University Press, 1990.
Denning, Michael. *The Cultural Front: The Laboring of American Culture in the Twentieth Century*. London: Verso, 1997.
———. *Mechanic Accents: Dime Novels and Working-Class Culture in America*. London: Verso, 1987.
Dickstein, Morris. "Hallucinating the Past: *Jews without Money* Revisited." *Grand Street* 9.2 (Winter 1990): 155–68.
Dime. Review of *Come On In*. *Variety*, 27 September 1918, 44.
Dos Passos, John. "Did the New Playwrights Theatre Fail?" *New Masses* 5.3 (August 1929): 13.
———. *U.S.A.* 1938. Reprint, New York: Library of America, 1996.
Douglas, Ann. *The Feminization of American Culture*. New York: Knopf, 1977.
———. *Terrible Honesty: Mongrel Manhattan in the 1920s*. New York: Farrar, Straus and Giroux, 1995.
Drucker, Sally Ann. "Yiddish, Yidgin, and Yezierska: Dialect in Jewish-American Writing." *Yiddish* 6.4 (1987): 99–113.
Dubey, Madhu. *Signs and Cities: Black Literary Postmodernism*. Chicago: University of Chicago Press, 2003.
Du Bois, W. E. B. "The Browsing Reader." *Crisis*, November 1928, 374, 390.
———. "Criteria of Negro Art." *Crisis*, October 1926, 290–97.
———. *The Philadelphia Negro: A Social Study*. Philadelphia: University of Pennsylvania Press, 1899.
———. Review of *Nigger Heaven*, by Carl Van Vechten. *Crisis*, December 1926, 81–82.
Duffield, Marcus. "The Pulps: Day Dreams for the Masses." *Vanity Fair*, June 1933, 26–27, 51, 60.
Dunne, Finley Peter. *Mr. Dooley in Peace and in War*. Boston: Small, Maynard, 1898.
Durham, Philip. "The *Black Mask* School." In *Tough-Guy Writers of the Thirties*,

edited by David Madden, 51–79. Carbondale: Southern Illinois University Press, 1968.

Eagleton, Terry. *Against the Grain: Essays, 1975–1985*. London: Verso, 1986.

Earle, David M. "Faulkner and the Paperback Trade." In *William Faulkner in Context*, edited by John T. Matthews, 231–45. New York: Cambridge University Press, 2015.

———. *Re-covering Modernism: Pulps, Paperbacks, and the Prejudice of Form*. Burlington, VT: Ashgate, 2009.

Eble, Connie C. Introduction. *American Speech* 75.3 (2000): 227–28.

Eliot, T. S. *The Waste Land: Authoritative Text, Contexts, Criticism*. Edited by Michael North. New York: Norton, 2001. First published by Boni & Liveright, 1922.

Ellison, Ralph. *The Collected Essays of Ralph Ellison*. Edited by John F. Callahan. New York: Modern Library, 2003.

Emerson, John, and Anita Loos. *Breaking Into Movies*. New York: McCann, 1921.

———. *How to Write Photoplays*. New York: McCann, 1920.

English, Daylanne. "W. E. B. Du Bois's Family *Crisis*." *American Literature* 72.2 (2000): 291–319.

English, James F. "Cultural Capital and the Revolutions of Literary Modernity, from Bourdieu to Casanova." In *A Handbook of Modernism Studies*, edited by Jean-Michel Rabaté, 363–77. Hoboken, NJ: John Wiley & Sons, 2013.

Entin, Joseph B. *Sensational Modernism: Experimental Fiction and Photography in Thirties America*. Chapel Hill: University of North Carolina Press, 2007.

Eysteinsson, Astradur. *The Concept of Modernism*. Ithaca, NY: Cornell University Press, 1990.

Faulkner, William. *Novels, 1926–1929*. New York: Library of America, 2006.

———. *Novels, 1930–1935*. New York: Library of America, 1985.

———. *Selected Letters of William Faulkner*. Edited by Joseph Blotner. New York: Random House, 1977.

Feaster, Patrick "'The Following Record': Making Sense of Phonographic Performance, 1877–1908." PhD diss., Indiana University, 2007.

———. "Framing the Mechanical Voice: Generic Conventions of Early Phonograph Recording." *Folklore Forum* 32.1/2 (2001): 57–102.

Fecher, Charles A. *Mencken: A Study of His Thought*. New York: Knopf, 1978.

Ferraro, Thomas. "Avant-Garde Ethnics." In *The Future of American Modernism: Ethnic Writing between the Wars*, edited by William Boelhower, 1–31. Amsterdam: Free University Press, 1990.

———. *Ethnic Passages: Literary Immigrants in Twentieth-Century America*. Chicago: University of Chicago Press, 1993.

Fisher, Rudolph. "The Caucasian Storms Harlem." *American Mercury*, August 1927, 393–98.

———. *The Collected Stories of Rudolph Fisher*. Edited by John McCluskey Jr. Columbia: University of Missouri Press, 1987.

———. *The Walls of Jericho*. 1928. Reprint, Ann Arbor: University of Michigan Press, 1994.
Fishkin, Shelley Fisher. *Was Huck Black?* New York: Oxford University Press, 1993.
Fitzgerald, F. Scott. *The Crack-Up*. Edited by Edmund Wilson. New York: New Directions, 1945.
Foley, Barbara. *Radical Representations: Politics and Form in U.S. Proletarian Fiction, 1929–1941*. Durham, NC: Duke University Press, 1993.
Forter, Greg. *Murdering Masculinities: Fantasies of Gender and Violence in the American Crime Novel*. New York: NYU Press, 1999.
Fowler, Doreen, and Ann J. Abadie, eds. *Faulkner and Popular Culture*. Jackson: University Press of Mississippi, 1990.
Fred. Review of *A Wild Girl of the Sierras*. *Variety*, 16 June 1916, 26.
Freeman, Joseph. *An American Testament: A Narrative of Rebels and Romantics*. New York: Farrar & Rinehart, 1936.
Frost, Laura. *The Problem with Pleasure: Modernism and Its Discontents*. New York: Columbia University Press, 2013.
Gaines, Kevin K. *Uplifting the Race: Black Leadership, Politics, and Culture in the Twentieth Century*. Chapel Hill: University of North Carolina Press, 1996.
Gardner, Erle Stanley. "Getting Away with Murder." *Atlantic Monthly*, January 1965, 72–75.
Gates, Henry Louis, Jr. *Figures in Black: Words, Signs, and the "Racial" Self*. New York: Oxford University Press, 1989.
———. *The Signifying Monkey: A Theory of African-American Literary Criticism*. New York: Oxford University Press, 1988.
Geismar, Maxwell, ed. *The Ring Lardner Reader*. New York: Charles Scribner's Sons, 1963.
Genette, Gerard. *Paratexts: Thresholds of Interpretation*. Translated by Jane E. Lewin. New York: Cambridge University Press, 1997.
Gilroy, Paul. *The Black Atlantic: Modernity and Double Consciousness*. Cambridge, MA: Harvard University Press, 1993.
Glazener, Nancy. *Reading for Realism: The History of a U.S. Literary Institution, 1850–1910*. Durham, NC: Duke University Press, 1997.
Gold, Michael. "3 Schools of U.S. Writing." *New Masses* 4.4 (September 1928): 13–14.
———. *120 Million*. New York: International Publishers, 1929.
———. *Change the World!* New York: International Publishers, 1936.
———. "Floyd Dell Resigns." *New Masses* 5.2 (July 1929): 10–11.
———. *Hoboken Blues*. In *The American Caravan: A Yearbook on American Literature*, edited by Van Wyck Brooks et al., 548–626. New York: Literary Guild of America, 1927.
———. *Jews without Money*. 1930. Reprint, New York: Carroll & Graf, 2004.
———. "Let It Be Really New!" *New Masses* 1.2 (June 1926): 20, 26.

———. *Mike Gold: A Literary Anthology.* Edited by Michael Folsom. New York: International Publishers, 1972.

———. *Money.* In *One-Act Plays,* edited by Barrett H. Clark and Thomas R. Cook, 203–29. Boston: D.C. Heath, 1929.

———. "Notes of the Month." *New Masses* 6.4 (September 1930): 3–5.

———. "Notes on Art, Life, Crap-Shooting, Etc." *New Masses* 5.4 (September 1929): 10–12.

———. "Theater and Revolution." *Nation,* 11 November 1925, 536–37.

Gosciak, Josh. *Claude McKay and the Romance of the Victorians.* New Brunswick, NJ: Rutgers University Press, 2006.

Goulart, Ron. *The Dime Detectives.* New York: Mysterious Press, 1988.

Grace, Sherrill E. *Regression and Apocalypse: Studies in North American Literary Expressionism.* Toronto: University of Toronto Press, 1989.

Graham, T. Austin. *The Great American Songbooks: Musical Texts, Modernism, and the Value of Popular Culture.* New York: Oxford University Press, 2013.

Grant, Madison. *The Passing of the Great Race; or, The Racial Basis of European History.* 4th rev. ed. New York: Charles Scribner's Sons, 1921.

Gray, W. Russel. "Jimmying the Back Door of Literature: Dashiell Hammett's Blue-Collar Modernism." *Journal of Popular Culture* 41.5 (2008): 762–83.

Grebstein, Sheldon Norman. "The Tough Hemingway and His Hard-Boiled Children." In *Tough-Guy Writers of the Thirties,* edited by David Madden, 18–41. Carbondale: Southern Illinois University Press, 1968.

Gregory, Sinda. *Private Investigations: The Novels of Dashiell Hammett.* Carbondale: Southern Illinois University Press, 1985.

Gruber, Frank. *The Pulp Jungle.* Los Angeles: Sherbourne Press, 1967.

Guillory, John. *Cultural Capital: The Problem of Literary Canon Formation.* Chicago: University of Chicago Press, 1993.

Gunning, Tom. "The Cinema of Attractions: Early Film, Its Spectator, and the Avant-Garde." In *Early Cinema: Space/Frame/Narrative,* edited by Thomas Elsaesser, 56–62. London: BFI, 1990.

Guttmann, Allen. *The Jewish Writer in America.* New York: Oxford University Press, 1971.

Hackett, Francis. "The Living Speech." In *Critical Essays on H. L. Mencken,* edited by Douglas C. Stenerson, 55–57. Boston: G. K. Hall, 1987.

Hagemann, E. R. "'The Cleansing of Poisonville' to *Red Harvest.*" *Clues* 7.2 (Fall–Winter 1985): 115–32.

Hammett, Dashiell. "The Advertisement IS Literature." *Western Advertising,* October 1926, 35–36.

———. *Complete Novels.* New York: Library of America, 1999.

———. *Crime Stories and Other Writings.* New York: Library of America, 2001.

———. *Selected Letters of Dashiell Hammett, 1921–1960.* Edited by Richard Layman and Julie M. Rivett. Washington, DC: Counterpoint, 2001.

———. *Lost Stories*. Edited by Vince Emery. San Francisco: Vince Emery Productions, 2005.
Hammill, Faye. *Women, Celebrity, and Literary Culture between the Wars*. Austin: University of Texas Press, 2007.
Hapgood, Hutchins. *Types from City Streets*. New York: Funk & Wagnalls, 1910.
Hansen, Miriam. "The Mass Production of the Senses." *Modernism/Modernity* 6.2 (1999): 59–77.
Harrison, Henry. "Anzia Yezierska: An Inspiration." *Writer's Digest*, March 1926, 10–12.
Harrison, James A. "Negro English." *Anglia* 7 (1884): 232–79.
Harrison-Kahan, Lori. "'Drunk with the Fiery Rhythms of Jazz': Anzia Yezierska, Hybridity, and the Harlem Renaissance." *Modern Fiction Studies* 51.2 (Summer 2005): 415–36.
———. "No Slaves to Fashion: Designing Women in the Fiction of Jessie Fauset and Anzia Yezierska." In *Styling Texts: Dress and Fashion in Literature*, edited by Cynthia Kuhn and Cindy Carlson, 313–33. Youngstown, OH: Cambria, 2007.
Haycraft, Howard. *Murder for Pleasure: The Life and Times of the Detective Story*. New York: D. Appleton-Century, 1941.
Hefner, Brooks E. "'Any Chance to Be Unrefined': Cinematic Modes in Anita Loos's Fiction." *PMLA* 125.1 (2010): 107–21.
———. "'I Used to Be a Highbrow, but Look at Me Now': Phrenology, Detection, and Cultural Hierarchy in S. S. Van Dine." *Clues: A Journal of Detection* 30.1 (Spring 2012): 30–41.
Hegeman, Susan. *Patterns for America: Modernism and the Concept of Culture*. Princeton, NJ: Princeton University Press, 1999.
———. "Taking *Blondes* Seriously." *American Literary History* 7.3 (Autumn 1995): 525–54.
Hemingway, Ernest. *Death in the Afternoon*. 1932. Reprint, New York: Scribner, 2003.
———. *Green Hills of Africa*. 1935. Reprint, New York: Scribner, 2003.
———. *A Moveable Feast*. 1964. Reprint, New York: Scribner, 2003.
———. *The Sun Also Rises*. 1927. Reprint, New York: Scribner, 2006.
Henricksen, Louise Levitas. *Anzia Yezierska: A Writer's Life*. New Brunswick, NJ: Rutgers University Press, 1988.
Hersey, Harold. *The Pulpwood Editor: The Fabulous World of the Thriller Magazines Revealed by a Veteran Editor and Publisher*. New York: Frederick A. Stokes, 1937.
Hitchcock, H. Wiley. *Music in the United States: A Historical Introduction*. Englewood Cliffs, NJ: Prentice-Hall, 1969.
Hobson, Fred C. *Serpent in Eden: H. L. Mencken in the South*. Chapel Hill: University of North Carolina Press, 1974.

Hoffman, Frederick J. *The Twenties: American Writing in the Postwar Decade.* New York: Free Press, 1965.
Holcomb, Gary Edward. *Claude McKay, Code Name Sasha: Queer Black Marxism and the Harlem Renaissance.* Gainesville: University Press of Florida, 2007.
Howard, June. *Form and History in American Literary Naturalism.* Chapel Hill: University of North Carolina Press, 1985.
Howells, William Dean. "Editor's Study." *Harper's New Monthly Magazine,* December 1887, 153–56.
Hughes, Langston. *The Big Sea.* 1940. Reprint, New York: Hill and Wang, 1993.
———. "The Negro Artist and the Racial Mountain." *Nation,* 23 June 1926, 692–94.
Hughes, Rupert. "Our Statish Language." *Harper's,* May 1920, 846–49.
Hurston, Zora Neale. *Folklore, Memoirs, and Other Writings.* New York: Library of America, 1995.
———. "Story in Harlem Slang." *American Mercury,* July 1942, 84–96.
Hutchinson, George. *The Harlem Renaissance in Black and White.* Cambridge, MA: Belknap Press of Harvard University Press, 1995.
Huyssen, Andreas. *After the Great Divide: Modernism, Mass Culture, Postmodernism.* Bloomington: Indiana University Press, 1986.
Irwin, Theodore T. "Slanguage: 1929." *transition* 16/17 (June 1929): 32–34.
James, Henry. *Hawthorne.* 1879. Reprint, New York: Harper and Brothers, 1901.
———. *The Question of Our Speech, The Lesson of Balzac: Two Lectures.* Boston: Houghton Mifflin, 1905.
Jameson, Frederic. *The Political Unconscious: Narrative as a Socially Symbolic Act.* Ithaca, NY: Cornell University Press, 1981.
Jenkins, Henry. *What Made Pistachio Nuts? Early Sound Comedy and the Vaudeville Aesthetic.* New York: Columbia University Press, 1992.
Johnson, James Weldon. *The Autobiography of an Ex-Colored Man.* 1912. Reprint, New York: Penguin, 1990.
———, ed. *The Book of American Negro Poetry.* New York: Harcourt, Brace, 1922.
———. *Complete Poems.* New York: Penguin, 2000.
———. "Romance and Tragedy in Harlem—A Review." Review of *Nigger Heaven,* by Carl Van Vechten. *Opportunity,* October 1926, 316–17, 330.
Jolas, Eugene. "The King's English Is Dying—Long Live the Great American Language." *transition* 19/20 (1930): 141–46.
———. "Logos." *transition* 16/17 (June 1929): 25–30.
[———]. "Proclamation." *transition* 16/17 (June 1929): 13.
———. "What Is the Revolution of Language?" *transition* 22 (February 1933): 125–26.
Jolo. Review of *Hit-the-Trail Holliday. Variety,* 14 June 1918, 29.
Jones, Gavin. *Strange Talk: The Politics of Dialect Literature in Gilded Age America.* Berkeley: University of California Press, 1999.
———. "Twain, Language, and the Southern Humorists." In *A Companion to*

Mark Twain, edited by Peter Messent and Louis J. Budd, 125–40. Malden, MA: Blackwell, 2005.
Josephson, Matthew. "Toward a Professional Prose." *Broom* 5.1 (August 1923): 59–61.
Kane, Elisha K. "The Jargon of the Underworld." *Dialect Notes* 5 (1927): 433–67.
Kaplan, Amy. *The Social Construction of American Realism*. Chicago: University of Chicago Press, 1988.
Katz, Mark. "Sound Recording: Introduction." In *Music, Sound, and Technology in America: A Documentary History of Early Phonograph, Cinema, and Radio*, edited by Timothy D. Taylor, Mark Katz, and Tony Grajeda, 11–28. Durham, NC: Duke University Press, 2012.
Katz, Wendy R. "Untying the Immigrant Tongue: Whitman and the 'Americanization' of Anzia Yezierska." *Walt Whitman Quarterly Review* 21.3–4 (2004): 155–65.
Kenner, Hugh. *The Counterfeiters: An Historical Comedy*. 1968. Reprint, Normal, IL: Dalkey Archive Press, 2005.
———. *The Pound Era*. Berkeley: University of California Press, 1971.
Keough, William. *Punchlines: The Violence of American Humor*. New York: Paragon House, 1990.
Keresztesi, Rita. *Strangers at Home: American Ethnic Modernism between the World Wars*. Lincoln: University of Nebraska Press, 2005.
Kershner, R. B. *Joyce and Popular Culture*. Gainesville: University Press of Florida, 1996.
Kittler, Friedrich A. *Gramophone, Film, Typewriter*. Translated by Geoffrey Winthrop-Young and Michael Wutz. Stanford, CA: Stanford University Press, 1999.
Klein, Marcus. *Foreigners: The Making of American Literature, 1900–1940*. Chicago: University of Chicago Press, 1981.
Kobal, John. *People Will Talk*. New York: Knopf, 1985.
Konzett, Delia Caparoso. *Ethnic Modernisms: Anzia Yezierska, Zora Neale Hurston, Jean Rhys, and the Aesthetics of Dislocation*. New York: Palgrave Macmillan, 2002.
Krapp, George Philip. "The English of the Negro." *American Mercury*, June 1924, 190–95.
Labaree, Mary Fleming. "Our Book Shelf." *Opportunity*, August 1929, 254–55.
Lardner, Ring W. *How to Write Short Stories (With Samples)*. New York: Scribner, 1925.
———. *Selected Stories*. Introduction by Jonathan Yardley. New York: Penguin, 1997.
———. *The Story of a Wonder Man*. New York: Scribner, 1927.
———. *The Young Immigrunts*. Indianapolis, IN: Bobbs-Merrill, 1920.
Levenson, Michael. *A Genealogy of Modernism: A Study of English Literary Doctrine, 1908–1922*. Cambridge, UK: Cambridge University Press, 1984.

———. *Modernism*. New Haven, CT: Yale University Press, 2011.
Leverage, Henry. "Dictionary of the Underworld." *Flynn's*, 3 January 1925, 690–93.
———. "Dictionary of the Underworld." *Flynn's*, 17 January 1925, 1056–57.
———. "Dictionary of the Underworld." *Flynn's*, 28 February 1925, 1150–51.
———. "Dictionary of the Underworld." *Flynn's*, 4 April 1925, 818–19.
Levinson, Julian. *Exiles on Main Street: Jewish American Writers and American Literary Culture*. Bloomington: Indiana University Press, 2008.
Levinson, Marjorie. "What Is New Formalism?" *PMLA* 122.2 (2007): 558–69.
Lewis, David Levering. *W. E. B. Du Bois: The Fight for Equality and the American Century, 1919–1963*. New York: Henry Holt, 2000.
———. *When Harlem Was in Vogue*. New York: Oxford University Press, 1981.
Lewis, Wyndham. *Time and Western Man*. London: Chatto and Windus, 1927.
Lichtblau, Joseph. "The NEW Gangster Story." *Writers' Digest*, September 1930, 11ff.
Lindsay, Vachel. *The Art of the Moving Picture*. Rev. ed. New York: Macmillan, 1922.
———. *The Art of the Moving Picture*. New York: Modern Library, 2000.
Loeb, Harold. *The Way It Was*. New York: Criterion Books, 1959.
Lood. Review of *A Temperamental Wife*. *Variety*, 19 September 1919, 54.
———. Review of *A Virtuous Vamp*. *Variety*, 21 November 1919, 55.
Loos, Anita. *A Girl Like I*. New York: Viking Press, 1966.
———. *Gentlemen Prefer Blondes; and, But Gentlemen Marry Brunettes*. New York: Penguin, 1998.
Lott, Eric. *Love and Theft: Blackface Minstrelsy and the American Working Class*. New York: Oxford University Press, 1993.
Lukács, Georg. "Realism in the Balance." In *Aesthetics and Politics: Debates between Bloch, Lukács, Brecht, Benjamin, Adorno*, 28–59. London: Verso, 1977.
———. *The Theory of the Novel: A Historico-Philosophical Essay on the Forms of Great Epic Literature*. Translated by Anna Bostock. Cambridge, MA: MIT Press, 1971.
Lutes, Jean Marie. "Authoring *Gentlemen Prefer Blondes*: Mass-Market Beauty Culture and the Makeup of Writers." *Prospects* 23 (1998): 431–60.
MacShane, Frank. *The Notebooks of Raymond Chandler*. New York: Harper, 2006.
Marcus, Steven. "Dashiell Hammett and the Continental Op." *Partisan Review* 41.3 (1974): 363–77.
Marling, William. *The American Roman Noir: Hammett, Cain, and Chandler*. Athens: University of Georgia Press, 1995.
———. "The Style and Ideology of *The Maltese Falcon*." *Proteus* 6.1 (1989): 42–50.
Martin, Gretchen. *The Frontier Roots of American Realism*. New York: Peter Lang, 2007.
McCann, Sean. *Gumshoe America: Hard-Boiled Crime Fiction and the Rise and Fall of New Deal Liberalism*. Durham, NC: Duke University Press, 2000.

———. "'A Roughneck Reaching for Higher Things': The Vagaries of Pulp Populism." *Radical History Review* 61 (Winter 1995): 4–34.
McGann, Jerome J. "Keats and the Historical Method in Literary Criticism." *MLN* 94.5 (1979): 988–1032.
———. *The Textual Condition*. Princeton, NJ: Princeton University Press, 1991.
McGurl, Mark. *The Novel Art: Elevations of American Fiction after Henry James*. Princeton, NJ: Princeton University Press, 2003.
McKay, Claude. *Banjo: A Story without a Plot*. New York: Harcourt Brace Jovanovich, 1929.
———. *Home to Harlem*. 1928. Reprint, Boston: Northeastern University Press, 1987.
McKible, Adam. "'Life Is Real and Life Is Earnest': Mike Gold, Claude McKay, and the Baroness Elsa von Freytag-Loringhoven." In *Little Magazines and Modernism: New Approaches*, edited by Suzanne W. Churchill and Adam McKible, 197–213. Burlington, VT: Ashgate, 2007.
McMillan, Dougald. *Transition: The History of a Literary Era, 1927–1938*. New York: George Braziller, 1976.
Mencken, H. L. *The American Language: A Preliminary Inquiry into the Development of English in the United States*. New York: Knopf, 1919.
———. *The American Language: An Inquiry into the Development of English in the United States*. Rev. ed. New York: Knopf, 1921; 3rd ed., 1923; 4th ed., 1936; Supplement II, 1948.
———. "Criticism of Criticism of Criticism." *Smart Set* 52 (August 1917): 138–44.
———. *H. L. Mencken's* Smart Set *Criticism*. Edited by William H. Nolte. Washington, DC: Regnery, 1987.
———. "The Life of the Poor." Review of *Jews without Money*, by Michael Gold. *American Mercury*, March 1930, 381–82.
———. *Mencken's America*. Edited by S. T. Joshi. Athens: Ohio University Press, 2004.
———. "Nothing Dead about Language U.S. Boys Take to the Trenches." *New York Evening Mail*, 28 September 1917, back page.
———. *Prejudices: A Selection*. 1958. Reprint, Baltimore: Johns Hopkins University Press, 2006.
———. *Prejudices: Third Series*. New York: Knopf, 1922.
———. *A Second Mencken Chrestomathy*. Edited by Terry Teachout. Baltimore: Johns Hopkins University Press, 2006.
———. "Spoken American." *Baltimore Evening Sun*, 19 October 1910, 6.
———. "The Two Englishes." *Baltimore Evening Sun*, 6 October 1910, 6.
Miller, Joshua L. *Accented America: The Cultural Politics of Multilingual Modernism*. New York: Oxford University Press, 2011.
Mitchell, Lee Clark. "'Nobody but Our Gang Warn't Around': The Authority of Language in *Huckleberry Finn*." In *New Essays on* Adventures of Huckleberry

Finn, edited by Louis J. Budd, 83–106. New York: Cambridge University Press, 1995.

———. "Verbally *Roughing It:* The West of Words." *Nineteenth-Century Literature* 44.1 (1989): 67–92.

Montanye, C. S. "Looking Out for Orchid." *Black Mask,* May 1920, 104–11.

Moretti, Franco. *Signs Taken for Wonders: On the Sociology of Literary Forms.* 1983. Reprinted, London: Verso, 2005.

Morey, Anne. "'Would You Be Ashamed to Let Them See What You Have Written': The Gendering of Photoplaywrights, 1913–1923." *Tulsa Studies in Women's Literature* 17.1 (Spring 1998): 83–99.

Morrisson, Mark S. *The Public Face of Modernism: Little Magazines, Audiences, and Reception 1905–1920.* Madison: University of Wisconsin Press, 2001.

Moseley, Merritt. "Ring Lardner and the American Humor Tradition." *South Atlantic Review* 46.1 (January 1981): 42–60.

Mott, Frank Luther. *A History of American Magazines, Volume 3: 1865–1885.* Cambridge, MA: Belknap Press of Harvard University Press, 1938.

Munson, Gorham. *The Awakening Twenties: A Memoir-History of a Literary Period.* Baton Rouge: Louisiana State University Press, 1985.

Murphy, James F. *The Proletarian Moment: The Controversy over Leftism in Literature.* Urbana: University of Illinois Press, 1991.

Naremore, James. "Dashiell Hammett and the Poetics of Hard-Boiled Detection." In *Art in Crime Writing: Essays on Detective Fiction,* edited by Bernard Benstock, 49–72. New York: St. Martin's, 1983.

"The Negro in Art: How Shall He Be Portrayed: A Symposium." *Crisis,* March 1926, 219–20; September 1926, 238–39.

Nelson, Raymond. "Babylonian Frolics: H. L. Mencken and *The American Language.*" *American Literary History* 11.4 (Winter 1999): 668–98.

Nettles, Elsa. *Language, Race, and Social Class in Howells's America.* Lexington: University Press of Kentucky, 1988.

Nicholls, Peter. *Modernisms: A Literary Guide.* Berkeley: University of California Press, 1995.

Nolan, William F. *The Black Mask Boys: Masters in the Hard-Boiled School of Detective Fiction.* New York: Mysterious Press, 1987.

North, Michael. *Camera Works: Photography and the Twentieth-Century Word.* New York: Oxford University Press, 2005.

———. *The Dialect of Modernism: Race, Language, and Twentieth-Century Literature.* New York: Oxford University Press, 1994.

———. *Machine-Age Comedy.* New York: Oxford University Press, 2009.

———. *Reading 1922: A Return to the Scene of the Modern.* New York: Oxford University Press, 1999.

Orvell, Miles. *The Real Thing: Imitation and Authenticity in American Culture, 1880–1940.* Chapel Hill: University of North Carolina Press, 1989.

Orwell, George. "Raffles and Miss Blandish." In *As I Please, 1943–1945*, 212–24. New York: Harcourt, Brace, 1968.
Parrington, Vernon L. *Main Currents in American Thought. Vol. 2, The Romantic Revolution in America, 1800–1860*. 1927. Reprint, Norman: University of Oklahoma Press, 1987.
Patrick, Walton R. *Ring Lardner*. New York: Twayne Publishers, 1963.
Perloff, Marjorie. "Pound/Stevens: Whose Era?" *New Literary History* 13.3 (Spring 1982): 485–514.
Phelps, Wallace, and Philip Rahv. "Problems and Perspective in Revolutionary Literature." *Partisan Review* 1.3 (June–July 1934): 3–10.
Poirier, Richard. "The Difficulties of Modernism and the Modernism of Difficulty." In *Images and Ideas in American Culture: The Functions of Criticism; Essays in Memory of Philip Rahv*, edited by Aurthur Edelstein, 124–40. Hanover, NH: Brandeis University Press, 1979.
Porter, Dennis. *The Pursuit of Crime: Art and Ideology in Detective Fiction*. New Haven, CT: Yale University Press, 1981.
Potter, Rachel, and David Trotter. "Low Modernism: Introduction." *Critical Quarterly* 46.4 (2004), iii–iv.
Pound, Ezra. *The Literary Essays of Ezra Pound*. New York: New Directions, 1968.
Powdermaker, Hortense. *Hollywood, the Dream Factory: An Anthropologist Looks at the Movie-Makers*. Boston: Little Brown, 1950.
Rabinowitz, Paula. *Black & White & Noir: America's Pulp Modernism*. New York: Columbia University Press, 2002.
Raczkowski, Christopher T. "From Modernity's Detection to Modernist Detectives: Narrative Vision in the Work of Allan Pinkerton and Dashiell Hammett." *Modern Fiction Studies* 49.4 (Winter 2003): 629–59.
Rainey, Lawrence. *Institutions of Modernism: Literary Elites and Public Culture*. New Haven, CT: Yale University Press, 1998.
Reynolds, David S. *Beneath the American Renaissance: The Subversive Imagination in the Age of Emerson and Melville*. New York: Knopf, 1988.
Rideout, Walter B. *The Radical Novel in the United States, 1900–1954: Some Interrelations of Literature and Society*. 1956. Reprint, New York: Columbia University Press, 1992.
Robinson, Henry Morton. "The Wood-Pulp Racket." *Bookman*, August 1928, 64–67.
Rogin, Michael. *Blackface, White Noise: Jewish Immigrants in the Hollywood Melting Pot*. Berkeley: University of California Press, 1996.
Rosen, Marjorie. *Popcorn Venus: Women, Movies, and the American Dream*. New York: Coward, McCann & Geoghegan, 1973.
Rosenwald, Lawrence. *Multilingual America: Language and the Making of American Literature*. New York: Cambridge University Press, 2008.

Rourke, Constance. *American Humor: A Study of the National Character.* 1931. Reprint, New York: New York Review Books, 2004.
Ruehlmann, William. *Saint with a Gun: The Unlawful American Private Eye.* New York: NYU Press, 1974.
Sanders, Judith. "Her Literary Dowry: Anzia Yezierska Reconsidered in the Context of Yiddish Literature." *Yiddish/Modern Jewish Studies* 13.4 (2004): 1–9.
Santayana, George. *The Genteel Tradition: Nine Essays.* Edited by Douglas L. Wilson. Cambridge: Harvard University Press, 1967.
Schachter, Allison. *Diasporic Modernism: Hebrew and Yiddish Literature in the Twentieth Century.* New York: Oxford University Press, 2012.
Schatz, Thomas. *The Genius of the System: Hollywood Filmmaking in the Studio Era.* New York: Pantheon, 1988.
Schmidt, Karl. "The Handwriting on the Screen." *Everybody's Magazine,* May 1917, 622–23.
Scholes, Robert. *Paradoxy of Modernism.* New Haven, CT: Yale University Press, 2006.
Schrader, Richard J. "'But Gentlemen Marry Brunettes': Anita Loos and H. L. Mencken." *Menckenia* 98 (Summer 1996): 1–7.
Scott, Thomas L., and Melvin J. Friedman, eds. *Pound/The Little Review: The Letters of Ezra Pound to Margaret Anderson: The Little Review Correspondence.* New York: New Directions, 1988.
Seldes, Gilbert. *The 7 Lively Arts.* 1924. Reprint, Mineola, NY: Dover, 2001.
Sewell, David R. *Mark Twain's Languages: Discourse, Dialogue, and Linguistic Variety.* Berkeley: University of California Press, 1987.
Shaw, Joseph T. Introduction to *The Hard-Boiled Omnibus: Early Stories from Black Mask.* Edited by Joseph T. Shaw, v–ix. New York: Simon and Schuster, 1946.
Singal, Daniel Joseph. "Towards a Definition of American Modernism." *American Quarterly* 39.1 (Spring 1987): 7–26.
Slotkin, Richard. *The Fatal Environment: The Myth of the Frontier in the Age of Industrialization, 1800–1890.* New York: Atheneum, 1985.
———. *Gunfighter Nation: The Myth of the Frontier in Twentieth-Century America.* Norman: University of Oklahoma Press, 1998.
Smethurst, James Edward. *The New Red Negro: The Literary Left and African American Poetry, 1930–1946.* New York: Oxford University Press, 1999.
Smith, Erin A. *Hard-Boiled: Working-Class Readers and Pulp Magazines.* Philadelphia: Temple University Press, 2000.
Smith, Henry Nash. *Virgin Land: The American West as Symbol and Myth.* Cambridge, MA: Harvard University Press, 1950.
Smith, Jacob. "The Frenzy of the Audible: Pleasure, Authenticity, and Recorded Laughter." *Television & New Media* 2 (2005): 23–47.
Smitherman, Geneva. *Word from the Mother: Language and African Americans.* New York: Routledge, 2006.

Sollors, Werner. *Beyond Ethnicity: Consent and Descent in American Culture.* New York: Oxford University Press, 1986.
———. *Ethnic Modernism.* Cambridge, MA: Harvard University Press, 2008.
"Something New for You." *Black Mask,* October 1922, 65.
Sonne, Owen E. "The Crime and Detective Story." *Writer's Digest,* June 1925, 18ff.
Stein, Gertrude. *Everybody's Autobiography.* 1937. Reprint, Cambridge, UK: Exact Change, 1993.
———. *Writings, 1932–1946.* New York: Library of America, 1998.
Stowe, William W. "From Semiotics to Hermeneutics: Modes of Detection in Doyle and Chandler." In *The Poetics of Murder: Detective Fiction and Literary Theory,* edited by Glenn W. Most and William W. Stowe, 366–83. San Diego: Harcourt Brace Jovanovich, 1983.
Strychacz, Thomas F. *Modernism, Mass Culture, and Professionalism.* New York: Cambridge University Press, 1992.
Symons, Julian. *Mortal Consequences: A History from the Detective Story to the Crime Novel.* New York: Shocken Books, 1972.
Teachout, Terry. *The Skeptic: A Life of H. L. Mencken.* New York: Harper Perennial, 2002.
Thaggert, Miriam. *Images of Black Modernism: Verbal and Visual Strategies of the Harlem Renaissance.* Amherst: University of Massachusetts Press, 2010.
Thompson, Jon. *Fiction, Crime, and Empire: Clues to Modernity and Postmodernism.* Urbana: University of Illinois Press, 1993.
Thoreau, Henry David. *Walden and Other Writings.* New York: Modern Library, 2000.
Thurman, Wallace. "Fire Burns: A Department of Comment." *Fire!! A Quarterly Devoted to the Younger Negro Artists* 1.1 (November 1926): 47–48.
———. "Negro Artists and the Negro." *New Republic,* 31 August 1927, 37–39.
———. "A Stranger at the Gates." Review of *Nigger Heaven,* by Carl Van Vechten. *Messenger,* September 1926, 279.
Tibbetts, John C., and James M. Welsh. *His Majesty the American: The Cinema of Douglas Fairbanks, Sr.* South Brunswick, NJ: A. S. Barnes, 1977.
Tillery, Tyrone. *Claude McKay: A Black Poet's Struggle for Identity.* Amherst: University of Massachusetts Press, 1992.
Toomer, Jean. *Cane: Authoritative Text, Contexts, Criticism,* 2nd ed. Edited by Rudolph P. Byrd and Henry Louis Gates Jr. New York: Norton, 2011.
Tucker, Jean E. "Voices from the Silents." *Quarterly Journal of the Library of Congress* 37.3–4 (1980): 387–412.
Tuerk, Richard. "Michael Gold's *Hoboken Blues:* An Experiment That Failed." *MELUS* 20.4 (Winter 1995): 3–15.
Twain, Mark. *Adventures of Huckleberry Finn.* 125th anniversary edition. Edited by Victor Fischer et al. Berkeley: University of California Press, 2001.
———. *Collected Tales, Sketches, Speeches, and Essays.* New York: Library of America, 1992.

———. *The Gilded Age and Later Novels*. New York: Library of America, 2002.
———. *Pudd'nhead Wilson and Those Extraordinary Twins*. New York: Norton, 2005.
———. *Roughing It*. 1872. Reprint, Berkeley: University of California Press, 1996.
Valgemae, Mardi. *Accelerated Grimace: Expressionism in the American Drama of the 1920s*. Carbondale: Southern Illinois University Press, 1972.
Van Dine, S. S. *I Used to Be a Highbrow, but Look at Me Now*. New York: Scribner, 1929.
Van Doren, Carl. "Beyond Grammar; Ring Lardner: Philologist among the Lowbrows." *Century*, July 1923, 471–75.
Van Patten, Nathan. "The Vocabulary of the American Negro as Set Forth in Contemporary Literature." *American Speech* 7.1 (October 1931): 24–31.
Van Vechten, Carl. *Nigger Heaven*. 1926. Reprint, Urbana: University of Illinois Press, 2000.
Vials, Chris. *Realism for the Masses: Aesthetics, Popular Front Pluralism, and U.S. Culture, 1935–1947*. Jackson: University Press of Mississippi, 2009.
Vogel, Shane. *The Scene of Harlem Cabaret: Race, Sexuality, Performance*. Chicago: University of Chicago Press, 2009.
Vološinov, V. N. *Marxism and the Philosophy of Language*. Translated by Ladislav Matejka and I. R. Titunik. Cambridge, MA: Harvard University Press, 1986.
Wald, Alan M. *Exiles from a Future Time: The Forging of the Mid-Twentieth-Century Literary Left*. Chapel Hill: University of North Carolina Press, 2002.
Wald, Priscilla. *Constituting Americans: Cultural Anxiety and Narrative Form*. Durham, NC: Duke University Press, 1995.
Ward, Sterling. "Under the Crimson Skull." *Black Mask*, April 1921, 29–36.
Weber, Brom. "The Misspellers." In *The Comic Imagination in American Literature*, edited by Louis D. Rubin Jr., 127–37. New Brunswick, NJ: Rutgers University Press, 1973.
Weber, Donald. *Haunted in the New World: Jewish American Culture from Chan to The Goldbergs*. Bloomington: Indiana University Press, 2005.
Wenska, Walter. "'There's a Man with a Gun over There': Faulkner's Hijackings of Masculine Popular Culture." *Faulkner Journal* 15.1–2 (1999): 35–60.
Williams, William Carlos. *The Selected Essays of William Carlos Williams*. New York: New Directions, 1969.
———. *Spring and All*. 1923. Reprint, New York: New Directions, 2011.
Wilson, Edmund. *Axel's Castle: A Study of the Imaginative Literature of 1870–1930*. 1931. Reprint, New York: Farrar, Straus, and Giroux, 2004.
———. "H. L. Mencken." *New Republic*, 1 June 1921, 10–13.
———. *The Shores of Light: A Literary Chronicle of the Twenties and Thirties*. New York: Farrar, Straus, and Young, 1952.
Wintz, Carrie D. *Black Culture and the Harlem Renaissance*. Houston: Rice University Press, 1988.

Wirth, Louis. *The Ghetto.* 1928. Reprint, Chicago: University of Chicago Press, 1956.
Wirth-Nesher, Hana. *Call It English: The Languages of Jewish American Literature.* Princeton, NJ: Princeton University Press, 2006.
Wood, Clement, and Gloria Goddard. *A Dictionary of American Slang.* Girard, KS: Haldeman-Julius, 1926.
Wood, James Playsted. *Magazines in the United States.* 2nd ed. New York: Ronald Press, 1956.
Woolf, Virginia. *The Essays of Virginia Woolf, Volume 3: 1919–1924.* Edited by Andrew McNeillie. San Diego: Harcourt Brace Jovanovich, 1988.
———. *The Essays of Virginia Woolf, Volume 4: 1925–1929.* Edited by Andrew McNeillie. London: Hogarth Press, 1994.
Worpole, Ken. *Dockers and Detectives: Popular Reading, Popular Writing.* London: Verso, 1983.
Yardley, Jonathan. *Ring: A Biography of Ring Lardner.* Lanham, MD: Rowman & Littlefield, 2001.
Yezierska, Anzia. *Bread Givers.* 1925. Reprint, New York: Persea Books, 2003.
———. *How I Found America: Collected Stories of Anzia Yezierska.* New York: Persea Books, 1991.
———. *Hungry Hearts.* 1920. Reprint, New York: Penguin Books, 1997.
———. "Mr. Lewisohn's 'Up Stream.'" *New York Times Book Review and Magazine,* 23 April 1922, 22.
Zaborowska, Magdelena J. *How We Found America: Reading Gender through East European Immigrant Narratives.* Chapel Hill: University of North Carolina Press, 1995.
Zhang, Quan. "Behind *Black Mask:* The Marketplace and *Black Mask* Fiction of the 1920s and 1930s." PhD diss., University of Maryland–College Park, 1993.

Index

Ade, George, 104; *Fables in Slang*, 67, 68, 231n18; Mencken on, 67–68

Adventures of Huckleberry Finn (Twain), 29, 37, 44–48, 84; "evasion" plot, 47, 48; Mencken's literary assessment, 38; unreliable frame narrative in, 44–46, 66, 83

African American urban fiction: of Fisher, 192–202; as genre, 28–29, 32–33, 61, 181; of McKay, 202–13; skin color of protagonists in, 201–2, 212

African American vernacular: class and, 181–83; glossaries and descriptions of, 20–21, 32, 188–91, 197, 208, 248n58; Harlem Renaissance school's debate on, 183–92; Mencken's neglect of, 53, 179–80, 197, 230–31n68; racist views of, 179–81, 200–201, 230n65; Twain's depiction of, 48–49

African American writers: canon of, 109–10; music as used by, 209; nineteenth-century, 102; politics of representation, 32, 106, 191–92, 196–97, 203, 213, 246n14, 247n26

Aldington, Richard: "English and American," 57–58; "A Young American Poet," 57

Allen, Frederick Lewis: *Only Yesterday*, 51

American Brahminism, 17

American Caravan, The (anthology), 131, 239n67

American Language, The (Mencken), 20, 35, 49, 52–61, 93, 220; African American vernacular ignored by, 53, 179–80, 181, 189, 197, 230–31n68, 248n58; appendix "Non-English Dialects in America," 217; appendix "Specimens of the American Vulgate," 59; baseball slang in, 21, 22, 59; changes in editions, 55–56; chapter on "American Slang," 58–59; charting of vulgate's entry into American literature, 56–57; editions of, 29–30; evolution of project, 52, 54; first edition, 52, 57, 104; fourth edition, 52, 55, 217, 230n56; Hammett's familiarity with, 168; importance of, 53–54; influence of, 19; Jolas's reference to, 36, 56; Josephson's reference to, 36, 56; Lardner and, 79; postscripts, 52; research for, 29; reviews of, 52; second edition, 52, 57–58, 59–60, 179; third edition, 52, 59, 179; Twain's influence on, 37, 39, 43, 49; on welcoming nature of American language, 115, 230n58; Yiddish words in, 104

American Magazine, 86, 157, 158

American Mercury (journal): cost of, 24; excerpts of Gold's *Jews without Money* published in, 132; Fisher's "Caucasian Storms Harlem" published in, 193; *Harper's Bazar* contrasted with, 24, 93; Hurston's "Story in Harlem Slang" published in, 179, 248n58; Knopf as publisher of, 25; Mencken as editor of, 23–24, 37, 50, 52; Mencken's commentary in, 51; prestige of, 23–25, 26; racist views of African American vernacular in, 180; Yiddish dismissed in, 237n25

American Speech (journal), 19–20, 189, 190–91
Anderson, Margaret, 224n19
Anderson, Sherwood, 76, 110, 136, 185; *Dark Laughter*, 25; *Winesburg, Ohio*, 118, 207, 248n54
Anolik, Ruth Bienstock: "All Words, Words about Words," 113
Antin, Mary, 30–31, 103, 109; assimilation and, 105–6; first-person narration used by, 116; *The Promised Land*, 104, 105–6, 112–13; realist aesthetic of, 111, 113, 114–15, 120, 133, 135
anti-Semitism: growth of, 106; of Mencken, 50, 51, 53
Arac, Jonathan: "Babel and Vernacular in an Empire of Immigrants," 39–40
Ashford, Daisy: *The Young Visiters*, 83, 233n59
Atlantic group, 16
Atlantic Monthly (magazine), 57, 192, 194
Auerbach, Erich: *Mimesis*, 225n42
Avery, Todd: "'The Girls in Europe Is Nuts over Ball Players,'"232n44

Bakhtin, M. M.: dialogic practice, 8; heteroglossia notion, 15; "zone of contact" notion, 46, 65
Baldwin, James, 195
Baltimore Evening Sun (newspaper), 37, 52
Banks, Ruth: "Idioms of the Present-Day American Negro," 189
Barnes, Djuna: *Nightwood*, 133
Barrie, J. M., 83
Barthes, Roland, 176, 177
Bartlett, John Russell: *Dictionary of Americanisms*, 226n66
baseball slang: Lardner's use of, 21, 22, 30, 59, 61, 74, 79–80, 94, 228n106, 233n50; Mencken on, 58; in Wood and Goddard's dictionary, 21, 82
Baum, L. Frank: *The Wizard of Oz*, 86
Beard, Charles and Mary: *The Rise of American Civilization*, 229–30n44
Bellow, Saul, 111
Belluscio, Steven S.: *To Be Suddenly White*, 237n24
Benjamin, Walter: "The Author as Producer," 153; *Understanding Brecht*, 163
Bennett, Arnold, 227n89
Berghaus, Günther: *Theater, Performance, and the Historical Avant-Garde*, 127–28

bibliographical codes, 25, 26
blackface minstrelsy, 131–32, 200–201, 239n67, 239n69, 248nn62–63
Black Mask (pulp magazine), 31–32, 61, 150–53; Daly and Hammett as most popular writers, 153, 154; Daly's stories in, 145, 153–63, 167; "Daytime Stories" series, 156; editors of, 150–52, 157, 167, 171; emergence of hard-boiled style in, 139, 141, 145–46, 150–51, 155; founding of, 150; Hammett's stories in, 163–64, 169; Lardneresque stories in early issues, 86; Mencken's editorial involvement in, 244n67; psychological *noir* in, 155–57
Blair, Walter: *Native American Humor*, 231n10
Blakemore, Steven: "Huck Finn's Written World," 48
Bleiler, E. F., 231n18
Boas, Franz, 20, 179, 189
Bok, Edward: *The Americanization of Edward Bok*, 107, 112–13
Bone, Robert: *The Negro Novel in America*, 185, 246n19
Boni & Liveright: as experimental publisher, 25; publication of Eliot's *Waste Land*, 110; publication of Loos's *Gentlemen Prefer Blondes*, 25–26, 236–37n20; publication of Yezierska's *Salome of the Tenements*, 110
Bonner, Sherwood, 180
Bourdieu, Pierre: *The Field of Cultural Production*, 23, 24, 25
Bourne, Randolph: "Trans-National America," 9, 115–16
Bowser, Eileen: *The Transformation of Cinema*, 71
boxing, 159, 244n70
Bradbury, Malcolm: "Modernisms/Postmodernisms," 5
Braddock, Jeremy: *Collecting as Modernist Practice*, 20
Brawley, Benjamin, 185; *The Negro Genius*, 246n19, 249n66
Brecht, Bertolt, 128, 130
Breu, Christopher: *Hard-Boiled Masculinities*, 155, 156, 218
Bridgman, Richard: *The Colloquial Style in America*, 10, 15, 73, 76
Brief Stories (pulp magazine), 167, 170–71
Brodhead, Richard H.: *Cultures of Letters*, 28

INDEX / 273

Brody, Alter: "Yiddish in American Fiction," 237n25
Brooks, Cleanth: *William Faulkner*, 250n7
Brooks, Van Wyck: *America's Coming-of-Age*, 17, 38–39, 115
Broom (little magazine), 36
Brown, Charles Brockden: *Edgar Huntly*, 241n15
Brown, Sterling, 32; *Negro in American Fiction*, 246n19; *Southern Road*, 247n44
Browne, Charles Farrar: *Artemus Ward*, 231n2; Artemus Ward persona, 65, 78, 231n10
Bruun, Laurids, 227n89
Bürger, Peter: *Theory of the Avant-Garde*, 23
Burns, Philip: "Fabrication and Faultline," 42

Cable, George Washington: *The Grandissimes*, 225n49
Cahan, Abraham, 30–31, 61, 103, 109; assimilation and, 104–5, 106; realist aesthetic of, 111, 113, 114–15, 125, 133, 135; *The Rise of David Levinsky*, 104, 105, 106, 112–13, 122; *Yekl*, 104–5; as Yiddish-language newspaper editor, 104
Cahan, Mary: first-person narration used by, 116; *Yekl*, 117
Cain, James M., 142
Cain, Paul, 152
Calloway, Cab: *Hepster's Dictionary*, 189
Calverton, V. F., 35
Camlot, Jason: "Early Talking Books," 70
Campbell, Joseph: *A Skeleton's Key to Finnegans Wake* (with Robinson), 226n75
Carey, Gary: *Anita Loos*, 233n66, 234n74
Carkeet, David: "Dialects in *Huckleberry Finn*," 229n26
Castronovo, Russ: *Beautiful Democracy*, 16
Cather, Willa, 64, 110
Cawelti, John G.: *Adventure, Mystery, and Romance*, 142, 144, 172, 241n7
Century magazine, 110, 114
Chandler, Raymond, 142, 152, 176, 218, 242n21, 249n77; Hammett's influence on, 177–78; Library of America edition, 241n10; "Red Wind," 241n10; "The Simple Art of Murder," 139–40, 148, 149, 168
Chaplin, Charlie, 164
Chesnutt, Charles W., 15, 187, 194, 201; *The Conjure Woman*, 205, 206

Chicago as center of American humor, 65–67, 72, 75, 79
Chinitz, David E.: *T. S. Eliot and the Cultural Divide*, 13
Christie, Agatha, 176
Churchwell, Sarah: "Lost among the Ads," 235n89
Classical Hollywood Cinema, The, 89
Cmiel, Kenneth: *Democratic Eloquence*, 16, 99
Cody, Phillip C., 151, 152, 157, 167
Cohen, Octavus Roy, 212
Coleman, Julie: *History of Cant and Slang Dictionaries*, 19, 189, 226n66
Colliers (magazine), 86
Come On In (film), 92
comic monologues, recorded, 69
Connolly, Cyril: *Enemies of Promise*, 9, 224n22
Conrad, Joseph, 108; *Heart of Darkness*, 12
Cooper, Wayne F.: *The Passion of Claude McKay*, 204
Corrothers, James D.: *The Black Cat Club*, 205, 231n11
Cosmopolitan (magazine), 142
Cowley, Malcolm, 226n75; *After the Genteel Tradition*, 17–18; "The Middle American Style," 9–10
Cox, James M., 39
Crane, Hart, 102
Cream, Mildred, 227n89
crime fiction, hard-boiled: 1920s as period of experimentation in, 152–53; 1920s social issues in, 161, 244n76; of Daly, 153–63; destabilization of plot structure in, 172–73; of Faulkner, 218; as form of modernism, 145–47; gendering of, 240n3; as genre, 27–28, 31–32, 138, 139–40; of Hammett, 163–78; hardback publications, 152–53; illegibility and unreliable narrators in, 146–49, 162–63; language in, 148–49; major characteristics of, 151; Mencken on, 61; objections to, 151–52; publication of, 141–42; slang in, 21, 22, 148–49, 160–62, 171; speed of writing, 146; stylistic narration of, 148; trial-and-error model of investigation in, 143–44, 146–47; vernacular narrative voice in, 157–58, 162–63, 170–71, 177, 212; viewed as lowbrow fiction, 142

criminal slang: dictionaries of, 21, 149, 160, 171; in hard-boiled crime fiction, 21, 22, 148–49, 160–62, 171
Crisis (journal), 32; "Criteria of Negro Art," 186, 187; Fisher's *Walls of Jericho* reviewed in, 187–88; "The Negro in Art: How Shall He Be Portrayed," 181, 185–88, 191, 194, 199; "Pictures of 500 Children," 247n26; Van Vechten's *Nigger Heaven* reviewed in, 187–88
Crockett, Davy, 10
Crosby, Harry: "The New Word," 2
Cullen, Countee, 185
"cultivated music," 11
cultural anthropology, 20, 179, 189
cultural production, zones of, 22–26, 27–28

Daly, Carroll John: aesthetic of, 140; *The Amateur Murderer*, 153; on craft of writing, 154–55; crime fiction of, 31–32, 152, 153–63; critical neglect of, 153–54; destabilizing realism in work of, 153–63; "Dolly," 155–57, 167; "The False Burton Combs," 155, 156, 157, 159–61; "Half-Breed," 161; *The Hidden Hand*, 174; "I'll Tell the World," 161–62; "Kiss-the-Canvas Crowley," 158–59; "Knights of the Open Palm," 154, 161, 244n76; Lardner's influence on, 158–59; *Man in the Shadows*, 174; modernization of crime fiction genre, 28, 162–63; "Paying an Old Debt," 157–58, 219; Prohibition's influence on plots, 228n106; Race Williams stories, 154–55, 156, 158, 159, 161–63, 168, 174; "Say It with Lead," 159; *The Snarl of the Beast*, 154, 174; stories published in *Black Mask*, 145, 153–63, 167; "Three Gun Terry," 157; "Three Thousand to the Good," 161; vernacular used by, 156, 158–63, 196; *The White Circle*, 156
Damon, Maria, 108; *Dark End of the Street*, 236n15; "Gertrude Stein's Jewishness," 236n15
Daudet, Alphonse: *Sappho*, 208
Dearborn, Mary V.: "Anzia Yezierska," 109
decadence, detective fiction and, 142–43, 241n12
Denning, Michael: *The Cultural Front*, 6–7, 9, 12, 215, 245n109; *Mechanic Accents*, 149
Detective Fiction Weekly (pulp magazine), 21, 149

detective stories: Carter stories, 144–45, 162, 242nn19–21; of Doyle, 141, 142, 144, 174, 241n16; of Faulkner, 27, 141, 217–18; of Gardner, 242n20; genealogy of, 141–42; Hammett's style contrasted with, 139–40; Harlem Renaissance, 193; of Poe, 141, 142, 143–44, 162, 241n13, 241n16; realism and, 139–40, 142–45, 151; reason and, 143–45; 172–73, 241n16; romanticism and, 142–43; Stein and, 26, 141, 164–65; of Twain, 49, 141, 169. *See also* crime fiction, hard-boiled
Dewey, John, 114, 126, 238n47
Dial (magazine), 1, 76
dialect literature: Ade and, 67–68; class-marking of characters through, 15–16, 40, 42–43, 46–47, 65; critiques of, 106; Dunne and, 65–67, 78; eye dialect and misspellings, 47, 65, 78, 231n10; Harlem-based fiction, 32–33; Jews and, 102–3, 104–8; of nineteenth-century white southerners, 180; objectification of dialect characters, 16; realism's reliance on, 15, 40–41, 63; rise of, 39–40; semiotics of, 67; stereotyping and, 103; Twain and, 36–37, 39–47, 78; vernacular distinguished from, 10–11, 77; Yezierska's relationship with, 108–26
Dialect Notes (journal), 19
Dickstein, Morris: "Hallucinating the Past," 130
Dime Detective (pulp magazine), 161
dime novels: critical neglect of, 14; detective characters in, 144–45, 162, 242nn19–21; machinelike output of, 149; multiaccentuality in, 12; overblown language in, 176; as pulp fiction, 149–50
Dos Passos, John, 13, 17, 75, 101, 127, 129, 205, 217, 226n71; *The 42nd Parallel*, 216; *Airways, Inc.*, 239n69; *U.S.A.* trilogy, 88, 216
Doyle, Arthur Conan: Holmes stories, 141, 142, 174, 241n16
Dreiser, Theodore, 17, 18, 102, 110; *An American Tragedy*, 14, 25; Mencken's views on, 49, 50
Drucker, Sally Ann: "Yiddish, Yidgin, and Yezierska," 112
Dubey, Madhu: *Signs and Cities*, 183
Du Bois, W. E. B., 32; aesthetic principles, 191, 196; "Criteria of Negro Art," 186, 187, 247n26; *The Dark Princess*, 193; as editor of *Crisis*, 185–88; Fisher's *Walls of Jericho*

reviewed by, 193, 198; *The Philadelphia Negro*, 186–87
Duchamp, Marcel, 3
Dunbar, Paul Laurence: *The Sport of the Gods*, 248n53
Dunne, Finley Peter, 64, 78, 104, 231n18; *Mr. Dooley in Peace and in War*, 63, 65–67, 84
Durham, Philip: "The *Black Mask* School," 154

Eagleton, Terry: *Against the Grain*, 5
Earle, David M.: *Re-covering Modernism*, 166
Egan, Michael, 39
Eliason, Norman E.: "Some Negro Terms," 189
Eliot, T. S., 177, 203, 217; popular culture's influence on, 13; *The Waste Land*, 21, 25, 57, 76, 110, 123, 226n75, 228n102, 233n60, 240n79, 248n60
Ellison, Ralph, 110, 195
Ellsworth, Fanny, 243n56
Emerson, John, 89, 90, 93
English, James F.: "Cultural Capital and the Revolutions of Literary Modernity," 22–23
ethnic studies, 109–11, 113, 235n90
Evening Mail (newspaper), 55
expressionism: Gold and, 127–28, 140, 240n80; hard-boiled crime fiction and, 140, 174–78
Eysteinsson, Astradur: *The Concept of Modernism*, 6, 7, 146

Fairbanks, Douglas, 86, 88, 89, 90–92, 93
fascism, 9
Faulkner, William: *Absalom, Absalom!*, 226n75; admiration for Loos's *Gentlemen Prefer Blondes*, 26; *If I Forget the Jerusalem*, 218; integration of vernacular and high modernism in works of, 217–20; *Intruder in the Dust*, 27, 141, 217–18; *Knight's Gambit*, 141, 218; letter to Loos, 86, 98; Loos viewed by, 101; maps and genealogies, 21; *The Portable Faulkner*, 226n75; pulp formulas used by, 27; *Pylon*, 27, 218; as reader of pulp fiction, 26; *Sanctuary*, 27, 218; *Soldier's Pay*, 218; *The Sound and the Fury*, 33, 218–20; Twain's *Huckleberry Finn* viewed by, 38; World War I and, 75; Yezierska's interest in, 110

Fauset, Jessie, 184, 185, 194, 202, 204, 246n14; *There Is Confusion*, 195
Faust, Frederick, 245n93
Feaster, Patrick: "Framing the Mechanical Voice," 69, 70, 232n24, 232n27
Fecher, Charles A.: *Mencken*, 229n43
Ferraro, Thomas J.: "Avant-Garde Ethnics," 102, 111, 122; *Ethnic Passages*, 238n49
films. *See* silent films; sound films
Fire!! (little magazine), 184, 192, 212, 247n35
Fisher, Rudolph: "The Caucasian Storms Harlem," 179, 193; "The City of Refuge," 193, 194–96, 202; *The Conjure-Man Dies*, 193; "Ezekiel," 202; "Introduction to Contemporary Harlemese," 21, 208, 248n56; "The Promised Land," 202; street slang in works of, 181, 184, 191, 192–94, 213. *See also Walls of Jericho, The*
Fitzgerald, F. Scott, 88, 110; *The Great Gatsby*, 240n79; "Ring," 72, 73, 74–75, 216; *This Side of Paradise*, 173
Flynn's (pulp magazine), 21, 149, 160, 171
Forum, 117
frame narration: of Cahan, 104; gentility and, 45–46; humor writing and, 66–67, 68, 71; of Lardner, 78–79; of Loos, 94; of McKay, 205–6; in realist writings, 15; removing, 18; of Twain, 44–46; of Van Vechten, 249n75
Frank, Waldo: *Our America*, 229n44
Freeman, Joseph: *An American Testament*, 3, 4, 10, 20
Freytag-Loringhoven, Elsa von, 2
Frost, Laura: *The Problem with Pleasure*, 22

Gaines, Kevin K.: *Uplifting the Race*, 187
Galsworthy, John, 108
Gardner, Erle Stanley, 151–52, 155, 157; Jenkins stories, 242n20
Gates, Henry Louis, Jr.: *Figures in Black*, 180, 246n9, 247n44; *The Signifying Monkey*, 197, 217
Geller, Todros, 240n80
Genette, Gerard: *Paratexts*, 21, 227n77
genteel and gentility: African American "uplift" and, 187, 191; class and ethnic identity and, 18, 40, 46–47, 103, 183, 235n90; in conflict with vernacular values, 38–39, 56–57, 174; frame narration and, 45–46, 66–67, 71; Golden Age detective stories and, 139–40; Loos's critique

genteel and gentility (*continued*)
 of, 95–97; realism and, 14, 15, 16–18, 104, 148; revolt against, 17–18; sentimentality and, 184; slang dictionaries and, 19; as terms, 16–17
Gentlemen Marry Brunettes (film), 87
Gentlemen Prefer Blondes (Loos), 92–101; as cross-media phenomenon, 25–26, 86–87; Dorothy character in, 97–100; genteel language caricatured in, 95–97, 170; Hollywood conventions in, 93–94; Mencken mentioned in, 98–99; narrative interplay in, 30, 88–89, 92–93, 97–98, 100, 101; publication history, 23–26, 86; slang in, 98, 99–100; structure of, 94
Gentlemen Prefer Blondes (film), 86
George, W. L., 227n89
Gilbert, Stuart, 2, 220; *James Joyce's "Ulysses,"* 226n75
Gilroy, Paul: *The Black Atlantic*, 203
Glaspell, Susan, 127
Glazener, Nancy: *Reading for Realism*, 16, 17
glossaries and dictionaries of slang, 19–22, 226n66, 226n68; academic interest, 19–20; as analogues to paratext, 21; baseball slang, 21, 82; connections with manifestos, 36; criminal slang, 21, 139, 149, 160, 175; early, 243n32; Harlem slang, 20–21, 32, 188–91, 197, 208, 248n58; Jolas's "Revolution of the Word Dictionary," 2–3; in literary works, 20–21; as paratextual keys, 21–22, 149, 188–89, 197, 248n60; pre-twentieth-century history of, 19; "Slanguage: 1929," 2, 3, 8, 23, 27, 33, 35, 36, 56, 77, 148, 160, 215, 218, 220
Goddard, Gloria: *A Dictionary of American Slang* (with Wood), 19, 20, 21, 82, 175, 248n60
Gold, Michael, 101; *120 Million*, 31, 217, 240n78; aesthetic of, 31, 103, 107–8, 126–38; "Change the World" column, 126–27, 128; critiques of modernist writers, 126–27; *Down the Airshaft*, 238n56; as editor of *New Masses*, 128, 129–30, 132, 135; experimental works, 127–28; "Faster, America, Faster!," 127; "Gertrude Stein: A Literary Idiot," 126, 130; *Hoboken Blues*, 31, 127, 131–32, 133, 137, 239n69; *Ivan's Homecoming*, 238–39n56; *La Fiesta*, 238–39n56; "Let It Be Really New!," 126; "Love on a Garbage Dump," 127; *Money*, 130–31, 133, 238–39n56; "Proletarian Realism," 240n78; Proust and, 239–40n78; "Theater and Revolution," 131; theatrical works of, 127, 130–33; "Towards Proletarian Art," 128–29, 130, 137; vernacular expressionism and, 126–38, 140, 240n80. See also *Jews without Money*
Goulart, Ron: *The Dime Detectives*, 153, 154
Grace, Sherrill E.: *Regression and Apocalypse*, 133, 240n81
Graham, T. Austin: *The Great American Songbooks*, 13
Grant, Madison: *The Passing of the Great Race*, 235n90
Greeley, Horace, 41
Griffith, D. W., 86, 87, 88, 89, 90, 94–95
"grim readers" concept, 22, 81, 100, 146, 160
Gruber, Frank: *The Pulp Jungle*, 242n27
Guillory, John: *Cultural Capital*, 25
Gunning, Tom: "The Cinema of Attractions," 70
Guttmann, Allen: *The Jewish Writer in America*, 109

Hagemann, E. R.: "'The Cleansing of Poisonville' to *Red Harvest*," 154
Haldeman-Julius, E., 19
Hammett, Dashiell, 4; "$106,000 Blood Money," 171, 173–74; as ad copywriter, 167–69; aesthetic of, 140, 176–78; "The Big Knock-Over," 171–73, 178; Continental Op stories, 166, 169–78; "The Creeping Siamese," 167; *The Dain Curse*, 165, 176; Faulkner and, 219; "From the Memoirs of a Private Detective," 169–70; "The Girl with the Silver Eyes," 165; *The Glass Key*, 146, 165, 166, 177; Hemingway and, 242n26; "highbrow" publications and, 32, 155, 157, 164, 166–67; "Itchy," 170–71, 174, 175; "The Jargon of the Underworld," 171, 245n104; letter to Blanche Knopf, 163, 166, 167, 171; Library of America edition, 241n10; *The Maltese Falcon*, 142, 152, 164, 166, 177; modernists' appreciation of, 32, 164–65; modernization of crime fiction genre, 28, 165–73, 177–78; "The Nails in Mr. Cayterer," 165; "Poisonville," 166, 174–78; Prohibition's influence on plots, 228n106; pseudonym used by, 167, 169; realism critiqued by, 168–69; *Red Harvest*, 32, 147, 163, 166,

174–78, 216, 244n70, 245n109; "The Road Home," 243n55; role of thieves' slang in, 22; "Slippery Fingers," 169–70, 171; Stein and, 164–65, 219; stories published in *Black Mask*, 145, 153, 157, 163–64, 167, 169–74; stream-of-consciousness method, 166, 171–72, 249n77; style contrasted with Golden Age detective writers, 139–40; style of, 148–49; "Tulip," 244n85; vernacular used by, 168–69, 173, 175–78
Hansen, Miriam: "Mass Production of the Senses," 88
Hapgood, Hutchins, 106–7; *Types from City Streets*, 110
Harcourt Brace, 164
Harlem-based fiction, 32–33, 181–213
Harlem Renaissance, 181–92; propaganda and, 186; "uplift" tradition, 32, 181, 182–83, 186–87, 191, 195–96, 200–201, 205–6, 213, 247n35
Harman, Thomas: *Caveat or Warening for Commen Curtesors*, 243n32
Harper, Frances E. W., 194
Harper's Bazar (magazine, later *Harper's Bazaar*): *American Mercury* contrasted with, 24; British version, 227n92; changes during 1920s, 227n89, 233n64; cost of, 24; Hughes article "Our Statish Language," 59; Loos's serialization in, 24–25, 86, 93, 234–35n89
Harris, Joel Chandler, 67, 180
Harrison, James A.: "Negro English," 180, 189
Hawthorne, Nathaniel, 64
Haycraft, Howard: *Murder for Pleasure*, 142, 241n7
H.D., 57; *The Collected Poems of H.D.*, 25
Hearst, William Randolph, 227n89
Hearst's International-Cosmopolitan (magazine), 87
Hegeman, Susan: "Taking *Blondes* Seriously," 95
Hemingway, Ernest, 3, 10, 75, 205, 217; *Death in the Afternoon*, 242n26; Gold's views on, 126, 130; *Green Hills of Africa*, 38; hard-boiled crime fiction style and, 145–46; *To Have and Have Not*, 27; "The Killers," 145; *In Our Time*, 25, 118; pulp formulas used by, 27; as reader of pulp fiction, 26, 32, 242n26; sound films' influence on, 224n22; Stein and, 109; *The Sun Also Rises*, 229n38; Twain's *Huckleberry Finn* viewed by, 38
Henriksen, Louise Levitas: *Anzia Yezierska*, 108
Hersey, Harold: *The Pulpwood Editor*, 242n27
Hersey, John, 10
Herskovits, Melville: *The Myth of the Negro Past*, 179
Heyward, Du Bose, 185
Hichens, Robert, 227n89
highbrow/lowbrow notion, 17, 23, 28, 38–39, 71, 141–42, 153, 164–67, 221
His Picture in the Papers (film), 91–92
Hitchcock, H. Wiley: *Music in the United States*, 224n28
Hit-the-Trail Holliday (film), 92
Hoffman, Frederick J.: *The Twenties*, 52
Holcomb, Gary Edward: *Claude McKay, Code Name Sasha*, 204
Home to Harlem, (McKay), 32–33, 191, 193, 204–10, 213, 248n54; experimental moments in, 209–10; language differences as subject in, 207–8; as picaresque, 205, 249n73; as proletarian novel, 249n67; transnationalism in, 9; use of music in, 209–10; working-class protagonists in, 192, 204–5
Hopkins, Pauline, 194
Hot Dog (magazine), 21
Howard, June: *Form and History in American Literary Naturalism*, 15
Howe, E. W., 68
Howells, William Dean, 68, 102; literary realism of, 39–40, 140; *My Mark Twain*, 40, 41; on realist writers, 16, 187; *The Rise of Silas Lapham*, 15, 40; Twain associated with, 40–41
Hughes, Langston, 32, 185, 204; on 1920s fascination with African American culture, 28; *The Big Sea*, 192; *Fine Clothes to the Jew*, 209, 248n61; "The Negro Artist and the Racial Mountain," 184, 199–200; poetry of, 247n44; *The Weary Blues*, 210, 248n61
Hughes, Rupert: "Our Statish Language," 59
humor writing: blurred notion of authorship in, 66–67; class and, 65; comic monologues and, 69; frame narration rejected in, 71; as genre, 27–28, 30; James on, 62; of Lardner, 72–85, 159, 160; modernization of, 63; realist aesthetics and,

humor writing (*continued*)
63–72; regional types, 64, 65; slapstick comedy and, 69–71; Southwestern, 41, 44–45, 62, 65, 66, 217; studies of, 63–64; subject-object relationships in, 71, 77–82; Twain and, 41–44, 48–49, 62–63; vaudeville and, 69–70

Hungry Hearts (Yezierska), 31, 109, 112, 117–22; "The Free Vacation House," 117–18, 119; "How I Found America," 121–22; "Hunger," 117; "The Lost 'Beautifulness,'" 117, 119; "The Miracle," 118–20, 119–20, 124; recurring characters in, 118–20; "Soap and Water," 119, 121–22, 136; "Where Lovers Dream," 118, 119, 120–21, 122; "Wings," 117

Hurston, Zora Neale: "Characteristics of Negro Expression," 179, 246n16; *Folklore, Memoirs, and Other Writings*, 190; "How It Feels to Be Colored Me," 210; modernism and, 195; "Story in Harlem Slang," 20–21, 179, 188–89, 190, 230–31n65, 248n58; studies of, 113; vernacular language used by, 217; works used as background for the study of high modernism, 109–10

Huyssen, Andreas: *After the Great Divide*, 13, 22

immigrants and immigration: assimilation problems, 30–31, 103, 104–26; English-only education for, 20, 53, 230n58; of Jews, 102–3; modernism and, 28–29, 31, 56, 61; multiethnicity of American society and, 115–16; nativism and, 28, 106, 107, 125, 230n58; older groups as genteel writers, 18; realist writing and, 17, 39–40, 102–3, 105–6

Immigration Acts of 1921 and 1924, 28
Intolerance (film), 90, 94–95
Irish humor, 65–67
Irwin, Theodore D.: "Slanguage: 1929," 2, 3, 8, 23, 27, 33, 35, 36, 56, 77, 148, 160, 215, 218, 220

James, Henry: *The American Scene*, 103; *Hawthorne*, 62; humor writing of, 64; literary realism of, 140; modernist aesthetics influenced by, 62–63; "The Question of Our Speech," 103; *The Question of Our Speech*, 16

jazz, Mencken's views on, 50
Jazz Singer, The (film), 131, 248n63
Jenkins, Henry: *What Made Pistachio Nuts?*, 69

Jewish American fictional memoir: of Antin, 105–8; break with realism, 102–38; of Cahan, 104–8; as genre, 28–29, 30–31, 61; of Gold, 126–38; of Yezierska, 108–26

Jewish Americans: blackface performances of, 201, 248nn62–63; early films depicting, 235n2; literary canon of, 109; politics of representation, 106–7, 184; realism and assimilation, 103, 104–8; stereotyping and ethnographic depictions, 103; vernacular language of, 3, 30–31. *See also* Yiddish

Jews without Money (Gold), 31, 132–38, 240n81; conclusion of, 132, 137; descriptions in, 136–37; legacy of, 130; structure of, 135–36; vernacular in, 127, 128, 133–35; woodcuts for, 133, 137, 240n80

Johnson, James Weldon, 181, 194, 202; *The Book of American Negro Poetry*, 183; *God's Trombones*, 183; McKay's letter to, 249n67; Van Vechten's *Nigger Heaven* viewed by, 188, 190; vernacular condemned by, 32

Jolas, Eugene: as editor of *transition*, 1–4, 8; "The King's English Is Dying—Long Live the Great American Language," 35–36, 102, 126, 148; "Logos," 223n3; "Proclamation," 1–2, 3, 14, 18, 35, 56, 115, 116, 211, 229n23, 237n35; "Revolution of the Word Dictionary," 2–3

Jolson, Al, 131, 248n63
Jones, Gavin: *Strange Talk*, 15, 17, 40, 42
Josephson, Matthew: "Towards a Professional Prose," 36, 56
Joyce, James, 3, 207, 220; admiration for Loos's *Gentlemen Prefer Blondes*, 26; Faulkner influenced by, 219; *Finnegans Wake*, 1, 27, 226n75; Gold's views on, 130; Loos viewed by, 101; lowbrow culture references in, 3; *A Portrait of the Artist as a Young Man*, 50, 76–77, 84; Roth influenced by, 111, 217; *Ulysses*, 21, 27, 50, 58, 75–76, 77, 130, 164, 241n8

Kane, Elisha K.: "The Jargon of the Underworld," 245n104
Kaplan, Amy: *The Social Construction of American Realism*, 16

Katz, Mark: "Sound Recording," 70, 232n27
Katz, Wendy R.: "Untying the Immigrant Tongue," 110
Kennedy, R. Emmet: *Gritny People*, 191
Kenner, Hugh, 30; *The Pound Era*, 51
Kirkland, Caroline: *A New Home, Who'll Follow?*, 233n47
Kirkland, David, 86
Klein, Marcus: *Foreigners*, 236n16
Knopf, Alfred A., 25, 32, 151, 164, 166, 174, 185, 216
Knopf, Blanche, 163, 166, 167, 171
Kollwitz, Kathe, 240n80
Konzett, Delia Caparoso: *Ethnic Modernisms*, 113
Krapp, George Philip: *The English Language in America*, 180; "The English of the Negro," 180, 181, 188
Kreymborg, Alfred, 129

Labaree, Mary Fleming, 248n48
"language of the streets": experimentation of, 27, 29, 145, 148, 190, 198, 219; Freeman on, 3, 10, 20; Jolas on, 2–3, 10; narrator and, 72; Thompson on, 178; value given to, 18
Lardner, Ring, 4; aesthetic changes of, 73–74, 85; "Baseball-American," 21, 22, 59; *The Big Town*, 73; career of, 72–74, 216; "Champion," 159; Daly influenced by, 158–59; "The Golden Honeymoon," 73; *Gullible's Travels*, 73; "Ham-American," 59; Hammett influenced by, 168–69; "Harmony," 80; *How to Write Short Stories (with Samples)*, 62, 73, 75; impact on humor writing, 30; influence of, 86, 145, 216, 219; Jack Keefe baseball stories, 21, 73, 74, 77, 79–82, 94, 228n106, 233n50; Joyce compared to, 75–76; *The Love Nest and Other Stories*, 73; modernization of humor genre, 28, 61, 63, 64, 71–85; *My Four Weeks in France*, 75; nonsense plays of, 73; *Round Up*, 73–74, 85, 216; Scribner's publishing of, 75, 76, 82, 86, 216; as sportswriter, 72, 75; *The Story of a Wonder Man*, 232n40; subjectivity of narrator through self-representation, 77–82, 94, 100, 158, 194; *Treat 'Em Rough*, 75; Twain's influence on, 73, 85; Woolf's admiration for works of, 26–27, 76, 134, 216, 219, 232n44; Yezierska influenced by, 111, 117;

You Know Me Al, 30, 72, 73, 74, 76–82, 85, 100, 216; *The Young Immigrunts*, 74, 82–85
Larsen, Nella, 226n71; *Passing*, 248n48; *Quicksand*, 193, 210
Lawrence, D. H., 129, 207; *Studies in Classic American Literature*, 229n44
leftist literature, 9
Le Sueur, Meridel: *The Girl*, 236n17
Levenson, Michael: *Modernism*, 5
Leverage, Henry: "Dictionary of the Underworld," 21, 139, 149, 160, 171, 245n104
Levinson, Julian: *Exiles on Main Street*, 236n16, 237n33
Levinson, Marjorie: "What Is the New Formalism?," 7
Lewis, Sinclair, 17–18, 50, 64, 74, 76, 110, 142, 185
Lewis, Wyndham, 101, 177
Lewisohn, Ludwig: *Up Stream*, 112–13, 115, 125
Liberator (magazine), 3
Library of America, 51, 193, 241n10
Lindsay, Vachel, 185; *The Art of the Moving Picture*, 89–90
literary criticism: canonical writers privileged in, 7–8, 29, 110, 219–21; ethnic studies, 109–11; reconsiderations of canonized works, 13; trends in, 5–6, 13–14
little magazines, 1–4, 8, 22, 36, 130. See also specific titles
Little Review (little magazine), 1, 8, 23, 130, 207; mottos, 22
"local color," 40, 194. See also dialect literature
Locke, David Ross, 231n10
Loeb, Harold: *Doodab*, 14, 25
Loos, Anita: anthology of works by, 233n66; *The Better Things of Life*, 87, 100; "The Biography of a Book," 23–24, 93; *Breaking into the Movies*, 95–96; *But Gentlemen Marry Brunettes*, 86–87, 97–98, 100; Faulkner's letter to, 86, 98; Faulkner's views on, 219; *How to Write Photoplays*, 30, 61, 89, 90, 94, 95; influence of, 216; memoirs of, 233n66; modernization of humor genre, 28, 63, 64, 72; narrative style, 87–88; *No Mother to Guide Her*, 100; screenplays for talkies, 87; as silent film scenarist and intertitle writer, 86, 87, 90–92, 94, 97; theatrical and film adaptations of works by, 86–87; writings of, 86–87. See also *Gentlemen Prefer Blondes*

Lott, Eric: *Love and Theft*, 239n67
Lovecraft, H. P., 156
Lukács, Georg: "Realism in the Balance," 225n45

Macdonald, Ross, 177–78
Mackenzie, Compton, 227n89
Macon, J. A., 180
magazines, 1920s American, 23–25. *See also* little magazines; pulp magazines; *specific titles*
Marcus, Stephen, 165
Marling, William: "Style and Ideology of *The Maltese Falcon*," 245n106
Marsh, Mae, 91
Martin, Edward A.: *H. L. Mencken and the Debunkers*, 52
Matrimaniac, The (film), 92
Matthews, Brander, 115–16
McCann, Sean: *Gumshoe America*, 161, 244n76
McFall, Haldane, 185, 186
McGann, Jerome: "Keats and the Historical Method in Literary Criticism," 25
McGurl, Mark: *The Novel Art*, 13, 50, 166, 234n67
McKay, Claude, 4; *Banjo*, 9, 32–33, 191, 192, 202–3, 205, 206, 210–12, 213, 217; career of, 203–4; *Color Scheme*, 204, 212; street slang in works of, 181, 184, 191, 202–13, 204, 213; transnationalism of, 9, 22, 191, 212; *Trial by Lynching*, 204; varied output of, 203; works used as background for the study of high modernism, 110. *See also Home to Harlem*
Melville, Herman, 64
Mencken, H. L., 17; "The American: His Language," 1, 54–55, 58; *American Mercury* commentary, 51; articles on American English, 52, 54–55; *Baltimore Evening Sun* articles on American language, 37, 52; *Black Mask* and, 31–32, 61, 150, 244n67; career of, 37; debunking and, 51; as editor of *American Mercury*, 23–25, 50, 52; on Gold's *Jews without Money*, 132; Howells's genteel style criticized by, 41; influence of, 4, 215, 217, 219–20, 229n38, 229n40; interest in American vernacular, 8; Joyce's works viewed by, 50; Lardner and, 30, 64, 85; letters and contributions to *American Speech*, 19; literary preferences, 49–50; Loos influenced by, 64, 93, 234n88; Loos's mention of, in *Gentlemen Prefer Blondes*, 98–99; *A Mencken Chrestomathy*, 59; *Mencken's America*, 51; *Notes on Democracy*, 51; "Nothing Dead about Language U.S. Boys Take to the Trenches," 55; "On Being an American," 53; "On Realism," 49–50; political and anti-Semitic views, 50, 51, 53; on portrayal of African Americans in art, 185; *Prejudices*, 51, 67–68; range of work, 51–52; *A Religious Orgy in Tennessee*, 51; scholarship on, 50–51; Twain's influence on, 16, 29, 36–49; vernacular translation of the American Declaration of Independence, 59–60, 160; Victorianism of, 51–52. *See also American Language, The*
Metropolitan (magazine), 110
Meyerhold, Vsevolod, 128, 130, 131
Micheaux, Oscar, 234n68
Miller, Joshua L.: *Accented America*, 19, 20, 50, 53, 224n28, 226n71, 230n58
Mitchell, Lee Clark: "Nobody but Our Gang," 229n30; "Verbally *Roughing It*," 41
modernism: American language as *lingua franca* of, 36, 55–56; cultural conceptualization, 5–8; formal movements, 6–7; hard-boiled crime fiction and, 145–48; "high modernism," 3–4, 12, 21, 33, 56–57, 115, 207–8, 217; immigration and, 28–29, 31, 56; influence directions in, 7–8, 12, 27, 33, 219–21, 228n102; James's influence on, 62–63; Jazz Age social changes, 145; literary studies of, 5–6; little magazines and, 1–4; manifestos of, 1–2, 4, 36, 60, 116, 128–29, 130; McKay viewed as modernist, 203–4, 212; paratexts in, 21–22, 149, 188–89, 226n75, 248n60; pessimism and, 146; plurality of practices in, 5–8; politics and, 224n25n35; pulp, 166; realism in opposition to, 14–18, 225n42, 225n45, 241n12; redefinition of pleasure and, 22–23; slang and, 3–4; slapstick comedy and, 30, 69, 70–71; taste and, 26–27; unreliable narrators, 79–81; Van Vechten's *Nigger Heaven* and, 188; zones of cultural productions, 22–23. *See also* vernacular modernism
Modernism/Modernity (journal), 6
Modern Library, 32, 142, 164
Modern Quarterly (magazine), 35
Montanye, C. S.: "Looking Out for Orchid," 158

Moretti, Franco: *Signs Taken for Wonders*, 241n16
Morrisson, Mark S.: *The Public Face of Modernism*, 13
Moseley, Merritt: "Ring Lardner and the American Humor Tradition," 78
Mosley, Walter, 177–78
Mott, Frank Luther: *A History of American Magazines*, 227n77
Move On (film), 235n2
multiaccentuality concept, 12–13
Munson, Gorham: *The Awakening Twenties*, 25
musicology: cultivated vs. vernacular distinction in, 11

Naremore, James: "Dashiell Hammett and Poetics of Hard-Boiled Detection," 146, 165
Nathan, George Jean, 23–25, 31–32, 61, 150, 167
Nation (journal), 130, 199
nativism, 28, 106, 107, 125, 230n58
Neal, Joseph, 10
Nebel, Frederick, 152
Nelson, Raymond: "Babylonian Frolics," 52
Nettles, Elsa: *Language, Race, and Social Class in Howells's America*, 40
New Masses (magazine), 3, 128, 129–30, 132, 135, 238n53, 239n69, 240n78, 240n80
New Modernist Studies, 6
New Playwrights Theatre, 127, 239n69
New York City Ghetto Fish market (film), 235n2
New Yorker (magazine), 52
New York Hat, The (film), 89
New York Times (newspaper), 193–94, 197
New York Times Book Review and Magazine, 115–16
Nicholls, Peter: *Modernisms*, 5, 6, 127
nickelodeons, 71, 103
Nolan, William F.: *The Black Mask Boys*, 154
Norris, Frank, 16–17
North, H. C., 154
North, Michael, 30; *Camera Works*, 88; *The Dialect of Modernism*, 13, 107, 110, 203, 212; *Reading 1922*, 125, 159–60
Norton Anthology of American Literature, The, 241n10
Nye, Bill, 65, 231n18

Olsen, Tillie: *Yonnondio*, 236n17
O'Neill, Eugene, 127; *Plays*, 25
Opportunity (journal), 188, 248n48
Orvell, Miles: *The Real Thing*, 140, 240–41n4
Orwell, George: "Raffles and Miss Blandish," 244n79
Ovington, Mary W., 185

paratexts, 21–22, 83–84, 149, 188–89, 197, 226n75, 227n77
Parrington, Vernon: *Main Currents in American Thought*, 17, 230n44
Partisan Review (magazine), 3, 165, 215
Patterson, Michael, 240n81
Peterkin, Julia, 185–86
Phelps, Wallace: "Problems and Perspective in Revolutionary Literature," 215
pleasure, redefinition of, 22–23
Poe, Edgar Allan, 64; Daly influenced by, 155–56; Dupin stories, 141, 142, 143–44, 162, 241n13, 241n16
Poetry (journal), 57–58
Poirier, Richard: "The Difficulties of Modernism and the Modernism of Difficulty," 22, 81, 146
Popular Detective (pulp magazine), 161
Porter, Dennis: *The Pursuit of Crime*, 176
Porter, Katherine Anne, 110
Porter, William T.: *The Spirit of the Times*, 65
Pound, Ezra, 9, 63, 127, 129, 177, 203, 217, 224n19, 233n60; *Cantos*, 21
Pound, Louise, 19
Powdermaker, Hortense, 88
primitivism, 11, 21, 129, 200–201, 240n81
proletariat: in American culture, 215, 238n53, 240n81, 245n109; McKay's writings and, 204; as narrators and protagonists, 9; "Proletarian Realism," 128–29, 130, 133, 137, 240n78
Proust, Marcel, 225n42, 239–40n78
Provincetown Players, 31, 127, 130–31, 238–39n56
pulp magazines: crime stories, 31–32, 149–50, 157; critical neglect of, 14; dime novels and, 12, 14, 149–50; Faulkner and Hemingway as readers of, 26, 27, 218; Mencken on, 61; ridicule of readers, 23; writing practice, 149–50, 243n35. See also specific titles

Queen, Ellery, 241n6

Rabinowitz, Paula: *Black & White & Noir*, 244–45n90
Raczkowski, Christopher T.: "From Modernity's Detection to Modernist Detectives," 166
Rahv, Philip: "Problems and Perspective in Revolutionary Literature," 215
Rainey, Lawrence: *Institutions of Modernism*, 22
"reading communities," 12–13
realism: aesthetics and American humor, 63–72; African American "uplift" and, 187; "Americanness" and, 102–3; *Atlantic* group, 16; class and racial differences in nineteenth-century America, 16, 40, 42–43, 46–47; detective fiction and, 142–43, 151; dialect literature and, 15, 39–41, 49, 63; exploitation of racial difference in plots, 106–7; Hammett's critique of, 168–69; hard-boiled crime fiction and, 139–40; of Howells, 39–40, 140; immigrants and, 102–3, 105–6; Jewish American fictional memoir and, 102–38; Mencken's views on, 49–50; modernism in opposition to, 14–18, 225n42, 225n45, 241n12; narrator's language in, 15, 40, 42–43, 65, 66–67; political engagement and, 14; proletarian, 128–29, 130, 133, 137, 204, 215, 240n78; racial critiques and, 184; social construction of, 16–17; socialist, 238n53; subject-object relationships in, 16, 18, 71, 148
Rhodes, Chip: *Structures of the Jazz Age*, 50
Rhys, Jean: studies of, 113
Robinson, Henry Morton: *A Skeleton's Key to Finnegans Wake* (with Campbell), 226n75; "Wood-Pulp Racket," 243n35
Rogers, Marion Elizabeth, 51
Rogin, Michael: *Blackface, White Noise*, 131, 248n62
Rosenwald, Lawrence: *Multilingual America*, 105
Roth, Henry, 109, 111; *Call It Sleep*, 130–31, 217, 237nn22–23; modernist aesthetic of, 111
Roth, Philip, 111
Rourke, Constance: *American Humor*, 64, 230n44

Samuels Jewelry Agency, 167
Sanders, Judith: "Her Literary Dowry," 236n19

Santayana, George: *Character and Opinion in the United States*, 229n44; "The Genteel Tradition in American Philosophy," 17
Sapir, Edward, 20
Sappho, 208
Saturday Evening Post, 24, 79, 82, 86, 157, 158
Schafer, R. Murray, 70
Schatz, Thomas: *Genius of the System*, 91
"schizophonia" notion, 70
Schmidt, Karl, 91
Scholes, Robert: *Paradoxy of Modernism*, 28
Schomburg, Arthur, 204
Schulberg, Budd, 88
Schuyler, George S.: "The Negro-Art Hokum," 246n2
Scopes trial, 51
screenplays, 1930s, 87–88
Scribner's, 75, 76, 82, 86, 216
Scribner's (magazine), 145
Seldes, Gilbert: *The Seven Lively Arts*, 72, 75–76, 76–77, 219
Sewell, David R.: *Mark Twain's Languages*, 39, 48, 228n10
Shaw, George Bernard, 108
Shaw, Henry W., 231n10, 231n18
Shaw, Joseph T., 150–51, 167, 171; *The Hard-Boiled Omnibus*, 139, 145, 152, 154, 157
silent films, 68–69; cultural assumptions surrounding, 95–96; humor writing and, 63, 100; intertitles for, 61, 86, 88, 89–92, 94, 234n76, 234n85; Loos's theories on writing for, 30, 61, 87–88, 94; slang used in intertitles, 91; slapstick comedy, 30, 69–71
Simon, Howard, 133, 137, 240n80
Singal, Daniel Joseph: "Towards a Definition of American Modernism," 6
slang lexicography. *See* glossaries and dictionaries of slang
slapstick comedy: modernism and, 30, 69, 70–71
Smart Set (magazine): "The American: His Language," 54–55; Hammett and, 155, 157, 167, 168, 169–70; Joyce's *Portrait of the Artist as a Young Man* reviewed in, 50; losses incurred by, 31, 150; Mencken and Nathan as coeditors of, 23, 37, 50, 52
Smashing Detective Stories (pulp magazine), 161
Smedley, Agnes: *Daughter of Earth*, 236n17
Smith, Charles Henry, 231n10

Smith, Erin A.: *Hard-Boiled*, 149–50, 240n3
Smith, Henry Nash: *Virgin Land*, 38–39
Smitherman, Geneva: *Word from the Mother*, 180
socialist realism, 238n53
Sollors, Werner: *Beyond Ethnicity*, 107, 182, 236n15; *Ethnic Modernism*, 237n22
Sonne, Owen E.: "Crime and Detective Story," 243n33
sound films, 87, 224n22
sound recordings: humor and, 63, 68–70, 78, 232n24
Southwestern humor, 41, 44–45, 62, 65, 66, 217
Spanish-American War, 66
Spingarn, J. E., 185
Stearns, Harold: *Civilization in the United States*, 229n44
Stein, Gertrude, 203, 217, 226n71; aesthetic of, 120, 121, 124; as aficionado of detective fiction, 26, 32, 139, 164–65, 219; *The Autobiography of Alice B. Toklas*, 11, 164; *Blood on the Dining-Room Floor*, 27, 141, 165; *Everybody's Autobiography*, 164; "Four Saints in Three Acts," 1, 2, 77, 164, 220; Gold's views on, 126, 130; James's influence on, 63; Jewishness of, 236n15; as a Jewish writer, 108; Loos's writing compared to, 101; *The Making of Americans*, 112, 120, 121, 145, 164; *Three Lives*, 120; vernacular used by, 10; "What Are Master-Pieces and Why Are There So Few of Them," 139; "Why I Like Detective Stories," 227n92; writing style of, 76; Yezierska's visit with, 108–9, 126
Stewart, Cal, 69, 78
Stoddard, Lothrop, 235n90
Stoker, Bram: *Dracula*, 228n102
Stowe, Harriet Beecher: *Uncle Tom's Cabin*, 233n64
Stowe, William W.: "From Semiotics to Hermeneutics," 143
"straight man," 69–70, 71
Strychacz, Thomas: *Modernism, Mass Culture, and Professionalism*, 13, 14
Symons, Julian: *Mortal Consequences*, 142, 241n7

Talmadge, Constance, 86, 92
Talmadge, Norma, 86
Teachout, Terry: *The Skeptic*, 230n46

Temperamental Wife, A (film), 86
Thaggert, Miriam: *Images of Black Modernism*, 185
Thompson, Jim, 218
Thompson, Jon: *Fiction, Crime, and Empire*, 146, 165–66, 178
Thrilling Detective (pulp magazine), 161
Thurman, Wallace: *The Blacker the Berry*, 192; *Harlem: A Melodrama of Negro Life*, 192; *Infants of the Spring*, 192; "Negro Artists and the Negro," 184; Van Vechten's *Nigger Heaven* viewed by, 247n35. See also *Fire!!*
Tibbetts, John C.: *His Majesty the American* (with Welsh), 90–91
Toklas, Alice, 164
Toomer, Jean, 32, 226n71; *Cane*, 181–83, 184, 207, 211, 237n22, 247n44, 248n54
transition (little magazine), 9; commentary on Joyce's *Finnegans Wake*, 226n75; Gold's praise for, 130; Irwin's "Slanguage: 1929" published in, 2, 3, 8, 23, 27, 33, 35, 36, 56, 77, 148, 160, 215, 218, 220; Joyce's *Finnegans Wake* excerpts published in, 1, 220; "Revolution of the Word" issue, 1–4, 8, 26, 27, 33, 35–36, 56, 59, 77, 79, 115, 116, 148, 160, 164, 215, 218, 220; Stein's "Four Saints in Three Acts" published in, 1, 2, 220, 848
transnationalism: of McKay, 22, 191, 212; vernacular modernism and, 9, 115–16
Triangle–Fine Arts, 90, 91
Tuerk, Richard: "Michael Gold's *Hoboken Blues*," 239n68
Twain, Mark: "Concerning the American Language," 37; as debunker, 38, 39; dialect writing of, 15, 16, 29, 36–37, 39–47, 63, 78, 170, 208, 216, 228n10; Faulkner influenced by, 217, 219; *The Innocents Abroad*, 49; "Jim Smiley and His Jumping Frog," 45, 62; Lardner influenced by, 73, 85; Mencken influenced by, 16, 29, 36–49, 68; *Pudd'nhead Wilson*, 49, 141, 169; *Tom Sawyer, Detective*, 49; *Tom Sawyer Abroad*, 46, 48. See also *Adventures of Huckleberry Finn*; *Roughing It*
Roughing It (Twain), 29, 48, 49; importance of language in, 36–37, 41–44, 45; Mencken's literary assessment, 37–38

"Uncle Josh" recordings, 69, 70, 71, 78, 82

Valgemae, Mardi: *Accelerated Grimace*, 133
Van Dine, S. S. *See* Wright, Willard Huntington
Vanity Fair (magazine), 23, 87, 153
Van Patten, Nathan: "The Vocabulary of the American Negro as Set Forth in Contemporary Literature," 190–91, 248n58
Van Vechten, Carl: *Nigger Heaven*, 32, 187–88, 189–90, 191, 194, 197, 201, 204, 206, 208, 212–13, 247n35, 249n75; on portrayal of African Americans in art, 185
Variety (trade journal), 92
vaudeville, 69–70
vernacular modernism: African American, 193–213; anthropology and, 20, 189; assimilation and, 108–26; class or ethnic identity and, 18, 28–29, 40, 42–43, 46–47, 65–67, 106–8, 113, 235n90; creative powers of American language, 55–56, 58; crime fiction and, 139–78; dialect literature distinguished from, 10–11; ethnic studies and, 109–11; experimentation in, 29, 33; expressionism and, 126–38, 140, 240n80; Faulkner and, 217–20; formal innovations in, 11–12, 13–14; genteel writing in conflict with, 38–39; glossaries as paratextual keys, 21–22, 149, 188–89, 197, 248n60; humor writing and, 62–101; impurity and, 35; Jewish American fictional memoirs and, 102–38, 184; malapropisms, 84–85; as model for writers in 1930s, 215–21; multiaccentuality and, 12–13; objectification of language and, 68; overlapping (s)languages in, 22; politics of representation, 32, 106–7, 183–92, 196–97, 203, 246n14, 247n26; psychological *noir*, 155–57; racial essentialism and, 124; readership of, 8–9; silent film narration and, 88–92, 100; sound films and, 224n22; subject-object relationships in, 18, 77–82, 148, 175; as term, 4, 8, 9–10; toward a theory of, 8–14, 220–21; transnational dimension of, 8–9, 212; Twain as pioneer for, 39–47, 62; "twisted" nature of, 76; vernacular narrative voice in, 30, 44–45, 88–89, 92, 100–101, 120–22, 157–58, 162–63, 170–71, 177, 206; Yiddish and, 104–8. *See also specific authors and subjects*
"vernacular music," 11
Vials, Chris: *Realism for the Masses*, 14

Virtuous Vamp, A (film), 86
Vogel, Shane: *The Scene of Harlem Cabaret*, 184, 186–87
Vološinov, V. N., 12

Wald, Alan M.: *Exiles from a Future Time*, 131–32, 239n56
Wald, Priscilla, 108; *Constituting Americans*, 112
Walls of Jericho, The (Fisher), 32, 196–202; critical invisibility of, 193–94; dispersal of narrative centrality, 191–92, 196; glossary in, 20–21, 190, 197–98; street speech in, 197–99, 208; title of, 202; uplift in, 196–97, 200–202
Walrond, Eric: *Tropic Death*, 191
Ward, Artemus. *See* Browne, Charles Farrar
Ward, Harold: "Under the Crimson Skull," 155
Weaver, John V. A., 59, 227n89
Weber, Brom: "The Misspellers," 65, 231n10
Weber, Donald: *Haunted in the New World*, 236n16
Weinberg, Robert, 154
Wells, H. G., 108
Welsh, James M.: *His Majesty the American* (with Tibbetts), 91
West, Nathanael: *The Day of the Locust*, 88
Western Advertising (trade journal), 168
Wharton, Edith: admiration for Loos's *Gentlemen Prefer Blondes*, 26, 101
White, Walter, 184, 185, 194, 202, 204, 246n14; *Fire in the Flint*, 195
Whitfield, Raoul, 152; "Murder in the Ring," 244n70; *The Virgin Kills*, 241n8
Whitman, Walt, 110; Gold influenced by, 127, 133, 136
Wild and Woolly (film), 234n85
Wild Girl of the Sierras, A (film), 91
Will, Barbara, 108, 236n15
Williams, William Carlos, 14, 129, 217; *In the American Grain*, 229n44; Mencken's fourth edition of *American Language* reviewed by, 230n56; *Spring and All*, 116
Wilson, Edmund, 73, 76; *Axel's Castle*, 216; on Dos Passos, 216; "H. L. Mencken," 50; "Who Cares Who Killed Roger Ackroyd?," 142
Wilson, Harry Leon: *Merton of the Movies*, 96
Wirth, Louis: *The Ghetto*, 102, 240n80

Wirth-Nesher, Hana: *Call It English*, 236n16
Wood, Clement: *A Dictionary of American Slang* (with Goddard), 19, 20, 21, 82, 175, 248n60
Wood, James Playsted: *Magazines in the United States*, 24
Woolf, Virginia, 225n42; "Character in Fiction," 14; interest in American vernacular, 8; James's influence on, 63; Lardner's works admired by, 26–27, 76, 134, 216, 219, 232n44
Woolrich, Cornell, 243n56
World War I, 74–75
Worpole, Ken: *Dockers and Detectives*, 145, 242n25
Worringer, Wilhelm, 240n81
Wright, Richard, 195
Wright, Willard Huntington, 23, 141–42, 241n6, 241n10
Writer's Digest (trade journal), 21, 79, 152

Yardley, Jonathan: *Ring*, 81–82
Yezierska, Anzia, 4, 101; aesthetic of, 30–31, 103, 107–8, 111–15, 118, 123–26, 133, 135, 194, 217; *Arrogant Beggar*, 112, 117, 122; *Bread Givers*, 108, 109, 112, 113, 117, 122–26; *Children of Loneliness*, 114; critical appraisal of, 236n16; ethnic pigeonholing of works, 110; on flexibility of American language, 20, 22, 113–14, 211; mix of first- and third-person narrative voices used by, 116–17, 122–26; "Mostly about Myself," 108, 123; "Mr. Lewisohn," 116, 125, 237n36; *The Open Cage*, 109; on personal costs of assimilation, 112; rediscovery of, 109; *Salome of the Tenements*, 110, 112, 122, 124, 125, 236–37n20, 238n48; scholarship on, 109–10; in subcanon of ethnic women's writing, 108–9, 113; "To the Stars," 114–15, 116; vernacular modernism of assimilation, 108–26; visit with authors in Europe, 108–9; working practice, 123–24; works as critique against gentility, 111–12. See also *Hungry Hearts*
Yiddish, 3, 31, 61, 103–4, 109, 111, 113, 117, 123, 134, 217, 226n11, 237n23, 237n25

Zaborowska, Magdalena J.: *How We Found America*, 122, 238n49
Zangwill, Israel, 108
"zone of contact" notion, 46, 65

www.ingramcontent.com/pod-product-compliance
Lightning Source LLC
Chambersburg PA
CBHW021348300426
44114CB00012B/1133